S T U D I E S   I N

Platonic Political Philosophy

DATE DUE			

LEO STRAUSS

STUDIES IN
Platonic Political Philosophy

With an Introduction by
Thomas L. Pangle

THE UNIVERSITY OF CHICAGO PRESS

CHICAGO & LONDON

Leo Strauss, 1899–1973, was the Robert Maynard
Hutchins Distinguished Service Professor of
Political Science at the University of Chicago.

The University of Chicago Press, Chicago 60637
The University of Chicago Press, Ltd., London

Library of Congress Cataloging in Publication Data

Strauss, Leo.
  Studies in Platonic political philosophy.

  Bibliography: p.
  1. Plato—Political science—Addresses, essays,
lectures. I. Title.
JC71.P62S87   1983   320'.01   83-5064
ISBN 0-226-77703-0

Contents

Foreword

A year or so before his death, Professor Leo Strauss requested that the writings contained in this book be gathered together and published in their present order and under the title that now appears at their head. He did not live to write a projected paper on Plato's *Gorgias* that was to have been placed after the paper on the *Euthydemus* and that would have brought to three the number of essays on Platonic dialogues; nor did he live to write the introduction that would, I believe, have explained his choice of this title for a book that, however suffused with the influence of Plato, devotes many pages to other authors. Rather than abandon the unexpected title, the decision was taken to retain it as being the authentic even if puzzling indication of the author's intention in forming this collection, and also to obtain an introduction that would, so far as possible, replace the statement that the author was prevented from writing. Professor Thomas Pangle's brilliant essay does that as well, I believe, as anything written by any living author could do.

Grateful acknowledgment is made for permission to reprint the pieces that have already been published (chapters 1–9 and 12–15). For details, see the unnumbered footnotes on the opening pages of those chapters.

JOSEPH CROPSEY

Introduction
Thomas L. Pangle

The University of Chicago Press and Joseph Cropsey, Leo Strauss's literary executor, asked me to write this introduction in lieu of the introduction Strauss intended to write but had not begun at the time of his death. Naturally, what I say will by no means qualify as a substitute for what Strauss would have said. I must go further: I am certain that I do not yet have a completely clear understanding of the fundamental intention which guided Strauss in this and all his mature works. My introduction must therefore be regarded as provisional—though it is a product of some years' reflection on Strauss's thought.

The work before us is made up of essays, notes, and reviews written over a number of years on widely varying topics. None of the pieces, it would seem, was originally written as a chapter for this book. Yet, looking back, Strauss apparently found that these writings, arranged in this order and selected from numerous others that he might have included, fell into place as parts of a coherent whole. The book thus exemplifies, and recalls, the deceptively unsystematic and even errant appearance of the path Strauss's investigations traced over the years. Of course, that appearance is not altogether misleading: Strauss certainly "wandered" through the Western tradition. But on close inspection his wanderings betray the mark of the inspired explorer. Strauss exploited more fully than did anyone else the shattering of traditional horizons, and of inherited preconceptions, to which the twentieth century was the reluctant heir. He approached the history of Western thought as if it were uncharted. He never ceased trying to "find his bearings," and did so repeatedly "from the beginning"—from various points, or questions, whose choice or whose coming to sight was not wholly planned and hence not free from arbitrariness. In retrospect, his wanderings prove to

1

have described ever more surely and startlingly the undeniable, hidden contours of this spiritual continent upon which the rest of us sleepily dwell. Surely it is not unreasonable to expect that in this, the book he likely knew would be his last, he meant to help us discern more sharply the guiding themes that had come to seem most significant to him.

The title Strauss chose is at first sight parodoxical. For, as is obvious from the table of contents, this book is devoted only in small part to studies of or about the work of Plato. Like Xenophon's titles, Strauss's forces the reader to puzzle a bit, and to turn to the contents with an initial, specific question: how do they constitute "studies in Platonic political philosophy?" It seems to me that, as we consider these pieces and look back at the earlier writings of Strauss to which they sometimes refer, an answer soon begins to take shape. Each one of Strauss's essays is a study in Platonic political philosophy inasmuch as each is an execution of, a model for, such philosophizing. The title of the present work, I would even suggest, stands as a kind of signature to Strauss's lifework, which ripened into nothing other than the demonstration of what it means to engage in philosophizing of this kind.

Strauss's New Interpretation of the "Ideas"

To carry on Platonic political philosophizing, as Strauss understands it, is not to limit oneself to studying the works of Plato, although such study may be situated near the heart of the enterprise. What then is that heart, which determines the focus of all Strauss's inquiries? Down through the ages, Platonists and commentators on Plato have generally agreed that what most of all distinguishes Plato's philosophy and political philosophy is his doctrine of the *ideas*, and especially the ideas of justice and the good.[1] The reader who first encounters Strauss by way of this volume, or who hopes through it to dispel some of the perplexity left by earlier encounters, is therefore likely to begin by wondering what stand Strauss takes toward what is often called Plato's "idealism." Strauss's several remarks here about the ideas are emphatic but so brief and allusive that they obviously require interpretation in the light of his previous writings. If we peruse those earlier writings, and especially the most recent, we come away with the impression that Strauss agrees with the traditional consensus. He does indeed raise, but only to reject, "considerations such as . . . would lead to the result, unacceptable to most people, that there are no ideas of the virtues"; as a result, he is "forced to conclude that the ideas retain in the *Laws*, if in a properly subdued or muted manner, the status which they occupy, say, in the *Republic*" (*AAPL* 183–84). When we turn, however, to Strauss's commentary on the *Repub-*

---

1. The outstanding exception is Farabi, who writes of Plato as if Plato had no doctrine of ideas; see FP (works of Strauss will be referred to by abbreviations—see p. 27).

lic, we find that he is extremely skeptical about whether Plato seriously meant the explicit teaching about the ideas he has Socrates present to the young boys there: "It is utterly incredible, not to say that it appears to be fantastic . . . no one has ever succeeded in giving a satisfactory or clear account of this doctrine of ideas" (*CM* 119). What Strauss finds unaccountable is the notion that the ideas, and in particular the idea of justice, are "self-subsisting, being at home as it were in an entirely different place from human beings." He suggests that Socrates is here continuing the theological myths he had earlier put forward as the most salutary basis for the education of young people. Still, these severe doubts about what we may call the theological dimension of the doctrine do not extend to what we may call the natural dimension. Strauss does take the doctrine seriously insofar as it appears to provide a sound way of conceiving our experience of the nature of things.

Strauss's unorthodox interpretation of the ideas begins from the observation that when Socrates speaks of an idea or form, he is referring to that to which the question "What is . . .?" points (e.g., What is Man? What is Number? What is Justice?). When we are overcome with perplexity as to what something is, we are aware that we need first to assign it to its proper class or kind, and then to understand that kind in its relations to other kinds or species. The Socratic "method" thus begins from what is perfectly commonsensical, if not banal. What distinguishes the method according to Strauss is its intransigent adherence to the direction given by this original experience of wonder. That is, Socrates refuses ever to abandon as mere abstraction the attempt to ascend from the many local and temporary particulars to their universal and lasting (transhistorical, though not necessarily eternal) class characteristics; and, on the other hand, he resists or at least brakes the tendency of his philosophic predecessors to forsake the species experienced by common sense (and expressed in ordinary language) in the name of a quest for hypothetical "elemental" causes from which the whole and every species in it is supposed to be generated. To understand how any or all of the kinds of beings have come into being, even to be able to reproduce that process, is not yet to understand what the fully evolved beings are—how they behave, what they need if they are alive, how the species are related to one another. The understanding sought for by the "What is . . . ?" questions "cannot be the reduction of one heterogeneous class to others or to any cause other than the class itself; the class, or the class character, is the cause *par excellence*" (*CM* 19). Now at least in the case of those things that are of most immediate importance to us (the good and the bad, the just and the unjust, the noble and the base), our most promising inlet into the classes that constitute reality is through the opinions held among men, and above all through the most serious, trusted, authoritative opinions of the various societies. These opinions, considering the experiences and the evidence they point to, almost always make a great deal of sense; but they also contain important ambiguities, obscurities, and contradictions—most important of all, they contradict one another. The path toward the truth about the natural species of things begins from the warring opinions and their confrontation, and proceeds in the direction of the needed resolutions to which the confrontations point. The universals employed and sought by what Socrates calls his "dialectics" or "art of conversation" differ fundamentally, then, from the universals employed and sought by modern scientific method. Among other things, the ideas are not conceived as mental constructs—conscious or unconscious. This is the case despite the affinity between the ideas and the mathematical objects, and despite the fact that the ideas are in a way—in a divinatory way—known a priori. According to the Socratic assessment of what might be termed man's "noetic situation" we have no sufficient grounds for supposing that the character of reality "in itself" is wholly or forever screened from our everyday experience, and we are hence not justified in doubting radically (as opposed to transcending dialectically) the common-sense articulations of the universe (*NRH* 121–125, 169–76; *CM* 19–20; *AAPL* 17, 35; *XSD* 148).

Yet if it is true that the soul, which carries out and apprehends these articulations, is not properly conceived as a "subject" beholding its "objects," it is also true that the soul occupies a unique status, "noetically," within the universe: "the soul, while akin to the ideas, is for this reason not an idea" (*AAPL* 183).[2] Moreover, if anything can be said to cause the ideas, it seems it can only be "the idea of the good, which is in a sense the cause of all ideas as well as of the mind perceiving them." As higher than the ideas, the good can only with reservation be called an idea itself: it "becomes questionable whether the highest as Plato understands it is still properly called an idea" (*CM* 119).

It is very difficult to see what Strauss would have us conclude from this. Perhaps the most important by-product of Strauss's attempt to interpret the ideas in light of the "What is . . . ?" questions is the dissolution of one of the chief purported differences between Xenophon's portrait of Socratic philosophy and Plato's. If we consult then what Strauss says about the good in the course of his analysis of Xenophon's Socrates, we find that he seems to suggest that for Socrates the good is not a being—"the good is primarily what is good for a given individual in these or those circumstances, but being is primarily the 'what' of a class or tribe of beings." What is more, Socrates does not know the good which is not good for something: "things are good in relation to needs; something that does not fulfill any need cannot therefore

2. In *CM* 119, Strauss had said that "the mind which perceives the ideas is *radically* different from the ideas themselves" (my italics)—but that was in the context of speaking of the ideas as separate substances.

be known to be good" (*XS* 119, 75; cf. *CM* 29). I would suggest that this implies the following. For Socrates, the soul's knowledge of the beings is directed—therefore, in a sense, caused—by a matrix of need (or *eros*) about which the soul can become ever more self-conscious but outside of which it can never wholly step, except in this moment of awareness of limitation. The soul, this would mean, as the being which looks not only at the beings but at itself looking, exists and is known in a way different from the other beings— more immediately but, as a consequence, in the greater fullness of its mystery. For the soul is so situated that it can become aware of its strongest, permanent needs but at the same time must recognize that those needs shape its every awareness—including its self-awareness. And since all other beings are known only by or through the soul, the enigma of the soul would then become the clearest signal of the elusiveness of the whole for man.

But then Strauss's affirmation that "the class, or the class character, is the cause *par excellence*" would seem to require some qualification. Perhaps it helps to observe that the cause *par excellence* is not the cause simply. After all, in the very next sentence Strauss avers that "the roots of the whole are hidden" (*CM* 19). The classes and their characters cannot be fully understood apart from their relations to one another, to the soul, and to the good. They cannot be understood, that is to say, apart from their status as parts of the whole. And while the whole can be known through its parts, it is a question whether it can be fully known in this way or whether it is not also necessary, at some point, to seek the "roots of the whole" (*WIPP* 39–40; cf. *AAPL* 146ff.). From this it would follow that the distinctive Socratic way, insofar as it is the way preoccupied with the ideas, remains admittedly imperfect or in need of supplement: "The elusiveness of the whole necessarily affects the knowledge of every part" (*CM* 21; cf. MITP 114). At this juncture we take note of the fact that in calling the class the cause *par excellence* Strauss did not characterize it as a "final cause"; he did not say it involved a purpose: "One is . . . tempted to wonder whether the Xenophontic Socrates was not, like the Platonic Socrates, dissatisfied with the simple teleology—anthropocentric or not—which at first glance seems to supply the most rational solution to all difficulties, and turned for this reason to the 'What is . . . ?' questions or to the separating of beings according to kinds" (*XSD* 149; cf. *NRH* 145–146).

The Idea of Justice

From all this we are in a better position to understand why Strauss sometimes identified "the unchangeable ideas" with "the fundamental and permanent problems" (*WIPP* 39; cf. *OT* 210). Given our imperfect knowledge of the whole, the object of a "What is . . . ?" question remains ineluctably problematic; and this remains true even in those cases where we make the greatest progress in properly separating the beings. This holds to a special degree of the virtues, and of justice in particular: when we raise the "What Is . . . ?" question about other things, we do not mean to bring into doubt the very existence of the thing in question; but in asking about the virtues, and especially about justice, we recognize that our questioning can have this more radical thrust. Serious and thoughtful men, whose opinions are reported with respect in the Platonic dialogues, were led to deny that justice exists, apart from human assertion, wish and illusion. They were led to the view that the principles of sharing and mutual assistance, which it is claimed are requisite if society is to survive and satisfy man's deepest natural needs, are always in fact no more than the mechanisms whereby some are exploited by others—consciously or unconsciously. In other words they held that what is said to exist as "justice," like what is said to exist as Zeus, exists *only* in speech or opinion—in convention or custom—and not at all in or by nature. We express the special status of the idea or problem of justice when we name it the idea of "natural justice," or "natural right": the question of what distinguishes and constitutes justice or righteousness is accompanied or at least shadowed by the question of whether there is a thing of such a nature. To the extent that political thought takes for granted either the existence or the nonexistence of justice, and proceeds on this basis to clarify "what we mean by justice," it has not yet reached the level of Socratic political philosophy or dialectics.

What then is Plato's conception of the problem of justice, according to Strauss? Justice in the fullest sense comes to sight, in what men say about it, as an object of aspiration: as the "common good" which binds men together in mutual dedication in a political community. Most of the time, to be sure, the concern with justice is limited to much more partial questions about mine and thine. But these questions depend on some implicit answer, however imprecise, to the question of the overriding purposes of the community. These highest goals cannot be adequately defined in terms of the requirements which are ubiquitous in social life and which, for this reason as well as because of their urgency, present themselves as at first sight the most reasonable candidates for primacy—viz., the needs for physical comfort and safety. Man is such a being as cannot orient himself merely by the good, understood as what is useful for survival, health, and material ease. He is always aware of sacred restraints on the means he may employ to pursue these needs; what is more, he is aware that it is sometimes necessary, nay, praiseworthy and admirable, to relinquish or sacrifice the satisfaction of these needs. The choice of means, and the capacity for sacrifice, is dictated by the human concern for virtue or excellence. The virtues are indeed useful, for the pursuit of the mundane goals mentioned; but they are also valued as ends in themselves. They are honored as being noble. It is this dimension of what man values—the noble, the estimable or precious that cannot be reduced to the good or useful—which displays man's peculiarly moral mode of being. It is no accident that in Greek the word for noble (*kalon*) designates at the same time "beautiful." The noble and the beautiful originally belong together. We experience the noble as preeminently deserving of or calling for adornment and enshrinement; and the decorative or "aesthetically" pleasing we experience as in need of a seriousness which it finds only in association with the noble. Hence the *kalon* comes into its own in the works of the artists, and especially the poets: the *demiourgoi*, the "public workers" of the highest order. It is there that a people sees in the least fleeting and least nebulous way what kinds of human beings it reveres. Nevertheless, the peculiar luminosity of the virtues as they appear in the "imitations" of the artists does not necessarily promote a clear account of the noble. It remains much easier to point to particular instances of the noble or virtuous than to explain what the noble as such is; and the noble is never free for long from controversy. The source of the dispute is usually not doubt as to whether the virtues exist, or even what they are in general: there is remarkably broad agreement on the nobility of attributes such as courage, generosity, wisdom, law-abidingness, and so on. Battles tend to develop rather over the specifications and, what is graver, the relative ranking of the virtues (e.g., the virtues of war vs. those of peace; humility vs. pride; generosity and love of leisure vs. thrift and industry). These quarrels mingle with, at once elevating and intensifying, the more frequent causes of discord arising from competition for scarce resources. The disputes thus become, in more concrete terms, disputes over the superiority of distinct human types or classes and their claims to highest moral and political authority: priests, soldiers, merchants, small farmers, gentry, lawyers, wage laborers, etc., vie for preponderance in the political order. Insofar as each of these factions possesses a comprehensive vision of the proper distribution of goods and the ordering of the ways of life in the whole community, each is understood, in Platonic terms, to represent a specific "regime" (*politeia*). The conflicts among the various "regimes" are the decisive conflicts at the root of all political life; and it is the aim of Platonic political philosophy in the narrow or strict sense to arbitrate these conflicts.

It does so chiefly by setting forth a single standard, the "best regime by nature," in the light of which the competing regimes that emerge in history can be judged, categorized, and—in favorable circumstances—"mixed" in judicious compromises. What is involved in elaborating the best regime Plato shows in the *Laws*, his "most political work" or indeed "his only political work" ("the *Republic* does not in fact present the best political order but rather brings to light the limitations, the limits, and therewith the nature of politics"—*AAPL* 1; cf. *CM* 29 and *WIPP* 29). The political philosopher tries to discover the best regime by critically cross-examining, and bringing into debate, intelligent spokesmen for the historical regimes widely regarded as the most respectable; he seeks to go beyond these spokesmen in the direction seemingly indicated by their contradictions and deficiences. In thus acting as "umpire" or as teacher of statesmen and founders, the Platonic political philosopher proceeds in a manner very different from that of the present-day social scientist or the "modern" philosopher like Hobbes or Hegel. He does not begin with "methodological" or "epistemological" considerations. He does not try to move from the "abstract" to the "concrete." Instead, he tries to look with the eyes of the shrewd practicing statesman and to speak his language, but to look further afield and to describe both what exists and what might come into being with greater precision. He even tries to protect such a statesman's perspective from distortions caused by the puzzling questions of sophisticated adults and young people who lack either the public spirit or the firsthand experience of the statesman (*WIPP* 27–29).

But this implies that the Platonic political philosopher adopts the perspective of the statesman through a conscious decision; that his decision is undertaken from a perspective very different from the statesman's; and that the decision to become a "political" philosopher in the strict sense entails a deliberate narrowing, a "dimming" of the philosopher's vision (*WIPP* 32). Even though Artistotle and Plato succeeded in making the ascent from the statesman's outlook to that of the philosopher appear, in hindsight, continuous and even "natural," we must not be deceived by that appearance into supposing that political philosophy actually emerges out of the disputes of statesmen. Nor ought we allow ourselves to fall into the error of understanding the Platonic political philosopher as some kind of continuation, or superior version, of the statesman and lawgiver (*AAPL* 106; *OT* 212). Strauss never tired of reminding his readers of the "almost overwhelming difficulties which had to be overcome before philosophers could devote any serious attention to political things," or of the fact that "Socrates himself, the founder of political philosophy, was famous as a philosopher before he ever turned to political philosophy" (*WIPP* 92). Strauss was far from regarding this sequence of Socrates' life as a mere historical contingency or accident. On the contrary: in Strauss's view, Socrates' life is emblematic of the permanent truth that philosophy is not "naturally" political; that it must be "compelled" to turn its attention back to "the human things," "the just and noble things" (*CM* 13–14; cf. 124–25, 127–28).[3] The problem that is thus revealed, which Strauss called "the problem of Socrates," involves in the first place the question "why pre-Socratic philosophy was able or compelled to dispense with political philosophy" and, in the second place, the

---

3. One of the severest criticisms Strauss ever leveled against Hobbes was that "Hobbes accepted on trust the view that political philosophy or political science is possible or necessary" (*NRH* 167); Hobbes thereby showed that he had paid insufficient attention, from the very beginning, to the fundamental question.

question why the Platonic and Xenophontic Socrates was enabled or compelled to found "political" philosophy (*SA* 3–8, 314). These questions, which point to two alternative conceptions of the nature of the philosophic life, must be answered if there is to be a genuine understanding of the problem of justice. For the emergence of philosophy, understood as a distinct form of excellence in its own right, radically alters our comprehension of what might conceivably be the good for man, and hence our comprehension of the common good. It is not true, for Plato and Xenophon at least, that philosophy is merely the most powerful instrument by which man, as "the political animal," furthers political society's pursuit of the just and the noble. We will never grasp adequately what Strauss, following Plato and Xenophon, means by "philosophy" so long as we try to conceive of philosophy as merely a method of thought, or an assemblage of intellectual tools, or even as the most comprehensive sort of reflection which culminates in a "total world-view": *philosophy is, above all, a unique way of life; and the authentic philosophers are human beings of a different kind from all other human beings* (*WIPP* 91). In order to avoid misunderstandings, one must hasten to add that "such men are extremely rare. We are not likely to meet any of them in any classroom. We are not likely to meet any of them anywhere. It is a piece of good luck if there is a single one alive in one's time." Hence, to say the least, "it is as absurd to expect members of philosophy departments to be philosophers as it is to expect members of art departments to be artists" (*LAM* 3, 7).

The Problem of Socrates

In *Natural Right and History* Strauss did not pretend to offer an adequate exposition of the Socratic way of life (see esp. 142, 145–46, 151–52); at the beginning of his discussion of "classic natural right" he declared that "the full understanding of the classic natural right doctrine would require a full understanding of the change in thought that was effected by Socrates"; but he then confessed immediately, "such an understanding is not at our disposal." It is difficult to say to what extent Strauss felt he had remedied this deficiency in subsequent years. What we do know for certain is that twenty years later Strauss had come to believe that the book could have been rewritten in an improved version. His own understanding of "natural right and history" had "deepened" in the interval; and apparently the most important aspect of the deepening had resulted from his "concentration on the study of 'classic natural right,' and in particular on 'Socrates'" ("Preface to the 7th Impression"). The "concentration" on Socrates evidently continues in the present volume—not only in the chapters discussing the *Apology of Socrates, Theages, Crito*, and *Euthydemus*, but, less conspicuously, in several of the other chapters as well. Strauss brings out early on the fact that the *Apology of Socrates*, the most comprehensive and public presentation of Socrates' whole life and way of life, spotlights the perplexing character of the relation between Socrates' mature thought or activity and his earlier investigations into nature and rhetoric. Socrates insists from the beginning that the official indictment is wholly derivative from an older, unofficial, but far more dangerous accusation which links him directly with other philosophers. He stresses the importance of the comic poet Aristophanes in the genesis of that first accusation. Yet as Strauss demonstrates, Socrates' purported refutation of the "first accusers" is so astonishingly ambiguous and weak that it has the necessary effect of heightening, rather than laying to rest, the wonder of the attentive reader. In order to appreciate the background of Strauss's highly compressed scrutiny of the *Apology*, a scrutiny guided by this wonder, it is helpful, if not essential, to have in view at least a brief summary of Strauss's previous reflections on what was involved in the eruption of philosophy out of prephilosophic life.

The Quarrel between Philosophy and Poetry

From a long study of the evidence available Strauss concluded that philosophy originally represents a thoroughgoing, if muted, rebellion against the spiritual authority of civil society (*NRH*, chap. 3). The seeds of the rebellion are sown by meditation on the seemingly endless disagreements among and within societies over the character of the just and the noble. To these disquieting thoughts are joined doubts engendered by dilemmas men encounter no matter what they believe to be noble. Always, the relation between the noble and the good (the pleasant, the useful, the healthful) appears problematic. Virtue seems to shine forth in its purest nobility when it entails painful sacrifice; yet we are aware that the whole good for man, the good that embraces but transcends virtue, is happiness. There must then be some positive correlation between virtue and happiness: but what can that be? Then again, we honor the virtuous not only for their pure intentions but for their solid accomplishments—virtue is understood to be good or useful as well as noble. Indeed, it is only with a view to its intended accomplishments that virtue seems to find measure: courage is guided by the need to conclude battles, moderation is guided by the need for health, generosity is guided by the requirements of the potential recipients, and so forth. But by its very usefulness, by its becoming limited in this way, virtue always verges on becoming, if not a mere means, then at any rate something of subordinate value.

Prior to the emergence of philosophy, questions of this kind are answered through appeals to antiquity (the ancestral) and to divinity. The principles of right and wrong embodied in a people's laws and customs are said to be good because they are old; but the old is said to be good because it leads back to

God or the gods, who created, or talked to, or in fact were, the oldest ancestors. The divine is immortal and either omnipotent or at least extraordinarily powerful. With its power it upholds the just and the noble, though in ways not always intelligible to men. Even if it fails fully to resolve the paradoxes of humanity's moral existence, it allows a glimpse of a realm which transfigures the human, and thus makes dimly comprehensible the reason why man's life can achieve only a truncated, reflected perfection. The restricted access men have to the divine is mainly by way of the ancient sacred writings and the songs of prophetic men who are inspired; among the Greeks in particular, it was especially the poets, inspired by the Muses, who revealed the ways of the gods and hence were accorded the honor of being held wise.

Now the men who foreshadow the philosophers are the men who find that the pronouncements of the poets, singers, or prophets do not remove but instead magnify and compound the moral conundrums. For such men, the accounts told of God or the gods only make plainer the disturbing disproportion between the answers men need and the arbitrariness, as well as the disgraceful lack of unanimity, exhibited by the highest authorities. Philosophy itself is born in the time when men perplexed to this degree no longer seek for better sources of poetic or prophetic wisdom, but instead uncover, and finally apply even to the poets' works, the criterion of nature. The discovery of nature grows out of the intransigent insistence upon two distinctions: in the first place, between knowledge based on hearsay and knowledge derived from experiences available to everyone; and, in the second place, between things that come into being as a result of imaginative human artifice and things (including man and his capacity to construct artifacts) that exist or grow by themselves. When viewed in the light of this distinction between what is by nature and what is by artifice or convention, the gods appear to be merely the fictions of the poets and their sponsors or listeners. Belief in the gods is seen to veil from man the evidence whose reasonable interpretation would lead toward knowledge of the true causes of things. In particular, it seems plausible to suppose that the gods are needed as supporters of nobility and justice because nobility and justice lack intrinsic support in the hearts of men—in their natural and not simply imagined needs and inclinations. After all, that which men incontrovertibly seek and need is not the noble but, rather, personal pleasure, security, and comfort. The concern for the noble can best be explained on the basis of speculations about its origins. Then one recognizes that the noble was in all likelihood the semiconscious invention of primitive men, who congregated and gradually devised civil societies in order to further their several individual interests: in the process, they found that it was necessary to encourage, through praise, honor, and habituation, some among themselves to sacrifice their original, natural good for the sake of the good of others. Over long ages, and given the plastic power of custom, the concern with being held to be noble or at least not ignoble has gained such strength that it now competes with man's natural, spontaneous, and uninvented desires, and obfuscates the calculation which naturally serves and guides the latter. Yet through piercing, uncompromising thought and iron self-discipline some men can liberate themselves from the sway of opinion and learn to content themselves with the pursuit of the pleasures that are truly or intrinsically sweet. Since man does, by nature, need the assistance of society, the truly free man will continue to dwell among and profit from his deluded neighbors; but spiritually he will live a life apart.

Many who hear and are affected by the teaching of the philosophers leap to the conclusion that the best life according to nature is that of the tyrant, who dominates his fellow men in order to reap honor and enjoy luxury. But the philosophers themselves are as scornful of the need for honor and luxury as they are of the need for myths about gods and an afterlife; for them the tyrant is as much a slave as the subjects over whom he wastes his energies and worries. Man's material requirements are by nature few, and he who understands this can devote most of his life to the deepest genuine pleasure—that of the thinking which liberates itself from every delusion or false hope, and thus comes to bask in the austere light shed by increasing knowledge of the unfailing nature of things.

This great rebellion of the philosophers against divine wisdom, against the wisdom of the poets, did not go unanswered. The most important document available to us from what Plato's Socrates calls "the old quarrel between philosophy and poetry" (*Republic* 607b) is Aristophanes' comedy *The Clouds*—a work which happens to be directed against none other than Socrates himself. We must content ourselves with singling out three salient points from Strauss's rich presentation of the Aristophanean critique of philosophy. First, the philosopher is absurdly lacking in prudence or practical wisdom. He depends on the law-abidingness and decency of the city and the family, while he gives expression to teachings which corrode the irreplaceable moral foundations of civilized society. His attempts, through subtle rhetoric, to cloak his true doctrines and to defend himself and his associates are wholly inadequate. The principal reason for this inadequacy is to be found in his second massive failing: he is laughably ignorant of the human soul and its remarkable heterogeneity. Above all, the philosopher is ignorant of his own soul and its needs. He fixes his gaze aloft and devotes himself almost fanatically to the passionate unraveling of the mysteries of the cosmos without inquiring adequately into what it is that makes it good or attractive for him to seek the causes of things. Insofar as his soul is truly dead to love—love of pleasure, as well as love of beauty or nobility—the philosopher lacks a crucial awareness, or else has so suppressed and sublimated part of his awareness that he has mutilated himself without realizing it. Moreover, he never reflects enough on his need for students, admirers, and friends, or on the necessary attachment this entails to the well-being of the city and its civic education and family upbringing. But for Strauss, if not for Aristophanes himself, these first two criticisms open the door to a third and even graver challenge. Socrates denies the existence of Zeus; and behind this blasphemy, Aristophanes shows, there stands an unqualified atheism— an atheism even more radical, in some ways, than that of other "pre-Socratic" philosophers like Parmenides and Empedocles (*SA* 173). Now given Socrates' ignorance about the soul, can his cosmology—however plausible—provide sufficient grounds for such atheism? Or is not Socrates' atheism, and his contempt for Divine Law, his greatest piece of boasting? For the truth is, the philosopher's purported knowledge of nature culminates (at best) in barely plausible and very incomplete hypotheses about the ultimate roots of things: the cosmology thus makes only more apparent or likely the ultimate indecipherability of the whole for man. Hence it leaves still unsolved not only the question of the existence of the divine, but also the problem of the nature—or, put more cautiously, the "godness"—of god or the gods (*SA* 52–53, 313). When Aristophanes, speaking on behalf of poetry and especially comic poetry, proclaims his superiority in wisdom, he does so without any trace of moralism: for he accepts and shares the philosopher's longing for independence from the opinions of the city. He in fact succeeds where the philosophers fail. He does so because he knows the limitations of authentic human independence. The comic poet can in public poke fun at the city's beliefs because he shows that he ultimately makes a genuine bow to some version of them. He lampoons the city's faith in its gods, and the hopes and longings expressed in that faith, but he does so without pretending to be himself altogether free of those hopes and longings, and without simply denying the existence of the divine—however it may wish, or may allow itself, to be named from time to time.

The Socratic Turn

Strauss was convinced that the key to understanding the works of Plato and Xenophon was the recognition that they were intended, in part, as a response to Aristophanes' powerful attack on philosophy. The response concedes a great deal of ground. In other words, Plato and Xenophon defend a conception of the philosophic life that has been altered in the light of what was learned from Aristophanes; they portray a "Socrates become beautiful and new" (*Second Letter* 314c). Yet the closer one looks the more difficult it becomes to spell out precisely in what the newness consists. In his reading of the *Apology* Strauss shows that the impression one first receives, or at any rate the impression traditionally handed down, of Socrates as the "citizen-philosopher" is in need of considerable qualification (cf. *NRH*

120–121; *LAM* 269). The mature, Platonic Socrates did not abandon a dedication to a life of inquiry so consuming as to make him appear very, very strange—even inhuman (31b); he did not rejoin the regular citizenry as an enlightened leader, or as an active follower, or even as a political adviser or commentator or historian. Nor did he ever become a teacher of civic virtue (and therefore, he insists, he cannot be held responsible for the morals of any of those who hung around listening to him "talking and minding my own business"–33a).

What *is* new is Socrates' emphatic admission that his idiosyncratic way of life has to be justified according to standards acceptable to the city and its moral-religious beliefs. In presenting this justification, however, Socrates does not limit himself to showing how, as "Gadfly," he recalled the city to the highest aspirations it already recognized. He goes on to make the claim that his life is in fact the unexpected summit of human existence—to which the good citizens, the gentlemen or the pious ones, have always more or less unknowingly looked up (38a). Socrates supports or leads up to what Strauss calls this "momentous statement" by developing a new interpretation of the tradition, including its greatest hero (Achilles) and its foremost contemporary mouthpiece (the Delphic Oracle). One may suggest that he alloys the gods of the poetic tradition with the gods of the philosophers. He surely maintains that the man who lives as Socrates does is the man most favored by the gods. This, it seems, is the principal way in which the Platonic philosopher assists the city and justifies himself before it: by offering the life of the philosopher—or a noble image in speech of that life—as the otherwise unrecognized standard in the light of which the disagreements over the just and the noble can be arbitrated and the relation of the noble to the good (to happiness) clarified. The moral virtues ultimately draw their dignity from the fact that they can be so interpreted as to become akin to, dim reflections of, even in some measure openings to, the philosophic life. It is here that we find the deepest ground on which Plato and Aristotle rest when they rank and explicate the political and moral virtues. They do not deny that those virtues are experienced as noble ends in themselves; but they doubt whether morality's elavation can be sustained unless it is conceived as somehow an adumbration of the quasi-divine experiences and pleasures of the philosopher. Yet if this is true, if there is even a likelihood that the philosophic life may be the polestar of human existence, it becomes all the more urgent that we arrive at a more than formulaic understanding of what that life is.

From what has been brought out so far, one might conclude that the revolution in thought effected by the Platonic Socrates involves more an attempt to transform the nature of the beliefs underlying civil society than a change in the beliefs and life of the philosopher. Yet not for one moment does Socrates suppose that moral and political virtue can be made philosophic, or that a healthy society can become rational, and thus cease to be a "closed" society. He knows he cannot hope to do more than induce in a few of the nonphilosophers (namely, the gentlemen or "true guardians" of the city) a respect for a certain poetic image of philosophy. The new Socrates has learned the lesson in political and psychological prudence that Aristophanes sought to teach. He has recognized his manifold dependence (both erotic and calculative) on those who are not philosophic, and accordingly acknowledges the unwritten, natural law which compels him to interest himself in their concerns. This means of course that the content of the philosophic life must undergo considerable change: Socrates must sympathize with and enter into the lives of human beings whom he cannot hope will ever partake of philosophic friendship or teach him much of anything. The most obvious sign of this great change is the fact that the new Socrates is married and has children.

It is true that Socrates is revealed to be not a very assiduous husband or father. Xenophon, who according to Strauss presents Socrates' marriage as a kind of image of his relation to the city, depicts that marriage as comic, and even "goes so far as not to count the husband of Xanthippe among the married men" (*OT* 210, 221; *XS* 41–42, 147, 178; *XSD* 132ff.). Analogously, the dialogue which is "*the* Platonic dialogue about politics" is the sole dialogue from which Socrates is totally absent. Yet, while Strauss emphasizes that the *Laws* is "sub-Socratic," he also demonstrates, through his interpretation of the *Crito*, that Socrates' absence is less "total" than it at first seems (cf. below, chap. 2, with *WIPP* 31–33; *AAPL* 2). Indeed it is the *Crito*, Strauss here shows, which provides us with the most vivid lesson in how the life of the Platonic political philosopher entails dealing with, and even caring for, fellow citizens who are utterly without philosophic interest or promise. As always, Strauss insists that one cannot understand a Platonic dialogue unless one attends first and foremost to the drama, to the characters or character types Socrates is shown encountering and to what that encounter reveals about the place of the philosophic impulse in the whole economy of human existence. Crito represents *the* unerotic or prosaic soul, the soul largely uninspired and unmoved by piety, poetry, and wonder. It is primarily with a view to men of this kind that Plato develops what one may call his "doctrine of legal obligation" or, better expressed, his view of the most reasonable bases for the law-abidingness of most men in most of the available lawful regimes. The *Crito*, Strauss concludes, proves that Hobbes "committed a grave exaggeration" (i.e., that he did not simply tell a lie) when he accused Socrates and those who follow him (e.g., Strauss) of being anarchists.

In Strauss's view, a full appreciation of Crito's character, and therewith an accurate assessment of the teaching conveyed by the *Crito*, requires that one turn to the only other dialogue in which Crito is the interlocutor: the *Euthydemus*. Who Crito is and what relation he bears to Socrates in the

Platonic portrayal becomes clearer when he is seen reacting to Socrates'
recounting of a previous encounter with two other human types situated, so
to speak, at equidistant poles from one another and from Crito in the field of
the Platonic Socrates' acquaintances. Through Socrates' narrative, we hear
now Socrates comports himself toward, in the first place, a beautiful and
promising boy (Kleinias), and, secondly, two particularly frivolous representatives of the "sophistic" movement. As regards the two sophists, they
seem at first blush to represent the limit case, or to reveal the complete lack
of seriousness toward which sophistry can lead: the "virtue" they pride
themselves on teaching is an art of speaking which makes no discernible
contribution to anything worthwhile, and certainly not to the speeches and
deeds expected of men in political life. Unfortunately, Socrates is absolutely
exuberant in his admiration of these dubious characters, whose pupil he
intends to become. Strauss warns the reader against brushing this exuber-
ance aside as "mere irony." At the same time, he also warns us against
adopting too hastily Crito's attitude of disappointment or even censure at
Socrates' expression of respect. The fact is, the *Euthydemus* provides
perhaps the most arresting testimony to a truth that will disappoint many
and that runs counter to the impression Socrates gives in his public speech
when on trial: the settings of the Platonic dialogues show that Plato's
Socrates was far more likely to be found conversing on good terms with
foreign sophists and those drawn to them than with statesmen, poets,
craftsmen, and serious Athenian gentlemen in other walks of life (cf. *CM*
57). A major reason for this proclivity is revealed by the drama of the
Euthydemus, as well as by the drama of many other dialogues. Socrates
shares with the sophists a deep dissatisfaction with conventional civic and
paternal education, and seeks to rescue some of the young—especially the
most truly capable—from its deadening effects. The *Euthydemus* affords a
rare, capital example of Socrates' protreptic: of the sort of speech by which
he tries to test the most promising sons of his fellow citizens, and then lead a
very few (like Kleinias perhaps) away from politics and the family toward a
life like his own, while moderating or making more "gentle" the "manly"
civic spirit of the rest (like Ctessipos). The outstanding difference between
Socrates and the sophists is that the various sophists resemble the city in
claiming to know what virtue is and how the young can be led to it. The fact
that Socrates has very great doubts about this claim in no way excludes the
possibility that he may learn a great deal by spending time with intelligent
men who have the daring to make such an assertion. These reflections help
explain why Socrates is, in the *Euthydemus* and in general, much more a
defender of the sophists (even or especially the ones who are least "serious") than some might wish—while at the same time he attempts to
admonish those same sophists, and suggest to them that they temper some of
their imprudent zeal.

One thing assuredly has now become clear: the new "political" philos-ophizing originated by Socrates is preoccupied to an unprecedented extent with mastering and practicing the art of rhetoric or communication. The new philosopher is keenly conscious of how delicate—how dangerous and yet how eminently useful and necessary—is the task of communicating with the extraordinarily diverse nonphilosophic society he and his kind must always inhabit. We must therefore deplore the fate which prevented Strauss from executing his proposed essay on the *Gorgias*—the principal Platonic dia-logue on political rhetoric. From the few remarks Strauss had already made in print about the *Gorgias*, it may be surmised that he would not have treated that dialogue without some reference to the *Phaedrus*; because it was his understanding that Plato's teaching on rhetoric or communication cannot be grasped unless one follows carefully the distinction which dictates the dualism of treatment represented by these twin works: namely, the distinction between private, erotic rhetoric and public, political rhetoric (*NRH* 152n; *AAPL* 2, 62; *CM* 52–53; *WIPP* 299–302). This dichotomy is intimately linked to the dichotomy between conversations Socrates engaged in out of a spontaneous need rooted in the heart of his philosophic activity, and conversations he was led to engage in out of necessity or compulsion—be it imposed from the outside or self-imposed. But reflecting on this last observation allows us to see that in Strauss's interpretation of the twin dialogues *Crito-Euthydemus* we have an illustrative foreshadowing of what he would have thought or said about the dyad *Gorgias-Phaedrus*. Among other things, the protreptic conversation with "the child Kleinias" may be said to provide at least an anticipatory glimpse of Socrates' erotic rhetoric. This rhetoric, as exemplified here, contains what Strauss characterizes as a "ruthless questioning of what Aristotle would have called the moral vir-tues." It leads up to Socrates' repeated indication that "philosophy and the political art have different ends" or that there is a "radical distinction between dialectics and the kingly art." In contradistinction to the political or kingly art, dialectics is the art which makes use of the discoveries made by mathematicians and astronomers.

We are thus forced to confront squarely the question around which we have been circling: to what extent was the *core* of Socratic philosophizing affected by the Socratic turn? On this, after all, hinges the meaning of "Platonic political philosophy." Let's return for a moment to the beginning or to the surface: to the words "political philosophy." They bespeak an ambiguity which runs throughout the thought of Socrates, and of Strauss. The words may mean: that philosophizing which takes as its principal subject matter politics—the human things, the just and noble things; but it may also mean: that philosophizing which continues to pursue the inquiry into nature as a whole—including man, as a part of nature—but does so now in a political or politic manner. Taken in this latter sense, the word *political* is at least tinged with a "derogatory" connotation (*WIPP* 93 n. 24). Despite this, Strauss holds that it is this latter sense which is the "deeper meaning of 'political philosophy'" (*WIPP* 93–94). Strauss can thereby be understood to imply that the core of Socratic philosophy was not decisively altered by the Socratic turn. In harmony with such a conclusion, we find Strauss suggesting—on the basis of what he learns from Xenophon—that the mature Socrates, when not under the obligation to keep company with gentlemen-citizens, pursued investigations into the paradoxical nature of light and of liquids, and into the question "Are the beings numbers?" When engaging in such investigations it seems likely that Socrates departed much earlier, and more sharply, from the ordinary opinions that were always his starting point than he did when he was investigating the nature of, say, justice. Xenophon, as Strauss puts it, only "points to the center of Socrates' life—a center of which he does not speak owing to the limitation he has imposed on himself." The pointing occurs, for example, by way of metaphor—as when Xenophon has the subtle and erotic Charmides attest to the truth he stumbled upon by accident one day: Socrates loves to dance alone, in a room with seven empty couches. Such a hint about the radically "solitary" life of the "philosophizing hermit," the "barbarian" Socrates, is even more remarkable than Xenophon's unmetaphorical report of Socrates' declaration to the effect that when he is with his "good friends" they read and inquire into old books together—an activity never once depicted by Xenophon (*XS* 8–9, 29–30, 116–17, 124, 148, 159–60, 169–70; *PAW* 136–41; below, p. 00).

Yet it seems to me at least that these interpretative reflections by Strauss do not necessarily imply that the true, hidden Socrates remained largely "undialectical" and untouched by his "political" accommodations when it came to his chief study, the study of the natural cosmos. I would submit, rather, that Strauss means this: though Socrates remained in his deepest thinking essentially solitary, and though he did not turn away from cosmology, he nevertheless "originated a new kind of the study of the natural things—a kind of study in which, for example, the nature or idea of justice, or natural right, and surely the nature of the human soul or man, is more important than, for example, the nature of the sun" (*HPP* 5; cf. *XS* 21; *SA* 314; *CM* 16). But then what exactly is the ground for the new importance of the human soul in the context of the study of the whole cosmos? What is the crucial thought that Plato and Xenophon believed had been missed by thinkers of the rank of Heraclitus, Parmenides, and the young Socrates?

The Theological-Political Problem

I cannot supply the answer to these questions. I can only offer some heuristic reflections and some tentative beginnings of answers which I believe may help explain, and thus find confirmation in, the selection and ordering of the following essays. I begin from two seemingly disparate points whose inner connection I was taught to see by Christopher Bruell. In the first place, let us note that all but one of the previous paragraph's references to Strauss's interpretation of the Xenophontic Socrates are to a book which is explicitly and emphatically a sequel. That to which it is a sequel is Strauss's commentary on Xenophon's *Oeconomicus*. The latter work deserves, according to Strauss, to be called "*the* Socratic discourse." Strauss's commentary on it, one might then conclude, deserves to be called *the* Straussian discourse.[4] At any rate, the *Oeconomicus* is "the most revealing" of Xenophon's Socratic writings because in it Socrates recounts (to Critobulus, the wayward son who is shown to be Crito's chief concern in Plato's *Euthydemus*) the conversation that occurred on the very day he made his famous turn. For the first time in his philosophic career, Socrates on that day examined a citizen-farmer who was or who was purported to be a perfect gentleman; he did so with a view to discovering what constitutes gentlemanliness, nobility, or morality. In the course of the conversation the differences between the philosopher ("pre-Socratic" and "Socratic") and the decent or noble citizen-gentleman attain an unprecedented clarity. Especially pregnant in its import is the difference that emerges between the two men as regards their understanding of the place of man in the whole. The moral gentleman teaches that the divine, and the unwritten law that somehow derives from the divine or from "nature" infused with the divine, endows "nature" with an order and meaning in the absence of which life and the world would be, for him, senseless. Simultaneously, the gentleman cannot help but disclose the deeply rooted longings or hopes upon which his conviction rests: the grounding in these "psychic" needs becomes manifest because the conversation reveals the logical and empirical inadequacy of the arguments which claim to furnish the grounding. Now the conversational activity by which Socrates brought all this to light, together with the activity by which he now recounts that bringing to light, to himself and to young men like Critobulus and the silent witness Xenophon, seems to constitute the Socratic dialectic *par excellence*.

Bearing this in mind, let us turn to the second point: to Strauss's declaration, in 1965, that since the time of his first work on Spinoza (i.e., since his mid-twenties) "the theological-political problem has remained *the* theme of my investigations" (*PPH*; cf. AP). This pronouncement obviously raises a host of questions. To begin with, what does Strauss mean by "the theological-political problem?" The phrase is drawn, as Strauss often noted with gratitude, from Spinoza; it signifies, most simply put, the apparently irresolvable conflict between the claims of reason and of revelation. That conflict, Strauss learned first from Spinoza, is as much a political as it is a

---

4. For what follows, cf. Christopher Bruell, "Strauss on Xenophon's Socrates," forthcoming in the *Political Science Reviewer*.

"theological" or "philosophic" problem. For revelation cannot be adequately understood if it is approached merely as "religious experience" in the sense of William James and other "psychologists of religion." Revelation is the authoritative disclosure to man of Divine Law—the Torah, the *Chari'a*, the "Old Law" and the "New Law"; this rule of law claims to give the ultimate direction to the whole of man's existence, collective as well as individual or familial. Strauss absolutely denied that the theological-political problem was a problem that arose only with the advent of monotheism or of the biblical religions and the "holy" God. By way of Spinoza, he learned from Maimonides and eventually from Farabi that the heart of revelation is the phenomenon of the "prophet," the human lawgiver who through his oratory or poetic speech orders the community and the nation or nations in the name of divine authority; and Strauss learned from the same teachers to appreciate the words of Avicenna, the words Strauss chose as the epigraph to his last published work, on Plato's *Laws*: "the treatment of prophecy and the Divine Law is contained in . . . the *Laws*." Strauss did not overlook, he rather brought out and stressed, the enormous differences between biblical thought and the thought of the Greek poets; but he regarded those differences as, in the final analysis, secondary. What is most essential in the quarrel between Plato and the Bible is already present in the quarrel between Plato and the poets or in the muted dispute between Socrates and Ischomachus. Strauss seems to have regarded Yehuda Halevi as perhaps the greatest directly antiphilosophic thinker in Judaism; and of Halevi he concluded, "His basic objection to philosophy was not then particularly Jewish, nor even particularly religious, but moral." In this connection Strauss also remarked: "Moral man *as such* is the potential believer" (my italics; *PAW* 140–41).

Why then does the theological-political problem dominate the project of Platonic political philosophy as Strauss understands it, and just what form does that problem assume? To come at least within hailing distance of the answer we must return, it seems to me, to the topic with which we began. The doctrine of ideas as Strauss interprets it is a doctrine that makes clear not the precise limits (in a Kantian sense), but the radical substantive limitedness, of human knowledge. To know the ideas is to be an expert, as Socrates says in the *Theages* and *Symposium*, in only one small respect: in *erotics* or love matters, in awareness of the neediness of the human condition. But this expertise is, as Socrates in the *Apology* has it, a "certain wisdom," or even "human wisdom." To know that one does not yet have satisfactory answers to the most important questions, to know that one has only more or less solid opinions (*doxai*) about what is just and noble, is to know that one has progressed from an earlier condition of far greater ignorance; it is to know that the awareness of this progress is accompanied by a deep if austere pleasure; above all, it is to know that the thing most needed is to continue this progress. This means, however, that one has an answer to the most important question for man: while it is true that, strictly speaking, one cannot claim to know the health of the soul, or its perfection, or the complete fulfillment and happiness of man, it is also true that one can rightly lay claim to know what is, in the carefully chosen expression of Socrates, "the greatest good" for man—the best available or conceivable: "It so happens that the greatest good for a human being is this, each day to make arguments about virtue and about the other matters concerning which you hear me conversing and examining myself and others; and the unexamined life is not worth living for a human being." All men other than the philosopher, one may say, live lives that are tragic or comic or both: the rest of us are all in the most important respects deluded boasters, skaters on thin ice who are unwilling or unable to look down for very long at what lies under our feet.

Yet this formulation of Socrates' human wisdom remains incomplete because it omits mention of the Delphic Oracle. Whatever Socrates' tale about the Oracle may mean, in its Platonic version it surely seems to suggest at least this: the Socratic turn involved a new hearkening to the voice of authoritative piety, a hearkening which took more seriously than anyone ever had before that voice's speech about the paltriness of human knowledge—took it seriously in the sense of refusing either to accept it or ignore or bypass it but instead attempting, as Socrates says, to "refute" it. Out of that attempted refutation grew Socrates' certainty as to his own peculiar wisdom and, concomitantly, his belief in the Oracle's correctness (insofar, that is, as the oracle was enabled or compelled to make Socrates its interpreter and spokesman). Let me try to express this in unmetaphorical language. The apparent unassailability of the Socratic position as to the "greatest good" for man would seem to be dissipated by the very existence of other intelligent men claiming to be guided by prophetic inspiration. Their claim, properly put, is not abashed by the disclosure, under Socratic questioning, of its total lack of sufficient reasons. Piety does not pretend to have grounding in what is comprehensible to unassisted human reason and experience. It appeals to a being, a realm, and experiences which exist and act in terms of what the philosophers call the "miraculous" or the "supernatural." Confronted with this appeal or claim, philosophy appears to be truly embarrassed. Every attempt by any philosopher to refute the claim, and hence the commands, of any revelation—even the most "fundamentalist" interpretations of revelation—fails, or can be shown to relapse into logical fallacy. In every case, the philosopher cannot escape the need to begin by assuming as a premise precisely what he is supposed to be demonstrating as a conclusion; in one way or another, the philosopher always assumes that his human reason can rule out, or at least discover the fixed limits of, what he calls the "miraculous." (The attempts by neo-Darwinians to limit the claims to knowledge, and hence the access to the education of the young, of so-called "Creation-ists" are painfully stark contemporary examples of the bluster and unscien-tific indignation into which rationalism collapses in these cases.) Now as Strauss was wont to point out, there is only one indisputable, logical proce-dure by which the philosopher can achieve a decisive refutation of the claims of piety or revelation that will allow him to put this dispute behind him and get on with his own business: he can show that in principle he has a clear and exhaustive explanation of how and why everything in the entire cosmos is as it is and behaves as it does. Then and only then can he honestly assert that he knows there is no room or place from which the miraculous can erupt to transform everything or anything in ways conceivable and inconceivable. The mature Socrates seems to have been the first philosopher who realized not merely that such a comprehensive account of things eludes man, but how dire are the consequences of this fact for the claims of philosophy. For this situation seems to imply that the philosopher's refusal to obey Divine Law, and to limit his thinking to the service of that law—his rejection of revelation in favor of reason—is finally rooted in an act of faith, of arbitrary will or decision, and not in reasoning. The ground of philosophy and the philo-sophic life is not superior to, it is basically the same as, a variant of, piety. But then philosophy is trapped in self-contradiction: philosophy claims that life can and should be based on reason, but this claim is itself not based on reason. Religious piety, which frankly confesses its own intellectual limita-tions, which submits to and obeys that which is beyond and above, would seem to admit more honestly, think through more fully, and understand better, the meaning of the experience of faith; moreover, religious piety would seem to remain closer to those simple, original experiences of right and wrong which are the root of the philosopher's humanity and his very concern for discovering the right way to live. Philosophy stands revealed then as a degenerate form of piety—querulous, exiguous, vain, and insuf-ficiently self-reflective (MITP; see below, chapter 7 and the beginning of chapter 12).

It is the theological-political problem so understood which forces itself to the permanent center of the Socratic philosopher's attention. The choice to live as a philosopher ceases to be simply an act of faith or of will if and only if it is a choice to live as a philosopher preoccupied with the serious examina-tion of the phenomena and the arguments of faith: if and only if, that is, the philosopher never completely ceases engaging in conversational scrutiny of those who articulate most authoritatively and compellingly the claims of the faithful, and if and only if through that perscrutation he repeatedly shows to his own satisfaction and to that of others that he has, not a definitive, but a fuller account of the moral experiences to which the pious point as their most significant experiences. The theme of such dialogues will always be in one way or another the human soul and the needs or longings of the soul which, the pious claim, allow us an intimation of the divine. In examining the needs of the soul the philosopher must perforce examine the needs of his own soul; he must try to become more fully aware of the perhaps hidden presuppositions about the noble or the good which may constitute an unexamined "faith" motivating his philosophizing.[5] In short, he must become an even more subtle and open-minded expert in erotics. Though Socrates may frequently and for considerable periods devote his thoughts to problems far from the life of man, it would seem he cannot ever leave altogether behind his wondering about the soul's needs and about the way those needs shape his wondering in general.

Conclusion

There is doubtless much more to be said about the nature of the dialectic that lies at the heart of Platonic political philosophy. But the preceding attempt to locate the nerve of Strauss's argument suggests that in his view a considerable portion of the Platonic philosopher's energies will be devoted to a painstaking, critical examination of intelligent spokesmen for, and students of, the various forms of piety. Accordingly, we find that the chapters on Plato are followed by a consideration or reconsideration of what Thucydides has to say about the Greek gods and the piety they solicit. Strauss then proceeds to a discussion of the quasi-autobiographical masterpiece of the Socratic who involved himself most directly and vigorously in the political world dominated by belief in these and in other, non-Greek, gods. The enormous demands—of concentration, careful reading, and questioning thought—that Strauss imposes on the reader in these two essays are partly intended, I surmise, to help us appreciate the effort we must make if we are to retrieve the original issues at stake in the confrontation between Socratic philosophy and the "natural" or prephilosophic life-world of politics, morality, and faith. The very success of Plato's rhetoric, deployed and inflated in ways he could not have precisely foretold, helped make it possible for the permanent problems, as Plato conceived them, to become overlain and obscured. Sometimes, of course, what laid down the new sediment of thought was a new theological-political understanding which plausibly claimed to be superior to (even while a continuation of) Plato: in such cases, these claims must be addressed and taken seriously by him who philosophizes in a Platonic manner. In his fifth chapter, Strauss therefore presents an introductory survey of the many forms assumed by that way of thinking which is the most long-lived, and perhaps the most powerful, of the stepchildren or rivals of the Platonic-Xenophontic Socrates: the Natural Law tradi-

---

5. Cf. Christopher Bruell, "On the Original Meaning of Political Philosophy: An Interpretation of Plato's *Lovers*, in *Shorter Dialogues of Plato*, ed. Thomas Pangle" (forthcoming).

tion. This way of thinking reaches one of its two highpoints in the writings of the greatest Christian political theologians; the investigation of Natural Law is thus at the same time Strauss's investigation of the Christian attempt to reconcile and incorporate philosophy.

From Natural Law Strauss ascends to what he evidently regards as the most profound and intransigent version of the alternative to philosophy posed by revelation: to the source of the faith of his fathers, to the Torah. His "preliminary reflections" on "the incompatible claims of Jerusalem and Athens" would seem to constitute his own enactment of at least the crucial first stages in the dialogue between Socratic philosophy and biblical prophecy. Strauss here follows, in a manner appropriate to our historical epoch, the trail blazed by the Platonist Jew Maimonides (cf. FP 357–60; QR 1–6; OA 95–99); as subsequent chapters plainly attest, for Strauss the encounter with the Bible is never widely distant from ever-renewed reflection on the writings of this supreme teacher of the Jews. Like Maimonides, Strauss in his dialogue with the prophets demonstrates the error of supposing that the choice between reason and faith must be left at the level of mere commitment or decision. Moreover, in this chapter he proves in deed, *ad oculos*, that Socratic philosophy is fully capable of meeting biblical faith, without requiring the assistance of any supplements from the later "history of thought." In fact, he demonstrates, the tools provided by Socratic dialectic are decisively superior to the tools employed by the "biblical criticism" of modern theology, philosophy, philology, and science; the latter are in some measure impediments to a truly open-minded appreciation of and argument with the message of the prophets. Incidentally, then, this chapter furnishes one of Strauss's most important criticisms or refutations of the historicism grounded in Heidegger and Nietzsche.

Yet Strauss did not arrive at the position from which he was able to deliver this criticism without great assistance from those who are its targets. Strauss could not have discovered the hidden maps left behind in *The Guide of the Perplexed* if he had not questioned radically all the most sacred presuppositions of modern scholarship and scientific rationalism. One of the champions of that scholarship and that rationalism, Strauss here reminds us, was Hermann Cohen, "the greatest representative of German Jewry and spokesman for it"; while on the other hand, "the man who started the questioning was Nietzsche."

Still, this observation does not explain, or even prepare us for, the next segment of the ordered route along which Strauss conducts us. It does not explain why, at the very center of his last work, Strauss seemingly interrupts his central theme, the confrontation between Platonic rationalism and Revelation, in order to confront "the most beautiful of Nietzsche's books," "the only book published by Nietzsche, in the contemporary preface to which he presents himself as the antagonist of Plato." Is it possible that, for Strauss, Nietzsche continues and surpasses biblical thought in some critical respect?

In his interpretation of *Beyond Good and Evil* Strauss focuses on "das religiöse Wesen." He justifies this emphasis by showing that the plan of the book reveals that for Nietzsche "the fundamental alternative is that of the rule of philosophy over religion or the rule of religion over philosophy; it is not, as it was for Plato or Aristotle, that of the philosophic and the political life." In contrast to the Socratics, Nietzsche elevates religion at the expense of politics. Even this does not go far enough. Strauss, who is not exactly given to repetitiveness, repeats within the space of three pages the assertion that "the doctrine of the will to power is in a manner a vindication of God." This reminds us of one of the most striking remarks of the opening chapter. For in trying to understand the importance Strauss assigns to Nietzsche we must not neglect any longer the synopsis of the most profound strands in twentieth-century philosophy with which Strauss begins this volume. In this first chapter of his final work Strauss makes it clear once again that for him *the* thinker of our age is Heidegger. It is only in Heidegger's writings that one finds the true justification for the fact that "political philosophy has lost its credibility," and has been replaced by "ideology," "value judgments," or "the view according to which all principles of understanding and of action are historical." What is this justification? The reason why "there is no room for political philosophy in Heidegger's work . . . may well be . . . that the room in question is occupied by gods or the gods." It would seem that in this crucial respect, as in so many others, Heidegger embodies the radicalization of his teacher Nietzsche. Heidegger and Nietzsche, one might gather, brought into being an unprecedented way of thinking in which philosophy goes over to the side of, and vindicates, the gods—the gods of the poets—and in doing so seeks to transform dramatically the meaning of poet, god, and philosopher.

If I am not mistaken, Strauss means to suggest that the undeniable greatness of Heidegger is magnified in its appearance because of the senescent condition of the contemporary rationalism or scientism which in its various forms stands as the only living alternative. This is true even of the most respectable version of contemporary rationalism, Husserl's "philosophy as rigorous science." Only near the end of his life did Husserl begin to glimpse the need for, and grope toward, the recovery of political philosophy. Strauss shows in his first chapter how urgent was the need for that groping—however inadequate it proved to be—in order to indicate the cogency, the pressing necessity, of entertaining in candor the possibility explored in the succeeding chapters: the possibility of returning to Platonic political philosophy.

One cannot understand the reasons for the decay that has overtaken rationalism in our time, and the resultant twilight of our modern Western civilization founded on this rationalism, until one has traced step by step, and without preconceptions for or against, the evolution of the modern political philosophy begun by Machiavelli. In his last four chapters Strauss reminds us of, and adds to, the studies of modern political philosophy which constituted such a large portion of his life's work. At the beginning of the chapter on Machiavelli, Strauss suggests, it appears to me, that "at the bottom" of modern philosophy is the understandable impulse to resolve the conflict between philosophy and faith, not by continuing the endless tenuous attempts of each protagonist to subsume the other, but by turning away and transcending the plane of the whole controversy. Modern philosophy would then be animated by the hope of dissolving the "conflict which has prevented Western thought from ever coming to rest"; having finally been brought to rest as regards the fundamental issue, thought could be put into the service of resolute and unhesitating action. Political philosophy could be reborn as "political theory," as a thinking which understood itself to be nothing more and nothing less than the guide to the revolutionary or lawful action of citizens.

Given that the Jewish people can plausibly be understood to be defined by "the idea of 'the chosen people,' " an idea which "expresses 'what Matthew Arnold called the Jewish passion for right acting as distinct from the Greek passion for right seeing and thinking,' " there is a discernible kinship between the hopes of modern philosophy and the hopes for the Messiah. In the hands of the penetrating and truly noble Kantian Jew Hermann Cohen, that kinship became the leitmotif of a new, supposedly superior or "historically progressive" grand synthesis of Jerusalem and Athens. Strauss closes his last work by returning again to Cohen and demonstrating, with the greatest respect but with relentless clarity, what a delusion was thus constructed by the man who had been in a sense the hero of Strauss's youth.

> Finite, relative problems can be solved; infinite, absolute problems cannot be solved. In other words, human beings will never create a society which is free of contradictions. From every point of view it looks as if the Jewish people were the chosen people in the sense, at least, that the Jewish problem is the most manifest symbol of the human problem as a social or political problem. (AP 6)

> It seems to me that this antagonism must be considered by us in action . . . It seems to me that the core, the nerve of Western intellectual history, Western spiritual history, one could almost say, is the conflict between the biblical and the philosophic notions of the good life . . . It seems to me that this unresolved conflict is the secret of the vitality of Western civilization. The recognition of two conflicting roots of Western civilization is, at first, a very disconcerting observation. Yet this realization has also something reassuring and comforting about it. The very life of Western civilization is the life between two codes, a fundamental tension. There is therefore no reason inherent in the Western civilization itself, in its fundamental constitution, why it should give up life. But this comforting thought is justified only if we live that life, if we live that conflict. (POR 44)

Abbreviations
Works by Leo Strauss Cited in the Introduction

AAPL	*The Argument and the Action of Plato's Laws* (Chicago: University of Chicago Press, 1975)
AP	Autobiographical Preface to *Spinoza's Critique of Religion* (New York: Schocken, 1965)
CM	*The City and Man* (Chicago: Rand McNally, 1964)
FP	"Farabi's Plato," in *Louis Ginzberg Jubilee Volume* (New York: American Academy for Jewish Research, 1945)
HPP	*History of Political Philosophy*, ed. Leo Strauss and Joseph Cropsey (Chicago: Rand McNally, 1963)
LAM	*Liberalism Ancient and Modern* (New York: Basic Books, 1968)
MITP	"The Mutual Influence of Theology and Philosophy," *Independent Journal of Philosophy* 3 (1979)
NRH	*Natural Right and History* (Chicago: University of Chicago Press, 1953)
OA	"On Abravanel's Philosophical Tendency and Political Teaching," in *Isaac Abravanel*, ed. J. B. Trend and H. Loewe (Cambridge: Cambridge University Press, 1937)
OT	*On Tyranny* (New York: Free Press of Glencoe, 1963)
PAW	*Persecution and the Art of Writing* (Glencoe, Ill.: Free Press, 1952)
POR	"Progress or Return?" *Modern Judaism* 1 (1981)
PPH	New preface to the publication of the German original of *The Political Philosophy of Hobbes*: see *Interpretation* 8:1 (1979)
QR	"Quelques remarques sur la science politique de Maïmonide et de Farabi," *Revue des Etudes Juives* 100 (1936)
SA	*Socrates and Aristophanes* (New York: Basic Books, 1966)
WIPP	*What is Political Philosophy?* (Glencoe, Ill.: Free Press, 1959)
XS	*Xenophon's Socrates* (Ithaca: Cornell University Press, 1972)
XSD	*Xenophon's Socratic Discourse* (Ithaca: Cornell University Press, 1970)

1

Philosophy as Rigorous Science and Political Philosophy

Whoever is concerned with political philosophy must face the fact that in the last two generations political philosophy has lost its credibility. Political philosophy has lost its credibility in proportion as politics itself has become more philosophic than ever in a sense. Almost throughout its whole history political philosophy was universal while politics was particular. Political philosophy was concerned with the best or just order of society which is by nature best or just everywhere or always, while politics is concerned with the being and well-being of this or that particular society (a polis, a nation, an empire) that is in being at a given place for some time. Not a few men have dreamt of rule over all human beings by themselves or others but they were dreamers or at least regarded as such by the philosophers. In our age on the other hand politics has in fact become universal. Unrest in what is loosely, not to say demagogically, called the ghetto of an American city has repercussions in Moscow, Peking, Johannesburg, Hanoi, London, and other far away places and is linked with them; whether the linkage is admitted or not makes no difference. Simultaneously political philosophy has disappeared. This is quite obvious in the East where the Communists themselves call their doctrine their ideology. As for the contemporary West, the intellectual powers peculiar to it are neo-positivism and existentialism. Positivism surpasses existentialism by far in academic influence and existentialism surpasses positivism by far in popular influence. Positivism may be described as the view according to which only scientific knowledge is genuine knowledge; since scientific knowledge is unable to validate or invalidate any value judgments, and political philosophy most certainly is concerned with the

Reprinted from *Interpretation: A Journal of Political Philosophy* 2, no. 1 (1971).

validation of sound value judgments and the invalidation of unsound ones, positivism must reject political philosophy as radically unscientific. Existentialism appears in a great variety of guises but one will not be far wide of the mark if one defines it in contradistinction to positivism as the view according to which all principles of understanding and of action are historical, i.e. have no other ground than groundless human decision or fateful dispensation: science, far from being the only kind of genuine knowledge, is ultimately not more than one form among many of viewing the world, all these forms have the same dignity. Since according to existentialism all human thought is historical in the sense indicated, existentialism must reject political philosophy as radically unhistorical.

Existentialism is a "movement" which like all such movements has a flabby periphery and a hard center. That center is the thought of Heidegger. To that thought alone existentialism owes its importance or intellectual respectability. There is no room for political philosophy in Heidegger's work, and this may well be due to the fact that the room in question is occupied by gods or the gods. This does not mean that Heidegger is wholly alien to politics: he welcomed Hitler's revolution in 1933 and he, who had never praised any other contemporary political effort, still praised national socialism long after Hitler had been muted and Heil Hitler had been transformed into Heil Unheil. We cannot help holding these facts against Heidegger. Moreover, one is bound to misunderstand Heidegger's thought radically if one does not see their intimate connection with the core of his philosophic thought. Nevertheless, they afford too small a basis for the proper understanding of his thought. As far as I can see, he is of the opinion that none of his critics and none of his followers has understood him adequately. I believe that he is right, for is the same not also true, more or less, of all outstanding thinkers? This does not dispense us, however, from taking a stand toward him, for we do this at any rate implicitly; in doing it explicitly, we run no greater risk than exposing ourselves to ridicule and perhaps receiving some needed instruction.

Among the many things that make Heidegger's thought so appealing to so many contemporaries is his accepting the premise that while human life and thought is radically historical, History is not a rational process. As a consequence, he denies that one can understand a thinker better than he understood himself and even as he understood himself: a great thinker will understand an earlier thinker of rank creatively, i.e. by transforming his thought, and hence by understanding him differently than he understood himself. One could hardly observe this transformation if one could not see the original form. Above all, according to Heidegger all thinkers prior to him have been oblivious of the true ground of all grounds, the fundamental abyss. This assertion implies the claim that in the decisive respect Heidegger understands his great predecessors better than they understood themselves.

In order to understand Heidegger's thought and therefore in particular his posture toward politics and political philosophy, one must not neglect the work of his teacher Husserl. The access to Husserl is not rendered difficult by any false step like those taken by Heidegger in 1933 and 1953. I have heard it said though that the Husserlian equivalent was his conversion, not proceeding from conviction, to Christianity. If this were proven to be the case, it would become a task for a casuist of exceptional gifts to consider the dissimilarities and similarities of the two kinds of acts and to weigh their respective demerits and merits.

When I was still almost a boy, Husserl explained to me who at that time was a doubting and dubious adherent of the Marburg school of neo-Kantianism, the characteristic of his own work in about these terms: "the Marburg school begins with the roof, while I begin with the foundation." This meant that for the school of Marburg the sole task of the fundamental part of philosophy was the theory of scientific experience, the analysis of scientific thought. Husserl however had realized more profoundly than anybody else that the scientific understanding of the world, far from being the perfection of our natural understanding, is derivative from the latter in such a way as to make us oblivious of the very foundations of the scientific understanding: all philosophic understanding must start from our common understanding of the world, from our understanding of the world as sensibly perceived prior to all theorizing. Heidegger went much further than Husserl in the same direction: the primary theme is not the object of perception but the full thing as experienced as part of the individual human context, the individual world to which it belongs.[1] The full thing is what it is not only in virtue of the primary and secondary qualities as well as the value qualities in the ordinary meaning of that term but also of qualities like sacred or profane: the full phenomenon of a cow is for a Hindu constituted much more by the sacredness of the cow than by any other quality or aspect. This implies that one can no longer speak of our "natural" understanding of the world; every understanding of the world is "historical." Correspondingly, one must go back behind the one human reason to the multiplicity of historical, "grown" not "made," languages. Accordingly there arises the philosophic task of understanding the universal structure common to all historical worlds.[2] Yet if the insight into the historicity of all thought is to be preserved, the understanding of the universal or essential structure of all historical worlds must be accompanied and in a way guided by that insight. This means that the understanding of the essential structure of all historical worlds must be understood as essentially belonging to a specific historical context, to a specific historical period. The character of the historicist insight must corre-

1. Cf. *Sein und Zeit* sect. 21 (pp. 98–99).
2. For this and what follows see H. G. Gadamer, *Wahrheit und Methode* 233–34; cf. 339–40; pp. xix and 505 of the second edition.

spond to the character of the period to which it belongs. The historicist insight is the final insight in the sense that it reveals all earlier thought as radically defective in the decisive respect and that there is no possibility of another legitimate change in the future which would render obsolete or as it were mediatise the historicist insight. As the absolute insight it must belong to the absolute moment in history. In a word, the difficulty indicated compels Heidegger to elaborate, sketch or suggest what in the case of any other man would be called his philosophy of history.

The absolute moment may be the absolute moment simply or the absolute moment of all previous history. That it is the absolute moment simply had been the contention of Hegel. His system of philosophy, the final philosophy, the perfect solution of all philosophic problems belongs to the moment when mankind has solved in principle its political problem by establishing the post-revolutionary state, the first state to recognize the equal dignity of every human being as such. This absolute peak of history, being the end of history, is at the same time the beginning of the final decline. In this respect Spengler has merely brought out the ultimate conclusion of Hegel's thought. No wonder therefore that almost everyone rebelled against Hegel. No one did this more effectively than Marx. Marx claimed to have laid bare with finality the mystery of all history, including the present and the imminent future, but also the outline of the order which was bound to come and in which and through which men would be able or compelled for the first time to lead truly human lives. More precisely, for Marx human history, so far from having been completed, has not even begun; what we call history is only the pre-history of humanity. Questioning the settlement which Hegel had regarded as rational, he followed the vision of a world society which presupposes and establishes forever the complete victory of the town over the country, of the mobile over the deeply rooted, of the spirit of the Occident over the spirit of the Orient; the members of the world society which is no longer a political society are free and equal, and are so in the last analysis because all specialization, all division of labor, has given way to the full development of everyone.

Regardless of whether or not Nietzsche knew of Marx' writings, he questioned the communist vision more radically than anyone else. He identified the man of the communist world society as the last man, as man in his utmost degradation: without "specialization," without the harshness of limitation, human nobility and greatness are impossible. In accordance with this he denied that the future of the human race is predetermined. The alternative to the last man is the over-man, a type of man surpassing and overcoming all previous human types in greatness and nobility; the over-men of the future will be ruled invisibly by the philosophers of the future. Owing to its radical anti-egalitarianism Nietzsche's vision of a possible future is in a sense more profoundly political than Marx' vision. Like the typical Continental European conservative Nietzsche saw in communism only the completion of democratic egalitarianism and of the liberalistic demand for freedom which is not a "freedom for" but only a "freedom from." But in contradistinction to those conservatives he held that conservatism as such is doomed, since all merely defensive positions, all merely backward looking endeavors are doomed. The future seemed to be with democracy and nationalism. Both were regarded by Nietzsche as incompatible with what he held to be the task of the twentieth century. He saw the twentieth century as an age of world wars leading up to planetary rule. If man were to have a future, that rule would have to be exercised by a united Europe. The enormous tasks of this unprecedented iron age could not possibly be discharged by weak and unstable governments depending upon public opinion. The new situation called for the emergence of a new nobility—a nobility formed by a new ideal: the nobility of the over-men. Nietzsche claimed to have discovered with finality the mystery of all history, including the present, i.e. the alternative whch now confronts man, of the utmost degradation and the highest exaltation. The possibility of surpassing and overcoming all previous human types reveals itself to the present, less because the present is superior to all past ages than because it is the moment of the greatest danger and chiefly for this reason of the greatest hope.

Heidegger's philosophy of history has the same structure as Marx' and Nietzsche's: the moment in which the final insight is arriving opens the eschatological prospect. But Heidegger is much closer to Nietzsche than to Marx. Both thinkers regard as decisive the nihilism which according to them began in Plato (or before)—Christianity being only Platonism for the people—and whose ultimate consequence is the present decay. Hitherto every great age of humanity grew out of *Bodenständigkeit* (rootedness in the soil). Yet the great age of classical Greece gave birth to a way of thinking which in principle endangered *Bodenständigkeit* from the beginning and in its ultimate contemporary consequences is about to destroy the last relics of that condition of human greatness. Heidegger's philosophy belongs to the infinitely dangerous moment when man is in a greater danger than ever before of losing his humanity and therefore—danger and salvation belonging together—philosophy can have the task of contributing toward the recovery or return of *Bodenständigkeit* or rather of preparing an entirely novel kind of *Bodenständigkeit: a Bodenständigkeit* beyond the most extreme *Bodenlosigkeit*, a being at home beyond the most extreme homelessness. Nay, there are reasons for thinking that according to Heidegger the world has never yet been in order, or thought has never yet been simply human. A dialogue between the most profound thinkers of the Occident and the most profound thinkers of the Orient and in particular East Asia may lead to the consummation prepared, accompanied or followed by a return of the gods. That dialogue and everything that it entails, but surely not political action of any kind, is perhaps the way.[3] Heidegger severs the connection of the vision with politics more radically than either Marx or Nietzsche. One is inclined to say that Heidegger has learned the lesson of 1933 more thoroughly than any other man. Surely he leaves no place whatever for political philosophy.

Let us turn from these fantastic hopes, more to be expected from visionaries than from philosophers, to Husserl. Let us see whether a place for political philosophy is left in Husserl's philosophy.

What I am going to say is based on a re-reading, after many years of neglect, of Husserl's programmatic essay "Philosophy as Rigorous Science." The essay was first published in 1911, and Husserl's thought underwent many important changes afterward. Yet it is his most important utterance on the question with which we are concerned.

No one in our century has raised the call for philosophy as a rigorous science with such clarity, purity, vigor, and breadth as Husserl. "From its first beginnings philosophy has raised the claim to be a rigorous science; more precisely, it has raised the claim to be the science that would satisfy the highest theoretical needs and in regard to ethics and religion render possible a life regulated by pure rational norms. This claim . . . has never been completely abandoned. [Yet] in no epoch of its development has philosophy been capable of satisfying the claim to be a rigorous science . . . Philosophy as science has not yet begun . . . In philosophy [in contradistinction to the sciences] everything is controversial."[4]

Husserl found the most important example of the contrast between claim and achievement in "the reigning naturalism." (In the present context the difference between naturalism and positivism is unimportant.) In that way of thinking the intention toward a new foundation of philosophy in the spirit of rigorous science is fully alive. This constitutes its merit and at the same time a great deal of its force. Perhaps the idea of science is altogether the most powerful idea in modern life. Surely nothing can stop the victorious course of science which in its ideal completion is Reason itself that cannot tolerate any authority at its side or above it. Husserl respects naturalism especially for keeping alive the notion of a "philosophy from the ground up" in opposition to the traditional notion of philosophy as "system." At the same time he holds that naturalism necessarily destroys all objectivity.[5]

By naturalism Husserl understands the view according to which everything that is forms part of nature, "nature" being understood as the object of (modern) natural science. This means that everything that is is either itself

3. *Was heisst Denken?* 31, 153–54; *Der Satz vom Grund* 101; *Einführung in die Metaphysik* 28; *Wegmarken* 250–52; *Gelassenheit* 16–26.
4. *Philosophie als strenge Wissenschaft*, ed. W. Szilasi, sects. 1, 2, 4 and 5. I have made use of the English translation by Lauer in Husserl, *Phenomenology and the Crisis of Philosophy*, Harper Torch Books, pp. 71–147.
5. Sects. 7–8, 11, 13, 14, 17, 65.

"physical" or if it is "psychic" it is a mere dependent variable of the physical, "in the best case a secondary parallel accompaniment." As a consequence, naturalism "naturalizes" both the consciousness and all norms (logical, ethical and so on). That form of naturalism which called for Husserl's special attention was experimental psychology as meant to supply the scientific foundation of logic, theory of knowledge, esthetics, ethics, and pedagogic. That psychology claimed to be the science of the phenomena themselves, or of "the psychic phenomena," i.e. of that which physics in principle excludes in order to look for "the true, objective, physically-exact nature," or for the nature which presents itself in the phenomena. Stated in very imprecise language, psychology deals with the secondary qualities as such which physics, solely concerned with the primary qualities, excludes. In more precise language, one would have to say that the psychic phenomena precisely because they are phenomena are not nature.[6]

As theory of knowledge naturalism must give an account of natural science, of its truth or validity. But every natural science accepts nature in the sense in which nature is intended by natural science, as given, as "being in itself." The same is of course true of psychology which is based on the science of physical nature. Hence naturalism is completely blind to the riddles inherent in the "givenness" of nature. It is constitutionally incapable of a radical critique of experience as such. The scientific positing or taking for granted of nature is preceded by and based upon the prescientific one, and the latter is as much in need of radical clarification as the first. Hence an adequate theory of knowledge cannot be based on the naive acceptance of nature in any sense of nature. The adequate theory of knowledge must be based on scientific knowledge of the consciousness as such, for which nature and being are correlates or intended objects that constitute themselves in and through consciousness alone, in pure "immanence"; "nature" or "being" must be made "completely intelligible." Such a radical clarification of every possible object of consciousness can be the task only of a phenomenology of the consciousness in contradistinction to the naturalistic science of psychic phenomena. Only phenomenology can supply that fundamental clarification of the consciousness and its acts the lack of which makes so-called exact psychology radically unscientific, for the latter constantly makes use of concepts which stem from every-day experience without having examined them as to their adequacy.[7]

According to Husserl it is absurd to ascribe to phenomena a nature: phenomena appear in an "absolute flux," an "eternal flux," while "nature is eternal." Yet precisely because phenomena have no natures, they have essences. Phenomenology is essentially the study of essences and in no way

6. Sects. 14, 15, 19, 42, 46–48.
7. Sects. 20–27, 29, 30, 32–42.

of existence. In accordance with this the study of the life of the mind as practiced by the thoughtful historians offers to the philosopher a more original and therefore more fundamental material of inquiry than the study of nature.[8] If this is so, the study of men's religious life must be of greater philosophic relevance than the study of nature.

Philosophy as rigorous science was threatened in the second place by a way of thinking which under the influence of historicism was about to turn into mere *Weltanschauungsphilosophie*. *Weltanschauung* is life-experience of a high order. It includes not only experience of the world but also religious, esthetic, ethical, political, practical-technical etc. experience. The man who posseses such experience on a very high level is called wise and is said to possess a *Weltanschauung*. Husserl can therefore speak of "wisdom or *Weltanschauung*." According to him wisdom or *Weltanschauung* is an essential ingredient of that still more valuable habitus which we mean by the idea of perfect virtue or by the idea of humanity. *Weltanschauungsphilos-ophie* comes into being when the attempt is made to conceptualize wisdom or to give it a logical elaboration or, more simply, to give it the form of science; this ordinarily goes together with the attempt to use the results of the special sciences as materials. This kind of philosophy, when taking on the form of one or the other of the great systems, presents the relatively most perfect solution of the riddles of life and the world. The traditional philos-ophies were at the same time *Weltanschauungsphilosophien* and scientific philosophies since the objectives of wisdom on the one hand and of rigorous science on the other had not yet been clearly separated from one another. But for the modern consciousness the separation of the ideas of wisdom and of rigorous science has become a fact and they remain henceforth separated for all eternity. The idea of *Weltanschauung* differs from epoch to epoch while the idea of science is supra-temporal. One might think that the realizations of the two ideas would approach each other asymptotically in the infinite. Yet "we cannot wait"; we need "exaltation and consolation" now; we need some kind of system to live by; only *Weltanschauung* or *Weltanschauungsphilosophie* can satisfy these justified demands.[9] Surely philosophy as rigorous science cannot satisfy them: it has barely begun, it will need centuries, if not millennia, until it "renders possible in regard to ethics and religion a life regulated by pure rational norms," if it is not at all times essentially incomplete and in need of radical revisions. Hence the temptation to forsake it in favor of *Weltanschauungsphilosophie* is very great. From Husserl's point of view one would have to say that Heidegger proved unable to resist that temptation.

The reflection on the relation of the two kinds of philosophy obviously belongs to the sphere of philosophy as rigorous science. It comes closest to

8. Sects. 49–50, 54, 56, 57, 59, 72.
9. Sects. 13, 67, 75–79, 81, 82, 90, 91.

being Husserl's contribution to political philosophy. He did not go on to wonder whether the single-minded pursuit of philosophy as rigorous science would not have an adverse effect on *Weltanschauungsphilosophie* which most men need to live by and hence on the actualization of the ideas which that kind of philosophy serves, in the first place in the practitioners of philosophy as rigorous science but secondarily also in all those who are impressed by those practitioners. He seems to have taken it for granted that there will always be a variety of *Weltanschauungsphilosophien* that peacefully coexist within one and the same society. He did not pay attention to societies that impose a single *Weltanschauung* or *Weltanschauungsphilosophie* on all their members and for this reason will not tolerate philosophy as rigorous science. Nor did he consider that even a society that tolerates indefinitely many *Weltanschauungen* does this by virtue of one particular *Weltanschauung*.

Husserl in a manner continued, he surely modified the reflection we have been speaking about, under the impact of events which could not be overlooked or overheard. In a lecture delivered in Prague in 1935 he said: "Those who are conservatively contented with the tradition and the circle of philosophic human beings will fight one another, and surely the fight will take place in the sphere of political power. Already in the beginnings of philosophy persecution sets in. The men who live toward those ideas [of philosophy] are outlawed. And yet: ideas are stronger than all empirical powers."[10] In order to see the relation between philosophy as rigorous science and the alternative to it clearly, one must look at the political conflict between the two antagonists, i.e. at the essential character of that conflict. If one fails to do so, one cannot reach clarity on the essential character of what Husserl calls "philosophy as rigorous science."

10. *Die Krisis der europäischen Wissenschaften und die tranzendentale Phänomenologie*, second edition, Haag 1962, 335.

2

On Plato's *Apology of Socrates* and *Crito*

I

The *Apology of Socrates* is the only Platonic work with Socrates in the title. Yet Socrates is visibly or invisibly the chief character in all Platonic dialogues: all Platonic dialogues are "apologies" of or for Socrates. But the *Apology of Socrates* is the portal through which we enter the Platonic kosmos: it gives an account of Socrates' whole life, of his whole way of life, to the largest multitude, to the authoritative multitude, to the city of Athens before which he was accused of a capital crime; it is *the* dialogue of Socrates with the city of Athens (cf. 37a4–7).

In the prooemium Socrates contrasts the manner in which he will speak with the manner of his accusers: the accusers spoke most persuasively and at the same time as untruthfully as possible; he on the other hand will say the whole truth, for the virtue of the speaker consists in saying the truth while the virtue of the judge or juryman consists in concentrating on whether what the speaker says is just. For the speaker will not merely state the facts—what he did—but also that they were innocent—that what he did was justly done. It is because Socrates trusts in the justice of what he has done that he will say the whole truth.

Socrates characterizes the manner of his speaking as artless: he who says the whole truth and nothing but the truth, he who has nothing to conceal, does not need any art; Socrates' speech will be altogether transparent. His accusers who had spoken most persuasively, had spoken artfully (*technikos*). One wonders whether the virtue of the speaker does not also consist in speaking persuasively. Must he not say the truth in an orderly and lucid

Reprinted from *Essays in Honor of Jacob Klein* (Annapolis: St. John's College Press, 1976).

fashion? Must he not arrange his argument properly and choose his words with some care? In brief, must he not speak artfully? Socrates' accusers had said that he is a clever speaker, and it was generally believed that he was a most artful speaker—that he could render the weaker speech the stronger (18b8–c1). It was therefore imperative that he should state right at the beginning that he will not speak artfully. He suggests that his inexperience in forensic diction prevents him from speaking properly before the court: he cannot speak artfully. But he also says that it would not be becoming for a man of his age to come before the court like a youth with fabricated speeches, *i.e.*, with lies; he does not say that he could not do this if he wished to: he can speak artfully.

Socrates shows how persuasive and artful his accusers are by sketching the background of the accusation. For this purpose he makes a distinction between the first untrue charges and the first accusers on the one hand, and the later charges and the later accusers on the other. The first accusers are more dangerous than the later ones, *i.e.*, than those who have formally indicted him, because they have persuaded the majority of the jurymen or of the Athenians while all or many of them were still children, because they are many, and because they have accused him for a long time. (The old accusers were in many cases the fathers of the jurymen.) They have accused Socrates untruthfully of being a wise man, a thinker on the things aloft, one who has investigated all things beneath the earth, and one who renders the weaker speech the stronger. Although this charge is untrue, it is not extreme; the first accusers did not accuse Socrates of having investigated all things aloft. Nor did they say that he does not respect, or believe in, gods; that he does not believe in gods was inferred by the listeners (in many cases children) who believed that those who do the things mentioned by the accusers also do not believe in gods. If one or the other comic poet raised the charges mentioned, he did not do it maliciously, and did not believe in them. As for the others, the first accusers proper, they cannot be identified and therefore cross-examined: Socrates can do hardly more than flatly deny their charges. On the other hand, the first accusers cannot defend their charges against Socrates' denials.

Before turning to the refutation of the first accusers, Socrates makes it clear that "you"—the whole jury, all Athenians—are prejudiced against him and thus indicates that his case is well-nigh hopeless. He defends himself against the charge of impiety before a jury that is convinced of his impiety. He would wish that he could liberate the Athenians from their prejudices if this is in any way better both for them and for him: one of the many things he does not know is whether it is not better for the Athenians to keep their prejudice intact.

Socrates restates the slander of the first accusers by framing it as a formal indictment. As a consequence, it becomes more responsible than the slander itself: it does not speak of Socrates' having investigated all things beneath the earth, but of his investigating the things beneath the earth. The formal indictment is as silent as the original slander on Socrates' not worshipping, or not believing in, gods. But Socrates adds now that "Socrates teaches others these very things," namely, the things beneath the earth, the heavenly things, and rendering the weaker speech the stronger: if Socrates did not teach the incriminated things, it would not be known that he had anything to do with them. By making this addition he lays as it were the foundation for the bipartition made in the official accusation (impiety and corrupting the young): the official accusation is derivative from the first accusation.

As we learn from Socrates, the first accusation was familiar to his audience from Aristophanes' *Clouds* in which he was presented as doing many ridiculous things—things of which he understands nothing. He does not despise this kind of knowledge—far from it—but he does not possess it. He does not make it as clear as he easily could have made it whether he regards the knowledge possessed by the Aristophanean Socrates as ridiculous nonsense or as respectable. He is of course completely silent about the fact that Aristophanes had presented him as denying the existence of the gods. Accordingly he asks the jury who are under the spell of an inveterate prejudice to free themselves from that prejudice by trusting the testimony of their senses: they should tell one another whether they have ever heard him conversing about subjects of this kind, for many of them have heard him talk in the market place, at the money changers' tables; yet Socrates also talked "elsewhere" when he was not heard by many of them (cf. 17c7–9). Surely their knowledge of what Socrates conversed about had not hitherto made the slightest dent on their prejudice.

Socrates devotes twice as much time, or space, to the refutation of the charge or the rumor that he is teaching others as to the refutation of the charge that he investigates the things beneath the earth and the heavenly things and that he renders the weaker speech the stronger, and this despite the fact that that rumor is not a general rumor. He proceeds like Xenophon in the *Memorabilia*, who devotes much more space to the refutation of the incredible corruption charge than to the refutation of the more credible corruption charge than to the refutation of the more credible impiety charge. Plato's Socrates discusses the rumor according to which he attempts to educate human beings and charges money for it. Again he flatly denies the truth of what is said about him. But this time he does not ask the jury to tell one another whether they have ever heard (or seen) him attempting to educate human beings while charging money for it; such transactions may be strictly private. He praises what Gorgias, Prodikos and Hippias—alien "sophists"—do or attempt to do, as noble, and he shows why their art aiming at the production of the virtue of the human being as well as of the citizen deserves being praised. He does not mention Protagoras. He casts some doubt on the possibility of that art: he had not cast any doubt on the possibility of the study of the things aloft and the like.

Socrates' refutation of the charge of the first accusers is so complete, so devastating as to become in a sense unintelligible. He lends words to "one of you" who might perhaps retort and say: if you do nothing more out of the common than the others, how does it happen that you have been slandered in such an extraordinary manner? must there not be some fire where there is so much smoke? The retort is fair and Socrates will try to show to the jury how he has become the butt of this slander. He is aware that by giving his explanation he will appear to be joking to part of the audience; nevertheless he will tell the whole audience the whole truth. He does have some kind of wisdom—that kind which is perhaps human wisdom as distinguished from the superhuman wisdom of the sophists (and of the physiologists). He is aware that by what he is going to say he could appear to be boasting (and thus involuntarily to be joking). For the speech that he will pronounce is not his but will be traced by him to a speaker who is trustworthy to the audience. That speaker is the god in Delphi or, more precisely, Chairephon, who was his comrade from his youth and at the same time (what Socrates could not say of himself) a comrade of the multitude, a sound democrat and therefore trustworthy to the audience. As they know, Chairephon was impetuous and accordingly once, when having come to Delphi, dared to ask the oracle whether anyone is wiser than Socrates. The Pythia replied that no one is wiser. The truth of this story is guaranteed, not by the god, nor by the Pythia, nor even by Chairephon, who is no longer alive, but by Chairephon's brother. The story of the Delphic oracle is new to the audience, just as the story told by Socrates shortly before, regarding Kallias and Euenos (20a2–c1).

Chairephon's question presupposed that he regarded Socrates as wise, as singularly wise, before he consulted the oracle. That wisdom of Socrates had nothing whatever to do with the wisdom which he discovered or acquired as a consequence of the Delphic utterance. It was pre-Delphic. In the light of his post-Delphic wisdom his pre-Delphic wisdom may be sheer madness but it was possessed by him or possessed him. He is completely silent about it in his defense before the jury. He gives a hint as to its character by his reference to the *Clouds*, in which Chairephon is presented as Socrates' companion *par excellence*. But Socrates presents Chairephon as a believer in the Delphic oracle, as pious; his piety strengthens the belief in his revered master's piety. Or could his consulting the oracle have had a non-pious motive? We are not told why he consulted the oracle. His question is not free from ambiguity: is anyone—man or god—wiser than Socrates? The Pythia's answer does not remove this ambiguity.

Socrates understood the god to have said that Socrates is most wise. He naturally believed in the god's veracity, to say nothing of his knowledge, or wisdom. On the other hand he was sure that he, Socrates, was not at all wise.

To solve the riddle he engaged in a certain kind of inquiry. He examined the people thought by him or by others to be wise. In examining them he examined indeed also the god: he tried to refute the oracle. He found out that while the people questioned by him believed that they possessed knowledge, they lacked it, whereas Socrates did and does not believe that he knows anything worthwhile of the most important things. He thus came to see the truth of the oracle: his attempt to refute the god turned into assistance to the god and whole-hearted service to him. Socrates examined the politicians, the poets whose "wisdom" does not appear to be different from that of the prophets and of those who delivered oracles, and the craftsmen. He does not say explicitly that he examined the farmers (perhaps farmers did not claim to be wise—cf. Xenophon, *Oeconomicus* 15), the gentlemen who mind their own business, or the sophists (and physiologists). His examination of the men believed to be wise, and especially of the politicians, aroused very deep hatred of him, and that hatred is at the bottom of the slander to which he has been exposed for a long time. People slanderously call him wise because those present at his examination of the so-called or would-be wise believed that he was wise regarding the most important things regarding which he examines the others. But this is a complete misunderstanding: Socrates is wise only in the sense that he knows that he knows nothing. And this is the meaning of the enigmatic oracle regarding Socrates: human wisdom is of little or no account, but a human being who posseses it, as Socrates does, is most wise. The god shows that he, the god, is truly wise by hinting at the truth about the worth or rather worthlessness of human wisdom and its purely negative content.

The animosity against Socrates was aggravated and acquired an opportunity to vent itself because the young men who accompany him enjoy listening to his examination of human beings and even frequently imitate him. Thereupon those examined by the young are angry at Socrates, not at themselves, and say that Socrates corrupts the young. (In the light of the facts that what was particularly aggravating was what Socrates' young followers did and that they engaged in their irritating pastime in his absence, it is understandable that he does not even know the names of the first accusers, although he knows the names of at least some whom he himself examined; cf. 18c8–d1 with 21c3.) Since this slander is obviously not sufficient, they say that he corrupts the young by doing and teaching the things for which all who philosophize are commonly blamed, namely, "the things aloft and beneath the earth," "not believing in gods" and "rendering the weaker speech the stronger." "Not believing in gods" had previously been presented by Socrates as an inference on the part of those who listen to the first accusers and therefore as even less borne out by evidence than the two other charges. But this he did before speaking of the Delphic oracle. In the meantime he has shown that whatever wisdom he possesses was elicited by the Delphic oracle, *i.e.*, that there was no pre-Delphic wisdom and hence there is no need any more for distinguishing between *physiologia* and atheism. In other words, he has shown that the primary charge concerns his corruption of the young and that the other three charges are pure inventions thought out in order to give some plausibility to the corruption charge; hence there is no longer any need for assigning a different status to the impiety charge on the one hand and the other two charges on the other. Socrates has also shown that he is hated not only by those whom he refutes but also by many of those who are present at the refutation (21d1; cf. 23a4); for the listeners believe that they know the truth about the most important things no less than those whom he examines; the distinction between the first accusers and the listeners breaks down: practically all Athenians are the first accusers. And the present accusers are merely the spokesmen for the so-called first accusers (24b7).

At the end of his refutation of the "first accusers" Socrates has succeeded in making intelligible the official accusation as he chooses to read it: the corruption charge precedes the impiety charge, and the impiety charge contains no reference to "the things aloft" and the like. Instead he makes the impiety charge to read that "he does not believe in the gods in whom the city believes but in other daimonic things (*daimonia*) that are new." He has not prepared us for the *daimonia*.

By accusing Socrates of corrupting the young the accuser Meletos claims to know what badness and goodness are. Socrates' knowledge of ignorance could be thought to imply that he does not know what goodness and badness are, and that the Athenians who believe that they know are mistaken: is not this precisely the corruption of the young of which he is accused — that, doubting himself, he makes the young doubt of what is held by all Athenians to be good and bad? is he not the sole corruptor (25a9–10)? One could say that in denying the corruption charge Socrates claims to know what badness and goodness are and hence seems to contradict his assertion that his knowledge is of little or no worth. This difficulty can be disposed of, on the basis of what we have learned hitherto, in two ways. 1. Socrates denies that he or anyone else possesses knowledge of the greatest things (22d5–8); perhaps badness and goodness as pertinent to the discussion with Meletos do not belong to the greatest things. 2. Meletos asserts that Socrates makes the young bad by teaching them not to believe in the gods of the city; the corruption charge is therefore reducible to the impiety charge. The impiety charge means more precisely this: Socrates does not believe in the existence of those gods in whose existence the city believes. Meletos walks into a trap which Socrates laid by asking him whether according to him Socrates is altogether godless or merely a denier of the gods of the city; Meletos cannot resist the temptation to say that Socrates is a complete atheist and therewith to contradict his own indictment according to which Socrates believes in certain daimonic things. This refutation is so beautiful because it leaves entirely open whether Socrates believes in the gods of the city.

The refutation of Meletos is followed, just as the refutation of the first accusers was, by "someone" possibly making a retort and Socrates extensively replying to it. The replies (and the retorts) are, judged according to their form, digressions: the defense proper consists of the refutations of Meletos and the first accusers which must therefore be given their due weight. In the first digression, Socrates spoke of his Apollon-inspired mission, thus incidently supplying the sole proof of his believing in the gods of the city. The second digression continues, deepens, modifies the first. It replies to the possible question of whether Socrates is not ashamed of having engaged in a pursuit through which he is now in danger of dying. Socrates treats with contempt the question and the one who might raise it: what one has to consider is exclusively whether one's deeds are just or unjust and those of a good man or a bad. He refers to the example of Achilleus, the son of a goddess, who without hesitation chose—not commanded by that goddess—to avenge the unjust killing of his comrade Patroklos by Hektor and to die soon afterwards rather than to live in disgrace. He does not mention Achilleus by name; nor does he speak of courage (andreia); nor does he seem to notice the slight incongruity of comparing his dying in ripe old age with Achilleus' dying young. The principle applying equally to Achilleus and to Socrates is this: "Wherever someone stations himself believing that it is best or is stationed by a commander, there he must, as it seems to me, remain and run risks, in no way taking into account either death or anything else before disgrace." Socrates remained at his post and braved death like everybody else wherever the Athenian military commanders stationed him; above all, he remained at the post where the god stationed him. Achilleus' action was not commanded to him by any man or god: does the comparison with Achilleus not suggest that Socrates' way of life was not imposed on him by any command but originated entirely in his thinking that it is best? (When speaking of his remaining at his post wherever his military commanders stationed him, he mentions the battles of Potidaia, Amphipolis and Delion. The battles mentioned first and last were Athenian defeats; at Amphipolis the Athenians first won a victory and then were defeated—Thucydides V 3.4 and 10.10. In the case of the defeats, courage consisted less in remaining or staying than in honorably withdrawing or fleeing. Cf. 28d8 and e3 with *Laches* 181b2, 190e5–191a5 and Xenophon, *Oeconomicus* 11.8.)

Socrates says now that the god's oracles commanded him to spend his life philosophizing and examining himself and others. In the first digression the emphasis was altogether on his examining others. Is philosophizing the same as realizing one's ignorance regarding the most important things? As appears from the present context, knowledge of one's ignorance goes together with the knowledge Socrates possesses that acting unjustly and disobeying one's better, be he man or god, is bad and disgraceful: human wisdom is more than the insight into the worthlessness of human wisdom. He does not know what most people believe that they know, namely, that death is the greatest evil, for he does not have sufficient knowledge of the things in Hades (he has not investigated all things beneath the earth); for all he knows death may be the greatest good. Accordingly he would not consider an offer of the jury to release him on the condition that he no longer philosophize, because he will obey the god rather than the jury: he will disobey a ruling or a law forbidding him to philosophize because he will obey the god rather than the jury or the city; he does not say that he would obey his own judgment rather than the laws. His philosophizing goes together with his exhorting any Athenian he meets to concern himself with reason-ableness, truth and the goodness of his soul rather than with wealth, fame and honor, and his refuting those who claim to be concerned with the most valuable things without being so. His exhortation to be concerned with goodness of the soul consists in showing that virtue does not come from wealth but from virtue come wealth and all other things good for man in both private and public life. His philosophizing consists chiefly in exhorting people to virtue as the most valuable thing. Since it is virtue that makes all other things good for man, his accusers cannot harm him but the Athenians will harm themselves if by condemning him to die they deprive themselves of the god-given boon. For the god has given him to the city as a gadfly to a great and noble horse that because of its size is rather sluggish and needs to be awakened from its drowsiness. The comparison is, as Socrates says, rather ludicrous: he unceasingly pricks, not the city as city but every indi-vidual "the whole day everywhere"; he does, and does not, take care of the affairs of the city.

It could seem strange that he never engaged in political activity. In the first digression (23b8–9) he had given a then perfectly sufficient explanation for this abstention by the busy-ness imposed on him by the service to the god which consists in examining everyone whom he believes to be wise. But this explanation will no longer do after he has revealed himself as exhorting or refuting every Athenian and not only those whom he believes to be wise, or after his service to the god had proved to be identical with his service to the Athenians (31b3) or after the shift from the purely negative understanding of human wisdom to a more positive understanding indicated by the term "philosophizing." He traces now his abstention from politics to his *daimo-nion*—something divine and daimonic which comes to him. This is nothing new to the audience; he has spoken to them about it many times and in many places, and it has given occasion to Meletos to caricature him as believing in new *daimonia*. From his childhood this voice comes or arises to him, which when it arises always turns him away from doing what he is about to do and never urges him forward. It is this *daimonion* that opposes his political activity. This opposition seems to him to be altogether fair, for if he had attempted a long time ago to be politically active, he would have perished a long time ago and would not have been of any benefit to his fellow citizens or to himself: if a man fighting for the right wishes to preserve his life even for a short time, he must lead a private not a public life. The *daimonion* then enabled Socrates to perform the mission imposed on him by the Delphic oracle. It is, however, radically different from the Delphic oracle. Not to mention the fact that the *daimonion* was familiar to the audience while they knew nothing of the Delphic command addressed to Socrates, the *daimonion* was effective from his childhood while Apollo's command reached him when he was already known as wise; the *daimonion* never urged him forward while Apollo always did; and while his obedience to Apollo's commands made him hated and thus brought him into mortal danger, the *daimonion* by keeping him back from political activity saved him from mortal danger or preserved his life; it acted as it were on the premise that life is good and death is bad while the Delphic command proceeds from the opposite premise (cf. *Socrates and Aristophanes* 82, 114, 125). The digression which begins with voicing utter contempt for concern with self-preservation culminates in a vindication of self-preservation—of self-preservation that is in the service of the highest good. With a view to the primary purpose of Socrates' speech it is not superfluous to note that from what he says about the *daimonion* no argument can be derived for refuting the impiety charge.

[*Note*. The most intelligible account of the *daimonion* is found in the *Theages*, a dialogue now generally regarded as spurious. In that dialogue Theages and his father try to persuade Socrates to "be together" with young Theages who wishes to become an outstanding Athenian statesman. Socrates declares that he is useless for that purpose since he understands nothing of the blessed and noble things which Theages needs; he understands only a small piece of learning, namely, the erotic things; in this subject he claims indeed to be of outstanding competence. Theages finds that Socrates is jesting: he simply does not wish to spend his time with Theages as he does with some of Theages' contemporaries who improve greatly thanks to their intercourse with Socrates. Thereupon Socrates ceases at once to speak of his being an *erotikos* and never returns to that subject; instead he speaks of his *daimonion*. The *daimonion* intimates to him what he and his friends should refrain from doing. It intimates in particular with which (young) people he should not spend his time: he cannot spend his time with these. It is true that the silence of the *daimonion* does not yet guarantee that his intercourse with the individuals concerned will be profitable for them. But when the power of the *daimonion* contributes to the being together, instant progress is achieved. Socrates adduces as an example what Aristeides once told him about his experiences with him: he never learned anything from Socrates; but, being together with him in the same house, preferably in the same room, still more preferably sitting at his side and touching him, he was marvellously profited. If the *daimonion* or the gods do not oppose Socrates' being together with Theages, the latter may have a similar experience: he will never learn anything from Socrates. Socrates has recourse to his *daimonion* after the recourse to his being *erotikos* was of no avail; his *daimonion* replaces his being *erotikos* because it fulfills the same function—because it *is* the same. Socrates cannot profitably be together with people who are not promising, who are not attractive to him. But not a few who are not attractive to him are attracted by him. He cannot well explain his refusal to be together with them by saying that he does not "love" them: he refers to a mysterious power to which everyone must bow and which cannot be asked questions; recourse to the *daimonion* is needed only for justifying refusals (to act). The *daimonion* is the forbidding, the denying aspect of Socrates' nature, of his natural inclinations; its full or true aspect is his *eros* as explained in the *Symposium*: *eros* is daimonic, not divine. "The nature of the other animals is daimonic, but not divine . . . Dreams then would not be god-sent but indeed daimonic" (Aristotle, *De div. per somnia* 463b14).]

Socrates shows next that in the two cases in which he acted politically, he came into mortal danger since he acted according to right or law. This happened once under the democracy and once under the oligarchy: he was neither a democrat nor an oligarch. One could find it strange that the *daimonion* did not turn him back from the two dangerous actions. Perhaps the *daimonion* is not indifferent to right and wrong. Or, more simply, the two actions could not have been avoided by him. When speaking of his action under the democracy, he identifies the jury, the whole jury, with the Assembly that committed the judicial murder of the generals in command at the battle of Arginousai. Accordingly when he says at the end of this passage that "you will have many witnesses for these things," he may refer only to what he did under the oligarchy; otherwise the reference would be ironic (as in 19d1–7). His proof that in his two political actions he stood up for the right leads him naturally to a somewhat muted discussion of the somewhat muted accusation that made him responsible for the misdeeds of his so-called pupils (especially Kritias and Alkibiades). Socrates simply denies that he ever had any pupils. If someone, be he young or no longer young, desired to listen when he spoke and minded his business—*i.e.*, when he philosophized—he never denied this to anyone; nor did he demand money for conversing but he offered himself to be questioned by everyone, rich or poor and, if they wished, they might hear what he said by answering his questions. He never gave private or secret instruction to anyone. It is true that there are some well-to-do young men who always accompany him. They seek his company—not indeed in order to be exhorted to virtue or to be deflated, but because they enjoy hearing how others, namely those who believe themselves to be wise without being wise, are examined, for to hear this is not unpleasant: it is not pleasant to be exhorted to virtue. Socrates says that it is not unpleasant: it is not unpleasant not only for possibly frivolous youths but simply; it is not unpleasant for Socrates himself. He does not say anything to the effect that that enjoyable examination consists in people being asked "what is?" regarding the human things, but he does not exclude it. However this may be, what he says to people or what he leads them to—people in general or his constant followers in particular—*i.e.*, what he does at the god's command which came to him through oracles, dreams and in any other manner of divine dispensation—the Delphic reply to Chairephon long ago ceased to be the single epoch-making event in his life—cannot be called the corruption of the young. If he corrupted any young men, either they themselves having become older or their fathers or other relatives should come forward and give testimony against him. He sees many of them in court. He mentions seven of his followers and seven of their fathers or brothers by name; altogether he mentions seventeen names. In the enumeration Plato appears in the company of Apollodoros. But none of the followers or their relatives come forward as witnesses for the accusers; the reason is obvious: the accusation is false. Socrates does not have recourse here to the argument which he used for silencing Meletos, namely that no one would voluntarily corrupt anyone (25c5ff.).

This is the end of the apology proper which is admittedly not exhaustive (34b7), one reason being that it deals chiefly with the corruption charge although the chief charge was that of impiety (cf. 35d1–2). In the conclusion Socrates justifies himself for not appealing to the pity of the jury as was the custom. That justification is in a way a digression in the sense previously defined, but it differs from the two digressions proper because it is not introduced as a reply to what "someone might perhaps say" (cf. 34d1–2 with 20c4 and 28b3). Socrates could beg for mercy in the customary manner since he too, as was said to and of Odysseus, is not born of an oak or a rock, and has relatives and in particular three male children, but he refuses to comply with the common practice, in the first place because he is concerned with his reputation as an outstanding Athenian and therewith with the reputation of Athens, and then because it would be unjust and impious to try to influence the jury to break their oath: in the act of defending himself against the charge of impiety he would reveal himself as impious in the eyes of all.

Socrates had expected to be condemned by a large majority; hence he spoke as if the whole jury were convinced of his guilt or hostile to him. To his surprise he was condemned by a small majority. If he judged rightly of the initial mood of the jury, his defense must have convinced not a few of its members. We have no right to assume that there were no members of the jury who regarded him as innocent or were friendly to him from the beginning. Socrates adds that if Meletos alone had accused him, if Anytos and Lykon had not come forward to accuse him, he would have been acquitted. One may therefore deplore that he refuted only Meletos.

"This was . . . a case in which no penalty was prescribed by law" and in which "the court had to choose between the alternative penalties proposed by the prosecution and the defense." (Burnet) Meletos had proposed the death penalty. Socrates proposes what he deserves. In order to determine it, he must consider both his merit and his need. As for his merit, he has never in his life kept quiet but neglected the things to which the many never cease to devote themselves—money-making, management of the household, generalships, success in political oratory, other kinds of political pre-eminence, conspiracies and seditions. As he indicates by this enumeration, all these activities are tainted by injustice. He regarded himself as in truth too good to attend to preserving himself by such activities by which he could not be of any use to the Athenians or to himself; the only plausible motive for going into politics is the concern with self-preservation (cf. *Gorgias* 511a4ff.). Previously Socrates had traced his abstention from politics to the *daimonion*, if not to the Delphic oracle, without openly voicing contempt for the political life; but now he speaks of his unique merit and is therefore silent on both kinds of superhuman promptings, while being very vocal on the low rank of political (and economic) activity. Instead of doing the things which the many do, he conferred the greatest benefit on each man by exhorting him to virtue. But being poor he lacks the leisure for his beneficial work. For both reasons taken together—his outstanding merit and his ten-thousandfold poverty—he deserves to have his meals in the prytaneion. This honor is awarded to the victors in the Olympian games, but these men make the Athenians only seem to be happy, while Socrates makes the Athenians truly happy; and they do not need sustenance but Socrates does.

Socrates' proposal is shocking, not only from the point of view of the majority who had found him guilty. What he says on his merit is based on the premise that he makes the Athenians in fact happy, *i.e.*, virtuous, or that his activity is entirely successful: he was as little successful in making his fellow citizens as good as possible as Perikles, Kimon, Miltiades and Themistokles were, whom he blamed so severely for their failure (*Gorgias* 515b8–516e8); he deserved the signal reward which he claimed as little as the participants in the Olympian games who did not win. What he says on his need for public maintenance would make sense if his friends had suddenly decided no longer to come to his assistance—an assumption that he himself refutes in the context.

Socrates makes his shocking proposal because he regards the serious alternatives to the death penalty as worse than death. He has not voluntarily done injustice to any human being. The Athenians will not believe this, for "we have conversed with one another only a short time." But did he not converse with them for many years the whole day long? Be this as it may, he wishes to do injustice to himself still less than to others, and he would do so by saying that he deserves some evil. As for the alleged evil that Meletos had proposed, he asserts again that he does not know whether it is good or evil. The alternatives—prison, fine and exile—he knows to be evils (although not great evils—30d1–4) and therefore he cannot choose them. As for exile in particular, in any other city to which he might go he would have the same troubles as in Athens. The young men would listen to his speeches; if he were to chase them away, they would persuade their elders to expel him; if he would not chase them away, their fathers and other relatives would expel him for the sake of the young.

At this point Socrates sees himself again confronted with what "someone might perhaps say" and thus begins the third and last digression. The first two digressions dealt with his divine mission; the last digression also deals with it, if in a somewhat different manner. Someone might perhaps say whether Socrates, after having been exiled from Athens, could not be silent and rest quiet. Socrates knows that it is of all things the most difficult to persuade "some of you" that it is impossible for him to remain silent. We tentatively assume that those whom he cannot persuade are those who condemned him. He could give two different reasons why he cannot remain silent. He could say in the first place that by remaining quiet he would disobey the god; but if he said this, they would think that he uses dissimulation ("irony"). He could say in the second place that it is the greatest good for a human being to engage every day in speeches about virtue and the other things about which they heard him converse and thereby examine himself and others—he does not say here "all others"—and that the unexamined life is not worth living for any human being; but this reason would convince them even less than the first and therefore, we may add, it is in need of a more plausible substitute. Socrates explains here tacitly why he told the story of the Delphic oracle. It is no accident that this explanation occurs in the central part of the dialogue. The distinction between the two reasons is identical with the distinction between being stationed by a superior and stationing oneself where one believes it is best (28d6–8). The second reason is utterly incredible to Socrates' condemners; the first reason is less remote from their understanding. We may conclude tentatively that those who acquitted Socrates believed either in his Delphic mission or in the intrinsic supremacy of the philosophic life or perhaps both.

After having made his momentous statement Socrates returns to the question of which penalty he should propose. He returns to the central alternative to the death penalty, a fine, which he had previously dismissed with a view to his not possessing money. In the repetition he repeats that he is not accustomed to regarding himself as deserving any evil but adds that he does not regard loss of money as an evil. He proposes therefore the small fine which he can afford to pay and raises at once the amount to thirty times its value at the request of Plato, Kriton, Kritoboulos and Apollodoros who vouch for the payment. There is then and there always was an alternative to the death penalty: why then did Socrates make at all his shocking proposal which could only aggravate the hostility of the jury? The Platonic Socrates, as distinguished from the Xenophontic Socrates, does not explain his conduct at the trial by his view that in his advanced years it was good for him to die.

This is not the only question left unanswered by Plato's *Apology of Socrates*. In the *Gorgias* Socrates compares the situation in which he would find himself if he were tried by the city on the charge brought by some villain that he corrupts the young, to that of a physician tried by children on the charge brought by a pastry cook that the physician gives them bitter medicine; he could not tell them the truth which they would be unable to understand. Here Socrates speaks of the multitude as homogeneous. But in the *Apology of Socrates* he makes a distinction, justified by the vote, between the condemning and the acquitting part: will the acquitters have understood him? After he was condemned to death, Socrates addressed the condemners and the acquitters separately. To the condemners he said three things. 1. What induced them to condemn him was not that he lacked speeches—a reminder of the prooemium—but his refusal to beg meanly for their pity, a refusal stemming from his concern with honor, with what is becoming for him. He compares the proper conduct before a court of law (not the proper conduct in the performance of his mission—28d10–29a1) with the proper conduct in war: however profound the difference, or the antagonism, between Socrates and the non-philosophic citizens may be, in grave situations he identifies himself completely, as far as his body is concerned, with the city, with "his people." 2. Yet he makes a distinction between the condemners and the accusers: the disgrace consequent upon his condemnation falls on the accusers. 3. He predicts that what they expect from killing him will not come to pass. They expect by killing him to get rid of the necessity to give an account of how they live. But more will put them to that test after his death, namely those whom he restrained from doing so, and they, being younger, will be harsher on them than he; of this restraining influence of Socrates his condemners were unaware. Socrates had not mentioned it before. On the contrary, he had said before (30e1–31a2) that if they kill him, they are not likely to find another gadfly: did he at that time wish to induce them to kill him?

With the acquitters he would like to exchange speeches (*dialegesthai*); in fact he exchanges stories with them (*diamythologein*) by telling them stories or reminding them of them. He explains to them the meaning of what had happened. In his speech to the condemners he had uttered a divination as men do who are about to die. Now he speaks of his customary divination, the divination through the *daimonion*. The *daimonion* formerly opposed itself very frequently and even on very small matters whenever he was about to do something wrong or unfit. But now on the day of his trial "the sign of the god"did not oppose itself at any moment to anything he did and in particular never while he delivered his speech, although in other speeches it had stopped him in the middle: the *daimonion* opposes not only some actions but also some speeches. The silence of the *daimonion* on this day suggests that what happened to Socrates is something good: to be dead is not bad. This silence of the *daimonion* is all the more remarkable since its function seems to have been to preserve his life; this may be the reason why it is now called "the sign of the god," *i.e.*, why the distinction between the *daimonion* and Apollo's command is blurred. In his speech to his condemners he had not questioned their premise that death is a great evil.

Socrates does not then leave matters now at saying that he does not know whether death is an evil. But the silence of the *daimonion* might not prove more than that death is good for Socrates now because of his old age (cf. 41d4 and *Crito* 43b10–11). He shows therefore that there is great hope that death is simply good. To be dead is one of two things: it is either to be nothing and have no awareness of anything, or it is, in accordance with what is said, some change and migration of the soul from the place here to another place. In discussing the first alternative, Socrates is silent on death as complete annihilation and on the question of whether fear of death thus understood is not according to nature. He speaks only of death as a state of dreamless sleep. If death is this, it would be a marvelous gain: if someone had to pick out that night in which he slept so profoundly as not even to dream, and, contrasting it with the other nights and days of his life, were to say after due consideration how many days and nights in his life he has spent better and more pleasantly than that night, practically everyone would find that they are easy to count compared with the other days and nights. The ambiguous sentence intimates the doubtful character of the thought: Socrates the gadfly, the awakener from drowsiness, as the encomiast of the profoundest sleep. One could say of course that in dreamless sleep one does not believe that one knows what one does not know and is therefore in possession of that human wisdom which is of little or no worth. But, as we have seen, this negative account of Socrates' concern was gradually superseded by a more positive account according to which it is the greatest good for man to exchange speeches every day about virtue and kindred things or to "philosophize," and an unexamined life is not worth living for man.

Correspondingly Socrates speaks in the second place of what follows if death is, as it were, a going away from home, from one's people, to another place where, according to what is said, all the dead are; in that case there would be no greater good than death. In Hades one would find in the first place all the half-gods who were just during their life and among them in the

first place the true judges (Minos, Rhadamanthys, Aiakos and Trip-
tolemos); Socrates does not speak of the half-gods who were unjust during
their lives, nor of what the true judges will do to them and still less of what
they will do to men who acted unjustly here (like his accusers and condemners). Instead he speaks of another great boon: in Hades one might
come together with Orpheus, Mousaios, Hesiod and Homer—another
group of four, the group whom Adeimantos quotes or mentions together as
teachers of injustice (*Republic* 364c5–365a3). For Socrates it would be
wonderful to meet there Palamedes, Aias the son of Telamon and other
ancients, if any, who died because of an unjust judgment and to compare his
experiences with theirs (Aias committed suicide). But, most important, one
could there spend one's time examining and searching those there, as these
here, as to who among them is wise and who believes himself to be wise
without being so; to converse with, to be together with, and to examine the
one who led the great army against Troy, or Odysseus or Sisyphos or a
thousand others, men and women, would be unspeakable happiness; those
there presumably do not kill one on this ground at any rate, for they are
happier than the ones here in the other respects and in addition are henceforth immortal, if the things that are said are true. Life in Hades seems then
to be happy for all, especially for Socrates who will continue there the life he
led in Athens and improve on it without having to fear capital and probably
any other punishment. Is dying then bad? If it is not bad, Socrates will not be
happier there than he was here (cf. *Statesman* 272b8–d2), unless the examination of Homer and his heroes and heroines increases happiness.
Socrates had not spoken of his examining women in Athens.

Socrates does not mention Agamemnon by name, just as he did not
mention Achilleus by name (28c2–d4). He mentions by name altogether
twelve who dwell "there" just as he had mentioned by name in his enumeration of his companions and their fathers or brothers twelve who dwell
"here," *i.e.*, who are still alive (33d9–34a2). Hesiod and Homer not un-
naturally occupy the central place. The second from the end in the second
enumeration is Odysseus; the second from the end in the first enumeration is
Plato.

In conclusion Socrates exhorts the acquitters to be of good hope in regard
to death with special regard to the outstanding truth that nothing is bad for a
good man while he is alive or after his death, and his affairs are not neglected
by gods. He then applies this truth to himself: it is now better for him to die
and to be freed from troubles, as the *daimonion* intimated by its silence.
Immediately before this conclusion he had suggested that all the dead are in
Hades and happy there; from this it would seem to follow that no one has to
fear death. But the concluding remark is to the effect that only the good men
do not have to fear death, and it seems to assume that Socrates is a good man
which in the whole context of the work also means that he is innocent of the

crimes of which he was accused. Yet he infers that it is good for him to die not from his goodness but from the silence of his *daimonion*: and he infers from that silence, not that death is simply good but that death is good for him now.

It is no wonder that he is not very angry with his condemners and even his accusers although they intended to harm him. What may cause some wonder is that he entrusts to them, and not to the acquitters whom he describes as his friends (40a1), the concern with the virtue of his sons; if the condemners and accusers will annoy his sons as he annoyed the condemners and accusers, and for the same reason, both he and his sons will have suffered justice at their hands. He seems to expect his condemners and accusers to become his spiritual heirs at least as far as his sons are concerned. Yet by entrusting his sons to his condemners, he entrusts them to the majority, *i.e.*, to the city; and the city is concerned with virtue, if only with vulgar virtue: it can be expected to urge Socrates' sons toward that kind of virtue. He concludes with the remark that he is going away to die and they to live; and that whether he or they go away to a better lot is immanifest to everyone except to the god. One may say that he returns to his early protestation of ignorance as to whether death is good or bad. He surely does not tell his condemners stories about Hades.

II

While the *Apology of Socrates* is *the* public conversation of Socrates carried on in broad daylight with the city of Athens, the *Crito* presents a conversation which he had in the strictest privacy, secluded as he was from everyone else by the prison walls, with his oldest friend.

At the beginning of the dialogue (cf. 44a7–8) Socrates is in profound sleep, dreaming of a beautiful and well shaped woman who is clothed—we learn even the color of her clothes—and who calls him and says that "on the third day [he] would come to the most fertile Phthia." He awakens and has his conversation with Kriton which culminates in the *prosopopoiia* of the laws of Athens. What the Laws are made to tell him reduces him again to a quasi-somnolent state—a state in which he can as little hear what Kriton or anyone else may say as he could in the state in which he was at the beginning. Yet while the state in which he was at the beginning was tranquil and peaceful, at the end he is in a state which is comparable to that of people filled with Korybantic frenzy who believe that they hear flutes, and in which the speeches he has heard from the Laws make a booming noise in him.

When the conversation with Kriton begins, it is still quite dark. It is also still quite dark when Socrates' conversation with Hippokrates begins (43a4, *Protagoras* 310a8). But in the case of the conversation with Hippokrates we hear that during that conversation the day began to dawn so that the two could see one another clearly (312a2–3); we hear nothing to this effect regarding the conversation with Kriton: perhaps it took place in its entirety before dawn; perhaps Socrates and Kriton did not see one another clearly at all; the conversation surely did not take place in its entirety in broad daylight. Correspondingly in the *Crito* nothing is said about Socrates' rising from his bed, sitting, standing or walking. One does not sufficiently explain the difference between the situation in the *Crito* and that in the Hippokrates-section of the *Protagoras* by saying that the *Crito* is a performed and the *Protagoras* is a narrated dialogue, for who can doubt that Plato would have been able to make it clear even in a performed dialogue that the sun and Socrates had risen?

The *Crito* opens with six or seven Socratic questions to which Kriton possesses the full answers. The last of these answers leads up to the prediction, based on what certain (human) messengers say, that Socrates will die tomorrow. This prediction Socrates refuses to believe because his dream assured him that he will die on the third day.

In the dream a beautiful woman said to Socrates and about Socrates what in Homer Achilleus said about himself to Odysseus while refusing to be reconciled with Agamemnon, his ruler. Socrates, even the dreaming Socrates, had to change the Homeric text and context, for Achilleus threatened to leave the army—his post—and to go home to Phthia, or he disobeyed his ruler (cf. *Republic* 389e12–390a4). He made the necessary change on the basis of another Homeric passage. In a central passage of the *Apology of Socrates* (28c2–d5) where Socrates presents Achilleus as a model of noble conduct, he speaks of a beautiful woman, the goddess Thetis, saying to her son Achilleus that he will die straightway after Hektor; Achilleus chose to die nobly rather than to live in disgrace—which he would surely do by returning to Phthia. In Socrates' dream the two Homeric passages (*Iliad* 9.363 and 18.94ff.) are combined with the result that a beautiful woman prophesies to him that he would come to Phthia, or advises him to go to Phthia, *i.e.*, to Thessaly. As a matter of fact, Kriton will soon propose to Socrates that he should escape from prison and go, if he wishes, to Thessaly (45c2–4). If Socrates accepted this interpretation of the dream, he would go to Thessaly on a more than human initiative and therefore by his action disobey only his human rulers. But Phthia being Achilleus' fatherland, the dream could as well mean that Socrates will come on the third day to his true fatherland, *i.e.*, to Hades. It is this interpretation which he tacitly chooses as a matter of course.

Kriton is eager that Socrates obey him and save himself for the sake of Kriton. He adduces two reasons. He will lose by Socrates' death an irreplaceable friend and, above all, his reputation with the many who do not know him and Socrates well will irreparably suffer, for they will think that he failed to save Socrates because he did not wish to spend the money required for the purpose: it is disgraceful to be thought to esteem money more highly than friends. (This argument implies that the many who condemned Socrates to die also would condemn Socrates' friends for not illegally preventing his execution, for the many think that it is disgraceful to esteem money more highly than friends.) Socrates does not even attempt to comfort Kriton about the loss of his best friend (for he would incur that loss also if Socrates left Athens as a fugitive from justice) but he tells him that his concern with the opinion of the many is exaggerated; the fact that the many guided by their opinion condemned Socrates to death does not prove, as Kriton thinks, that they can inflict the greatest evils; they can do this as little as they can bestow the greatest goods: they cannot make men sensible or foolish. Socrates does not deny of course that they can inflict evils (cf. *Gorgias* 469b12). Kriton is thus compelled to set forth more serious considerations. He fears that Socrates does not wish to expose Kriton and his other friends to accusations by informers and hence to heavy fines; while he has asked Socrates to worry about Kriton's reputation, he asks him not to worry about the wealthy Kriton's property. Socrates had indeed not been unmindful of Kriton's possible financial sacrifices. Kriton shows him that there is no reason for being concerned with the matter. In the first place only a small amount of money is required for arranging Socrates' jail break and for assisting him afterwards. Secondly, the informers can be bought off with small amounts of money. Thirdly, if Socrates still worries about Kriton's sacrifice, however small, the expense does not have to be borne by Kriton at all; Simmias of Thebes could and would single-handedly bear it. Finally, Socrates should not worry about his way of life in his place of refuge; in many places he will find people who will esteem him highly; Kriton mentions by name Thessaly where he, Kriton, has good connections.

Kriton turns then from considerations which are more or less closely connected with his wealth to considerations of what is just for Socrates to do: by failing to save himself he would transgress his duty to himself and his duty to his children, for he would betray himself and his children. The father Kriton rebukes the father Socrates severely for being tempted to choose the easiest course regarding the rearing of one's children, namely desertion. He is silent about Socrates' duty to the city. The consideration of the just turns almost insensibly into a consideration of the noble, of what befits a manly man: Socrates and his friends will be thought to have mismanaged the whole affair from the beginning to the end through lack of manliness. This shift from the just to the noble is based on a specific view of justice: it is a man's first duty to preserve himself, to prevent his suffering injustice (cf. Kallikles' argument in the *Gorgias*). In conclusion Kriton urges Socrates to deliberate about his proposal while saying that there is no longer time for deliberation (for Socrates must escape during the coming night) or that there is no object of deliberation (for there is no imaginable alternative to flight during the coming night). He obviously does not believe in the prediction conveyed through Socrates' dream that he will die only on the third day.

The consideration of the just occupies externally the center in Kriton's argument. In Socrates' reply it becomes the primary and the chief, not to say the sole, consideration. To justify this change, he must question Kriton's fundamental premise that one must respect the opinion of the many because the many are so powerful. That premise had been rather summarily dismissed before (44d1–e1). Now he examines it at some length. He starts from the fact that he is always obedient to nothing other of what is his than the *logos* which appears best to him when he reasons (*logizetai*): he may obey *logoi*, or promptings, which are not properly speaking his, such as oracles (*Apology of Socrates* 20e5–6) or the *daimonion* or the laws (52c8–9). In the conversation with Kriton he barely alludes to the *daimonion*; he does not refer to the fact that the *daimonion* approved by its silence of his conduct at the trial (*Apology of Socrates* 40a4–c3)—that conduct which Kriton so severely blamed because of its apparent lack of manliness (45e4–5). Kriton was obviously as little impressed by the testimony of the *daimonion* as by the prediction conveyed through Socrates' dream: he did not believe in the *daimonion*. Apart from twice swearing "by Zeus," he never speaks of the gods. He is sober or rather pedestrian, therefore narrow and hence somnolent regarding the things which transcend his sphere, his experience.

The *logoi* that appear to Socrates best as a result of his reasoning are not necessarily unchangeable; they may be superseded by better *logoi*. He denies therefore that his present situation as such and especially the nearness of his death justify a revision of the *logoi* at which he had arrived previously, for that situation, brought about by the mysterious and sinister power of the many, had been taken into account by the former *logoi*. This applies also to the *logoi*, or at least to some *logoi* on which he and Kriton had previously reached agreement: Kriton too cannot give them up merely on account of the present situation. Socrates proposes that they discuss first Kriton's *logos* about the opinions—the *logos* that one must pay respect to the opinions of the many. Previously they held, in agreement with what was always said by those who believe that they are saying something worth while, that one must respect some opinions of human beings but not others. This could be thought to mean that one must respect some opinions of the many. Socrates here excludes this by adding that one must respect the opinions of some but not those of others, for the opinions that are respectable are the useful or good opinions and these are the opinions of those who are sensible, *i.e.*, of the few.

For instance, a man in gymnastic training who is serious about it, is swayed by the praise, the blame and the opinions, not of every man but of that single man alone who happens to be a physician or a trainer; he will act in a manner approved by the single expert rather than by all others; by respecting the *logoi* of the many who are not experts, he will suffer damage in his body, perhaps even ruin it. The opinions, not only of "the many" but of any "many" are to be disparaged in favor of the opinion of the single knower. And since by not listening to the physician or trainer one may ruin one's body, not only the man already seriously engaged in gymnastic training but everyone (who can afford it) must seek the expert's guidance. Accordingly in regard to the things just and unjust, base and noble, good and bad too one must follow the opinion of the single expert, if there is one, and not that of the others. Socrates thus forces us to wonder what one must do if no expert regarding the just, noble and good things is available, if the best that one can find among human beings is knowledge of one's ignorance regarding the most important things (*Apology of Socrates* 22d7 and context). Must one not, or at least may one not, in that case obey the opinions of non-experts, a kind of opinion of non-experts, the most authoritative kind, *i.e.*, the laws of one's city? Would the laws thus not be only "the way next to the best"? On the other hand, what should one do if there is an expert in such matters and his *logos* differs from that of the laws?

Socrates does not raise these questions explicitly. But he also does not limit himself to alluding to them, by using the conditional clause "if there is an expert." He intimates in addition why the availability of an expert cannot be taken for granted and at the same time the specific limitation of Kriton by studiously avoiding the word "soul." He uses instead periphrastic expressions like "whatever it is of the things belonging to us with which justice and injustice are concerned" and which deserves higher honor than the body. He thus intimates the difference between the expert regarding justice and the non-experts (and in particular the laws): the expert's *logoi* on what is just proceed from knowledge of the soul.

Socrates turns next to Kriton's *logos* that one must be concerned with the opinion of the many regarding the just, the noble and the good things and their opposites not because of its intrinsic worth but because the many have the power to kill us, *i.e.*, to ruin our bodies. It is not quite clear whether in taking issue with that *logos* Socrates presupposes the whole result of his refutation of Kriton's first *logos*. (Note the unusual density of adjectival vocatives—48a5, b3, d8, e2—in the transition from the first to the second argument.) Certain it is that he no longer speaks now of the single expert regarding the just things: might that expert not say that in certain circumstances one must cede to the power of the many or try to elude it (cf. *Republic* 496d–e)? Instead he ascertains that Kriton still agrees with what both had agreed upon previously or that those agreements still remain; the agreements of two take the place of the verdicts of the single expert. They agreed and agree that not life but the good life is to be valued most highly and that the good life is the same as the noble and just life. From this it follows that the only thing which they have to consider in regard to Kriton's proposal is whether Socrates' escape from prison against the will of the Athenians would be just on the part of Socrates and of Kriton; all other considerations are irrelevant. Socrates is willing to reconsider his opinion; he would not wish to act against the will of Kriton, just as he does not wish to escape against the will of the Athenians; he wishes to reconcile Kriton's will with that of the Athenians. He encourages him therefore to contradict him; if Kriton is able to do it successfully, he will obey him. At the same time he makes sure that Kriton still adheres to their former agreements by stressing how unbecoming it is for men of their old age to change opinions like little children.

Socrates explains what it means to act justly by first stating that one must in no manner voluntarily act unjustly or that to act unjustly is for him who acts unjustly both bad and base in every manner. He thus reminds us of the question as to whether anyone can voluntarily act unjustly (*Apology of Socrates* 25d5–26a7 and 37a5–6) or whether all acts of injustice do not stem from ignorance: only the knower, the expert regarding the just things, can act justly. He draws the conclusion that one must not when suffering injustice do injustice in turn. After some hesitation Kriton agrees. Socrates states secondly that inflicting evil on human beings, even if one has suffered evil from them, is unjust, for inflicting evil on human beings differs in nothing from acting unjustly. Kriton agrees without hesitation. One wonders whether one cannot act unjustly against the gods (cf. *Euthyphro* 11e7–12e9 and *Laws* 821c6–d4), *i.e.*, whether impiety is not a crime, and hence whether Socrates would not have committed an unjust act by not believing in the existence of those gods in whose existence the city believes, unless such unbelief harmed the city, *i.e.*, human beings. If those who comdemned Socrates and those who acquitted him regarded impiety as a crime while differing as to whether Socrates was guilty of it, Kriton would not belong to either group. It goes without saying that he did not belong with the condemners; as for the acquitters, they were people who could be assumed to believe in Socrates' *daimonion*. One wonders furthermore whether inflicting evil on human beings can be simply unjust if war is not simply unjust; but Socrates went to war whenever the city told him to go (51b4–c1) without making his obedience dependent on whether the war was just or not.

Socrates draws Kriton's attention to the gravity of the matter on which they agreed and still agree. Only some few share these opinions; and those who hold them and those who do not cannot deliberate in common; they have no common ground, and they are bound to despise one another's deliberations. *The* cleavage among men is no longer that between knowers and ignoramuses, or between the philosophers and the non-philosophers ("philosopher" does not occur in the *Crito*), *i.e.*, between the few who hold and the many who do not hold that the unexamined life is not worth living, but that between those who hold that one may not requite evil with evil and those who hold that one may, or even ought to, do it. One may wonder how there can be a city if there is no common deliberation between those few and these many. Or is it a pre-requisite of citizenship that one believe in the right of requiting evil with evil? But is then the city not radically unjust? Be this as it may, Socrates admits now as it were in passing that we may defend ourselves when we suffer evil, but he lays stress on the fact that in doing so we must not do evil in return.

The question which Socrates and Kriton have to decide is whether by going away "from here" without having persuaded "the city" "we" inflict evil on "some" and even on those whom one ought to harm least. The difference between Socrates and Kriton is now irrelevant. Previously Socrates had spoken of going away without the permission, or against the will, of the Athenians (48b2–c1, e3); now he replaces "the Athenians" by "the city," because "the Athenians" are "many" or even "the many." The place of "the Athenians" in the meaning which the expression has in the two indicated passages is taken in the sequel particularly by "the fatherland": "the Athenians" and "the fatherland" occur each seven times in the *Crito*. In the sequel Socrates speaks of "the fatherland" and much more frequently of "the city" (and derivatives) and "the laws" (and derivatives), *i.e.*, uses expressions which never occurred before, while there no longer occurs any reference to "the many." In acting without the permission of the city they harm "some": they do not harm all men.

Only at this place in the conversation does Kriton not understand a Socratic question: despite, or rather on the basis of, his agreement with Socrates on the principles he has no doubt that it would be just for Socrates to escape from prison and for him to assist him therein (45a1–3, c5ff.), for in doing so neither he nor Socrates would in his opinion inflict evil on human beings and least of all on those whom one ought to harm least, *i.e.*, relatives and friends. He does not think of the city, for he is not a political man (cf. Xenophon, *Memorabilia* I 2.48 and II 9.1). We may go one step further and say that the previous agreements between Socrates and Kriton did not extend to political things and especially the laws. Socrates does not answer or explain in his own name the question which Kriton had not understood. To counteract the scaring effect which the power of the many had on Kriton (cf. 46c4–5), he has recourse to a more noble action of a kindred kind. He asks him to visualize that when about to run away "from here," they would be stopped by the laws and the community of the city and asked to give an account of what Socrates intends to do. The relation of the laws and the community of the city is not explained but it is clear that while the city consists of human beings, the laws do not: the laws are in a sense superhuman. The appearance speaks of itself once in the singular, *i.e.*, means itself as the community of the city, and thereafter in the plural, *i.e.*, means itself as the laws. The Laws ask Socrates first whether he does not by his attempt intend to destroy "us laws and the whole city" so far as it lies in him, for a city will be destroyed if the judgments given by the courts are rendered ineffective by the actions of private men. Socrates asks Kriton whether they would reply that they have been wronged by the city which gave the wrong verdict; Kriton agrees eagerly, strengthening his assent by an oath. (There occurs only one other oath of Kriton; he replies to Socrates' question near the beginning why he had not awakened him by a "No, by Zeus.") He apparently thinks that in correcting by private action an injustice committed by the city, one does not inflict evil on human beings but rather bestows a benefit upon them.

The Laws do not respond to Socrates' and Kriton's justification. Instead they are made to counter with the admittedly strange question whether they and Socrates had not agreed that one must abide by the judgments given by the city's courts. When Socrates does not answer, they repeat their assertion that Socrates is attempting to destroy them and ask him on the basis of what charge against them and the city he does so. He seems to have answered that question earlier when he put it to himself and replied that the city wronged him by his condemnation. But the question which the Laws put to him concerns not his private complaint against a single act of theirs but his charge against Athenian laws in general. The question of Socrates' charge against Athenian laws in general is raised but not answered in the *Crito*. For Socrates, to say nothing of Kriton, is not given an opportunity to answer that question raised by the Laws.

The Laws seem now to begin at the beginning. They tell Socrates that they have generated him by virtue of the marriage laws and that they have reared and educated him by virtue of the laws which commanded his father to educate him in gymnastic and music. Socrates approves of these laws. He does not say that he agrees with the reasoning of the Laws. To say nothing of their claim to have generated him, they are understandably silent on the branches of education higher than music and gymnastic. (Cf. *Republic* 520a9–c1 and Cicero, *Republic* I 8.) The Laws draw the conclusion that through what they have done for him, he is their offspring and their slave and therefore that he and they are not equal in right: this is the reason why he cannot rightfully do to them what they do to him, even less than he could rightfully have done to his father what his father did to him or rightfully do to a master, if he were a slave, what his master does to him. For the fatherland is more venerable and more highly esteemed by gods and by men of sense than mother and father and all ancestors. The fatherland seems to communicate its immortality or unchangeability to the laws; therefore the Laws can say that through what they have done for Socrates he has become their offspring, he and his ancestors: the Athenian laws were not at all times the same. The Laws wisely do not refer to the principle that one must not do evil to human beings; it is sufficient for them to refer to the principle that every citizen belongs altogether to them; one would be tempted to say that every citizen belongs to the Laws body and soul, were it not for the fact that the *Crito* does not use the word "soul." Accordingly the *Crito* can only intimate that the soul is more venerable than the body and state that the fatherland is more venerable than father and mother: it does not force us to wonder whether or not the soul is more venerable than the fatherland (cf. *Laws* 724a1–727a2).

The Laws compare the relation between the citizen and the fatherland, the city, or the laws to the relation between children and their father, *i.e.*, to a relation not based on agreement or compact. How far does the duty of obedience to the law extend according to the Laws? They say nothing about any limits to that obedience. We must then assume that they demand unqualified obedience, passive and active. Yet the Laws may be mistaken in what they demand; they do not raise a claim to superhuman wisdom or to be of divine origin (cf. *Laws* 624a1–6 and 634e1–2) or to be divine—as little as does the woman who appeared to Socrates in his dream. (The Athenians are not presented in the *Crito* as generated and educated by gods; see *Timaeus* 24d5–6.) The Laws may believe that something is just without its being so; one may therefore try to persuade the fatherland or the city to desist from its demand, but if one fails therein, one must do as one is told. (They do not say here that one must try to persuade the Laws, for the things which one is legally commanded to do are frequently determined not by the laws as such but by political or judicial decisions.) The Laws refer to Socrates' special case: he claims to be truly concerned with virtue and is therefore under a special obligation. But precisely Socrates had touched on the question as to whether he would or could obey a law forbidding him, explicitly or implicitly, to philosophize, *i.e.*, to be truly concerned with virtue, and he said that he would not (*Apology of Socrates* 29c6–d5). As for the Laws' argument that one must unqualifiedly obey the laws even more than the son must obey his father, it is sufficient to think of the case of an insane father against whom one may use deception and even force in his own interest and to wonder whether cities are incapable of passing insane laws. Be this as it may, Kriton is fully satisfied that the Laws say the truth, as fully as that other father, Kephalos, would have been.

The Laws themselves seem to feel that the satisfactory character of the Athenian laws concerning marriage and elementary education or the obligations deriving from one's debt to them on account of these particular laws do not suffice to justify their demand for complete submission. Therefore they "might perhaps" make the following two additions. Firstly, they have given to Socrates, just as to all other citizens, a share in all the noble things at their disposal: Meletos may be right in saying that the Laws make human beings better (*Apology of Socrates* 24d10–11); they surely are as little able as the many to make a man sensible (cf. 44d6–10). Secondly, they permit every Athenian who is of age, if the Laws and the city displease him, to go to an Athenian colony or wherever he wishes, taking his property with him; no law prevents him from doing it, although something else might. But whoever stays in Athens, seeing how the Laws decide cases before the courts and administer the city in other respects, has agreed by deed to do what the Laws command, unless he persuades them, if they make a mistake, of what is intrinsically, naturally just; for the Laws are civilized and do not command in a savage, tyrannical manner but are willing to listen and to be persuaded. This agreement with the Laws takes the place formerly occupied by education through the Laws (cf. 51e4–7 with 50e2).

Unqualified obedience to the Laws has then two heterogeneous grounds: the fact that they have generated and reared the citizen and the fact that he has made an agreement with them; the former makes him the slave of the Laws, the other is the act of a free man; unqualified obedience to the Laws has its root in the co-operation of compulsion and consent. And the Laws take full responsibility for everything done by their authority: for the administration of justice and for the political administration in general; the Laws are the city, the citizen body, the Athenians; the distinction previously suggested between the Laws and the citizen body is here silently dropped. There is a twofold reason for this. Firstly, the Laws act only through being known to human beings (*Apology of Socrates* 24d11ff.), they act only through human beings and, above all, they originate in human beings or, more precisely, in the regime which in Athens is a democracy. Secondly, acting unjustly means inflicting evil on human beings; but the Laws are not human beings.

No Athenian, the Laws continue, made the agreement with the Laws in deed to such a singular degree as Socrates, for he hardly ever left Athens, he never even desired to know another city or other laws but the Laws and the city sufficed him; he showed by deed that the city pleased him. This reasoning of the Laws may explain why they are silent on Socrates' ever having attempted to persuade the Laws to change their course although he knew that they were defective in at least one important respect (*Apology of Socrates* 37a7–b1), for he could not have done this without engaging in political activity and, as the Laws doubtless knew, his *daimonion* prevented this (*ib.* 31c4–e6); the Laws are silent on this point because spelling out what persuading the Laws means would not be compatible with the *hypothesis* of their superhuman status. In the case of Socrates at any rate the duty of obeying the Laws was not limited by the right to persuade the Laws. This fact strengthens their contention that by trying to run away he would act against his tacit agreement with them and hence commit an unjust act; they are now silent on the other ground of obedience to them. They conclude this part of their argument by asking Socrates whether he has agreed to live as a citizen according to them. Kriton, asked by Socrates, replies that it is necessary for him and Socrates to agree to what the Laws say.

The Laws conclude their reasoning about the justice of Socrates' running away by emphasizing again that in doing so he would break his covenants with them—convenants into which he entered under no compulsion whatever and which therefore were just—they do not say that the Laws themselves are just—and that he was pleased with the laws. The latter fact is all the more remarkable since, as they mention now, he was in the habit of saying of Sparta and Crete (what he apparently did not say of Athens) that they are well-governed or have good laws; although he had no desire to know other cities and other laws, he nevertheless knew at least some of them. His hardly ever leaving Athens proves that the city pleases him and hence the Laws: for whom could a city without laws please? That no city which has no laws can please obviously does not prove that the pleasing city must have pleasing laws: a city may have other attractions than its laws; this is what Socrates meant when he made the Laws emphasize that no *law* prevented him from moving to another city. (One finds an extensive statement of Socrates' view of Athens' attractions and of her laws in his description of the democracy in the eighth book of the *Republic*.)

Without giving Kriton now or later an opportunity to voice his agreement or disagreement, the Laws show next that in escaping from prison Socrates would act not only unjustly but also ridiculously, for the action would be inept or not suitable to the ends which it is meant to achieve; it would not have the excuse of being at least a profitable crime. They thus counter the reasonings by which Kriton had supported his advice. They deal very briefly with the great risks run by Socrates' friends as too obvious to require explanation. They deal rather extensively with the risk run by Socrates himself. He could escape to one of the nearby cities like Thebes and Megara which are well-governed but he would come there as an enemy of their regime (for the regime is not democratic and Socrates is a law-abiding citizen of democratic Athens), and he would be regarded there at least by the patriotic citizens as a destroyer of laws and therefore presumably a corrupter of the young. The Laws discuss then very briefly the alternative that Socrates would avoid the well-governed cities and the most well-behaved of men and dismiss it at once on the ground that, if he did this, life would not be worth living. One wonders whether his life was not worth living in Athens which was not a well-governed city. The Laws return therefore to the first alternative: what kind of speeches will he make in the well-governed cities? the same as in Athens, to the effect that virtue and justice and the things established by law and the law are of the highest value to human beings? But if made by a fugitive from justice would they not discredit Socrates' life work? The Laws return then again to an alternative: that Socrates would avoid, not so much the well-governed cities as "these places" (*i.e.*, the region of Athens, Megara and Thebes) and go to Thessaly. There he would not be frowned upon for having transgressed the gravest laws because the people there live in the greatest disorder and dissoluteness and would probably be only amused if Socrates told them of the laughable details of his escape—things more truly laughable than his staying in prison which to Kriton seemed so laughable (45e5–46a1). But the mood of the Thessalians would change as soon as he annoyed any of them, as he could not help doing without ceasing to be Socrates (cf. *Apology of Socrates* 37d6–e2). Then they would make as much of the contrast between his deed and his speeches as the most respectable Thebans and Megarians would do. The disjunction used by the Laws—well-governed cities nearby and dissolute Thessaly far away—is not complete; there were well-governed cities far away from Athens, Sparta and especially Crete (52e5–6), where Socrates and his escape from prison might not be known. But, as the Laws and Socrates (43b10–11) say, he is an old man who is not likely to live for a long time anyway. The Laws have no reason to discuss whether another course of action would have been appropriate if Socrates had been younger.

According to Kriton it is a demand of justice that Socrates save himself to complete the rearing and education of his sons. The Laws treat this argument at the end of their reasoning concerning the expediency of Socrates' running away. They advise him to entrust the rearing and education of his children to his friends. Socrates himself had spoken only of what he would wish his condemners to do to his children after they reach puberty (*Apology of Socrates* 41e1–42a2).

In their conclusion the Laws speak of themselves only as Socrates' rearers; they are now silent on their having generated and educated him (cf. 54b2 with 51c8–9 and e5–6). In accordance with this limitation of their claim they now disclaim responsibility for the injustice which Socrates suffered; he has suffered that injustice at the hands, not of the Laws, but of human beings. It is of the utmost importance that the Laws themselves declare Socrates to be innocent of the crimes with which he was charged. They advise him to subordinate every other consideration to that of what is right so that, having come to Hades, he can plead in his defense before those who rule there all that the Laws have told him; shortly thereafter they in fact identify the rulers in Hades with the Laws in Hades: in Hades there is not the distinction between the laws and the rulers (those who execute the laws) which permits the Laws to say that Socrates has suffered injustice at the hands not of the Laws, but of those who execute the Laws; in Hades, miscarriage of justice is not possible. The thought of Hades surely strengthens their conclusion that Socrates would act unjustly if he followed Kriton's advice.

Both the content and the manner of the speeches of the Laws make it impossible for Socrates to listen to any other speeches and in particular to what Kriton might say. But Kriton has nothing else to say: the speech of the

Laws has entirely convinced him. Then, Socrates concludes, let us act in this way since it is in this way that the god leads. The voice of the Laws seems to be the voice of the gods.

Deeds are more trustworthy than speeches: Socrates did stay in prison, he chose to stay, he had a *logos* telling him to stay. But is this *logos* identical with the *logos* by which he persuades Kriton? We have indicated why this is not likely. There are then two different *logoi* leading to the same conclusion. The *logos* which convinces Socrates would not convince Kriton and vice-versa. Kriton is concerned above all with what the people of Athens will say if he has not helped Socrates to escape from prison: what Socrates tells Kriton, Kriton can and will tell the people.

Hobbes committed a grave exaggeration when he accused Socrates and his followers of being anarchists. The truth underlying that exaggeration is the fact that Socrates did not think that there could be an unqualified duty to obey the laws. But this did not prevent him from thinking, nay, it enabled him to think that the demand for such obedience is a wise rule of thumb as distinguished from an unqualifiedly valid law.

3

On the *Euthydemus*

From the *Crito* we are led to the *Euthydemus* by the consideration that the *Euthydemus* contains the only other conversation between Socrates and Kriton. The two dialogues stand indeed at opposite poles. The *Euthydemus* is the most bantering, not to say frivolous and farcical dialogue while the *Crito* is the most solemn one: the *Crito* is the only dialogue in which there occurs almost a theophany. Yet there is a remarkable kinship between the two dialogues in regard to structure. In the *Euthydemus* Socrates' performed conversation with Kriton surrounds and interrupts the conversation, narrated by Socrates, between Socrates, Euthydemos and others. The only other dialogue which has a comparable structure is the *Crito* in which Socrates' performed conversation with Kriton surrounds the quasi-conversation, evoked by Socrates, between Socrates and the Laws of Athens.

The farcical character of the *Euthydemus* stands in a superficial contrast with the fact that Socrates praises therein the patently absurd and ridiculous "art" of Euthydemos, not only to Euthydemos' face, but in his absence when speaking to Kriton, as very great wisdom; he even expresses his desire to become a pupil of Euthydemos. Everyone will say, everyone has said that this is "that customary irony of Socrates."[1] But Kriton, the direct addressee of Socrates' report about his conversation with Euthydemos, does not say this. Was Kriton unaware of that irony? Was he impervious to it? Would thus the *Euthydemus* not reveal to us Kriton's most important limitation? Would it thus not throw light retroactively or in advance on the *Crito*?

Reprinted from *Interpretation: A Journal of Political Philosophy* 1, no. 1 (1970).

1. *Republic* 337 a4–5.

I: The prologue: the initial conversation
between Kriton and Socrates
(271 a1–273 d8)

Kriton opens the dialogue by asking Socrates "Who was it, Socrates, with whom you conversed yesterday in the Lykeion?" Kriton is therefore responsible for the dialogue's taking place; the dialogue is as it were imposed on Socrates. Kriton's question "Who was . . . " reminds us of Socrates' "What is . . . " questions. Yet it is not philosophic but rather "anthropologic," i.e. belonging to the sphere of gossip, of ordinary curiosity. Kriton could hear and see that Socrates was conversing with someone, presumably a stranger, but a big crowd standing around Socrates and the man with whom he conversed prevented him from seeing everyone and hearing anything distinctly. Since the conversation in which Socrates was engaged is called philosophic by Socrates himself, we may say that Kriton's access to philosophy was blocked. He could see the man sitting next but one to Socrates on Socrates' right, and he could recognize the boy sitting between Socrates and that man; the boy reminded him of his son Kritoboulos who is more or less of the same age but the boy Kleinias had grown much lately and is beautiful and good to look at, while Kritoboulos is rather defective. We assume then that Kriton's initial question is inspired not by aimless curiosity but by paternal concern for Kritoboulos who gave him cause to worry. This assumption is borne out by the end of the dialogue.[2]

The stranger whom Kriton has seen was Euthydemos; he had not seen Euthydemos' brother Dionysodoros who had been sitting on Socrates' left. Kriton does not know either of them at all whereas Socrates has known them for quite some time. Kriton believes that they are sophists; he wishes to hear where they come from and what their wisdom is; he does not ask how much they charge.[3] Socrates is not certain as to their place of origin but he knows that they have been tossed around quite a bit among Greeks. As for their wisdom, they are the greatest masters in doing battle, i.e. winning battles, that Socrates has ever seen. Not only can they fight in heavy armor and enable others to do the same; they are also proficient in doing battle before law courts and in teaching others to speak before law courts and to compose speeches to be delivered before law courts. Above all, they have made themselves masters in the battle of speeches simply: they can refute everything that is said at any time regardless of whether it is false or true. Socrates speaks of pay only when he speaks of the two brothers' ability to teach the art of fighting in heavy armor. The reason becomes clear at the end of his account: he declares to Kriton that he contemplates handing himself over to the two men for instruction in their art. They will of course demand pay for it

2. cf. *Crito* 45 b4–6.
3. cf. *Apol. Socr.* 20 b7–8.

and Socrates is poor. He must therefore persuade Kriton to participate in the venture. Kriton gives him an opportunity for doing this.

Kriton is not convinced that Socrates' thought is wise: Socrates seems to be too old for the venture. The situation here is the reverse of that in the *Crito* where Socrates uses his old age as a reason for declining the venture proposed by Kriton.[4] Socrates replies that the two brothers themselves were already of advanced years when they took up that wisdom which he desires and which he now calls eristics. He grants that he and his hoped for teachers might become ridiculous to his boyish fellow pupils and that this must be prevented by all means since the two brothers are strangers. They might even refuse to accept Socrates as a pupil on this ground. But he has already an experience of how this difficulty can be overcome. He is also taking lessons in harp-playing together with boys; he got rid of the embarrassment caused to him and to the teacher by persuading some elderly men to become his fellow pupils. Socrates will therefore attempt to persuade some other elderly men—the combination of harp-playing and eristics is not suitable to most people—to become his fellow pupils at the two brothers'. He begins his attempt with Kriton: why does Kriton not go to school with him? As a bait they will take Kriton's sons to the two brothers. Kriton does not reject the proposal. He leaves the decision to Socrates. He surely does not show the eagerness he showed in the *Crito*.[5] He wishes to hear first from Socrates what kind of wisdom they will learn if Socrates decides on handing himself and Kriton over to the two brothers. Socrates is only too willing to comply with Kriton's wish, i.e. to give a full and truthful, if not verbatim report, of yesterday's conversation.

According to some divine dispensation Socrates was sitting alone in the dressing room, in the place in which the conversation was to take place a little later, and was already about to leave. Then unexpectedly, when he had already got up, the customary sign, the *daimonion*, occurred to him, whereupon he naturally sat down again. According to its wont the *daimonion* had then warned Socrates against what he was about to do. In so doing however it rendered inevitable the conversation with Euthydemos and the others. The conversation was then imposed on Socrates by his *daimonion*. Yet, as the sequel shows, the conversation was the opposite of compulsory. The *daimonion* forbade him to leave the dressing room, as the Laws forbade him to leave the prison. By forbidding him to leave, the *daimonion* permitted, nay, sanctioned the conversation that followed. No other conversation presented by Plato has so high an origin. The high origin could be thought to explain why the *Euthydemus* is so extraordinarily rich in Socratic oaths.

Shortly after Socrates had sat down again, Euthydemos and Dionysodoros with a train of many pupils entered without taking notice of Socrates.

4. *Crito* 52 e2–4, 53 d7–e1.
5. 46 b1.

A short while later Kleinias entered; he was followed by many lovers among whom Ktesippos stood out.[6] Socrates confirms Kriton's remark that Kleinias had grown much; he would never himself have made that remark to Kriton. Kleinias did take notice of Socrates who was still sitting alone, and hurried to him at once. Kleinias had barely sat down at Socrates' side when Dionysodoros and Euthydemos after a short deliberation joined Kleinias and Socrates. Kleinias, who attracts so many lovers, attracts also Dionysodoros and Euthydemos with their crowd of pupils and is in turn attracted by Socrates. It is in this way that Kleinias' bipartite train, whose parts were joined only by chance, becomes in a manner the train of Socrates. But most obviously Kleinias is the center.

II. The first series of the two brothers' speeches (273 c1–278 e2)

Socrates introduced the two brothers to Kleinias as men wise not in the small things but in the great ones: they understand everything pertaining to war which is needful for the future good general; they can also enable a man to help himself in the law courts if someone wrongs him. One sees at once that the description of the two brothers' arts which Socrates had given to Kriton is already considerably colored by what he learned from them soon afterwards. We note only that when speaking to Kriton Socrates had not mentioned the two brothers' mastery of the art of generalship: Kriton is less likely to be an aspirant to that art than Kleinias, the grandson of Alkibiades; besides he had mentioned to Kriton that they teach their arts for pay and that they teach one how to compose speeches to be delivered by others before law courts: if Kleinias keeps his promise, he will not need a speech writer, to say nothing of becoming one. Socrates' introduction met with contempt and laughter on the part of the two brothers; they teach the things mentioned by Socrates no longer as serious but only as by-work; their serious claim now is that they believe to be able to transmit virtue better and more quickly than any other human being.

What they understand by virtue becomes clear from Socrates' report to Kriton about their newly acquired power: they can refute whatever is said, be it false or true and they can enable anyone within a short time to do the same. This power is necessarily identical with virtue if virtue is wisdom and if wisdom in the proper sense—knowledge of the most important things—is impossible. For in that case the highest superiority of a man to others in speeches is eristic superiority. The brothers' view of virtue entails that in particular the art of generalship is not virtue, at least not the highest virtue.

6. Socrates speaks of Ktesippos "being beautiful and good in regard to his nature" (273 a8). Kriton speaks of Kleinias being beautiful and good in regard to sight (271 b4–5). Kriton never speaks of "nature."

Socrates seemed to be deeply impressed by the claims of the brothers. He wondered where they found their new possession; the last time they visited Athens they were experts in fighting in armor only; Socrates is now silent on the expertise in forensic rhetoric. We assume that Socrates had heard of their new claims during their present visit but in introducing the brothers to Kleinias deliberately refrained from mentioning their highest claim in order to hear that claim stated in public by the brothers themselves. Be this as it may, he then declared that if they truly possess the knowledge, the science, which they claim to possess, he ought to treat them like gods; only gods, it seems, could conceivably give men virtue. But considering the magnitude of the claim they must forgive Socrates' unbelief. The brothers were willing and even eager to exhibit their wisdom: they were on the lookout for pupils. No fee will be demanded for the exhibition. Socrates in his turn vouched that all those present who lack that wisdom—he, Kleinias, Ktesippos and all the other lovers of Kleinias—wish to acquire it.

Ktesippos happened to sit rather far away from Kleinias; when Euthydemos talked to Socrates, he happened to obstruct Ktesippos' view of Kleinias; thereupon Ktesippos who wished both to see his beloved and to hear what would be said, jumped up and took his stand opposite Socrates and the three others sitting with him; the others—both Kleinias' lovers and the brothers' comrades—did the same. It was then in the first place Ktesippos' desire to prevent the obstruction of his view of his beloved that led to the blocking of Kriton's access to philosophy. (Kriton is not an erotic man). As a result of Ktessippos' action the lovers and the pupils together formed a semi-circular wall around those who are neither pupils nor lovers.

Socrates appealed to the brothers to exhibit their wisdom since everyone present—not only Kleinias' lovers but also the brothers' comrades—are eager to learn: the brothers have a very large public. His appeal was greeted with great eagerness by Ktesippos and all the others. Apparently the brothers did not respond immediately. They surely gave Socrates the opportunity to address them once more. He asked them now to gratify the others and for his sake to exhibit their wisdom. He thus indicated that his interest in the exhibition differs from the interest in it taken by the others. The peculiarity of his interest appears from the question that he addressed to the brothers: can they transmit virtue only to someone who is already convinced that he ought to learn from them or also to someone who is not yet convinced of it because he does not believe that virtue can be taught or that they are teachers of virtue? There are reasons for believing that Socrates was doubtful whether virtue can be taught. Certainly the brothers must be able to dispel that doubt; they must possess an art which proves the teachability of virtue. But, Socrates wondered, that art will not necessarily prove that the brothers are excellent teachers of virtue. Dionysodoros assured him that one and the same art dispels both doubts: the teachibility of virtue stands or falls by the two brothers' teaching virtue most excellently.

Dionysodoros' reply encouraged Socrates to ask him whether the brothers would not be best, at least of all human beings living now, at urging people on toward love of wisdom (philosophy) and an active concern with virtue. He obviously assumed that virtue and wisdom are identical or at least inseparable. But it is not clear why he is concerned with exhortation. Perhaps he thinks that exhortation to virtue does not presuppose that the question regarding virtue's teachability he decided either way: even if virtue is acquired by means other than teaching, men must be encouraged to strive for it. On Dionysodoros' replying again in the affirmative Socrates asked the brothers to exhort Kleinias to philosophizing and to caring for virtue: he and Kleinias' lovers desire that the boy, the scion of a blessed house, should become as good as possible, and they fear that he might be corrupted. The youngest and most beloved member of the group is naturally in the greatest danger of being corrupted and therefore the fittest object of the brothers' exhortation to virtue. Far from warning Kleinias against the mischief which the two sophists might do to him, as he warns Hippokrates against Protagoras, Socrates hands him over to the two sophists for education in virtue or in order to prevent his corruption. This difference is not sufficiently explained by the facts that in the case of Kleinias the sophists are present and Socrates is courteous; perhaps Hippokrates is more corruptible than Kleinias. We must also not forget that Socrates tells the story of Hippokrates to a nameless comrade, while he tells the story of Kleinias to his old and familiar friend Kriton.

Euthydemos was not disturbed by Socrates' concern for Kleinias: he was not interested in Kleinias as Socrates is, with a view to the boy's virtue or incorruption; the only thing which is necessary according to Euthydemos is that the boy be willing to answer. (Euthydemos laid down no other condition than that laid down by Socrates on other occasions.) Socrates reassured him on that score. Before he goes on with his report, he expresses to Kriton his apprehension that his report might not do justice to the amazing wisdom of the brothers: like a poet he must call to his assistance not only Memory but the Muses as well. Just as the dialogue would never have taken place without the intervention of the *daimonion*, its narration too is not possible without superhuman help. The narration is a kind of epic poem; it is in a way as poetic as the speech of the Laws in the *Crito*.

The questioning was begun by Euthydemos who asked Kleinias which human beings are learners, the wise or the unwise? Kleinias was embarrassed and turned to Socrates who encouraged him as well as he could. While Kleinias was still silent, Dionysodoros, whispering into Socrates' ear, predicted that whatever the boy would answer, he would be refuted. Kleinias answered that the wise are the learners and when he was cross-examined by Dionysodoros, he was forced to admit that the unwise are the learners. Both answers were refuted by the brothers. The refutation is possible because of the equivocity of "unwise" which may mean both "stupid" and "ignorant"; the human beings who learn are those who are intelligent and do not (yet) know. The character of the reasoning was not made clear by Socrates or anyone else present. Socrates merely reports that the refutations were greeted with noisy laughter by the brothers' pupils whom he now calls their lovers: from admiration to love there is only one more or less long step. On the other hand, Socrates and the other friends of Kleinias, while filled with admiration for the brothers, were depressed. We on our part can hardly fail to notice that each of the two *elenchoi* looks like a Socratic *elenchos*. We may also note that if the fallacy is disregarded, the two refutations prove either that neither the wise nor the unwise learn, i.e. that learning is impossible, hence presumably that wisdom proper is impossible, and hence that the only wisdom possible is eristics; or they prove that both the wise and the unwise learn, i.e. that wisdom is not only possible but even most easy to acquire: while being the best it is the cheapest, like water (304 b 1–4). The contradiction between the two implicit results leads us to the question as to whether wisdom is possible. The final result leads then beyond the brothers' wisdom.

There followed a second round similar to the first; Euthydemos addressed a question to Kleinias, Kleinias replied; Euthydemos refuted the reply and, on being cross-examined by Dionysodoros, Kleinias reasserted what he had answered first. Yet this time there was apparently no laughter and applause. Euthydemos was about to start a third round when he was stopped by Socrates. As he tells Kriton, he did not wish that Kleinias be still further discouraged. But we must not forget that Socrates was unable to stop the brothers earlier since their perfect teamwork had obviously taken him by surprise. In the speech by which he stopped them and which he addressed in the first place to Kleinias, he showed himself a changed man. Gone was the depression which he had felt before and very little remained of his admiration for the brothers. Someone might say that Socrates was never depressed and that he never admired the brothers. But why did he say "we were depressed" and "we admired Euthydemos"? Why did he then identify himself with Kleinias' lovers and did no longer do so now? Socrates' narrative must be presumed to be coherent on all levels. The fact that the second round was hardly more than a repetion of the first surely contributed to the change. The full explanation however is that Socrates had understood in the meantime what the brothers were about. He explained this to Kleinias in an uninterrupted speech of unusual length: the two strangers have been doing to Kleinias what the Korybantes do to someone about to be initated; it was a play, a prelude to the initiation into the sacred rites of sophistry; for one must learn first of all the right use of words, as Prodikos says; in accordance with this the strangers showed Kleinias his unawareness in this respect; but all this is play, enabling one at best to practise boyish pranks on people, for even if one has full knowledge of the right use of words, he will not know the things a bit better. Socrates comes close to saying to the brothers to their face that they have been practising boyish pranks on Kleinias. The strangers will of course from now on act seriously and fulfill their promise to exhibit their art of urging people on to virtue. Socrates turned next to the brothers themselves with the same reminder: they should show Kleinias in what manner one ought to be concerned with wisdom as well as with virtue. There are then various manners of urging on: although the brothers did not claim that their preceding speeches were serious and in particular that those speeches were protreptic, Dionysodoros at any rate had said that eristics and protreptics are one and the same art. What he meant can be inferred from what he and his brother did: if virtue is above all superiority in speeches or the ability to refute every speech, the mere exhibition of this ability will urge on every ambitious youth toward virtue. Socrates indicated his disagreement by declaring that he will give the brothers a doubtless poor specimen of what he understands by a protreptic speech. The protreptic speech will no longer belong to the prelude; it will be part and parcel of the sacred rites of "sophistry" in the wide sense of that term.

III. Socrates' protreptic speech I (278 e2–283 a4)

Now Socrates asked Kleinias to answer his questions. In contradistinction to the brothers he begins at the beginning. The brothers' tacit premise had been that their potential pupils are ambitious, that they are filled with the desire for what they regard as a great, if not the greatest, good. Socrates began his protreptic speech by inducing Kleinias to state that premise and to correct it.

He asked him first whether we human beings—all of us—do not wish to do or act well. He went on from there to propose a list of the good things which we need in order to do or act well. Since he did not suggest to Kleinias any alternative, and not only for this reason, one can say that his questions are leading; he surely wished to encourage Kleinias. Kleinias agreed with every point Socrates made. In this way it was established that first being rich, second being healthy, beautiful and the like, and finally noble birth, power and honor in one's city are good things. The order would be one of ascent for an ambitious human being. Socrates did not ask Kleinias whether he thought the list is complete but he raised a question which would permit the answer that the list is complete. While he had divulged his own view in the former cases, he did not do so now. He asked the boy whether moderation, justice and courage are good things or not, adding that their being good could be disputed. It could be disputed on the ground that the only good things are those mentioned earlier and that the virtues are not necessarily needed for obtaining them. Nevertheless Kleinias replied that the three virtues are good. Only after Socrates had asked him whether wisdom belongs to the good things and had received an affirmative reply did he ask him whether in his view the list is complete; he thought that it is. Wisdom apparently belongs to another class of virtues than moderation, justice and courage. But then Socrates suddenly remembered the greatest of all goods, good fortune, which is universally and therefore of course also by Kleinias understood to be the greatest good. Yet with equal suddenness Socrates changed his mind by remembering that wisdom is good fortune, as even a child would know. But the child Kleinias did not know; he was astonished by Socrates' contention. Socrates made him agree with him by showing him that in all cases wisdom makes human beings fortunate. The cases which he mentioned are flute playing, letters, seafaring, generalship and medicine. In speaking of the central case he indicated most clearly that the wisdom in question does not always guarantee good luck. Kleinias who was not supposed to notice this, did not notice it. We have then reached the result that wisdom is, humanly speaking, omnipotent. In the words of Socrates, he and Kleinias eventually agreed together, he did not know how, that in the main a man who possesses wisdom does not in any way need good fortune in addition. But if this is so, what becomes of the goods of fortune in the wide sense, like wealth, health and political power which occupied so conspicuous a place in Socrates' list and which seemed to be indispensable for doing or acting well or for happiness? Socrates brought it about that Kleinias agreed to these propositions: we are happy on account of those goods only if they benefit us, and they benefit us only if we do not merely own them but use them; to convince Kleinias he used the examples of food and drink and then of a craftsman's (a carpenter's) tools and materials. (He implied that craftsmen using their tools and materials might act well but would not be happy.) Here the question arises whether we can use those goods if we do not own them and therefore whether a wise man who is poor or even a slave can be happy; in other words, the question arises whether good fortune is guaranteed by wisdom; needless to say, the question was not explicitly raised. Instead Socrates drew Kleinias' attention to the fact that the mere use of good things will not suffice for making a man happy; the use must be right use; while wrong use is bad, non-use is neither good nor bad; right use is brought about by knowledge. Knowledge then brings about the right use of the good things figuring in the beginning of the previous list. No possession whatever is of any benefit if its use is not guided by prudence, wisdom, intelligence; a man possessing little but using it intelligently is more benefitted than a man possessing much but using it without intelligence; hence a man without intelligence is better off if he is deprived of the good things previously listed than if he possesses them, for instance, if he is poor rather than rich, weak rather than strong, obscure rather than honored.[7] When Socrates asked next who would do less, a courageous and moderate man or a coward, and therewith which of the two is better off without intelligence, Kleinias replied "the coward", i.e., the coward without intelligence is better off than the courageous man without intelligence; Socrates gave Kleinias no opportunity to decide whether the unintelligent man is better off if he is moderate or if he is immoderate. He gave him even less opportunity to decide whether the unintelligent man is better off if he is just or if he is unjust; judging by the analogy of the other cases the answer would have to be that he is better off if he is unjust. But this thought verges on the absurd. It is much better to say that justice seems to be the only good, the only virtue that is beneficent (on the whole) even if not guided by intelligence, perhaps because the laws which the just man obeys supply the lack of intelligence in the man himself.[8] Accordingly Socrates' abstraction from justice here would be tantamount to an abstraction from law; he surely is silent about the laws in the *Euthydemus* as distinguished from the *Crito*. Be this as it may, the ruthless questioning of what Aristotle would have called the moral virtues,[9] served the purpose of bringing out the unique significance of wisdom: wisdom—and of course not honor or glory—is not only the greatest good; it is the sole good; only through the presence of wisdom and the guidance by it are the other goods good. This purpose is most appropriate in a speech meant to exhort to the practice of wisdom.

Socrates summarized the result of his preceeding conversation with Kleinias and drew the conclusion to which Kleinias assented that every man must strive in every way to become as wise as possible. In particular he must beseech his lovers, nay, every human being to let him partake of wisdom, gladly doing every menial service which is not base in return. Kleinias wholeheartedly agreed. Only one difficulty remained: they had not investigated whether wisdom is teachable, let alone reached agreement on this point. Speaking in a more lively manner than ever before, Kleinias proclaimed his opinion that wisdom is teachable. This pleased Socrates since it saved him a long inquiry on this subject; he did not say that he and Kleinias have reached agreement on it. Socrates drew the final conclusion that since our happiness depends altogether on our wisdom and if virtue can be acquired by learning, learning, striving for wisdom, philosophizing is the one thing needful.[10]

7. Compare what Socrates explains to Kriton's son Kritoboulos in the first chapter of the *Oeconomicus*.

8. That justice in contradistinction to courage and moderation cannot be misused is an important ingredient of the first paragraph of the text of Kant's *Foundations of the Metaphysics of Morals*.—Cf. *Republic* 491 b7–10 and *Meno* 88 a6–e4.

9. *Republic* 619 c7–d1 (and context).

10. Kleinias' threefold use of "O Socrates" (280 d4, 282 c4, d3) is a very obvious example of that use of vocatives that is prompted by self-confidence.

The premise of the two brothers' speech was that wisdom proper is impossible and therefore that its place is properly taken by eristics. Socrates seemed to be uncertain whether wisdom is teachable; it is not clear whether that doubt affects the possibility of wisdom. Yet the reasoning addressed to Kleinias seems to imply that in order to be wise one must know all the arts, and this does not seem to be possible for any one man; thus wisdom would be impossible. Socrates and the brothers agree as to virtue proper being different from "moral virtue". But as is indicated by Socrates' reference to the honorable services which the beloved boy may do in order to acquire wisdom, Socrates admits that there is some awareness of the honorable which antedates the acquisition of wisdom. His doubt of the teachability of wisdom may be connected with what he intimated regarding the limited power of wisdom in regard to luck or chance; perhaps one must be particularly "wellborn" in order to learn wisdom.

Socrates was pleased with his success in urging Kleinias on toward philosophy. He apologized again to the brothers for the inadequacy of his protreptic speech and asked them to repeat as craftsmen what he had done as a layman or else to continue his exhibition by discussing with Kleinias whether he must acquire every branch of knowledge or whether one who wishes to be happy and a good man needs to acquire a single branch of knowledge only and what this branch is. He also reminded them again of how important it is to him and the others that Kleinias should become wise and good.

This was the turning point in the dialogue. Socrates brings this out by addressing Kriton and stating to him that he was watching with the greatest attention what would happen next and observing in what manner the brothers would lay hold on the speech and from where they would start their exhorting Kleinias toward wisdom and virtue.

IV. The central series of the brothers' speeches (283 a5–288 d4)

It could be thought to be a good omen that it was Dionysodoros, the brother remotest in years from boyhood, who started the conversation. Socrates' and the others' expectations to hear something extraordinary were not disappointed: the speech was extraordinary as an exhortation toward virtue. Dionysodoros no longer addressed Kleinias nor did he pay any regard to what Socrates had said. He asked Socrates and Kleinias' lovers whether they are serious in wishing Kleinias to become wise. Thinking that it was the brothers' disbelief in their seriousness that had induced them to proceed so playfully before and fearing a repetition, Socrates assured them emphatically of their seriousness. This is all that Dionysodoros needed for his refutative speech: desiring that Kleinias become wise means desiring that he cease to be the one he is now—that he cease to be—that he perish; fine friends and lovers you are! Whatever else might have to be said about this speech, as an exhortation to virtue it is indeed extraordinary. Dionysodoros' thesis could be understood as a most shameless admission of the worst crime imputed to sophists: education in wisdom is corruption of the young (see 285 b1). Or did Dionysodoros think that his speech was protreptic since it refuted Socrates and Kleinias' lovers and thus enabled Kleinias to recognize the two brothers as the true teachers of wisdom? Was this the reason why he and his brother no longer addressed Kleinias himself?

We might have expected that Socrates would rebuke Dionysodoros for continuing with his boyish pranks. He failed to do so. This fact is of considerable importance for the understanding of the dialogue as a whole. The speeches of the brothers are obviously ridiculous and yet Socrates says to Kriton that he contemplates becoming their pupil and he even tries to induce Kriton to join him. Of the first series of speeches Socrates said in so many words that he could not take them seriously. His final judgment as stated to Kriton near the beginning of the dialogue makes sense only if at one point or another the conversation with the brothers had ceased to be playful and taken on a serious turn. We must watch to see how this change came about.

Did Socrates consider that philosophizing is learning to die? The obvious reason for his failure to rebuke Dionysodoros for his levity is that before he could say anything, Ktesippos vented his anger and indignation: Dionysodoros lied by imputing to him such an unholy wish. Euthydemos was not intimidated by Ktesippos' outburst; he asked him whether in his opinion it is possible to say a falsehood or to lie. Ktesippos replied of course in the affirmative. Euthydemos refuted him by starting from the fact that one can speak about, or say, only what is and not what is not; he led up to the explicit result that Dionysodoros must have said the truth when he drew the conclusion that angered Ktesippos. (If Euthydemos' reasoning were valid, all men would always think or say the truth whenever they think or speak; all men would be wise and there would be no need for wishing that Kleinias should become wise.) Ktesippos was not disconcerted by the refutation. He granted that Dionysodoros said somehow the things that are but not as they are. He tacitly presupposed that one can say the truth. It was this presupposition that was next questioned by Dionysodoros. (Dionysodoros' argument would lead to the conclusion that all men always think or say the untruth, i.e. that wisdom is impossible on the ground opposite to the one advanced by Euthydemos.) Ktesippos contended that gentlemen as well as other men speak the truth. Euthydemos rejoined: if the gentlemen say the truth, they speak ill of evil things and of evil human beings; do they also speak bigly of big men and hotly of hot men? Whereupon Ktesippos replied: they speak frigidly of the frigid and say of them that they frigidly converse. The brothers had no expedient left but for Dionysodoros to complain about abuse;

Ktesippos rejected that complaint as unfounded since Dionysodoros had so rudely said that Ktesippos wished the perdition of those whom he cherishes most. This round ended then clearly with a defeat of the brothers: Ktesippos' manliness got the better of their wisdom. It was to be expected that the sophists would arouse sooner or later the susceptibilities of a hot-tempered young gentleman.

At this juncture Socrates was forced to intervene in order to prevent a conflagration. In order to appease Ktesippos, he was forced to speak to him playfully: far from being able to blame the brothers for what could seem to be their continuing playfulness, the extreme seriousness of the situation that had arisen between Ktesippos and Dionysodoros forced him to become playful himself. He alluded to the fact that the issue was still merely verbal: the strangers insist on calling corruption what in ordinary parlance is called education to virtue and wisdom; if they know how to destroy human beings so as to make them good and sensible out of bad and senseless, let them destroy Kleinias and make him sensible and let them do the same to all of us; but if the young are afraid, let the strangers make their dangerous experiment on old Socrates. Therewith Socrates handed himself over to Dionysodoros to do to him whatever he pleased: Socrates' handing himself over to the sophists of which he speaks to Kriton as of being contemplated by him only, has already taken place to some extent the day before, and it took place then with a view to appeasing Ktesippos' wrath against the sophists.

Ktesippos, that generous youth, could not stay behind old Socrates and offered himself to the strangers for anything they might do to him provided their doings would end in him becoming altogether virtuous. He denied being angry at Dionysodoros: he only contradicted him. As if he had learned something from Prodikos, he pointed out that contradicting and abusing are two different things. The somewhat dangerous incident thus ended in perfect reconciliation between Ktesippos and Dionysodoros. We must not overlook the fact that Socrates established concord exclusively by influencing Ktesippos: the sophists were not angry. By speaking of contradicting, by taking it for granted that contradicting is possible, Ktesippos offered a flank to Dionysodoros. The fact that Dionysodoros and Ktesippos contradicted one another regarding contradicting was somehow noticed by Ktesippos. But Dionysodoros reduced him to silence. He did this by making use of the same point formerly used for showing the impossibility of lying; but the present case lacked the potential for anger or indignation which the former had.

Socrates was astonished by Dionysodoros' argument. As he told Dionysodoros, he was always astonished at that particular argument for he had heard it from many people and many times—Protagoras used it and even people before him. It astonished him because it is incompatible with the claim of the men who use it. If it is impossible to lie, to say or think a falsehood, all men are wise, and there is no need for teachers like the brothers. While Socrates expounded this argument, Euthydemos took the place of his brother. So it happened that it was Euthydemos, the wisest or cleverest of the brothers, whom Socrates decisively refuted. The decisive character of this event could easily remain unnoticed. Socrates did not put the slightest emphasis on his victory and as for Euthydemos having been reduced to silence we can only infer it from the fact that Dionysodoros took the word again immediately afterwards. He blamed Socrates for reminding the brothers of something which they had said earlier: their claim that they can refute what is said at any one time (272 b1) is to be taken quite literally. Eristics, mental wrestling, is a game which as such is constituted by certain arbitrary but inviolable rules. As appears from the sequel, another rule of this kind which Socrates unwittingly transgressed is that he who is questioned must not reply with questions of his own. Socrates bowed to this rule on the explicit ground that a man who is altogether wise regarding speeches determines reasonably whether to answer questions or not. Despite his compliance Socrates succeeded in refuting Dionysodoros and in fact the two brothers on fundamentally the same ground as before. This time Socrates put the proper emphasis on his victory. But this had the embarrassing consequence that Ktesippos became very abusive so that Socrates had to calm him again. The net result was therefore again that Socrates' refutation of the brothers could easily remain unnoticed.

Socrates calmed Ktesippos by a consideration that resembles the one by which he had encouraged Kleinias earlier. He spoke again of the brothers not being serious but on the other hand he studiously avoided the word "play" and derivatives from it. He spoke to Ktesippos of the brothers' witchcraft. Since the brothers imitated the Egyptian sophist Proteus, Ktesippos and Socrates ought to imitate Menelaos who forced Proteus to reveal his secret. Needless to say, Socrates will not use force. He proposed that he continue his protreptic speech: perhaps the brothers will from compassion with his serious endeavor be serious themselves.

V. Socrates' protreptic speech II (288 d5–290 e1)

Socrates asked Kleinias to remind him of where they left off but, without waiting for Kleinias' doing so, did the reminding himself: he had no faith in Kleinias' memory. Or did he have too great faith in it? They had finally agreed, he said, that one must philosophize. Strictly speaking they had not agreed on this since it followed from the premise, regarding which Socrates had suspended judgment, that wisdom is teachable. Be this as it may, philosophy is the acquisition of knowledge: of which knowledge? Not remembering their earlier discussion Kleinias regarded it as possible that kinds of knowledge which do not entail the good use of the knowledge concerned could be the desired knowledge. They agreed thereafter that they are in need of a kind of knowledge in which both the making (production) of something and the knowledge of how to use that something coincide. That knowledge as to how to make a thing which is not accompanied by knowledge of how to use it is insufficient for our happiness had become clear in the earlier exchange between Socrates and Kleinias; that knowledge of how to use a thing which is not accompanied by knowledge of how to make it or procure it is insufficient for our happiness was implicit in the earlier exchange; one could say that Socrates corrected in his second protreptic speech the defect of the first—the defect which consists in the abstraction from the power of chance. Using the criterion thus established they examined at Socrates' suggestion first the art of making speeches and then the art of generalship, i.e., the two arts of the brothers that are lower than eristics. Kleinias rejected the art of speech making on the ground that those who make (i.e. write) speeches to be delivered before courts of law and the like do not know how to use them: even regarding speeches the art of making them and the art of using them are different. What is at least as important as this judgement is the amazing, the wholly new self-confidence with which it was made by young Kleinias. Socrates agreed with Kleinias' main point that the art of speech making does not make men happy but he claimed that he had had great expectations from it: it is a marvelous art, not far inferior to the art of the enchanters; it bewitches crowds as the enchanters bewitch snakes, tarantulas and the like. All the more impressive is Kleinias' firm verdict. (We must not forget however that "the art of making speeches" is an ambiguous expression: the art of making speeches that Socrates possesses is inseparable from the art of using them.) Socrates turned then to generalship as an art most likely to make its possessor happy. This proposal was again firmly rejected by Kleinias: generalship is an art of hunting but no art of hunting is an art of using; for instance, geometers, astronomers, and calculators do not make the figures which they use but find or discover them, and since they do not know how to use them, they hand their findings over to the dialecticians for use. For this remark Kleinias was praised by Socrates very highly—as highly as never before or after. Socrates did not say a word to the effect that if Kleinias' statement were unqualifiedly true, dialectics, being neither a hunting nor a productive art but only an art of using, could not possibly be the desired science. The ironical character of his high praise did therefore not become quite obvious. Kleinias, obviously encouraged, went on to say that the generals hand over their conquests to the political men. But since he said nothing to the effect that the political men produce or hunt what they know how to use, he seems to imply without being aware of it that the political (or kingly) art too is not the desired science either. Within the context of the discussion the defect of dialectics and of politics (to say nothing of speech writing) cannot but redound to the benefit of eristics. And that defect was due to the use of a criterion established by Socrates.

Kriton suddenly interrupts Socrates' narrative. The reason for this is not that he is greatly concerned about the desired science but that he is concerned about his sons; Socrates' glowing report about Kleinias has reminded him of his domestic difficulty. But without Socrates' assistance or serious resistance he finds comfort in his unbelief; he is certain that Socrates' report about Kleinias' answers is a complete falsehood. He is then by no means incapable of becoming aware of Socrates' irony in any point. Socrates admits that Kleinias or even Ktesippos may not have given the clever answers that he ascribed to Kleinias but he insists on not having given them himself; he claims to have heard them perhaps from some higher being. Kriton's reaction to this claim is of the same force as if he had said in the *Crito* that not the laws but Socrates had made that impressive speech. Socrates provoked Kriton's intervention by his unfounded praise of Kleinias in order to put a stop to Kriton's hesitation to send his sons to some teachers of wisdom. As a matter of fact Kriton now takes it for granted that youths not as advanced as Socrates' fictitious Kleinias might be benefited by becoming Euthydemos' pupils.

Kriton's interest is not exhausted by his interest in Kleinias; he is also interested in the subject matter of the conversation; he is interested to know the sequel of Socrates' protreptic conversation with Kleinias and especially whether they found the art they were looking for. Limiting himself to the most important, Socrates tells him what happened to them when they examined the kingly art which is the same as the political art; the term "kingly art" is perhaps preferred because it corresponds to the splendor, the claim of the art in question. The kingly art seemed to them the art which by ruling all other arts makes all things useful. Yet they were hard put to it to tell what the work of the kingly art is. At this point Kriton has become a participant in the conversation, as it were, at the side of Kleinias. (How would Kriton have reacted to Socrates' protreptic questions if he had been in the place of Kleinias?) While he knows quite well what the work of his art—the art of farming—is, he is as unable as Kleinias to tell what the work of the kingly art is or what good it transmits. But Socrates and Kleinias had agreed that there is no other good but some knowledge. This deprives such good things as freedom of the claim to be the work of the political art; in the light of the premises agreed upon by Socrates and Kleinias, freedom as such is neither good nor bad. (Hence it is better to speak of the kingly art.) It likewise follows that the kingly art must make the human beings wise, for only wisdom makes men happy. The kingly art is then an art which both "makes" (produces) something and guarantees the good use of that something. Kriton regards it as necessary to make clear that these things were agreed upon by Socrates and Kleinias: we do not know where Kriton stands. At any rate there is agreement between Socrates and Kriton as to the kingly art not transmitting all arts, for the products of all arts other than the kingly art are neither good nor bad. But in what will the kingly art make the human beings wise and good? Kriton knows that Socrates and Kleinias were in a great predicament: he is not affected by it and he has no suggestion to make as to how that predicament could be overcome. Socrates tells him that in his despair he called on the two brothers for help, urging them to be serious. Kriton is curious to hear whether Euthydemos helped Socrates and Kleinias: he has noticed the superiority of Euthydemos to Dionysodoros; he has become mildly interested in Euthydemos' wisdom.

Socrates' effort to determine the science which makes human beings happy has ended in complete failure. He has confirmed by deed the view of some of his critics that he was most excellent in exhorting men to virtue but not able to guide men to it:[11] he proved to be excellent in exhorting Kleinias to strive for that wisdom which makes humans happy but was unable to tell what that wisdom is. Someone might say that the predicament arises solely from the almost complete disregard of dialectics: dialectics is obviously the desired art or science. But then one must explain why Socrates abstracted from dialectics. Looking at the result of his action, one will be inclined to say that the abstraction from dialectics redounds in the circumstances of the dialogue to the benefit of eristics. But why is eristics to be benefited?

VI. The final series of the brothers' speeches (293 a8–304 b5)

Euthydemos came to Socrates' assistance by putting Socrates' question on the broadest possible basis. Instead of continuing Socrates' questioning on the kingly art, he asked him whether there is anything which he does not know. In other words, he proved that Socrates possesses that science regarding which he and Kleinias were in a predicament for such a long time by proving that Socrates is omniscient. He proceeded as follows. Socrates admittedly knows some things, however trivial; he is therefore a knowing man; being a knowing man he cannot be a non-knowing man at the same time; hence he must know everything. Socrates raised no objection to this monstrous argument but he showed by deed that he had learned Euthydemos' art: he raised no objection because he had learned Euthydemos' art. Instead he tried to turn the tables on the brothers by compelling them to admit that they, nay, all human beings too know

11. Xenophon, *Memorabilia* I 4. 1 (Plato, *Clitopho* 410 b4 ff.).

everything. Dionysodoros made this admission without any ado. If we still remember the kingly art, we might be inclined to say that on the basis of Dionysodoros' admission the kingly art is compatible with democracy. Socrates made sure that the brothers were serious in raising the claim to omniscience; as a consequence Dionysodoros here used his only oath. When Ktesippos became aware of the exorbitant character of Dionysodoros' claim, he demanded a massive proof: does each of the brothers know how many teeth the other has? The brothers refused to comply with this demand since they believed that he was poking fun at them: they did not appeal to the rules of eristics since they were eager to answer any questions regarding the many skills however lowly they possessed. Socrates intervened by appealing from Dionysodoros to Euthydemos. Euthydemos succeeded in keeping Socrates properly obedient to the rules of eristics despite his knowing that Euthydemos wished to entrap him in merely verbal snares, i.e. despite his realizing the unserious character of the proceedings, for he was already resolved on becoming the pupil of Euthydemos, of that master in the dialectical art: the true dialectics was completely forgotten.

Socrates asked Euthydemos to begin his questioning again from the start. Thereupon Euthydemos asked him whether he knows what he knows by means of something. Socrates replied: yes, by means of the soul. This reply was not in conformity with the rules of eristics, for he had not been asked by means of what he knows. When Euthydemos pointed this out to him, Socrates became properly apologetic which did not prevent him from making a similar mistake immediately afterward. Socrates presents himself to Kriton as acting the part of a rather slow pupil—of a Strepsiades as it were. Accordingly, he was led to admit that he always knew all things: when he was a child, when he was born, when he was conceived, before heaven and earth had come into being. Socrates was being taught a caricature of the doctrine of recollection; it is a caricature of that doctrine especially since it is silent on the soul as well as on learning. Euthydemos concluded his argument by asserting that Socrates will also know everything in the future, if this is Euthydemos' pleasure. This is perfectly reasonable given his premises: only what he says (or thinks) is or will be, but since genuine wisdom is not possible, its place is taken by eristics so that only what is upheld by the master of that art is or will be.

Socrates next tried to entrap Euthydemos by asking him how he, Socrates, knows that the good men are unjust: if Euthydemos (we should remember the previous difficulty regarding justice) grants that Socrates knows it, he says something revolting; if he denies that Socrates knows it, he denies Socrates' omniscience which he had been at such great pains to establish. Dionysodoros walked into the trap by preferring the alternative that is not shocking; he was openly rebuked for this by his brother, so much so that he blushed. When Socrates thereupon asked Euthydemos whether his omniscient brother had not made a mistake, Dionysodoros quickly asked whether he, Dionysodoros, is Euthydemos' brother and thus forced him to answer this question and to forgo Euthydemos' answer to his own question. The brothers finally forced him to admit that he is fatherless. This gave Ktesippos an occasion to intervene. He tried to turn the tables by bringing up the question of the brothers' father. Yet Euthydemos gladly admitted that his father, being father, was a father of all men and all beasts while he himself as well as Ktesippos were the brothers of puppies and the like. Dionysodoros on his turn, proved to Ktesippos that by beating his dog who is a father and is his, he beats his father. (Socrates escaped the charge of father-beating only because he did not own a dog.) A somewhat insulting reply of Ktesippos led not to an intervention on the part of Socrates, but to Euthydemos telling Ktesippos that no human being needs many good things: the theme "father-beating" is followed by the theme "continence." Ktesippos refuted Euthydemos' first reasonable contention with the help of mythological examples. He defended the case for "having more" success-fully also against Dionysodoros. The themes "father-beating" and "conti-nence" remind us of the *Clouds* where Socrates is presented as a teacher of father-beating and as extremely continent. One is tempted to say that Socrates presents Euthydemos as a caricature of the Aristophanean Soc-rates. Socrates could not possibly have been the addressee of an argument in favor of continence, while Ktesippos was fitted for this role by his nature. Ktesippos was also successful in his ensuing argument with the brothers, so much so, that Kleinias was greatly pleased and laughed. As Socrates tells Kriton, he suspects that Ktesippos owed his success in the last argument to his having overheard the brothers discussing it among themselves, "for no other human being now living possesses such wisdom."

When Socrates asked Kleinias why he laughed about such serious and beautiful things, Dionysodoros asked Socrates whether he had ever seen a beautiful thing. He thus introduced the great theme of the relation of the beautiful things to beauty itself; according to Socrates things are beautiful by the fact that some beauty is present with each of them. Dionysodoros refuted this view by referring to the fact that Socrates does not become Dionysodoros by Dionysodoros' being present with him and repeated his question in this more incisive manner: how can the different be different by the presence of the different with the different? While pretending to be surprised by Dionysodoros' predicament which Dionysodoros himself traced to the non-being of the beautiful itself, Socrates was already trying to imitate the wisdom of the brothers since he longed for it. He imitated that wisdom to his satisfaction and thus and only thus defended "the doctrine of ideas" but admitted of course that otherwise the brothers are excellent craftsmen of the dialectical art which as every art finishes off its peculiar work. This gave Dionysodoros an occasion to perform another of his verbal somersaults which Socrates praises as the peak of wisdom: "will this wisdom ever become my own?" This question or exclamation induced Dionyso-doros to ask Socrates what he understands by his own. Somewhat rashly Socrates agreed that only those living beings are his own which he may sell, give away, or sacrifice to any of the gods. But what then is the status of Socrates' ancestral gods? Obviously Socrates may give them away, sell them, or sacrifice them to any of the gods he pleases. Socrates was knocked out and left speechless. Euthydemos had given him the knock out blow. The brothers acted like caricatures of Socrates' accusers: they did not seriously accuse him. Ktesippos who had tried to come to Socrates' help fell an easy victim to another of Dionysodoros' clowneries; he gave up the struggle with the words "the two men are unbeatable."

The whole show had ended with the complete victory of the brothers. This was the view not merely of Euthydemos' lovers but of the group around Kleinias and, above all, of Socrates as well: Socrates had never seen so wise human beings. Overwhelmed by their wisdom he turned to praising them. He praised them in the first place for their indifference to the many as well as to the great men who are thought to be something; only the few who resemble them like the brothers' speeches; all other men would be more ashamed to refute others with the help of speeches of this kind than to be refuted by them. This sense of shame has nothing to do with the awareness of unfair advantage, as appears from the second ground on which Socrates praises the brothers: their speeches are popular or populist and gentle; they reduce indeed everyone to silence by denying the obvious but they thus reduce themselves too to silence, so that their speeches cannot be resented. Finally, they have brought their art to such a perfection that anyone can learn it within a very short time. This fact, it is true, carries with it the inconvenience that a single public exhibition, which is meant to allure paying pupils, suffices for initiating people to their art; Socrates advised them therefore to abstain from public exhibitions. He concluded by asking the brothers to accept him and Kleinias as pupils.

Turning to Kriton, he encourages him to join him (and Kleinias) in going to school at the brothers': the only condition laid down by them is a payment of a fee, not natural gifts nor youth; and what is especially important for Kriton, the brothers' instruction does not in any way interfere with one's money-making.

VII. The epilogue: the final conversation between Socrates and Kriton (304 b6–307 c4)

Kriton politely declines Socrates' suggestion: he belongs to those who would rather be refuted by Euthydemian speeches than refute other men with their help. Aware of the difference of rank between himself and Socrates, he regards it as improper or ridiculous to rebuke him for his strange likes but he cannot abstain from telling him what he was told by somebody else. Quite by accident he met a man who had heard the exchange of speeches—a man with a high opinion of his wisdom and who is clever in regard to forensic speeches. That man had nothing but contempt for the brothers. Kriton defended the brothers' doings against him with the words "but philosophy is something graceful", i.e. he took it for granted that the brothers' speeches are philosophic. His nameless informer also disapproved of Socrates' absurd conduct toward the brothers; Kriton would have been ashamed of him. Kriton repeats his disagreement with the unqualified disapproval of the brothers' speeches but he feels that Socrates is to be blamed for publicly disputing with them.

Socrates is unable to reply properly to this detractor of philosophy before he knows to what kind of man he belongs. He learns from Kriton that he composes speeches to be delivered by orators proper. Men of this kind belong according to Prodikos and according to Socrates to the borderland between the philosophers and the politicians and regard themselves as superior to either; in order to be recognized universally as such, they denigrate the philosophers: the greatest threats to their renown are the masters of Euthydemian speeches. Socrates agrees with Kriton in describing Euthydemos' art as philosophy. The men in question regard themselves as supremely wise because they partake in the proper measure partly in philosophy and partly in political matters. Socrates' judgment on them is based on this principle: everything that is between two things and participates in both is inferior to the better and superior to the worse, if one of the two things is good and the other bad; if the two things are good and directed toward different ends the thing participating in both is inferior to both in usefulness for the ends in question; if the two things are bad and directed toward different ends, the thing participating in both is superior to both. Hence if both philosophy and political action are good but directed toward different ends, as the borderland people cannot help admitting, they are inferior to both the philosophers and the politicians. Socrates presupposes here that philosophy and the political art have different ends and hence are different arts; he tacitly repeats the radical distinction between dialectics and the kingly art. He asks that one not be angry with the detractors of philosophy; after all, they take hold of something reasonable: they are aware of the radical difference between philosophy and politics.

Socrates has successfully vindicated Euthydemos and what he stands for. Kriton neither denies nor admits this. Instead he turns to the subject of his greatest and constant predicament: his two sons, and especially his oldest son Kritoboulos. Whenever he meets Socrates, he becomes aware of the paramount importance of education but he cannot find an educator worthy

of the name. As a consequence, he does not know how to urge on Kritoboulos toward philosophy: he does not dream of asking Socrates to apply his
protreptic skill to Kritoboulos nor does Socrates offer it. One could say that
Socrates had candidly exhibited the limitation of his protreptic art; yet he
had at least tried to apply it to Kleinias. A more plausible reason is that
Kritoboulos' nature is less fit for the purpose than Kleinias' or, in other
words, Socrates' *daimonion* holds him back in the case of Kritoboulos as
distinguished from that of Kleinias.

Socrates reminds Kriton of a fact to be observed in regard to every
pursuit, the fact that the good practitioners are rare; just as this is no reason
for rejecting money-making or rhetoric, it is no reason for rejecting philosophy. One must carefully examine philosophy itself. If it seems to be a bad
thing, Kriton must keep everyone, not only his sons, away from it; but in the
opposite case the opposite course is to be taken.

We are still too much inclined to see the conflict between Socrates and
"the sophists" in the light of the conflict between the thinkers of the
Restoration and the thinkers who prepared the French Revolution or took
its side. In the *Euthydemus* Socrates takes the side of the two brothers
against Ktesippos and Kriton. Socrates was not the mortal enemy of the
sophists nor were the sophists the mortal enemies of Socrates. According to
Socrates, the greatest enemy of philosophy, the greatest sophist, is the
political multitude (*Republic* 492a5–e6), i.e. the enactor of the Athenian
laws.

4

Preliminary Observations on the Gods in Thucydides' Work

These observations "repeat," i.e., modify, some observations which I have made in the Thucydides-chapter of *The City and Man*. No necessary purpose would be served by stressing the differences between the first and the second statements.

For Thucydides the war between the Peloponnesians and the Athenians was, as he expected from the beginning, the most noteworthy motion—so to speak, the greatest motion of all times which affected all human beings. He gives a two-fold proof of his contention. The first and by far the most extensive (I.1–19) proves it by laying bare the weakness of the ancients and therewith the strength, the surpassing strength, of the men, especially the Greeks, of the present. Apart from a seemingly casual reference to the Delian Apollon (13.6), the first proof is silent regarding gods; this silence seems to be connected with the fact that the most famous speakers about antiquity are the poets, and the poets are in the habit of adorning their subjects by magnifying them (10.3): tracing happenings to the gods means precisely adorning the happenings by magnifying them. The second proof concentrates on the greatness of the sufferings brought on by the Peloponnesian War as contrasted especially with the sufferings due to the Persian War (23.1–3). Thucydides tacitly distinguishes the sufferings which human beings inflicted upon one another and those which were inflicted upon them by earthquakes, eclipses of the sun, drought, famine, and last but not least the plague. Following the guidance supplied by Thucydides' Perikles addressing the Athenians, we may call the second kind of happening or suffering "daimonic" (II.64.2), leaving it open whether the word

Reprinted from *Interpretation: A Journal of Political Philosophy* 4, no. 1 (1974).

always signifies, within the work, happenings of non-human or super-human origin (such as omens) or whether it is best understood as synonymous with "natural."

Let us then turn to Perikles' speeches or, more generally, let us consider a possible difference between Thucydides' narrative of the deeds on the one hand and the speeches of his characters concerning our subject on the other. In Book One he speaks in his narrative of the god in Delphi, of oracles, temples, and so on without making it clear whether he accepts or reveres them in the same manner as so to speak everyone else did. On the other hand, the first pair of speeches—those of the Korkyraians and the Korinthians in Athens (I.32–43)—contain no reference whatever to gods or to sacred things. (The same is true of the brief exchange between the Korinthian embassy and the Athenians in 53.2–9.) The situation is somewhat more complex and revealing in the four speeches delivered in Sparta by the Korinthians, the Spartan king Archidamos, and the ephor Sthenolaidas (68–86). The Korinthians, the accusers par excellence of the Athenians, appeal more emphatically to the gods who watch over the performance of oaths than the other speakers. The only speaker here who is completely silent on the gods is Archidamos, the only speaker here whom Thucydides singles out here by an explicit, if somewhat qualified, praise. In the next assembly of the Peloponnesians which again takes place in Sparta, there occurs only a single speech; in that speech the Korinthians refer to the oracle of the god (123.1). There follows a narrative of the final exchanges which deal chiefly with mutual recriminations regarding pollutions contracted by the two sides concerning gods; Thucydides abstains from judging on the merits of the two cases; he merely notes that the Spartans held their polluting action to be responsible for the great earthquake that happened in Sparta (128.1). Thucydides' account of the final fate of the Spartan and of the Athenian leaders in the Persian War—King Pausanias and Themistokles—contains literal quotations from the letters by the two men to the king of Persia, i.e., something approaching speeches by Thucydidean characters; those quotations contain no references to gods. On the other hand, the god in Delphi had a weighty word to say about the fitting burial of the Spartan king, traitor though he was (134.4).

We are now prepared for considering the next speeches, the Periklean speeches. There are altogether three such speeches (I.140–44, II.35–46 and 60–64). Perikles is, just like Archidamos, completely silent on the gods; only once in the Funeral Speech (38.1) does he refer to sacrifices. Archidamos remains for the time being unchanged. Before the first invasion of Attika he addresses a speech to the supreme commanders of the Peloponnesian troops without ever referring to the gods (II.11). Yet in a Periklean speech addressed to the Athenian Assembly which Thucydides reports without claiming to quote it, he makes that outstanding leader speak of "the goddess," meaning thereby the most valuable statue of Athena, for he is setting forth there in detail the financial resources of the city (13.5). On the other hand, Thucydides has to say quite a few things about gods and sacred matters in his narrative of the plague which follows immediately on Perikles' Funeral Speech, to say nothing of his narrative about early Athens (15.2–6).

The first exchange of speeches after Perikles' last speech concerns the conflict between the Spartans and the Plataians, who were allies of the Athenians. The exchange is based on a solemn oath still binding the two (or three) parties to the conflict. It is particularly worthy of note that the Spartan king Archidamos begins his final reply to the Plataians by calling on the gods and heroes who possess the Plataian land—to be witnesses to the justice of the Peloponnesian cause (79.2)—a justice which the reader might find rather dubious: the moral-political situation has undergone a profound change since the debate in Sparta.

We learn from Thucydides' narrative that after a victorious naval battle against the Peloponnesians the Athenians consecrated a captured enemy ship to Poseidon (84.4). In the ensuing speech of the Peloponnesian naval commanders to their troops, who were understandably disheartened by their preceding defeat caused by their insufficient naval training or experience, no reference is made to the gods (87). Yet the Athenian soldiers were also afraid: the Peloponnesian ships were more numerous than the Athenian ones. The Athenian commander Phormion restored their courage by a speech which is likewise silent regarding gods (88–89). In the second naval battle the Peloponnesians fought better than in the first but the final result was again a complete Athenian victory: experience and skill were again decisive. Toward the end of Book Two Thucydides tells a story, without vouching for its truth, about Alkmaion, matricide, who, thanks to Apollon's oracle, found a safe refuge in a district which did not yet exist at the time of the murder (102.5–6).

The next speech is the one which the Mytilenian ambassadors address to the gathering of the Peloponnesians and neutrals at Olympia in order to solicit help for their intended defection from the Athenian allies; the Mytilenians are compelled to show that their intended action is not unjust or ignoble (III.9–14). Toward the end of their speech they admonish their would-be new allies to be awed by the respect in which those would-be allies are held by the hopes of the Greeks and by the respect of the Olympian Zeus in whose temple they appear, as it were as suppliants. As Thucydides shows by his narrative, the Mytilenians' request and in particular the last-minute appeal to the Olympian Zeus remained without effect. He does not give a speech of reply. The reply is given by deed or to some extent by the two speeches exchanged in the Athenian Assembly after the Athenians' conquest of Mytilene. Prior to the actual conquest of Mytilene the Peloponnesian comander Teutiaplos of Elis addresses to his troops a brief speech which is, according to Gomme (*ad loc.*), the only one prefaced by *tade*, instead of the usual *toiade* (29–30). (One might add that after having quoted the brief speech, Thucydides notes that Teutiaplos had said *tosauta*—an expression which he uses quite frequently.) Teutiaplos' counsel was rejected by his Spartan fellow-commander Alkidas, obviously a stupid man who thus contributed to the failure of the Peloponnesian enterprise. In a meeting of the Athenian Assembly which takes place after the conquest of Mytilene Kleon passionately opposes the reconsideration of the capital punishment of all grown-up male Mytilenians—of a punishment resolved upon a few days earlier: the Mytilenians are simply guilty of an inexcusable injustice and must be dealt with accordingly. Kleon does not refer to the gods: he has no reason to refer in any way to the gods (37–40). The case for gentleness or rather for discrimination is made by Diodotos, who had already stated it in the preceding meeting of the Assembly (42–48); his speech is perhaps the most enigmatic speech in the whole work. Diodotos is likewise completely silent on the gods. But it is possibly not inappropriate to note that he speaks of the weakness of the passionately excited "human nature" as compared with "the force of laws or anything else awful" (45.7; cf. 84.2). Partly thanks to Diodotos' intervention the majority of the Mytilenians had a hair's-breadth escape.

Seen within the context of the whole, the fate of Mytilene and the speeches accompanying it are the foil of the fate of Plataiai at the hands of the Peloponnesians—an event illumined likewise by an exchange of speeches. The Plataians are eventually compelled to surrender their starved city to the Spartans, who accept the surrender with a reservation which, to me at least, is not a model of good faith. The Plataians know of course that the Spartans will give in to the demands of the Thebans, the Plataians' deadly enemies, but they make the manly effort to remind the Spartans of what the Spartans would have to do as good men. They naturally appeal to the gods, who in the Persian War consecrated the anti-Persian alliance in which the Plataians distinguished themselves. They remind the Spartans of the sacred duty incumbent upon the latter to respect the graves, always honored by the Plataians, of the Spartans' fathers who had fallen in the Persian War and had been buried in Plataian ground. They invoke the gods whom the Greeks worship on the same altars in order to persuade the Spartans not to give in to the Thebans' demand (53.5–9). The Thebans' hard and hateful reply is meant to show that the Plataians have always been unjust (61–67): hence the Thebans are completely silent about the gods (IV.67.1); as the Thebans imply, the Plataians' pious invocations do not deserve an answer.

The narration of the fate of Mytilene and of that of Plataiai prepares us sufficiently for Thucydides' account of the rising of the *demos* in Korkyra and of the fratricidal wars between the mighty and the *demos* in the cities in general. Cruel hatred took the place of friendship to the nearest of kin, led to complete disregard of the sanctity of asylum in the temples and to utter disregard of "the divine law": partnership in crime rather than respect for the divine law became the bond of good faith. Thucydides does not explain what the precise ground of the divine law is nor what its specific prohibitions (or commands) are, but he leaves no doubt that the partisans on both sides lost all piety (82.6–7).

When Thucydides, compelled or excused by the sequence of events, comes to speak of the first Athenian expedition against Sicily, he speaks first of a number of daimonic things, one of them a small volcano near Sicily; in the opinion of the local people the outbreaks are due directly to Hephaistos (87–88). Immediately thereafter he speaks at somewhat greater length than before of earthquakes, this time giving his own opinion about a related event; his own opinion contains no reference to gods (89). The Spartans on the other hand ask the god at Delphi regarding the foundation of a city; the god approves of the plan properly modified; although the modifications are accepted by the god, the foundation is not successful, not the least owing to the ineptitude of the Spartan magistrate (92.5–93). Shortly thereafter Thucydides avails himself of the opportunity to mention the violent death of Hesiod in the temple of the Zeus of Nemea: he had received in Nemea an oracle to the effect that this would happen to him there but Thucydides does not vouch for the truth of the story (96.1). Thucydides would have misled us greatly about Athens and hence about the Peloponnesian War if he had not added soon thereafter his account of the Athenians' purification of Apollon's island of Delos, the purification having been ordered by "some oracle or other." The truth about the original form of the Delian festival is vouched for by no less a man than Homer himself (104).

The end of the first part of the war is decisively prepared by the Athenian victory, due primarily to Demosthenes at Pylos (or Sphakteria), and by Brasidas' victorious march to Thrace. Near the beginning of the section Demosthenes addresses the hoplites under his command. In the situation, which is rather grave, not to say desperate, he urges them to be of good hope and not to be too greatly concerned with the calculation of chances. He does not mention gods (IV.9–10). His tactics prove to be highly successful. The Spartans are now willing to conclude an armistice and even a peace treaty in order to get back the Spartiates cut off by the Athenians and send ambassadors to Athens. In their speech to the Athenian Assembly those ambassadors go so far as to leave it open whether the Spartans or the Athenians started the war, i.e., broke the treaty (IV.17–20); they naturally do not mention any god: Apollon had promised to come to the Peloponnesians' help called or uncalled (I.118.3, II.54.4). Thanks chiefly to Kleon the

Athenians win a splendid victory. Nothing is said by anyone to the effect that the Spartans had asked for or received permission from the oracle to send ambassadors to Athens.

Before turning to Brasidas' expedition, Thucydides speaks of three actions which are particularly noteworthy with a view to our present purpose. The first is the pan-Sicilian gathering at Gela, which has at its high point the speech of Hermokrates that he quotes (IV.58–64). He warns his fellow-Sicilians of the danger threatening them at the hands of the Athenians: the Athenians intend to come to Sicily, not in order to help their Ionian kinsmen against the Dorians but in order to acquire the wealth of the whole of Sicily. He does not blame the Athenians for their desire, which belongs to human nature universally. He is completely silent about the gods, thus silently anticipating the argument of the Athenians on Melos. The second action is Brasidas' winning over the Akanthians, allies of Athens, to Sparta by a clever speech (IV.85–87). He presents the Spartans as the liberators of the Greeks from servitude to Athens and he disposes of any fear which the Akanthians might feel that the Spartans might misuse their victory, telling his audience that he has received from the Spartans' rulers the most solemn oaths to the desired effect: what stronger proof of Spartan good faith could be given? In addition, he counters a possible Akanthian argument that the Spartans have no right to liberate the Akanthians from the Athenians by force, by calling as witnesses the gods and heroes of the Akanthians' land: to force the Akanthians to be free and to contribute their share towards the liberation of Greece as a whole by the use of force for this purpose is not unjust. The third action is the Athenians' occupation and fortification of the Delion, a temple of Apollon near the border of Boiotia and Attika. The Boiotian leader Pagondas delivers a speech to his troops in which he tells them that the god whose temple the Athenians have lawlessly occupied will be on the side of the Boiotians and that the sacrifices which the Boiotians have offered are favorable (IV.92). The Athenian commander Hippokrates in his address to his troops is completely silent on gods and sacred things (IV.95): we could not expect differently. The battle ends of course with a very severe Athenian defeat. The impious actions of the Athenians, which consisted in fortifying, and living in, the sanctuary, enable the Boiotians, as they think, to demand from the Athenians the evacuation of the temple before they can claim the surrender of their dead. In the ensuing debate the Athenians claim that their allegedly impious action would be forgiven as an involuntary action even by the god (98.6).

When Brasidas comes to Toronte, he arranges there a meeting of the citizens, to whom he says things similar to those he had said to the Akanthians (114.3–5) but his speech to the Toronaians is only reported, not quoted. Thucydides did not need a further proof of Brasidas' rhetorical ability. In addition, Brasidas' action in Akanthos had established his credit among Athens' vacillating allies sufficiently. Finally, we cannot exclude the possibility that the Spartan authorities did not entirely approve of Brasidas' making solemn promises in their name (108.7; cf. 132.3). In the report of the speech to the Toronaians there naturally occurs no reference to the gods. Let us remind ourselves here of two earlier parallels. In I.72–78 Thucydides first reports and then quotes the speech of the Athenians in Sparta: gods are not mentioned in the report but they are mentioned in the quoted speech; the result is that of the four speeches delivered on the occasion only Archidamos' speech is silent about the gods. In II.88–89 Thucydides first reports and then quotes Phormion's speech to the Athenian troops; but Phormion, in contradistinction to the Peloponnesian commanders, does not reinforce his speech by threats of punishment (II.87.9).

As a consequence of Brasidas' successes the Spartans and the Athenians conclude an armistice. The first article of the armistice concerns the sanctuary and the oracle of the Pythian Apollon (IV.118.1–3). The same order is observed in the solemnly sworn so-called peace of Nikias (V.17end–18.2).

Book V opens with Thucydides' account of the correction by the Athenians of a neglect of which they had become guilty when they purified Delos. There soon follows the battle of Amphipolis with Brasidas in command of the Peloponnesians and their allies and Kleon in command of the Athenians; the battle leads to a severe defeat of the Athenians; the leaders of both armies are killed. Before the battle Brasidas addresses his speech, quoted by Thucydides, to his troops without referring to gods or sacred things (cf. also 10.5); on the other hand, he prepares a sacrifice to Athena (10.2). We note that no speech of Kleon is reported, let alone quoted. Kleon is too busy with "seeing," with observing the movement of Brasidas' army, to speak (7.3–4, 9.3, 10.2): a strange reversal of doings as between a Spartan and the then leading Athenian demagogue, a kind of comic equivalent to the fighting at Pylos. The citizens of Amphipolis honor Brasidas after his death with the honors of a hero. The death of the two commanders increased the influence of those leading men in Sparta and Athens who favor peace. To bring about this result in Sparta, the cooperation of the priestess in Delphi was important. This does not necessarily contradict Apollon's promise at the beginning of the war that he would come to the help of the Spartans called or uncalled, for the only oracle regarding the war which proved to be true concerned the war's lasting 27 years (V.26.3): the god had not promised that the Spartans would be victorious in "the first war." This is to say nothing of the fact that the armistice or peace was at that time a great help for Sparta.

Between Brasidas' last speech (9) and the dialogue on Melos at the end of V (84ff.) there occur no quoted speeches but only a few reported speeches or references to them. But in that twilight there occur mentions of gods and divine things, among which one may count earthquakes (45.4, 50.5), and of unfavorable sacrifices as causes why the Spartans broke off military operations (54.2, 55.3, 116.1). But the Athenians too of course obeyed the oracle of the Delphic god (32.1). Above all, Thucydides makes clear that the Spartans' flute playing prior to battle was not done "for the sake of the divine" (70).

It is easy for us to find that the references to "the divine law" in Thucydides' account of the civil wars (III.82.6; cf. II.53.4) and to the gods in the dialogue between the Melians and the Athenians are the most important or the most revealing statements occurring in his work as far as the gods are concerned. It is all the more necessary to realize that the theology of the Melian dialogue is in one sense of subordinate importance; the subject is brought up by the Athenians as it were in passing. In order to show the Athenians that they may have some hope against hope, the Melians remind them of the role played in war by chance: they trust, as far as chance is concerned, that "the divine" (*to theion*) will not disadvantage them, given the justice of the Melians—to say nothing of the fact that the Spartans are forced by sheer shame to come to the Melians' assistance. The Athenians reply that they, the Athenians, can count on the good will of "the divine," for they act within the limits of what human beings hold or believe regarding "the divine," for the Athenians (or all sensible human beings) believe as regards "the divine" what is generally thought about it and as regards the human they know clearly, namely, that the strong rules the weaker by nature and hence sempiternally with necessity. Thereupon the Melians drop the subject and speak only of their manifest or human hopes, i.e., the hope which they derive from their relation with Sparta. We note that in the Melian dialogue "the gods" are not mentioned but only "the divine," which is more general and more vague than "the gods." Of "the divine law" as distinguished from "the divine," Thucydides speaks in his own name; but he is in the case of the divine law, as in that of the divine, equally silent about the precise meaning of the expressions. He clearly disapproves of breaches of the divine law, whereas he refrains from passing judgment on the Athenians' theology as stated by their ambassadors on Melos.

Books VI and VII, which contain Thucydides' account of the Sicilian expedition, are related to the Melian dialogue as his account of the plague is to his Pericles' Funeral Speech. In his archaeology of Sicily he indicates the untrustworthy character of what is said about the Kyklopes and others (2.1–2). The first great event pertaining to the Sicilian expedition is the exchange of speeches, quoted by Thucydides, between Nikias and Alkibiades in the Athenian Assembly; there are two such speeches by Nikias and one by Alkibiades. In what could seem to be, especially in retrospect, a reversal of roles Nikias warns the Athenians against endangering what they possess for the sake of immanifest and future things (9.3), just as the Athenians had warned the Melians; there is this difference that the Melians were not, or at least not in the same way as the Athenians, in love with the faraway (13; cf. 24.3). But Nikias is not equal to Alkibiades in dexterity; he is defeated in the debate, in a way that resembles Nikias' (or his comrades') defeat by Kleon in the debate regarding Pylos. Neither Nikias nor Alkibiades mentions gods but Alkibiades refers to the oath which obliges the Athenians to come to the assistance of their Sicilian allies (18.1; cf. 19.1). Nikias' last word is to the effect that the fate of the expedition will depend on chance, which cannot be mastered by men, rather than on human foresight (23.3). While the expedition is being prepared according to the proposal of the sensible and hitherto always lucky Nikias, unknown individuals mutilate the Hermai which stand in front of private houses as well as temples; this and other impious deeds are regarded as a bad omen for the expedition and even for the established democratic regime; a strong suspicion falls on Alkibiades and quite a few others. In spite of this Alkibiades is left together with Nikias in command of the expedition; the Athenians have the greatest hope for future things as compared with what they already possessed (31.6). This hope was not unconnected with piety; when everything was ready for the departure of the armament, the customary prayers and libations were offered (32.1–2). As little as in the debate in the Athenian Assembly are the gods mentioned in the debate in the Syracusan Assembly. It is hard to say whether this silence is one of the shadows cast by the unsolved mystery of the mutilation of the Hermai and similar impieties.

The considerable disappointment which the Athenians with the exception of Nikias (46.2) experienced after their arrival in Sicily proves to be minor compared with the recall to Athens of Alkibiades who is now to be proceeded against on account of his alleged impiety. The action of the Athenian *demos* against Alkibiades enables or forces Thucydides to tell the true story of the alleged tyrannicide committed by Harmodios and Aristogeiton. We note in particular two things: the tyranny of Peisistratos and his family was on the whole mild and law-abiding and in particular pious; Hippias, the man who was in fact tyrant after the death of his father, Peisistratos, survived and after his expulsion a few years later from Athens by the Spartans and some Athenians found refuge with the Persian king and fought on the Persian side at Marathon (54.5–6, 59.4), thus foreshadowing in a manner the fate of Themistokles.

In the first battle, Nikias defeats the Syracusans after having encouraged his troops by reminding them of their military superiority to the enemy: the enemy army is inferior to Nikias' army in regard to knowledge (68.2, 69.1). There is no need for him to refer to gods and hence he does not refer to them. This is perfectly compatible with the fact that in both armies the soothsayers bring the usual sacrifices prior to the battle (69.2). The battle was accompanied by a thunderstorm and heavy rain—phenomena which increased the fear of those who had no previous battle experience while the more experienced men simply regarded them as a consequence of the season of the year (70.1): experience diminishes the frightening effect of the dai-monic things. Any discouragement which the Syracusans may have suffered on account of their defeat is removed by a speech of Hermokrates in their Assembly which Thucydides reports and which is not encumbered by an explicit reference to gods (72). Hermokrates is also the speaker for Syracuse in a gathering at Kamarina in which both belligerents sue for the favor of those Sicilians who have not yet taken sides; the speaker for Athens carries the characteristic name Euphemos. Both speeches are quoted and are silent on the gods. In a gathering of the anti-Athenian cities at Sparta Alkibiades succeeds in convincing the Spartans of the soundness of a broadly conceived anti-Athenian policy and strategy and at the same time of the perfect correctitude of his high treason. Alkibiades' speech is also quoted and is silent on the gods; its being quoted and its being silent on the gods have the same reason. While the Spartan and Korinthian relief force is already on its way to Syracuse, the situation of the Athenians on Sicily looks quite favor-able: Nikias is quite hopeful. Yet the only mishap which befell the Spartans was that they had to interrupt a military operation which they had started against Argos, because of an earthquake (95.1). As it seems to me, Book VI, which is rich in quoted speeches, also abounds in reported speeches.

Book VII can be said to bring the *peripeteia*: the leadership in the fight for Syracuse shifts from the Athenian gentleman Nikias with his half-Spartan turn of mind to the much more daring commanders Gylippos of Sparta and Hermokrates of Syracuse (cf., e.g., 3.3 and 8.3). The Athenians' situation in Sicily becomes grave; Nikias is compelled to send a letter to Athens with an urgent request for additional troops and supply. Apart from the fact that the letter was accompanied by oral messages, it has the status of a quoted speech (8.1–2, 10–15) to a greater degree than the excerpts from the letters of Pausanias and Themistokles to the king of Persia (I.129.3, 137.4). Nikias does not hesitate to tell the Athenians what he thinks of their "difficult natures" (VII.14.2 and 4). The reversal of fate which has taken place in Sicily resembles that at Pylos: while Athens has ceased to be the preponder-ant naval power, the anti-Athenian combination's naval power has in-creased (11.2–4, 12.3). Gods and the sacred things are not mentioned—at least not explicitly. For the greatest increase in the Spartans' power was caused by their holding now among other things that the Athenians had broken the treaty, whereas in the first war it had rather been the Spartans who had begun the war; the Spartans therefore believed that their misfor-tunes in the first war, like that at Pylos, were deserved or reasonable (cf. 18.2); they believed that good or bad fortune in war depends on the justice or injustice of the belligerents, i.e., on the rule of gods concerned with justice. This thought is ascribed by Thucydides to the Spartans, but it is no accident that it follows almost immediately his quotation of Nikias' letter; it is also a Nikian thought.

The operations urgently recommended by Alkibiades begin to hurt the Athenians considerably, although for the time being the harm which Athens suffered was as nothing compared with what happened to the small city of Mykalessos at the hands of Thracian mercenaries who were in the pay of Athens and whom the Athenians had to send home for fiscal reasons. Thereafter through an improvement in their naval tactics the Syracusans defeat the Athenians unmistakably in a naval battle; this was the turning point (41). Yet for the moment the Athenians' situation seems to be greatly improved by the arrival of the second Athenian expeditionary force that is commanded by Demosthenes. Demosthenes' daring attempt either to win a victorious decision practically at once or else to start at once with the preparation for the return home of the Athenian armament is spoiled in the first place by enemy resistance. Secondly, there is disagreement among the Athenian commanders and within the army: there seems to be no longer any hope. Demosthenes voted for immediate return to Athens. In the deliberations Nikias could not be as frank as Demosthenes since he was engaged in secret negotiations with the influential, wealthy Syracusans, who desired as much as he a speedy end of the enormously expensive war; he still has some hope. He voted therefore against Demosthenes' proposal. The reason by which he supported his vote was what he thought of the difficult nature of the Athenians: the very soldiers who clamor now for the immediate return to Athens will say after their return, when they have come again under the influence of the demagogues, that the Athenian generals have been bribed by the enemy: he for one would not prefer to perish unjustly at the hands of the Athenians rather than perishing at the hands of the enemy "privately," i.e., not unjustly. He does not consider the fact that his unjust death would contribute to the salvation of the Athenian armament. The exchange between Demosthenes and Nikias (47–49.3) is the most striking example in Thucydides' work of an exchange of reported speeches. Nikias' speech, though, does not simply express his thought since, as Thucydides makes clear, his hope prevents him from being completely frank. He clings to his opinion because he is swayed by hope based on his Syracusan connections rather than by fear of Athenian revenge, and his opinion wins out. The postponement of the Athenians' departure is due entirely to him. But at the time everything was ready for the departure of the whole armament by sea, an eclipse of the moon took place. Thereupon most of the Athenians and not the least Nikias himself, who was somewhat too much addicted to divination and the like, demanded further postponement of the departure: Nikias decided that according to the interpretation given by the soothsayers one ought not even to deliberate about the date of leaving before three times nine days had passed (50.4).

In the meantime the Syracusans gained a splendid naval victory, thus almost closing to the Athenians the exit from the harbor of Syracuse. The

Athenians' discouragement increased correspondingly and still more their regret about the whole expedition. Before they make a last desperate effort to break the Syracusan blockade, Nikias calls all soldiers under his command together and addresses to them a speech in which he shows them there is still hope, given the power of chance especially in war. Nikias' speech is paralleled by a speech of the enemy commanders to their troops: they have much better grounds for hope whereas the Athenians are reduced to putting their reliance altogether on fate (61–68). In these speeches, both of which are quoted, gods and sacred things are not mentioned, but the extreme danger in which the Athenians find themselves induces Nikias to address every single commander of a trireme and remind him, among other things, of the ancestral gods (69.1–2). The battle which follows and which consisted in the futile attempt of the Athenians to achieve a breakout through the blockading enemy navy was of unrivaled violence. The Athenians who could not embark were compelled to be spectators of the life-and-death struggle. Their participation was limited to their passionate response to the part of the fight which they could see from the place where each happened to stand: when they saw their own men vanquish the enemy, they caught courage and called on the gods; in the opposite case, they lost their courage and apparently also their willingness to call on the gods (71.3). Hope ceasing, piety ceases (cf. also 75.7). The Athenians' disaster prevents them from taking the customary loving care of their many dead, even from asking the victors for the surrender of the Athenian corpses (72.2): the contrast with the circumstances in which Perikles delivered his Funeral Speech is overpowering. Retreat into the interior of Sicily is rendered difficult and eventually impossible by a ruse of Hermokrates to which he was forced to have recourse because the Syracusans refused to continue fighting during the night: they just happened to celebrate a festival in honor of Herakles (73.2–74). Thucydides has described the miserable end of the Athenian army and its commanders—an event which surpasses description—as adequately as possible.

Shortly before the very end Nikias addressed a speech of encouragement to his troops which is quoted by Thucydides in full and which is the last speech quoted in full that occurs in the work. Nikias, still filled with hope, exhorts his soldiers to be hopeful. He declares truthfully that he is rather worse off than his comrades in arms although he has fulfilled the customary duties toward the gods and has always been just and modest towards human beings. The Athenians may have provoked the envy of the god by their expedition but they have been sufficiently punished for this; now they deserve the god's pity rather than his envy (77.1–4). Nikias' theology obviously differs from—nay, is opposed to—the theology stated by the Athenian ambassadors on Melos. According to Thucydides himself Nikias would have deserved a better fate than the one which fell to his lot, for he had applied himself more than any other of Thucydides' contemporaries to the exercice of that virtue which is praised and held up by the law (86.5)—as distinguished from another, possibly higher, kind of virtue—but his theology is refuted by his fate. It is almost unnecessary to say that the Athenians' hopeless retreat into the interior of Sicily was accompanied by thunderstorms and rain which, while being seasonal, were interpreted by the Athenians as pointing to misery still to come (79.3).

Thucydides' theology—if it is permitted to use this expression—is located in the mean (in the Aristotelian sense) between that of Nikias and that of the Athenian ambassadors on Melos.

Book VIII, the last Book is anticlimactic. What this expression means depends obviously on the character of the climax, i.e., in the first place on the character of Books VI–VII and then of the whole work. It has been plausibly suggested that the peculiarity of Book VIII is due to its incompleteness, perhaps to Thucydides having died before he was able to complete his work. But this is not more than a plausible hypothesis. The peculiarity of Book VIII must be understood in the light of the peculiarity or peculiarities of the bulk of the work. The most striking peculiarity of the bulk of the work is the speeches of the characters which are quoted in full and the way in which they are interwoven with the account of the deeds as well as with the speeches which are merely reported. There are no speeches quoted in full to be found in Book VIII. There is however a large section of Book V which has the same character: V.10–84. The absence of quoted speeches from this section heightens the power, the impact, of the dialogue on Melos (V.85–112) and the account of the Sicilian expedition (VI–VII). Is that power, that impact, not still more heightened by the absence of fully quoted speeches from Book VIII? Let this question also not be more than a plausible hypothesis. It has at least the merit of protecting us against the danger of mistaking a plausible hypothesis ratified by an overwhelming majority for a demonstrated verity.

Since the Athenians and their enemies preserve their turns of mind—their zealous quickness and their cautious slowness, respectively—despite what happened in Sicily, the Athenians were able to build up a new powerful force and to protect the largest part of their empire. Their initial anger when they learned of their disaster in Sicily was directed also against the diviners and soothsayers who had confirmed them in their hope that they would conquer Sicily. But the long-range reaction was rather in favor of thrift and moderation and of some form of rule by older men. One may doubt, however, whether any effort on the part of the Athenians would have been of any avail to them if there had not been frictions or dissensions among her enemies. Owing to Alkibiades' instigation an important part of Attika was under permanent occupation by an enemy army commanded by the Spartan king Agis, and Agis was or became a mortal enemy of Alkibiades. Owing to his command of a Spartan army Agis' power in Sparta had increased and he had thus increased or aroused dissensions with the other Spartan authorities. Alkibiades therefore had to depend on the support of these other Spartan authorities (5.3–4, 12.2, 45.1). But it was another division within the enemy combination which saved Athens and—incredible as it may sound—by the same stroke Alkibiades, who was condemned to death by Athens. The Athenian defeat in Sicily had made the king of Persia (and therewith his satrap Tissaphernes) and the Spartans the actual or potential heirs to that part of the Athenian empire which was located in Asia Minor and the islands nearby. Tissaphernes wished to use those rich financial resources, which were hitherto at Athens' disposal, for the king's services. This state of things naturally led to a Spartan-Persian alliance that was strongly urged by Alkibiades. While the war continued with more or less its old fury, the *demos* of Samos rose with the help of the Athenians against their oligarchic fellow-citizens, killing or expelling them and confiscating their property (21). Furthermore, the war still dragging on, the Peloponnesians felt that their treaty with Tissaphernes gave them less than they were entitled to expect; accordingly, a new treaty of alliance between the two powers was concluded. A change in the Spartan command brought the latent conflict between Sparta and Persia into the open. The Spartans who were now negotiating with Tissaphernes found it unbearable that the two treaties between Sparta and Persia restored to the king of Persia the right to all countries which he and his ancestors ever possessed, i.e., above all the Greek lands which Greeks had liberated from Persian domination. Tissaphernes became angry and was unwilling to continue paying the large sums of money which he had spent hitherto for the Peloponnesian navy. Precisely at this moment Alkibiades saw himself compelled to take refuge with Tissaphernes in order to find protection against his numerous and powerful enemies in Sparta. He took resolutely the side of Tissaphernes against the Spartans. He became the teacher of Tissaphernes is all things—especially regarding moderation: Tissaphernes ought to reduce the pay of the Peloponnesian sailors, whose high pay induces them to commit every kind of mischief and to ruin their bodies (45.1–2). Alkibiades, who was notorious for his *hybris* and incontinence, as teacher of moderation and continence: if this is not the greatest or most moving *peripeteia* recorded in Thucydides' work, it is surely the most astounding one. What an ancient critic observed with regard to Thucydides' account of the Kylon affair (I.126.2ff.)—here the lion laughed—can be applied with at least equal right to Alkibiades' timely conversion.

Politically the most important instruction which Alkibiades gave to Tissaphernes was to prevent the victory of either the Peloponnesians or the Athenians: a divided Greece could easily be controlled by Persia. If Persia had to make a choice between the two Greek powers she ought to prefer

Athens, which constituted less of a danger to Persia than the Peloponnesians. In this way Alkibiades prepared at the same time his reconciliation with the Athenians. For he held that the Athenians might turn to him if Tissaphernes appeared to be his friend. But this solution required the change of the Athenian regime from a democracy into an oligarcy: the Persian king could not be expected to put any reliance on a democracy. Very influential Athenians were won over to the plan to recall Alkibiades and to abolish the democracy. The popular opposition to the plan was silenced by the hope for the pay which the Persian king would give. Connected with Alkibiades' conspiracy but to some extent independent of it, there developed an anti-democratic conspiracy among the highest strata of the Athenian army on Samos, with the consequence that that army as a whole favored the abolition of democracy and the recall of Alkibiades. The Athenians on Samos sent an embassy to Athens with Peisandros as its leader. There was considerable opposition in Athens to the recall of Alkibiades, not the least on the ground of the fact that he had been condemned to death because of impiety. Yet the opponents were unable to suggest an alternative which might save Athens. Thereupon Peisandros told them clearly "there is none" except to make the government more oligarchic (53.3). This utterance of Peisandros—roughly six lines—is the only direct speech quoted in Book VIII. This does not necessarily mean that it is the most important utterance of a Thucydidean character that occurs in the last Book. But it clearly underlines, especially if taken in conjunction with the absence of any quoted speech by Alkibiades, the most striking characteristic of that Book: its anticlimatic character, as previously explained. One might also note the relative abundance of fully quoted treaties of alliance (18, 37, 58) as contrasted with the complete absence of fully quoted speeches proper.

The oligarchically minded Athenians other than Alkibiades, if not altogether inimical to him, established an oligarchy in Athens and wherever else they could in the Athenian empire. But the allies or subjects of Athens were less eager for oligarchy than for being independent of Athens. The regime now established in Athens was the government of 5,000 who were most able to help the city by their property and by themselves. This meant in fact that only members of the oligarchic clique were entitled to participate in the government and exercised a violent rule. At Peisandros' proposal the actual government was vested in 400 men out of the 5,000. The establishment of this regime in Athens was a remarkable achievement, the work of some of the most able and excellent Athenians. The oligarchic rulers naturally fortified their rule by prayers and sacrifices to the gods (70.1). They changed many of the provisions made under the democracy but they did not recall the men who had been exiled in order not to be forced to recall Alkibiades in particular. They tried to start negotiations with Agis; peace with Sparta rather than with Tissaphernes was their aim. But they achieved nothing. In addition, the Athenian army on Samos put down the oligarchy there. The democratic leaders obliged the soldiers and especially the oligarchically minded among them by the greatest oaths to accept the democracy and continue the war against the Peloponnesians (75.2). They were in favor of Alkibiades' recall and its implication: alliance with the King of Persia. This proposal was adopted by the Assembly of the soldiers on Samos, with the result that Alkibiades joined the Athenians on that island. He addressed a speech to that Assembly which Thucydides reports and which overstated the case for Alkibiades and his policy as strongly as possible (81.2–3). Thereupon he was elected general to serve together with the previous ones. He was now in a position to frighten the Athenians with his alleged or true influence on Tissaphernes and Tissaphernes with his power over the Athenian army. It was in this grave situation that Alkibiades seemed for the first time to have benefited his fatherland no less than any other man by preventing an ill-conceived attempt of the Athenians on Samos to leave that island and to sail straight into the Peiraeus. In fact there was at that time no one apart from him as capable to restrain the multitude. He abolished the rule of the 400 while preserving or rather restoring the rule of the 5,000. Just at this time, while the sharpest civic conflict raged in Athens, the Athenians suffered a severe naval defeat in the closest proximity to the city; the situation was graver even than immediately after the disaster on Sicily. But they showed again their old courage and resilience. The rule of the 5,000, i.e., the rule of the hoplites, was firmly established. Then the Athenians had for the first time during Thucydides' life a good regime: a right kind of mixture of oligarchy and democracy. Simultaneous with this salutary revolution Alkibiades was formally recalled (96–97) and therewith the hope for Athens' salvation restored. The hope came to nought, as other hopes spoken of by Thucydides had come to nought, but not through Alkibiades' fault. How it came to nought is told by Xenophon in the *Hellenika*. There seems to be a connection, not made explicit by Thucydides, between the first good Athenian regime that existed during Thucydides' lifetime and Alkibiades' unquestioned predominance.

5

Xenophon's *Anabasis*

Xenophon's *Anabasis* seems today to be regarded universally as his most beautiful book. I do not quarrel with this judgment. I merely wonder what its grounds are. The question is obviously reasonable; in the eighteenth century, quite a few judicious men would have assigned the highest place among Xenophon's writings to his *Memorabilia* rather than to his *Anabasis*. In other words, the fact that we judge the *Anabasis* to be Xenophon's most beautiful book does not yet prove that that judgment was shared by Xenophon. Before we can agree or disagree with the ruling opinion, we would have to know what the book meant for Xenophon, we would have to know the place and function of the book within the Corpus Xenophonteum and therewith possibly the full beauty of the *Anabasis*. Perhaps we have answered our question unwittingly and thoughtlessly, if truthfully, by speaking of Xenophon's Anabasis, of Xenophon's ascent.

The authentic title of the book is "Cyrus' Ascent," i.e., the expedition of the younger Cyrus from the coastal plain to the interior of Asia. The title is misleading, for Cyrus' ascent came to its end in the battle of Kunaxa in which he was defeated and killed; the account of his ascent fills at most the first of the seven Books of the *Anabasis*. The title of the *Anabasis* is not the only misleading title of Xenophon's works: *The Education of Cyrus* deals with the whole life of the older Cyrus while his education is discussed only in the first Book; the *Memorabilia* contains what Xenophon remembers of Socrates' justice and not Xenophon's memorable experiences as such.

This manuscript was left by Leo Strauss in its handwritten form. It was transcribed as carefully as possible by Joseph Cropsey, with assistance from Jenny and Diskin Clay. It was first published in *Interpretation: A Journal of Political Philosophy* 4, no. 3 (1975).

The *Anabasis* opens as follows: "Dareios and Parysatis had two sons born to them, of whom the elder was Artaxerxes and the younger Cyrus." The work begins as if it were devoted to a memorable incident in the royal family of Persia. This opening makes us see that Persia, apparently the strongest monarchy, was in fact a dyarchy in which the preference of the queen for her younger son had the gravest consequences. Yet while the *Anabasis* tells us a great deal about Persia, it tells us very little about the royal family of Persia; it cannot be said to be devoted to Persia, not even to the Persian-Greek conflict, except incidentally.

Perplexing and even misleading as the title and the opening of the *Anabasis* are, the identity of its author is no less enigmatic. When Xenophon recapitulates in his historical work, the *Hellenika*, with utmost brevity the events narrated in the *Anabasis*, he ascribes the account of those events to Themistogenes of Syracuse (III 1.1–2). Nothing is known about Themistogenes, not even regarding his ever having lived. One is entitled to assume that Themistogenes of Syracuse is a pseudonym for Xenophon of Athens. In the *Anabasis*, Xenophon speaks of his outstanding deeds and speeches only in the third person; he apparently wishes to preserve this kind of becoming anonymity as much as possible. Syracuse and Athens were the most outstanding commercial and naval powers of Greece; Xenophon might be thought to mean "slayer of strangers," while Themistogenes is "the offspring of Right"; Themistogenes could seem to be a somehow idealized Xenophon. In the same context in which he mentions Themistogenes, he mentions the name of the Spartan admiral who was ordered by the ephors to assist Cyrus in his expedition; his name was Samios. When he mentions him in the *Anabasis* (I 4.2), Xenophon calls him Pythagoras. It would not be surprising if the author of the *Memorabilia*, when hearing the name "Samios" thought at once of the most famous Samian philosopher, Pythagoras.

In the *Anabasis*, Xenophon appears on the center of the stage only at the beginning of Book Three. Let us first see what we learn about him and his intention from the first two Books by observing certain peculiarities of his manner of writing. As can be expected, he will say everything necessary about the cause as well as the circumstances of Cyrus' ascent, but it is not likely that he will forgo things worthy to be mentioned which came to his attention on the occasion of that ascent although they do not throw light on it directly. Still, it is doubtful whether what he says in particular about the fauna and flora of the countries through which he passed was not required by his interest in provisions for the army and concern with them.

In order to secure himself against disgrace and even mortal danger threatening him at the hands of his brother, the king, to whom he had become suspect, Cyrus resolved to make himself king; for this purpose he secretly assembled an army consisting of different contingents of Greek mercenaries, to say nothing of the Persian troops whose command had been entrusted to him by his brother. For his march inland he found a pretext which was plausible in the eyes of the king, but which did not fool the king's loyal satrap Tissaphernes. Xenophon mentions as the most important stations of the way the cities which he describes by a standard formula that is susceptible of characteristic variations. The first cities mentioned are "inhabited, prosperous and large." In the present context (I 2) the standard expression occurs three times, whereas the description of cities as "inhabited" with the omission of "prosperous and large" occurs five times; in one case the city in question is simply called "the last city of Phrygia." What this procedure means becomes clear from the description of Tarsos as a large and prosperous city; as is said immediately afterward, Tarsos was not inhabited, its inhabitants having fled at the approach of Cyrus' army. In the case of the last city of Phrygia, one wonders whether it was not uninhabited even before the rumor of Cyrus' approach reached it. This much is clear: the standard expression indicates the normal or optimal case; the variations indicate the various states of defectiveness. This has the consequence that Xenophon is not compelled to speak in many cases expressly of defects or that his general tone is less harsh, more gentle than it otherwise would be; he enables or compels himself to speak as much as possible in terms of praise rather than in terms of blame.

The inhabited, prosperous and large city is the first, in itself not important example of a practice of great importance. Let us think above all of the virtues. On a number of occasions Xenophon gives lists of virtues. Out of those lists one can easily construct a comprehensive list of all virtues which he regarded as such. In describing the character of a man who was not in all respects admirable but on the whole deserved praise, it is sufficient for Xenophon not to mention the virtues which the individual in question lacked; he does not have to speak explicitly of his blemish or blemishes. Here we mention only his silence on Cyrus' piety in his eulogy of Cyrus (I 9).

The second Xenophontic device which must be discussed at this point is his use of *legetai* (he, she, it is said to . . .). It makes a difference whether a human being is said to possess such and such qualities and whether he possesses them in fact. Artaxerxes and Cyrus are introduced as the sons of Dareios and Parysatis. When Xenophon speaks of the parents of the older Cyrus, in the *Education of Cyrus* (I 2.1), he says that Cyrus is said to be the son of Kambyses and that his mother is agreed upon to have been Mandanes. Was the paternity of Dareios known to a higher degree than was that of Kambyses? And in what way? And does this help to explain Parysatis' preference for Cyrus? We do not know. We do not have to seek the reason why Cyrus was said to have had intercourse with Epyaxa, the wife of the king of the Kilikians (I 2.12). When Xenophon speaks of a city located near the river Marsyas, he says: "There Apollon is said to have flayed Marsyas after having defeated him when he challenged him to a contest regarding wisdom, and to have hung up his skin in the cave from which the sources (of the river Marsyas) issue. . . . There Xerxes is said to have erected (magnificent buildings) when he returned from Greece after having been defeated in that battle" (I 2.8–9). Xenophon treats here a mythical and a non-mythical story as equally trustworthy or untrustworthy. The conflict between Apollon and Marsyas was foolishly provoked by Marsyas who received condign punishment; the conflict between Xerxes and the Greeks was foolishly provoked by Xerxes, who was of course much less severely punished: the object of the conflict between Xerxes and the Greeks was not wisdom. The parallel treatment of the two stories draws our attention to the broad and in a sense comprehensive theme "gods and men." Yet this theme is not strictly comprehensive, let alone all-comprehensive, because of the equivocity of "gods." For instance, "The Syrians held the big and tame fishes of the river Chalus to be gods, and did not permit anyone to harm them, nor doves" (I 4.9): are these Syrian gods regarded as gods also by the Greeks? or are only those gods truly gods that are said by the Greeks to be gods? and are the latter regarded as gods by Xenophon in particular? There is surely a very important agreement in this matter between the Greeks and the Persians, in particular as regards sacrificing and swearing (I 8.16–17; II 2.9). The conflict between Greeks and Persians after Cyrus' death turns precisely on the question as to which of the two sides broke the solemnly sworn treaty. When addressing Tissaphernes, the Greek general Klearchos takes it for granted that they both agree as to the sanctity of oaths and its ground: the universal rule of the gods (II 5.7, 20–21, 39). When Cyrus' army succeeded in crossing the Euphrates River on foot, the event seemed to the people living in that place to be divine, and the river plainly to have retired before Cyrus as the man who was to be the king. The omen soon proved to be misleading, just as Cyrus' interpretation of the predictions of the Greek soothsayer proved to be wrong (I 4.18; I 7. 18–19).

The points which we have stated or indicated are brought together at the end of Book Two. Xenophon had narrated how most of the Greek generals (*strategoi*) and quite a few Greek captains (*lochagoi*) had been treacherously murdered by the Persians, and is now describing the characters of the murdered generals. One of these generals, the Thessalian Menon, proves to have been a man of unbelievable wickedness; not only was he a deceiver, liar, and perjurer; he prided himself on using these qualities and ridiculed those men who were foolish enough to become their victims. He was the one who in a critical situation determined his fellow Greeks to follow Cyrus against the king (I 4.13–17). He was a friend, and guest friend of Ariaios, the commander of Cyrus' Persian troops, who after Cyrus' death betrayed Cyrus' Greek contingent to the Persian king (II 1.5; 2.1; 4.15). Klearchos at any rate suspected that Menon was responsible for the betrayal to the Persians of his fellow officers, whereas Ariaios makes the already murdered

Klearchos responsible while claiming that Menon and Proxenos, having denounced Klearchos' plotting, are greatly honored by the king (II 5.28, 38). Be this as it may, Xenophon concludes his statement on Menon as follows: "While Menon's fellow generals were killed for having campaigned against the king together with Cyrus, he was not killed although he had done the same things, but after the death of the other generals the king took revenge on him by killing him, not as Klearchos and the other generals who were beheaded, which is thought to be the quickest death, but, having been tortured alive for a year, is said to have met the end of an evil man" (II 6.29). The king of Persia punished most severely that Greek general whose crime, whose perjury, whose breach of solemnly sworn oaths, was most beneficial to him; Menon was punished for his impiety, not by any god, but by the human beneficiary of his crime. But this "is said" to have been done. It suffices to note that whereas in the case of the other murdered generals Xenophon tells us how old they were when they died, he is silent on this point in the case of Menon. The implicit premise of the justice or high-mindedness of the king of Persia is as credible as that of the gods' revenge of perjury. Through the quoted "he is said" sentence Xenophon is enabled to present things—all things, "the world"—as grander and better than they are (cf. Thucydides I 21.1) while indicating at the same time the difference between the naked truth and the adornment. He has succeeded, not indeed in mitigating his harsh condemnation of Menon—what useful purpose would have been served by such mitigation?—but nevertheless in speaking on the whole in terms of praise rather than in terms of blame.

With a slight exaggeration one may say that Book Two ends with Menon and Book Three begins with Xenophon taking the center of the stage. At any rate, the end of Book Two and the beginning of Book Three read as if they were meant to bring out the contrast between Menon and Xenophon, between the arch-villain and the hero. It remains to be seen whether Menon is truly the foil of Xenophon in the *Anabasis*.

In his first enumeration of the Greek contingents of Cyrus' army Xenophon mentions the generals of those contingents in this order: 1) Klearchos of Sparta, 2) Aristippos the Thessalian, 3) Proxenos the Boiotian, 4) Sophainetos the Stymphalian and Sokrates the Achaian (I 1.9–11); Menon is not mentioned here because he joined Cyrus' expedition after it had already begun its march inland (I 2.6). At any rate, the contingent led by Proxenos, and hence Proxenos, can well be said to occupy the central place in the initial enumeration. When describing the characters of the Greek generals at the end of Book Two, Xenophon speaks extensively only of three of them: Klearchos, Proxenos and Menon (II 6); Proxenos is again in the center. Why does Proxenos deserve that place?

Let us now see what we learn from the first two Books about Xenophon. It should go without saying that the "I" who is said to have said or written or thought something in the *Anabasis* (I 2.5; 9.22, 28; II 3.1; 6.6), unless this happens in a quotation from a speech explicitly ascribed to Xenophon, cannot be identified by anyone who has a decent respect for our author, with Xenophon, but only with Themistogenes of Syracuse. Xenophon himself occurs in these Books three times. In the first place he approaches Cyrus who is just passing by on horseback while surveying the two opposed armies and asks him whether he has any orders to give; Cyrus commands him to tell everyone that the sacrifices are favorable and that the entrails of the sacrificed beasts are fine. Xenophon was also fortunate enough to be able to satisfy Cyrus' curiosity regarding a similar point (I 8.15–17). This conversation is important, not so much because it takes place shortly before the fatal battle but because it is the only exchange between Xenophon and Cyrus recorded by Xenophon, just as there is only one exchange between Xenophon and Socrates in the *Memorabilia*; the former concerns sacrifices, the latter concerns the dangers inherent in kissing handsome boys. When Xenophon occurs in the *Anabasis* for the second time, he is in the company of Proxenos (II 4.15); when he occurs for the third time, he is in the company of two other generals (II 5.37, 41). In the central case, Proxenos is again somehow in the center.

But we must not completely overlook an occasion on which Xenophon is indeed not mentioned by name yet may very well have been meant. After the battle of Kunaxa, when Cyrus was already dead but his Greek mercenaries were victorious, the king sent heralds to the Greeks, one of them being the Greek traitor Phalinus, with the request to give up their arms. The chief speaker for the Greeks was in fact the Athenian Theopompos, who explains to Phalinus that the only good things which they have are arms and virtue, but their virtue would not be of any avail without the arms; with the help of their arms they might even fight with the Persians about the Persians' good things. When Phalias heard this, he laughed and said, "You resemble a philosopher, young man, and speak gracefully" (II 1.13–14). Theopompos' thesis is identical to the one most familiar to us from Aristotle: virtue, and especially moral virtue, is in need of external equipment (*Eth. Nic.* 1178a 23–25, 1177a 27–34; compare *Mem.* I 6.10 and *Oec.* II 1–4). Why Xenophon should appear for a moment in the guise of a Theopompos ("God-sent") will become manifest soon.

After the murder of their generals and of many of their captains the Greeks were utterly disheartened, when they considered the situation in which they found themselves; only few of them could take food, kindled a fire, or went to their arms. In spite or because of this, all of them settled down to rest for the night—with one exception: "There was in the army a certain Xenophon from Athens who went with the expedition without being a general, a captain, or a soldier of any sort but Proxenos, being a guest-friend of his for a long time, had sent for him who was then at home. He promised him if he came to make him a friend of Cyrus whom Proxenos himself said he regarded as better for him than his fatherland." We begin now to understand why Proxenos is assigned a central place: he was the one who had suggested to Xenophon to join Cyrus' army (III 1.1–4). Proxenos was then not unqualifiedly attached to Boiotia or for that matter to Greece; he was to some extent uprooted. Apparently he had no doubt that Xenophon was not unqualifiedly attached to Athens or even to Greece, that he too was to some extent uprooted, although he does not state why this was the case. To whom or what was then Proxenos attached? From his very youth he desired to become a man capable of doing the great things and for this reason he took paid instruction from Gorgias of Leontini. After his intercourse with Gorgias he had come to believe that he was now capable both to rule and, by being a friend of the first men, not to be inferior to them in requiting them for the benefits he received from them; in this state of mind he joined Cyrus. He believed to acquire through his actions with Cyrus a great name and great power and much money; but he was obviously concerned with acquiring those things only in just and noble ways. He was indeed able to rule gentlemen but he was unable to inspire the soldiers with awe and fear of himself; he obviously feared to become hated by the soldiers; he thought that it was sufficient for being and [being] regarded a good ruler that one praise him who acted well and not praise him who acted unjustly (II 6.16–20). Proxenos and Xenophon, in contradistinction to Menon and even to Klearchos, were amiable gentlemen. Proxenos seems to be more attracted to the noble acquisition of fame, great power and great wealth anywhere on earth than to his fatherland. Xenophon is clearly distinguished from Proxenos by the fact that he was tougher, wilier and wittier than the latter. One is tempted to trace this difference to the difference between their teachers, Gorgias and Socrates. But Gorgias was also the teacher of Menon. The difficulty cannot be disposed of by the assertion that Socrates was a philosopher and Gorgias a sophist, for how do we know that Gorgias was a sophist according to Xenophon or his Socrates? (cf. Plato, *Meno* 70a5–b2, 95b9–c8, 96d5–7; cf. *Gorgias* 465c1–5). This much however may safely be said, that this difference between Proxenos and Xenophon is likely to be connected with Xenophon's having been familiar with Socrates. Must we then understand Xenophon—the Xenophon presented in the *Anabasis*—in the light of Socrates?

When Xenophon had read the letter from Proxenos, he communicated with Socrates of Athens about the journey. (Socrates is called here "Socrates of Athens" because Xenophon of Athens is not the writer.) Xenophon was obviously aware of the gravity of the step which he contemplated and sought therefore the counsel of an older and wiser man. Socrates suspected that Xenophon might get into trouble with the city by becoming a friend of Cyrus, since Cyrus was thought to have warred zealously together with the Spartans against Athens in the Peloponnesian War. But of course he did not know. Nor did his *daimonion* give him any guidance, or if it did, it was not of any authority for the city, to say nothing of the fact that its verdict might be disputable (cf. Plato, *Theages* 128d8–e6). He therefore advised Xenophon to go to Delphi and to communicate with the god about the journey. Xenophon followed that advice and asked Apollon in Delphi to what god he should sacrifice and pray in order to make the contemplated journey in the most noble and best way and, after having performed noble actions, to return safely. Apollon told him to which gods he ought to sacrifice. Xenophon does not tell us why Apollon did not give him any guidance regarding the god or gods to whom he ought to pray. On his return to Athens, he reported at once to Socrates. Socrates was somewhat taken aback: instead of asking the god first whether it would be better for Xenophon to make the journey or to stay at Athens, he had by himself decided to go and asked the god only how he could make the journey in the most noble way. Xenophon must have thought that the question as to whether becoming a friend of Cyrus was in itself desirable, and in particular as to whether the Athenians' reaction to this was worth considering, could be answered by his own unassisted powers, but that no human being could know whether the journey would be beneficial to Xenophon (cf. *Mem.* I 1.6–8; cf. *Hellen.* VII 1.27). Perhaps Xenophon, as distinguished from Socrates, was rash in underestimating the hostile reaction of the city of Athens to his joining Cyrus. Socrates merely replied that after he had addressed to Apollon the second or secondary question, he must do what the god had commanded him to do. Therefore Xenophon sacrificed to the gods whom Apollon had mentioned and left Athens (III 1.5–8): he is as silent about prayers as Apollon.

The agreements as well as the disagreements between Xenophon and Socrates regarding the oracle make it all the more necessary for us to return to the question as to whether the Xenophon presented in the *Anabasis* must be understood in the light of Socrates, in other words, as to what precisely is the difference between the two men. Xenophon was a man of action: he did the political things in the common sense of the term, whereas Socrates did not; but Socrates taught his companions the political things with the emphasis on strategy and tactics (*Mem.* I 2.16–17; 6.15; III 1). What this difference means in simple practical terms appears when we remember the three ends which Proxenos so nobly pursued: a great name, great power and much wealth. Socrates, we know, was very poor and in no way dissatisfied with this condition. As to Xenophon, he returned from the expedition with Cyrus in very comfortable circumstances (V 3.7–10). This proves that he exercised successfully the economic art in the common sense of the expression. But this implies that Xenophon, as distinguished from Socrates, was desirous of wealth, of course only of nobly acquired moderate wealth. In this respect he resembles Ischomachos who taught Socrates the economic art, not exercised by Socrates, rather than Socrates; Xenophon also makes us think of his contemporary and friend Kritoboulos whom Socrates tried to teach the economic art, but in his case Xenophon leaves it open whether Socrates had any success (cf. the *Oeconomicus*). We hardly go too far by saying that the principle which individualizes Xenophon in the *Anabasis* comes to sight by the contrast between him and Socrates, and not by that between him and Proxenos, to say no further word of Menon.

Cyrus deceived Xenophon as well as Proxenos about the purpose of his expedition; he did not say a word to anyone about his plan to depose or kill the king except to Klearchos, the most renowned general in his employment. But after his army had come to Kilikia, everyone saw that the expedition was aimed against the king. Yet most of the Greeks—Xenophon being one of them—did not abandon Cyrus out of shame before one another or before Cyrus. Xenophon was as disheartened as everyone else after the Persians' treachery but then he had during a short slumber a most astounding dream. He dreamed that a lightning had struck his father's house and had set it altogether on fire so that no one could escape. This dream was in one respect comforting: Xenophon seemed to see a great light coming from Zeus; but on the other hand, Zeus is a king and might show by a dream what was awaiting those who had dared to attack the king of Persia (III 1.9–12; cf. I 3.8, 13, 21; 6.5, 9; II 2.2–5). The dream brought Xenophon, and Xenophon alone, to his senses: he must do something, and at once. He gets up and calls first Proxenos' captains together. He addresses to them a speech which is quoted in full and in which he sets forth clearly and forcefully the dangers to which they are exposed as well as the great benefits accruing to the Greeks from the Persians' treachery: the Greeks are now no longer under an obligation to comply with the treaty; they may now justly take of the Persians' possessions whatever and however much they like. The judges of the contest are the gods, who will be on the side of the Greeks, as is reasonable to assume; for the oaths were broken by the Persians while they were strictly observed by the Greeks. Xenophon mentions in this speech the gods five times. He concludes the speech by promising the captains his full cooperation and even more than that: if they wish him to lead them, he will not use his youth as a pretext for declining the leadership. He is naturally elected to be their leader, i.e., the successor to Proxenos, with the unanimity of all who were in fact captains and even Greeks (III 1.12–26). This is the beginning of Xenophon's ascent: through a single speech, spoken at the right moment, and in the right way, he has become from a nobody a general.

Proxenos' captains next called together the generals and other high commanders who had survived the bloodbath, of all Greek contingents. Introduced by the oldest of Proxenos' captains, Xenophon is asked to say to this more stately assembly what he had said to Proxenos' captains; but he does not simply repeat himself. The second speech is again quoted in full. He puts now the emphasis on the fact that the salvation of the Greeks depends decisively on the mood and conduct of the commanders; they must act as the models for the soldiers. Therefore, the most urgent thing to do is to replace the murdered commanders; for everything, especially in war, depends on good order and discipline. In this speech, the gods are mentioned only once. The officers then proceed to the election of five new generals, one of these being Xenophon (III 1.32–47).

Shortly after that election, when the next day was about to begin to break, the commanders decided to call an assembly of the soldiers. The soldiers were first briefly addressed by the Spartan Cheirisophos and then by the Arcadian Kleanor, who had been assigned the central place in Xenophon's enumeration of the newly elected generals (III 1.47). Kleanor's speech is about twice as long as Cheirisophos' and is devoted to a rehearsal of the Persian treachery, about which Cheirisophos had been silent. Accordingly, Cheirisophos refers only once to the gods, but Kleanor four times. Yet their speeches served only as preludes to the speech by which Xenophon addressed this most stately assembly before which he appeared in as stately an attire as he possibly could: he wished to be attired becomingly for victory as well as for death on the field of honor. When he mentioned the many fine hopes of salvation which they may have if they wage ruthless war against their enemies, a man sneezed. Thereupon all soldiers with one impulse made obeisance to the god (cf. Aristophanes, *Knights* 638–45). Xenophon grasped the opportunity thus offered with both hands or without any false shame; he interpreted the sneezing as an omen from Zeus the Savior and proposed that they vow to offer sacrifices to that god as soon as they come to a friendly land, but to make a vow also to offer sacrifices to the other gods according to every man's ability. He put this proposal to a vote; it was unanimously adopted. Thereupon they made their vows and chanted. After this pious beginning, Xenophon began his speech by explaining what he meant by the many fine hopes of salvation which the Greeks have. They are based in the first place on their having kept the oaths sworn by the god in contrast to the perjury committed by the enemy; hence it is reasonable to assume that the gods will be opposed to the Persians and will be allies of the Greeks, and the gods can of course be of very great help if they wish. Xenophon arouses the Greeks' hopes furthermore by reminding them of the deliverance of their ancestors with the gods' help from the Persians in the Persian wars. Even Cyrus' Greek contingents defeated the many more numerous Persians a few days ago with the gods' help and then the prize was Cyrus' kingly rule: but now the prize is the very salvation of the Greeks. Having arrived at this point, Xenophon ceases to mention the gods. As orator he had spoken of the gods in this third speech eleven times, whereas he had spoken of them in his first speech five times and in his central speech only once.

He turns next to purely human considerations or measures. In this connection he points out that if the Persians succeeded in preventing the Greeks
from returning to Greece, the Greeks might very well settle down in the
midst of Persia, so rich in all kinds of good things, not the least in beautiful
and tall women and maidens. Could the vision of himself as founder of a city
in some barbaric place be the second stage of his ascent? We recall that
Proxenos' invitation to join Cyrus could have implied his certainty as to the
lukewarmness of Xenophon's patriotism, not to say Xenophon's lack of
patriotism; this impression could seem to be reinforced by what Xenophon
says now to the army. Be this as it may, the final and by no means the least
important measures which he proposes to the army are the restoration and
even strengthening of the commanders' punitive powers, which must be
supported by the active and zealous assistance of every member of the army;
he demands that this proposal be put to the vote. He is strongly supported in
this matter by the Spartan Cheirisophos and the proposal is thereupon
unanimously adopted. Finally Xenophon proposes that Cheirosophos be
put in command of the van of the army on the march, and he and Timasion,
the two youngest generals, in command of the rear. This proposal too is
unanimously adopted. Xenophon has become quite informally, if not the
commander of the whole army, at least its *spiritus rector*. After the most
urgent matters have been settled, Xenophon reminds in particular those
who desire wealth that they must try to be victorious; for the victors will both
preserve what belongs to them and take what belongs to the defeated (III 2).
The economic art as the art of increasing one's wealth can be exercised by
means of the military art (*Oec.* I 15).

The Persians next tried with very minor success to corrupt the Greek
soldiers and even captains. They were more successful when they sent
bowmen and slingers against the Greek rear guard, which suffered considerable losses and were unable to retaliate. Xenophon thought of a device
which proved to be wholly useless. He was blamed by some of his fellow
generals and accepted the blame in good grace. By analyzing what had
happened more closely and by drawing on his knowledge of things military,
which he surely had not acquired during the present campaign, he found a
solution which promised to redress the Persians' superiority in slingers and
cavalry. Again his proposals were adopted.

In his speech to the soldiers Xenophon had explained to them that their
fear of being cut off from the way to Greece by the big and deep rivers, the
Tigris and Euphrates, was unfounded: all rivers, even though they are
impassable at a distance from their sources, become passable if one
approaches their sources (III 2.22). He had failed to mention there that this
solution brings up a new predicament: the predicament caused by mountain
ranges, by the ascent. After having defeated the Persians, the Greeks
reached the Tigris River at the deserted city of Larisa, originally Median,

which could not be taken by the Persians at the time when they conquered Media, until a cloud concealed the sun and the inhabitants thereupon fled from the city. The Greeks came next to another originally Median city, which the Persians also could not take until Zeus horrified the inhabitants with thunder. (Shortly before making this remark Xenophon uses the expression *legetai*: are we to think that Zeus' having caused the thunder is what was said as distinguished from what was known?) The Greeks continued their march while the Persians pursued them cautiously, especially after the Greeks had improved their tactical arrangements. Their situation improved in proportion as the country through which they had marched became more hilly, but whenever they had to descend from the hills to the plain, they suffered considerable losses. On one occasion there arose a difference of opinion between Cheirisophos and Xenophon which was soon amicably settled. The settlement required a strenuous uphill march, to which Xenophon, riding on horseback, encouraged the soldiers in question by a somewhat exaggerated promise. When one of the soldiers complained that the ascent was easy for Xenophon who was on horseback, while he was marching on foot carrying his shield, Xenophon leaped down from his horse, pushed the complaining soldier out of his place, took away the shield from him and marched on with it as fast as he could, although he had on his cavalry breastplate in addition to the infantryman's shield. But the rest of the soldiers sided with Xenophon, and by their striking and abusing the complaining soldier, forced him to take back his shield and to march on (III 4). Xenophon was not a Proxenos.

Another difference of opinion between Cheirisophos and Xenophon arose when the Persians began to burn down the villages near the Tigris which were well supplied with victuals. Xenophon seemed to be well pleased with the spectacle: as long as there was a treaty between the Greeks and the Persians, the Greeks were obliged to abstain from doing harm to the king's country but now the Persians themselves admit by their actions that the country is no longer the king's: therefore we ought to stop the Persian's incendiaries. Cheirisophos, however, thought that the Greeks too should set about burning, for in this way the Persians would stop the sooner. Xenophon, who may have remembered his thought that if the worst came to the worst, the Greeks could settle down in the midst of the king's possessions, did not reply. However this may be, the officers were greatly disheartened. Yet after the interrogation of the prisoners the generals decided to march north through the mountainous land of the Karduchians—a difficult land inhabited by a warlike people but not subject to the Persian king. This decision proved to be the Greeks' salvation. While it was taken by "the generals," its seed had been planted, as we have seen, by Xenophon's speech to the soldiers (III 5).

Books Two to Five and Seven begin with summaries which state very briefly what had been narrated before (but cf. also VI 3.1). In none of these summaries or introductions is the name of Xenophon mentioned. He may have wished to counteract the not involuntary but inevitable self-praise conveyed through the narration of his deeds and speeches. The introduction to Book Four is by far the most extensive, about as long as the introductions to Books Two, Three, Five and Seven taken together. Book Four is the central book. By failing to supply Book Six with an introduction, Xenophon brings it about that Book Four is the central Book also among the Books supplied with introductions. Is the doubly central position of Book Four justified by its content?

The Karduchians were no friends, let alone allies, of the Persian king. This does not mean that they gave the Greeks a friendly reception. On the contrary, when the Greeks entered their land, they fled into the high mountains, taking their women and children with them, and inflicted as many losses on the Greeks as they could. In fact, during the seven days during which they marched through the Karduchians' land, they had to fight all the time and suffered more evils than the king and Tissaphernes altogether had inflicted on them while they marched through Persia (IV 3.2). The difficulties were considerably increased by the snow which began to fall. Cheirisophos was now in sole command of the van and Xenophon of the rear. Communication between the van and the rear became very difficult especially since the rear was very hard-pressed by the enemy and the forward march of the rear began to resemble a flight. When Xenophon complained to Cheirisophos about his not having waited for the rear, the Spartan had a good excuse but could not suggest a solution; the solution was suggested by Xenophon, whose men had taken two prisoners. By having one of them slaughtered within the sight of the other, he induced the latter to help the Greeks to overcome the obstacles caused by his countrymen and to act as the Greeks' guide. The march through the land of the Karduchians reveals again the bravery and resourcefulness of the Greeks and especially of Xenophon. Despite the savage fighting with the barbarians, under a treaty Xenophon succeeded in recovering from them the Greek dead and burying those dead in a most becoming manner.

From the difficult and dangerous mountains of the Karduchians they descended to Armenia, which is lying in the plain and whose climate seemed to offer in every respect a relief from the hardship suffered from the former country and its inhabitants. Yet their entry into Armenia was blocked by a river difficult to cross, and the crossing was resisted by an army consisting of Persians and of Persian mercenaries, some of them Armenians. In addition, the Karduchians reappeared in force in the rear of the Greeks and likewise tried to prevent the Greeks' crossing the river. Thus the Greeks were again in great difficulties. In that situation Xenophon had a dream—just as in the night after Kunaxa—but the present dream was much less frightening, and when dawn came he reported it to Cheirisophos together with its favorable interpretation of Xenophontic origin. The good omen was confirmed by the sacrifices offered in the presence of all generals which were all favorable from the very beginning. Xenophon, who could always be easily approached by the soldiers if they had to tell anything related to the war, was now told by two young men that they had by accident discovered a ford. Xenophon showed his gratitude to the gods for the dreams and the other helps in the proper manner and informed Cheirisophos at once of the two young men's discovery of the ford. Before crossing the river, Cheirisophos put a wreath upon his head and the soothsayers were offering sacrifices to the river; these sacrifices too were favorable. In these circumstances it is not surprising that the Greeks succeeded in their enterprise. Contrary to what "Theopompos of Athens," who resembled a philosopher, had said, weapons and virtue were not the only good things within the power of the Greeks (II 1.12–13); or, if you wish, the gods' favor followed with a kind of necessity the Greeks' keeping their oaths. Yet if one wishes, one may also say that one of the virtues by which Xenophon distinguished himself was his piety, provided one adds that his piety is hard to distinguish from that combination of toughness, wittiness and wiliness which separated him from Proxenos and which revealed itself already to some extent in the query addressed by him to the god in Delphi. It surely differs *toto cælo* from the piety of a Nikias.

After their entry into Armenia the Greeks marched through western Armenia, which was ruled by Tiribazos, a "friend" of the king of Persia. Tiribazos tried to conclude a treaty with the Greeks. Despite their two experiences with Tissaphernes and the king, the Greek generals accepted the offer. But this time they were cautious enough to prevent another Persian treachery. The Greeks were helped and hindered by heavy snowfall. Xenophon's example showed them again a way out. Violations of the treaty had also been committed by some Greek soldiers who had wantonly burned down the houses in which they had been quartered; they were punished for their transgressions by having to live in poor quarters. Their further march through Armenia was again hampered by deep snow, and the north wind blowing full in their faces and freezing the men. Then one of the soothsayers told them to offer sacrifices to the wind; when this was done, it seemed quite clear to all that the violence of the storm abated (IV 5.4): "seeming quite clear to all" is more trustworthy than "what is said." Owing to the snow many of the human beings began to suffer from ravenous hunger; Xenophon did not know what the trouble was but when he learned it from an experienced man, he did the necessary things with the desired result.

While the march through the land of the hostile Karduchians inflicted many hardships on the Greeks, the march through Armenia was gay and the reception by the natives was very kindly. This was due to a great extent to an Armenian village chief (*komarchos*) with whom Xenophon succeeded in establishing a most cordial relation within the shortest time. Provisions and especially an excellent wine were ample. When Xenophon came the next day in the company of the village chief to look after the soldiers, he found them feasting, cheerful and most hospitable. With the help of the village chief Xenophon and Cheirisophos found out that the horses bred there were meant as a tribute to the king. Xenophon took one of the colts for himself and gave his own rather old horse to the village chief for fattening up and sacrifice, for he heard that it was sacred to Helios. He also gave colts to the other high commanders. (The number of horses bred for the king in Armenia was seventeen; the daughter of the village chief had been married nine days before, and nine is the center of seventeen. [IV 5.24]—Gods are mentioned by Xenophon as orator in his first three speeches by which he established his ascendancy seventeen times: III 1.15–2.39).

Perhaps we are now in a position to answer the question as to why Book Four—or at least the account of the march through the land of the Karduchians and through Armenia—is located in the center of the *Anabasis*. We might add here that Book Four is the only Book of the *Anabasis* in which no formal oaths (like "by Zeus," "by the gods," and so on) occur. The march through the Karduchians' country is the toughest and the march through Armenia is characterized by descriptions of gaiety: the Karduchians and the Armenians are in a way the two poles. When we turn from the *Anabasis* to the *Education of Cyrus* (III 1.14 and 38–39), we find in the latter work and only there a kind of explanation of the distinction accorded to Armenia in the *Anabasis*. The son of the king of Armenia had a friend, a "sophist," who suffered the fate of Socrates because the king of Armenia was envious of his son's admiring that "sophist" more than his own father and therefore accused that "sophist" of "corrupting" his son. Armenia seems to be the barbarian analogon to Athens. It is then not quite true that the Persian-Greek antagonism is of no or of only subordinate importance in the *Anabasis*.

From here we understand somewhat better than before the difference between Xenophon and Socrates. The Armenian analogon to Socrates is perfectly free from any desire for revenge with his pupil's father. More generally stated, he does not believe that virtue consists in surpassing one's friends in benefiting them, and in surpassing one's enemies in harming them; he tacitly rejects the notion of virtue which Socrates tries to instill into the mind of Kritoboulos (*Mem.* II 6.35; II 3.14), the gentleman's virtue, and which Cyrus is said to have possessed to an extremely high degree (*Anabasis* I 9.11,24,28; cf. ibid., V 5.20). The questionable character of this notion of virtue is pointed out not only by the Platonic Socrates (*Rep.* 335d11–12) but also by Xenophon's two lists of Socrates' virtues in whch courage (manliness) does not occur and in which justice is identified with never harming anyone in the slightest (*Mem.* IV 8.11 and *Apol. Soc.* 15–18).

The ascent of Xenophon or rather his native ascendancy showed itself in the sole serious rift between him and Cheirisophos. He had given to Cheirisophos the village chief as guide. Since the Armenian did not quite act according to Cheirisophos' wishes, the Spartan beat him without binding him; thereupon the Armenian ran away (IV 6.3). Proxenos would never have beaten the village chief; Cheirisophos beat him, just as Klearchos would have done, but failed to bind him; Xenophon would have beaten him if necessary but have taken the precaution of binding him; Xenophon keeps to the right mean.

When after some time their way was again blocked by hostile natives, Cheirisophos called together a council of generals. Two opposed proposals were made. Kleanor favored a straight attack on the barbarians' strong position. Xenophon also was no less eager to overcome the obstacle but to do it with the minimum loss of lives; he proposes to achieve the goal in the easiest way: the enemy position should be taken not by means of a frontal attack but by means of a feint, of "stealing." He appeals to the excellent training of the Spartan ruling class in stealing. After he has thus gained Cheirisophos' good will, the Spartan replies equally good-naturedly that the Athenians are outstanding in stealing public money, as is shown by the fact that they prefer to have the best thieves for their rulers. Xenophon's proposal is naturally adopted with a minor modification suggested by Cheirisophos and leads to an entire success. In a similar incident shortly thereafter it was again in the first place Xenophon's shrewd calculation, as distinguished from Cheirisophos' simple aggressiveness, which overcame the obstacle to the Greeks' onward march that was caused by other barbarian tribes (IV 7.1–14). After some further strenuous efforts the Greeks came finally within sight of the sea. Xenophon, who was in command of the rear, was so to speak the last Greek who was vouchsafed this deeply moving and beautiful sight. But this did not minimize in the least the greatness of his achievement: it was his prudent counsel which had saved the Greeks from the king's and the other barbarians' attempts to destroy them.

If there could be any doubt about this, it would be disposed of by the grand, solemn and gay celebration which the Greeks staged after having arrived at the Greek city of Trapezus, located at the Black Sea in the land of [the] Kolchians. They stayed for about thirty days in Kolchis where they found ample provisions partly by plundering and partly by buying from the Trapezuntianes. Thereafter they prepared the sacrifices which they had vowed. They sacrificed to Zeus the Savior and to Heracles the Leader as well as to the other gods to whom they had made vows. Here Xenophon seems to disclose the identity of the gods to whom the god in Delphi had advised him to sacrifice prior to his departure and which he had disclosed previously only to Socrates (III 1.6–8).

Next the question arose of how the army should continue its progress toward Greece proper. There was universal agreement that the rest of the journey should be made by sea. Cheirisophos promised that if he were sent to the admiral in command of the Spartan navy, he would bring back the ships required for the purpose. This proposal was approved by the army. Xenophon alone, who was the least sanguine, uttered a warning. He told the soldiers what they would have to do and how they would have to behave until Cheirisophos' return, and in particular that they could not be certain that Cheirisophos' mission would succeed. But when he drew their attention to the fact that they might have to continue their way by land and hence that the cities situated along the sea ought to be directed to repair the road, the soldiers protested loudly: under no circumstances would they continue to march by land. Xenophon wisely refrained therefore from putting his proposal to the vote but achieved what he regarded as indispensable by persuading the cities to take care of the roads; in addition, of the detachments which disregarded Xenophon's injunctions, some were destroyed by enemy action.

After Cheirisophos' departure Xenophon was in fact the chief commander of the whole Greek army. The Trapezuntianes did not wish to get into trouble with the Kolchians for the sake of approvisioning the Greek army and therefore led that army against the Drilai, the most warlike of the peoples of the Pontos who inhabited territory difficult of access. The Greeks' light armed troops could not take the enemy stronghold and it was quite impossible for them to retreat. In this situation Xenophon, asked for a decision, agreed with the view of the captains that an assault on the stronghold be made by the hoplites, for he put his reliance on the favorable sacrifices as interpreted by the soothsayers (V 2.9). The counsels of human prudence and the hints of the god proved to be in full agreement: the stronghold was taken by the hoplites. But this was not yet the end of the battle; an enemy reserve, apparently first observed by Xenophon, came to sight upon certain strong heights. That is to say: there was agreement between the view of the other commanders, and not of Xenophon in particular, and that of the soothsayers. The situation was as desperate as it was before Xenophon's intervention. Then quite unexpectedly and suddenly some god gave the Greeks a saving device: somebody—only god knows how and why—set a house on fire and this led to a panic on the part of the enemy; when Xenophon grasped the lesson supplied by chance, he gave orders that all houses, i.e., the whole city, be burned down. What was first called "some god," is now called "chance": *deus sive casus*. It is surely something different from human prudence or, from the point of view of the good pursuit of human prudence, something higher than human prudence which brought about the Greek victory (*Mem.* I 1.8). It was Xenophon's reliance on the superhuman, on the *daimonion*, which distinguished him from the other commanders and which showed itself with particular clarity after he had become in fact the commander-in-chief. One cannot help wondering how Xenophon's extraordinary piety went together with his extraordinary wiliness. As a human being he was surely less powerful than any god. But may he not have been wilier than any god? May not a slave be wilier than his master, however wily? Yet, the gods, in contradistinction to human beings, know everything (*Mem.* I 1.19, but compare *Symposium* 4.47); therefore, they will see through every human ruse. But is precisely the attribution of omniscience to the gods not part of a human ruse, of human flattering? The great difficulty which here remains in Xenophon or his Socrates is connected with the fact that according to him (or to them), the pious man is the man who knows the laws, or what is established by laws, regarding the gods, and that he never raises the question, "what is law?" (*Mem.* IV 6.4 and I 2.41–46). This difficulty cannot be resolved within the context of an interpretation of the *Anabasis*. It would be both simpler and less simple to say that Xenophon or his Socrates never raise the still more fundamental question, "what is a god?"

The Greeks were finally compelled to leave Trapezus by land. Only the least strong, led by the two oldest generals, were sent off by boat. Those who marched arrived on the third day in Kerasus, a Greek city on the sea where they stayed for ten days, made a review of the hoplites and counted them: 8,600 hoplites out of about 10,000 proved to have survived. Thereafter they distributed the money received from the sale of the booty. A tithe had been assigned to Apollon and to Artemis of Ephesus; each of the generals took his part to them in the place indicated by the god. Xenophon specifies how he applied the portion entrusted to him in honor of Apollon. As for the portion to be given by him in honor of Artemis, he ran into some difficulty because in the meantime he had been exiled by the city of Athens— presumably because he was fighting on the side of the Spartans against his fatherland—but the Spartans settled him in Skillus where he bought a plot of land for Artemis according to Apollon's oracular choice. The land was rich in beasts of chase; the hunting, to which the whole neighborhood was invited, took place in honor of the huntress-goddess. Xenophon had the temple to the goddess built as a replica of the Artemis-temple in Ephesus. It would indeed have been a shocking solecism if he had abandoned his piety or receded from its demands after his blessed return. His account of his life in Skillus is a fitting conclusion to his account of the supreme command which he exercised after Cheirisophos' departure.

From Kerasus the Greeks proceeded by sea or by land to the mountains of the Mossynoikians. The Mossynoikians to whom they came first attempted to prevent them from passing through their territory, but Xenophon arranged an alliance with those Mossynoikians who were enemies of the former. The attack upon the enemy stronghold led to a disgraceful defeat not only of the allied barbarians but also of those Greeks who had of their own free will accompanied them for the sake of plunder. On the next day however, the whole Greek army, properly prepared by sacrifices which were favorable, attacked and was entirely successful. The Greeks were naturally well received by the allied Mossynoikians. Those people were regarded by the soldiers as the most barbarous men whom they had met on their march, the most remote from the Greek laws, for they did in public what others would do only when they are alone, and when they were alone they would act as if they were in the company of others—talking to themselves, laughing by themselves, dancing wherever they chanced to be, as if they were giving an exhibition to others (V 4.33–34). We were previously led to believe that the Karduchians and the Armenians were the two poles whom the Greeks came to know on their march. We see now that the Mossynoikoi are more alien to the Greeks than either the Karduchians or the Armenians. This does not mean, as goes without saying, that the Mossynoikians lived in a "state of nature"; they lived under laws as well as all other tribes. All men live under laws; to this extent, law is natural to man or law belongs to man's nature. Yet it is nevertheless necessary to make a distinction between nature and law (cf. *Oec.* VII 29–30 and *Hiero* 3.9) and to preserve it. Some light falls on the seeming paradox if we observe the similarity of some traits of the most extreme barbarians with some traits of Socrates (cf. *Symposium* 2.18–19; cf. Plato, *Symposium* 175a7–b3, c3–d2, 217b7–c7, 220c3–d5).

When the Greeks came to the land of the Tibarenians, the generals were tempted to attack their fortresses but they abstained from this since the sacrifices were not favorable and all soothsayers agreed that the gods in no way permitted that war. So they marched peacefully through the Tibarenians' land until they came to Kotyora, a Greek city, a colony of the Sinopeans. There they stayed 45 days, in the first place sacrificing to the gods and each Greek tribe instituting processions and gymnastic contests. As for provisions, they had to take them by force, since no one sold them any. Thereupon the Sinopeans became frightened and sent an embassy to the army. The spokesman for the embassy was Hekatonymos, who was thought to be a clever speaker. He revealed his power of oratory by addressing to the Greek soldiers a few friendly words which were followed by a much more extensive and insulting threat to the effect that the Sinopeans might ally themselves with the Paphlagonians and anybody else against Xenophon's army. Xenophon disposed of the threat by not only contrasting the customs and actions of the Sinopeans with those of the Trapezuntians and even some of the barbarians through whose land they had passed, but by a much more effective counter-threat: the alliance with the Paphlagonians is at least as possible for Xenophon's army as for the Sinopeans. As a consequence of Xenophon's oratory Hekatonymos lost his standing among his fellow ambassadors and there was perfect harmony between the Sinopeans and the army. Xenophon had perfectly succeeded in defending the army against the charge of injustice; he had given a signal proof of his justice by presenting his possible recourse to war against Greeks in alliance with barbarians as an act of sheer self-defense.

Yet the harmony was not as perfect as it seemed at first. On the next day the generals called together an assembly of the soldiers and of the ambassadors from Sinope, in order to decide the question of whether the army should continue its journey by land or by sea; in either case they would need the help of the Sinopeans. Hekatonymos again made a speech. He asserted that to march through Paphlagonia was altogether impossible; the only way out was by sailing to Herakleia. Although the speaker was by no means trusted by all soldiers—some of them suspected him of being a secret friend of the king of the Paphlagonians—the soldiers voted to continue the journey by sea. Xenophon added this warning: the resolution is acceptable only if literally all soldiers will be embarked and accordingly if the necessary number of boats be provided. So new negotiations between the army and the Sinopeans became necessary. In this situation it occurred to Xenophon that, considering the magnitude of the Greeks' armed force in this out of the way region, it would be a resplendent thing if the soldiers were to increase the territory and power of Greece by founding a city. It would become a large city, considering the size of the army and the number of the people already settled in the region. Before talking to anyone, Xenophon sacrificed and consulted Cyrus' soothsayer. But that soothsayer was eager to return home—for he had his pockets filled with the money which Cyrus had given him for his true prophecy—and therefore betrayed to the army Xenophon's plan which he traced solely to the latter's desire to preserve for himself a name and power.

Here we seem to have reached, and already surpassed, the peak of Xenophon's ascent. Granted that the foundation of a great Greek city "in some barbaric place" (Plato, *Republic* 499c9) would have redounded to Xenophon's name and power, was that name and power not amply deserved? Would his action not have been beneficial, not only to him but to Greece and hence to the human race? Had he not justly and piously performed anything, and more than anything, that one could expect from someone who had joined the expedition of Cyrus as a nobody and apparently for rather frivolous reasons? Xenophon was fit to the highest degree not only to be the supreme commander of the army but to become the founder of a city, worthy of the greatest honor during his life and especially after his death: the honors awarded to the founder of a city. But then, in the last moment, that highest and so well-deserved honor is snatched away from him not by any divine ill-will but by a greedy soothsayer. It goes without saying that the gods did not come to Xenophon's assistance in that matter.

But perhaps we have not paid sufficient attention to the true difficulty. When the soldiers heard of Xenophon's still undivulged plan to found a city far away from Greece, the majority disapproved of it. In an assembly of the soldiers a number of men attacked the plan. Xenophon however listened in silence. Timasion, who officially was Xenophon's fellow commander of the rear (III 2.37–38), declared that one must not esteem anything more highly than Greece and hence not think of staying in the Pontos (V 6.22). Tacitly, perhaps unknowingly, Timasion was opposing Proxenos' invitation addressed to Xenophon to join Cyrus' expedition, for the invitation was based on the premise that it is perhaps right to regard Cyrus as better for oneself than one's fatherland (III 11.4). Xenophon fails to reply to that grave, if implicit, charge: was the thought that one can esteem a barbarian prince or king more highly than one's fatherland not an act of profound injustice, perhaps even the root of Xenophon's injustice?

But, to repeat, Xenophon remained silent. Only when he was reproached for trying to persuade the soldiers privately and for sacrificing privately, instead of bringing the matter before the assembly, was he compelled to stand up and to speak. He begins by stating that, as they knew through their own seeing, he sacrifices as much as he can both regarding the soldiers and himself in order to achieve by speaking, thinking and doing what will be most noble and best both for the soldiers and himself. In other words, the soothsayer's distinction or opposition between Xenophon's and the soldiers' interest is a vicious imputation. In the present case, Xenophon continues, he sacrificed solely in order to find out whether it would be better to speak to the soldiers and to do the required things or not to touch the matter at all (V 6.28). This means in plain English that he did not consult the sacrifices regarding the advisability of his thinking about the founding of a city. The case resembles his conduct toward Proxenos' invitation to join Cyrus' expedition when Xenophon, deviating from Socrates' counsel, asked the god in Delphi not whether he should join that expedition but what he should do in the way of sacrifices and prayers in order to make the journey in the most noble manner (III 1.7). Yet there is this important difference between the two cases: in the case of Proxenos' invitation, Xenophon himself made the decision to join Cyrus' expedition; in the case of the founding of a city, he found out from the soothsayer the most important thing, namely, that the sacrifices were favorable: so that there was nothing wrong with thinking about the founding of a city. But thinking is one thing; speaking and doing are entirely different things. Xenophon was prevented from consulting the sacrifices regarding speaking and doing, not by unfavorable sacrifices or by his own decision, but by the very soothsayer. This happened in the following manner. The soothsayer had told Xenophon the truth about the sacrifices since he knew of Xenophon's thorough knowledge in this field of human endeavor; but he added of his own the warning that, as the sacrifice revealed, some fraud and plot against Xenophon was being prepared; for he knew—not indeed from the sacrifices—that he himself was plotting to slander Xenophon before the soldiers by asserting that Xenophon intended to found a city without having persuaded the army. Xenophon has thus succeeded perfectly in refuting the soothsayer's charge. But now, he goes on, given the opposition of the majority, he himself abandons his plan and proposes that anyone who leaves the army before the end of the journey be regarded as having committed a punishable offense. His proposal was unanimously adopted. This decision naturally displeased the soothsayer greatly, for he was eager to go home with his money at once. His lone protest did not have the slightest effect on the generals. The case was different with some more powerful members of the army who had conspired with the Greeks of the Pontos against Xenophon. A rumor was launched that Xenophon had not given up his plan to found a city. There was a mutinous spirit abroad so that Xenophon found it advisable to call together an assembly of the army.

It was very easy for him to show even to the meanest capacity the stupidity of believing that he could deceive the whole army about his alleged plan to found a city in Asia while the large majority, if not all except himself, were eager to return to Greece. Regardless of whether the imputation of that folly was due to one man or to more than one, it stemmed from envy, a natural consequence of the great honors awarded to him which were the natural consequences of his great merits. He had never prevented anyone from acquiring the same or greater merits: by speaking, fighting or being awake (V 7.10). The tripartition "speaking, fighting, being awake" takes the place of the tripartition "speaking, thinking, doing" (V 6.28) but fighting now takes the place which thinking occupied in the earlier discussion, because thinking was there central for the reason given when we discussed that passage; "thinking" is now replaced by "being awake" since it is intended as "worrying," a special kind of thinking (*merimnai, phrontizein*). Xenophon is willing to cede his authority to anyone who shares his deserts but to a slight degree. This is the end of his defense. But he has an important point to add. The greatest danger that threatens the army does not come from a plan to found a city or similar things but from the lack of discipline in the army which has already led to terrible crimes, partly told to Xenophon now for the first time and as a whole told by him for the first time to the army; it will in the future inevitably lead to its destruction. Xenophon has turned from defense to attack, and this turn is entirely successful. The soldiers spontaneously move and resolve that henceforth those responsible for the crimes committed will be punished and that those who in the future will start illegal proceedings will be put on trial for their lives; the generals will be responsible for the proceedings against all crimes committed since Cyrus' death and the captains will form the jury. At Xenophon's advice and with the approval of the soothsayers, it is further enacted that the army be purified and the purification was performed.

This was not yet the end of Xenophon's defense turned into attack. It was resolved—Xenophon does not say at whose suggestion—that the generals themselves should be prosecuted for any offenses they might have committed. One of the generals accused of misconduct was Xenophon himself; he was accused by some of having beaten soldiers from *hybris*, i.e., without necessity. This means that at this time the difference between him and Proxenos becomes the theme. It was as easy for him to defend himself against the charge of acting against the soldiers from *hybris* as it was to defend himself against the charge that he would found a colony against the will of the army. In continuing he asks the soldiers to remember not only the harsh actions which he was compelled to perform for their benefit but also the kind ones. His speech ends with this memorable sentence: "It is noble as well as just and pious and more pleasant to remember the good things rather than the bad ones." It is pleasant to remember bad things after one has come safely through them, although even as regards the pleasures of memory the good things are preferable to the bad ones. At any rate, from every point of view there seems to be in the last analysis a harmony between the noble, the just, the pious and the pleasant. No wonder then that Xenophon speaks as much as possible in terms of praise rather than in terms of blame. It should go without saying that his audience complied with the advice with which he concluded his speech.

Xenophon's trial leads then to a complete acquittal. Perhaps nothing shows more clearly the difference between him and Socrates than the fact that Socrates' trial culminated in his capital punishment. But we must not forget that Xenophon's plan to found a city failed.

In Book Five there occurs a somewhat larger number of oaths pronounced by Xenophon himself than in all preceding Books.

The dissatisfaction of the army which led to Xenophon's accusation was not altogether unfounded. If we are not "excessively pious" (Herodotus II 37.1)—and nothing and no one forces us to be so—we may admit that Xenophon has indeed succeeded perfectly in vindicating his piety; but did he vindicate his justice? Did he meet the implicit charge that he esteemed something more highly than Greece? More than that: is full devotion to Greece the sole or even the highest ingredient of justice? Must one not, just as in the case of horses, prefer not the indigenous or homebred, the children of the fatherland, but the best human beings (*Cyropaedia* II 2.26. Dakyns *ad loc.* observes: "Xenophon's breadth of view: virtue is not confined to citizens, but we have the pick of the whole world. Cosmopolitan Hellenism.")? Xenophon has described an army, nay, a political society, which is constructed according to this highest standard in his *Education of Cyrus*. What then is the difference from the point of view of justice between the hero of *The Education of Cyrus*, the older Cyrus, and Xenophon? The older Cyrus achieved what he achieved partly by virtue of his descent, his inheritance: he was on both sides the heir of a long line of hereditary kings; Xenophon had no such advantages. Granted that from the highest point of view only knowledge of how to rule gives a man a right to rule—and not, for instance, inheritance (cf. *Mem.* III 9.10), does not knowledge of how to rule need some iron alloy, some crude and rough admixture in order to become legitimate, i.e., politically viable? Is, to use a favorite term of Burke, "prescription" not an indispensable ingredient of non-tyrannical government, of legitimacy? In a word, "justice" is an ambiguous term; it may mean the virtue of the man which consists in surpassing his friends in benefiting them and his enemies in harming them (*Mem.* II 6.35); but it may also mean the virtue of a Socrates whose justice consists in not harming anyone even in a little thing (*ibid.* IV 8.11). While Xenophon undoubtedly possessed the justice of a man, he can hardly be said to have possessed the justice of Socrates. This does not mean that his place is near to that of the older Cyrus. One fact settles this question to our full satisfaction: the enjoyment which Cyrus derived after his first battle from looking at the faces of the slain enemies was too much even for his own grandfather, the tyrannical king of Media, to bear (*Cyrop.* I 4.24); cruelty is indeed an indispensable ingredient of the military commander as such (*Mem.* III 1.6), but there is a great variety of degrees of cruelty. Xenophon stands somewhere in between the older Cyrus and Socrates. By this position he presents to us not a lack of decisiveness but the problem of justice: justice requires both the virtue of a man (and therewith the possible emancipation of cruelty) and the virtue of Socrates; the virtue of the man points to Socratic virtue and Socratic virtue requires as its foundation the virtue of the man; both kinds of virtue cannot coexist in their plenitude in one and the same human being. Xenophon may have regarded himself as the closest approximation best known to himself to their coexistence in one and the same human being. (Cf. Strauss, *Xenophon's Socrates*, 144.) Surely, Xenophon (does not equal Plato) presents himself in his difference from Socrates.

Shortly after Xenophon's acquittal and the restoration of military discipline as well as the conclusion of a peace treaty with the Paphlagonians, from whom the Greeks had for a time partly procured their provisions through robbery, Cheirisophos returned from his mission to the Spartan admiral Anaxibios. He did not bring the boats which he had promised or hoped to bring but he brought words of praise and a promise from Anaxibios that if the army would succeed in getting out of the Pontos, he would employ them as mercenaries. This increased the soldiers' hope for a speedy return to Greece and hence for possessions which they might take home. They thought that if they were to choose a single commander for the whole army, they would achieve their goal best because of the obvious advantages of monarchic rule (greater secrecy and dispatch and the like) for purposes of this kind. With this thought in mind they turned to Xenophon. The captains told him that the army wanted him to be sole commander and tried to persuade him to accept this position. He was not entirely adverse to the prospect of being sole, absolute ruler, not responsible to any one; he considered that this position would increase his honor among his friends and his name in Athens and perhaps he might do some good to the army. But when he considered how immanifest to every human being the future is, he saw that the exalted position offered him brought with it also the danger of his losing even the reputation which he had gained heretofore. Unable to make up his mind, he did what any sensible man confronted with such a dilemma would do; he communicated his difficulty to the god. He sacrificed two victims to Zeus the King. That god distinctly indicated to him that he should not strive for the position nor accept it if he were elected to it. The oracle was less clearly unfavorable. But instead of saying this directly, straightaway, Xenophon gives a brief survey of his earlier experiences with the omina related to his fate: his experience with his attempt to found a city and perhaps with his accusation throw a new light on the old omina. As for his consulting Zeus the King, this was the god who had been named to him by the Delphic oracle. Furthermore, he was the same god who, Xenophon believed, had shown him the dream when he set out to take care of the army together with others, i.e., after the murder of the generals; the dream was ambiguous (III 1.12) but originally Xenophon had taken it as rather a good omen. Finally, he remembered now that at the very beginning of his setting out from Ephesus to join Cyrus, a sitting eagle screamed upon his right; as a soothsayer explained to him, this omen was a great one, by no means befitting a nobody, indicating great fame but at the same time great toil, for birds are most apt to attack the sitting eagle; nor did that omen prognosticate the acquisition of great wealth, for the flying eagle is more likely than the sitting one to take what it wants.

For a moment one is tempted to believe that not the plan to become the founder of a Greek city in the Pontos but the election to supreme command of the whole army, to "the monarchy" (VI 1.31), would have been the peak of Xenophon's ascent (cf. *Cyropaidia* VIII 2.28; Aristotle, *Eth. Nic.* 1115a32). But can "monarchy" equal "foundation" in grandeur, in sacredness?

In an assembly of the soldiers all speakers said that one man should be elected commander of the whole army and after this proposal was approved Xenophon was proposed for that position. In order to prevent his election, which seemed to be imminent, he had to state the case against his election as clearly and as forcibly as he could. That case had been made in the required manner by the gods, but in his speech to the army he is to begin with silent on this theme; to begin with, he keeps his pious thought private, for himself. In his public speech, he speaks to begin with publicly, politically, as a political man. The reason seems to be this. He does not merely wish to prevent his own election but to give the army some guidance as to whom they should elect. As for that guidance he had no oracular indication. He had to make the decision himself—just as he had made the decision in Delphi as to whether or not he should accept Proxenos' invitation. Xenophon disapproves of the thought that the army would elect him as supreme commander when a Spartan was present and available; in the circumstances the election of Xenophon would be inexpedient both for the army and for Xenophon himself. As the Spartans have shown by their conduct in the late war, they will never permit leadership to go to a non-Spartan (cf. III 2.37). Xenophon assures the army that he will not be so foolish as to cause dissension if he is not elected: to rebel against the rulers while a war is going on means to rebel against one's own salvation. The seemingly casual observation of Xenophon regarding the Spartan preponderance and her concern with it must never be neglected; it helps to explain the partly true and partly alleged pro-Spartan bias of his writings. The immediate reaction to Xenophon's observation was indeed anti-Spartan; whether and to what extent that immediate reaction was intended by Xenophon perhaps as a warning to the irascible Spartan candidate against misuse of his power in case of his election it is impossible to say. The reference to the Peloponnesian War is also helpful and even more helpful for indicating the questionable character of fidelity to Greece as the sole or most important ingredient of justice. At any rate Xenophon is now compelled to counteract the effect of this seemingly pro-Spartan move. Swearing by all gods and goddesses he now states that the gods have stated to him in a manner which even a tyro in such matters could not misunderstand that he, Xenophon, must abstain from "the monarchy"; to accept that position would be bad for the army but in particular also for Xenophon (cf. *Mem.* I 1.8). It literally goes without saying that Cheirisophos is elected sole and absolute commander. He gladly accepts the honor and confirms Xenophon's suspicion that the Athenian would have had a very hard time with the Spartans. The fact that the choice lay only between Xenophon and Cheirisophos shows that the struggle for hegemony within Greece was still the Spartan-Athenian struggle and therefore that the identification of justice with fidelity to Greece remained questionable.

Under Cheirisophos' command the Greeks sailed on the next day along the coast to Herakleia, a Greek city. But the soldiers still had to settle the question whether they could continue their journey from there by land or by sea. The question was inseparable from that of how to approvision the army. One of the men who had opposed Xenophon's plan to found a city proposed that they should demand money from the Herakleotai: should one not send Cheirisophos, the elected ruler, and perhaps even Xenophon to Herakleia for that purpose? Both leading men strongly opposed the use of violence against a friendly Greek city. The soldiers elected therefore a special embassy. But they met only firm resistance on the part of the Herakleotai. This led to a mutinous mood of the majority of the Greek soldiers who were Achaians and Arcadians and refused to be dictated to by a Spartan or an Athenian. They separated therefore from the minority and elected ten generals of their own. In this way, the command of Cheirisophos was terminated about a week after his election: an indication of the impermanence of the Spartan hegemony. One sees in retrospect how well the gods had advised Xenophon regarding the rejection of "the monarchy." He was displeased with the splitting up of the army—a splitting up which, he thought, endangered the safety of all its parts. But he was persuaded by Neon, the commander immediately subordinate to Cheirisophos of the latter's contingent (V 6.36), to join, together with Cheirisophos and his contingent, the force commanded by Klearchos, the Spartan commander at Byzantion. Xenophon gave in to Neon's advice perhaps because it agreed with the oracular indication of Herakles the Leader; surely that indication was not, as far as we know, supported by any calculation or guesswork on the part of Xenophon. But is this quite correct? Xenophon was contemplating leaving the army and sailing home, but when he sacrificed to Herakles the Leader and consulted him, the god indicated to him that he should stay with the soldiers. Whether or to what extent Herakles' indication or Xenophon's or Neon's purely human persuading determined Xenophon, it is impossible to say. Thus the whole army was split into three parts: the Arcadians and Achaians, the troops of Cheirisophos, and those of Xenophon. Each part went in a different way in the direction of Thrace.

The Arcadians (and Achaians) disembarked by night at Kalpe Harbor; they immediately proceeded to occupy the villages of the neighborhood which abounded in booty; in fact the Greeks took a lot of booty. But when the Thracians recovered from the unexpected attack, they killed a considerable number of their assailants and cut off the retreat of their enemies. Cheirisophos, on the other hand, who had marched along the coast, arrived safely in Kalpe. Xenophon, the only Greek commander who had some cavalry, learned through his horsemen of the fate of the Arcadians. Thereupon he called his soldiers together and explained to them that their situation required that they save the Arcadians. Perhaps, he concluded, the god wishes to arrange things in this way that those who talked big are humbled whereas we, who begin with the gods, will have a more honorable fate. He made of course all the necessary arrangements. Timasion with the horses would be in the van; everything was to be done to create the impression that the troops relieving the besieged Arcadians were much more numerous than they in fact were; the first thing they did in the next morning was to pray to the gods. Eventually—be it through the wish of the god or through Xenophon's counsel or through both—the three parts of the army were reunited in Kalpe, which is located in Asiatic Thrace. The region was very fertile and attractive, so much so that the suspicion arose that the soldiers had been brought hither owing to the scheming of some who wished to found a city (VI 4.7). Yet the majority of the soldiers had joined Cyrus' expedition not from poverty at home but in order to make money in order to return to Greece loaded with riches. At any rate, after the failure of the Arcadians the whole army resolved that henceforth the proposal to split the army would be treated as a capital crime and that the generals elected by the whole army be restored to their power. The situation was further simplified by the death of Cheirisophos, who had taken a medicine for fever; his successor became Neon. In a way unforeseen by any human being Xenophon had thus become the "monarch," while the plan to found a city remained as abortive as before. The question is however unresolved of how the political difficulty obstructing an Athenian's monarchy in a period of Spartan hegemony can be overcome. As we shall see almost at once, it is resolved by an event which could be understood as an act of the god or Xenophon's piety.

As Xenophon next explained to an assembly of the soldiers, the army had to continue its journey by land, since no boats were available, and they had to continue it at once, since they had no longer the necessary provisions. Yet the sacrifices were unfavorable. This renewed the suspicion that Xenophon had persuaded the soothsayer to give a false report about the sacrifices because he still planned to found a city. The sacrifices continued to be unfavorable, so that Xenophon refused to lead out the army for approvisioning itself. An attempt made by Neon to get provisions from the nearby barbarian villages ended in disaster. Eventually provisions arrived by ship from Herakleia. Xenophon arose early in order to sacrifice with a view to an expedition and now the sacrifices were favorable. A soothsayer saw at about this time another good omen and therefore urged Xenophon to start the expedition against the enemy (Persians and their Thracian allies). Never before had the resistance of the gods to intended actions of the Greek army been so sustained. Needless to say, there were opportunities left to Xenophon to reveal his military and rhetorical skills. In the ensuing battle the Greeks were unmistakably victorious.

While the Greeks still waited for the arrival of Kleandros, they provisioned themselves from the nearby countryside, which abounded in almost all good things. Furthermore, the Greek cities brought things for sale to the camp. Again a rumor arose that a city was being founded and that there would be a harbor. Even the enemies tried to establish friendly relations with the new city which was alleged to be founded by Xenophon and turned to him with questions on this subject but he wisely remained in the background.

Eventually Kleandros arrived with two triremes but with no merchant ship. He arrived in the company of the Spartan Dexippus who had rather misbehaved in Trapezus. Thus it came to an ugly dissension between Kleandros and Agasias, one of the generals elected by the army. Despite all efforts of Xenophon and the other generals Kleandros took the side of Dexippus and declared that he would forbid every city to receive the Greek mercenaries, "for at that time the Spartans ruled all Greeks" (VI 6.9). Kleandros demanded the extradition of Agasias. But Agasias and Xenophon were friends. This precisely was the reason why Dexippus slandered Xenophon. The commanders called an assembly of the soldiers in which Xenophon explained to the army the gravity of the situation that had arisen: every single Spartan can accomplish in the Greek cities whatever he pleases. The conflict with Kleandros will make it impossible for the Greek mercenaries either to stay in Thrace or to sail home. The only thing to do is to submit to Spartan power. Xenophon himself, whom Dexippus had accused to Kleandros as responsible for Agasias' quasi-rebellion, surrenders to Kleandros for adjudication and advises every other man who is accused to do the same. Agasias swears by the gods and goddesses that he acted entirely on his own initiative: he follows Xenophon's example by also surrendering to Kleandros. Thanks to Xenophon's intervention the whole conflict is peaceably settled: he saved not only himself but so to speak all his comrades in arms, not only from the Persians and other barbarians but from the Spartans as well.

The Spartan admiral Anaxibios was induced by the Persian satrap Pharnabazus to arrange for the removal of the Greek army from Asia since it seemed to constitute a threat to his province. Anaxibios promised the commanders to hire the army as mercenaries in case they crossed over to Europe. The only man who was unwilling to consider Anaxibios' proposal was Xenophon, but he gave in when Anaxibios merely asked him to postpone his leaving the army until after the crossing. The soldiers next entered Byzantion but Anaxibios failed to give them the promised pay. On the other hand he wished to avail himself of the services of the mercenaries in a war with the Thracian Seuthes in which he was engaged. He succeeded in persuading the mercenaries to leave the city until they became aware that they were to be cheated of their pay; then they re-entered the city with the use of force. An ugly conflict threatened. Thinking not only of Byzantion and the army but also of himself, Xenophon intervened. When the soldiers saw him, they told him that here was his great chance: "You have a city, you have triremes, you have money, you have so many soldiers." He first attempted to quiet them down, and, after he had succeeded in this, called an assembly of the army and told them the following things: by avenging themselves on the Spartans for a deception attempted by a few Spartans and by plundering a wholly innocent city, they merely would make all Spartans and all allies of Sparta, i.e., all Greeks, their enemies; the experience of the Peloponnesian War has shown them all how mad their proceedings and intentions are; it will lead to a hopeless war between the small army of mercenaries and the whole power of Greece which is now under Spartan control; all justice is on the side of the Spartans, for it is unjust to take revenge on the Spartans for the deception attempted by a few Spartans and by plundering a wholly innocent city—the first Greek city which they occupied—while they never harmed a barbarian city; the mercenaries themselves will become exiled by their fatherland and hence their fatherlands' and even their kin's enemies. He urges them that being Greeks they obey those who rule the Greeks and thus try to obtain their rights. If they fail in this, they will at least avoid being deprived of Greece. On Xenophon's entreaty the army resolved to send to Anaxibios a properly submissive message. Xenophon knew both when to resist and when to give in. So it came to pass that ultimately through Persian treachery even those Greeks who were willing to esteem Cyrus more highly than Greece were compelled to restore Greece to her rightful place. But—to say nothing of the justice of Cyrus' expedition against his brother—this is not yet the end of the story.

Anaxibios' reply was none too gracious. This gave a Theban adventurer the opportunity to try to sabotage the arrangement which Xenophon had proposed. The next result however was that Xenophon by himself left Byzantion in the company of Kleandros. Thereafter there arose a dissension among the generals as to where the army should move; this led to a partial disintegration of the army—a result welcome to Pharnabazus and therefore also to Anaxibios. But Anaxibios was about to hand over the command of the Spartan navy to his successor and was therefore no longer courted by Pharnabazus. Therefore Anaxibios asked Xenophon to return to the army and to bring back to Asia by all means the bulk of Cyrus' mercenaries; the soldiers gave Xenophon a friendly reception, glad as they were to leave Thrace for Asia. Given the intra-Spartan jealousies, fidelity to Sparta and hence to Greece was not easy, if not altogether impossible.

In this situation Seuthes renewed an earlier attempt to win Xenophon over to his side. Kleanor and another general had already before wished to lead the army to Seuthes, who had won their favor with gifts, but Xenophon refused to give in to Seuthes' wish. The new Spartan commander in Byzantion, Aristarchos, forbade the return of Cyrus' mercenaries to Asia. Xenophon had to fear being betrayed by the Spartan commander or by the Persian satrap. He therefore consulted the god as to whether he should not attempt to lead the army to Seuthes. Anaxibios' plot against Xenophon becoming now most manifest and the sacrifices being favorable, he decided that it was safe for him and for the army to join Seuthes. In their first meeting Xenophon and Seuthes stated what kind of help each expected to receive from the other; Xenophon was especially concerned with what kind of protection against the Spartans Seuthes would offer to the mercenaries. In an assembly of the soldiers Xenophon stated to them, before they made up their minds, what Aristarchos on the one hand and Seuthes on the other promised to them; he advised them to provision themselves forthwith from the villages from which they could safely do so. The majority of the soldiers thought that Seuthes' proposal was preferable in the circumstances. Thus Cyrus' mercenaries became Seuthes' mercenaries. But it soon became clear that Seuthes was not quite honest. He had invited the commanders to a banquet but he expected to receive gifts from them and especially from Xenophon prior to the banquet. This was particularly awkward for Xenophon, who was practically penniless at the moment. Still, when his turn came, he had had already a drink which enabled him to find a graceful way out.

Xenophon and his Greeks kept their bargain with their Thracian allies faithfully; they did their best to help Seuthes in subjugating his Thracian enemies. Yet there was the exorbitant cold of the Thracian winter. Above all, Seuthes' friend or agent Herakleides tried to cheat the Greek mercenaries of part of their pay. When found out by Xenophon, he incited Seuthes against him and attempted to induce the generals to defect from Xenophon. Xenophon began now to wonder whether it was wise to continue his alliance with Seuthes. In addition, as the pay for the soldiers was not forthcoming, they became very angry with Xenophon. At this moment, the Spartans Charminus and Polynikus sent by Thibron arrived and told the army that the Spartans were planning an expedition against Tissaphernes for which Cyrus' former army was urgently needed. This gave Seuthes a splendid opportunity for getting rid of the mercenaries and his debts to them at the same time. In an assembly of the soldiers the two Spartan emissaries laid their proposal before the soldiers who were delighted with it, but one of the Arcadians got up straightaway to accuse Xenophon who allegedly was responsible for the mercenaries' having joined Seuthes and received all the rich benefits of the soldiers' toils from Seuthes; Xenophon deserves capital punishment. Xenophon's ascent has finally led to the lowest descent. But ought one not also say that Xenophon's apology, which refers to deeds and speeches well known to innumerable men, is infinitely easier and at the same time infinitely more effective than Socrates'? Seuthes made a last minute attempt to prevent Xenophon's reconciliation with the Spartans by calumniating the latter. But Zeus the King, whom Xenophon consulted, dispelled all suspicions.

There followed a somewhat ambiguous reconciliation between Xenophon and Seuthes and as its consequence the payment of the debt still owed to the mercenaries, and thereafter an unambiguous reconciliation between Xenophon and all mercenaries and between Xenophon and the Spartans. Xenophon eventually showed by deed that he esteemed Greece more highly than Cyrus and other barbarians (III 1.4). He failed to show that he esteemed his fatherland more highly than Cyrus or Sparta because the city of Athens had exiled him (V 3.7, V 6.22, VII 7.57), as he tells us, for reasons which he fails to tell us. Could Socrates' apprehension when he heard of Proxenos' invitation be vindicated by the *Anabasis* as a whole?

Xenophon begins at once to wage war against the Persians with a view to capturing booty. He was rather successful in this enterprise.

The density of references to god, of oaths and in particular of formal oaths pronounced by Xenophon himself is greater in Book VII than in all preceding Books.

6

On Natural Law

Natural law, which was for many centuries the basis of the predominant Western political thought, is rejected in our time by almost all students of society who are not Roman Catholics. It is rejected chiefly on two different grounds. Each of these grounds corresponds to one of the two schools of thought which are predominant today in the west, *i.e.* positivism and historicism. According to positivism, genuine knowledge is scientific knowledge and scientific knowledge can never validate value judgments; but all statements asserting natural law are value judgments. According to historicism, science (*i.e.* modern science) is but one historical, contingent form of man's understanding of the world; all such forms depend on a specific *Weltanschauung*; in every *Weltanschauung* the "categories" of theoretical understanding and the basic "values" are inseparable from one another; hence the separation of factual judgments from value judgments is in principle untenable; since every notion of good and right belongs to a specific *Weltanschauung*, there cannot be a natural law binding man as man. Given the preponderance of positivism and historicism, natural law is today primarily not more than a historical subject.

By natural law is meant a law which determines what is right and wrong and which has power or is valid by nature, inherently, hence everywhere and always. Natural law is a "higher law" but not every higher law is natural. The famous verses in Sophocles' *Antigone* (449–460) in which the heroine appeals from the man-made law to a higher law do not necessarily point to a natural law; they may point to a law established by the gods or what one may call in later parlance a positive divine law. The notion of natural law

Reprinted with permission of the publisher from the *International Encyclopedia of the Social Sciences*, David L. Sills, editor; vol. 2, pp. 80–90. ©1968 by Crowell Collier and Macmillan, Inc.

presupposes the notion of nature, and the notion of nature is not coeval with human thought; hence there is no natural law teaching, for instance, in the Old Testament. Nature was discovered by the Greeks as in contradistinction to art (the knowledge guiding the making of artifacts) and, above all, to *nomos* (law, custom, convention, agreement, authoritative opinion). In the light of the original meaning of "nature," the notion of "natural law" (*nomos tēs physeōs*) is a contradiction in terms rather than a matter of course. The primary question concerns less natural law than natural right, *i.e.* what is by nature right or just: is all right conventional (of human origin) or is there some right which is natural (*physei dikaion*)? This question was raised on the assumption that there are things which are by nature good (health, strength, intelligence, courage, etc.). Conventionalism (the view that all right is conventional) derived its support in the first place from the variety of notions of justice, a variety incompatible with the supposed uniformity of a right that is natural. Yet the conventionalists could not deny that justice possesses a core which is universally recognized, so much so that injustice must have recourse to lies or to "myths" in order to become publicly defensible. The precise issue concerned then the status of that right which is universally recognized: is that right merely the condition of the living together of a particular society, *i.e.* of a society constituted by covenant or agreement, with that right deriving its validity from the preceding covenant, or is there a justice among men as men which does not derive from any human arrangement? In other words, is justice based only on calculation of the advantage of living togther, or is it choiceworthy for its own sake and therefore "by nature"? The two possible answers were given prior to Socrates. For our knowledge of the thought of the pre-Socratic philosophers, however, we depend entirely on fragments of their writings and on reports by later thinkers.

Socrates' disciple Plato is the first philosopher whose writings proper have come down to us. While Plato cannot be said to have set forth a teaching of natural law (cf. *Gorgias* 483e and *Timaeus* 83e), there can be no doubt that he opposed conventionalism; he asserts that there is a natural right, *i.e.* something which is by nature just. The naturally just or right is the "idea" of justice (*Republic* 501b; cf. 500c–d and 484c–d), justice itself, justice pure and simple. Justice is defined as doing one's own business or rather doing one's own business "in a certain manner," *i.e.* "well" (433a–b; 443d). A man (or rather his soul) or a city is just if each of its parts does its work well and thus the whole is healthy; a soul or a city is just if it is healthy or in good order (cf. 444d–e). The soul is in good order if each of its three parts (reason, spiritedness, desire) has acquired its specific virtue or perfection and as a consequence of this the individual is well-ordered toward his fellow men and especially his fellow citizens. The individual is well-ordered toward his fellow citizens if he assigns to each what is intrinsically good for him and hence what is intrinsically good for the city as a whole. From this it follows that only the wise man or the philosopher can be truly just. There is a natural order of the virtues and the other good things; this natural order is the standard for legislation (*Laws* 631b–d). One may therefore say that the natural right in Plato's sense is in the first place the natural order of the virtues as the natural perfections of the human soul (cf. *Laws* 765e–766a), as well as the natural order of the other things by nature good. But assigning to each what is good for him by nature is impossible in societies as we find them anywhere. Such assigning requires that the men who know what is by nature good for each and all, the philosophers, be the absolute rulers and that absolute communism (communism regarding property, women and children) be established among those citizens who give the commonwealth its character; it also requires equality of the sexes. This order is the political order according to nature, as distinguished from and opposed to the conventional order (*Republic* 456b–c; cf. 428e). Thus natural right in Plato's sense also determines the best regime, in which those who are best by nature and training, the wise men, rule the unwise with absolute power, assigning to each of them what is by nature just, *i.e.* what is by nature good for him. The actualization of the best regime proves indeed to be impossible or at least extremely improbable; only a diluted version of that political order which strictly corresponds to natural right can in reason be expected. The establishment of the best regime is obstructed in the last analysis by the body, the only thing which is by nature private (*Laws* 739c; *Republic* 464d) or wholly incapable of being common. Accordingly, sheer bodily ("brachial") force must be recognized as having a natural title to rule—a title indeed inferior to that deriving from wisdom but not destroyed by the latter (*Laws* 690a–c). Political society requires the dilution of the perfect and exact right, of natural right proper: of the right in accordance with which the wise would assign to everyone what he deserves according to his virtue and therefore would assign unequal things to unequal people. The principle governing the dilution is consent, *i.e.* the democratic principle of simple equality according to which every citizen possesses the same title to rule as every other (*Laws* 756e–758a). Consent requires freedom under law. Freedom here means both the participation in political rule of those unwise men who are capable of acquiring common or political virtue, and their possessing private property; law can never be more than an approximation to the verdicts of wisdom, yet it is sufficient to delineate the requirements of common or political virtue, as well as the rules of property, marriage and the like.

It is in accordance with the general character of Aristotle's philosophy that his teaching regarding natural right is much closer to the ordinary understanding of justice than in Plato's. In his *Rhetoric* he speaks of "the law according to nature" as the unchangeable law common to all men, but it is not entirely certain that he takes that law to be more than something generally admitted and hence useful for forensic rhetoric. At least two of his three examples of natural law do not agree with what he himself regarded as naturally right (*Rhetoric* 1373b4–18). In the *Nicomachean Ethics* (1134b18–1135a5) he speaks, not indeed of natural law, but of natural right. Natural right is that right which has everywhere the same power and does not owe its validity to human enactment. Aristotle does not give a single explicit example but he seems to imply that such things as helping fellow citizens in misfortune into which they have fallen in consequence of performing a civic duty, and worshipping the gods by sacrifices belong to natural right. If this interpretation is correct, natural right is that right which must be recognized by any political society if it is to last and which for this reason is everywhere in force. Natural right thus understood delineates the minimum conditions of political life, so much so that sound positive right occupies a higher rank than natural right. Natural right in this sense is indifferent to the difference of regimes whereas positive right is relative to the regime: positive right is democratic, oligarchic, etc. (cf. *Politics* 1280a8–22). "Yet," Aristotle concludes his laconic statement on natural right, "one regime alone is by nature the best everywhere." This regime, "the most divine regime," is a certain kind of kingship, the only regime which does not require any positive right (*Politics* 1284a4–15, 1288a15–29). The flooring and the ceiling, the minimum condition and the maximum possibility of political society, are natural and do not in any way depend on (positive) law. Aristotle does not explicitly link up his teaching regarding natural right with his teaching regarding commutative and distributive justice, but the principles of commutative and distributive justice cannot possibly belong to merely positive right. Commutative justice is the kind of justice which obtains in all kinds of exchange of goods and services (it therefore includes such principles as the just price and the fair wage) as well as in punishment; distributive justice has its place above all in the assignment of political honors or offices. Natural right understood in terms of commutative and distributive justice is not identical with natural right as delineating the minimum conditions of political life: the bad regimes habitually counteract the principles of distributive justice and last nevertheless. Aristotle is no longer under a compulsion to demand the dilution of natural right. He teaches that all natural right is changeable; he does not make the distinction made by Thomas Aquinas between the unchangeable principles and the changeable conclusions. This would seem to mean that sometimes (in extreme or emergency situations) it is just to deviate even from the most general principles of natural right.

Natural law becomes a philosophic theme for the first time in Stoicism. It there becomes the theme primarily not of moral or political philosophy but of physics (the science of the universe). The natural or divine or eternal law is identified with God or the highest god (fire, aether, or air) or his reason, *i.e.* with the ordering principle which pervades and thus governs the whole by molding eternal matter. Rational beings can know that law and knowingly comply with it in so far as it applies to their conduct. In this application natural law directs man toward his perfection, the perfection of a rational and social animal; it is "the guide of life and the teacher of the duties" (Cicero, *On the Nature of the Gods* I 40); it is the dictate of reason regarding human life. Thus the virtuous life as choiceworthy for its own sake comes to be understood as compliance with natural law—with a law, and hence as a life of obedience. Inversely, the content of natural law is the whole of virtue. The virtuous life as the Stoics understood it is however not identical with the life of moral virtue as distinguished from the life of contemplation, for one of the four cardinal virtues is wisdom which is above all theoretical wisdom; the virtuous man is the wise man or the philosopher. One is tempted to say that the Stoics treat the study of philosophy as if it were a moral virtue, *i.e.* as something which could be demanded from most men. Justice, another of the four virtues, consists primarily in doing what is by nature right. The foundation of right is man's natural inclination to love his fellow men, *i.e.* not merely his follow citizens: there is a natural society comprising all men (as well as all gods). The inclination toward the universal society is perfectly compatible with the equally natural inclination towards political society which is of necessity a particular society. The unchangeable and universally valid natural law—a part of which determines natural right, *i.e.* that with which justice in contradistinction to wisdom, courage, and temperance is concerned—is the ground of all positive law; positive laws contradicting natural law are not valid. It is sometimes asserted that the Stoics differ from Plato and Aristotle by being egalitarians. Differing from Aristotle (but not from Plato) they denied that there are slaves by nature; but this does not prove that according to them all men are by nature equal in the decisive respect, *i.e.* as regards the possibility of becoming wise or virtuous (Cicero, *On the Ends of the Good and Bad Things* IV 56). The peculiarity of the Stoics in contradistinction to Plato and Aristotle which explains why the Stoics were the first philosophers to assert unambiguously the existence of natural law would seem to be the fact that they teach in a much less ambiguous way than Plato, to say nothing of Aristotle, the existence of a divine providence which supplies divine sanctions for the compliance or non-compliance with the requirements of virtue. (Cf. Cicero, *Laws* II 15–17 and *Republic* III 33–34.)

The Stoic natural law teaching is the basic stratum of the natural law tradition. It affected Roman law to some extent. With important modifications it became an ingredient of the Christian doctrine. The Christian natural law teaching reached its theoretical perfection in the work of Thomas Aquinas. It goes without saying that in the Christian version, Stoic corporealism ("materialism") is abandoned. While natural law retains its status as rational, it is treated within the context of Christian (revealed) theology. The precise context within which Thomas treats natural law is that of the principles of human action; these principles are intrinsic (the virtues or vices) or extrinsic; the extrinsic principle moving men toward the good is God who instructs men by law and assists them by His grace. Natural law is clearly distinguished from the eternal law—God Himself or the principle of His governance of all creatures—on the one hand, and the divine law, *i.e.* the positive law contained in the Bible, on the other. The eternal law is the ground of the natural law, and natural law must be supplemented by the divine law if man is to reach eternal felicity and if no evil is to remain unpunished. All creatures participate in the divine law in so far as they possess, by virtue of divine providence, inclinations toward their proper acts and ends. Rational beings participate in divine providence in a more excellent manner since they can exercise some providence for themselves; they can know the ends toward which they are by nature inclined as good and direct themselves toward them. Man is by nature inclined toward a variety of ends which possess a natural order; they ascend from self-preservation and procreation via life in society toward knowledge of God. Natural law directs men's action toward those ends by commands and prohibitions. Differently stated, as a rational being man is by nature inclined toward acting according to reason; acting according to reason is acting virtuously; natural law prescribes therefore the acts of virtue. Man possesses by nature knowledge of the first principles of natural law which are universally valid or unchangeable. Owing to the contingent character of human actions, however, those conclusions from the principles which are somewhat remote possess neither the evidence nor the universality of the principles themselves; this fact alone would require that natural law be supplemented by human law. A human law which disagrees with natural law does not have the force of law (*Summa theologica* 1 2 q.90ff.). All moral precepts of the Old Testament (as distinguished from its ceremonial and judicial precepts) can be reduced to the Decalogue; they belong to the natural law. This is true in the strictest sense of the precepts of the Second Table of the Decalogue, *i.e.* the seven commandments which order men's relations among themselves (*Exodus* 20: 12–17). The precepts in question are intelligible as self-evident even to the people and are at the same time valid without exception; compliance with them does not require the habit of virtue (*S.th.* 1 2 q. 100). A sufficient sanction is supplied by divine punishment for transgressions of the natural law but it is not entirely clear whether human reason can establish the fact of such punishment; Thomas surely rejects the gnostic assertion that God does not punish and the assertion of certain Islamic Aristotelians that the only divine punishment is the loss of eternal felicity. He does say that sin is considered by the theologians chiefly in so far as it is an offense against God, whereas the moral philosophers consider sin chiefly in so far as it is opposed to reason. These thoughts could lead to the view of some later writers according to which natural law strictly understood is natural reason itself, *i.e.* natural law does not command and forbid but only "indicates"; natural law thus understood would be possible even if there were no God (cf. Suarez, *Tractatus de Legibus ac de Deo Legislatore* II 6 sect. 3; Grotius, *De jure belli ac pacis*, Prolegomena sect. 11; Hobbes, *Leviathan* ch. 15 end; Locke, *Treatises of Civil Government* II sect. 6; Leibniz, *Théodicée* sect. 183). Thomas treats natural right (as distinguished from natural law) in his discussion of justice as a special virtue (*S. th.* 2 2 qu. 57). Therein he is confronted with the task of reconciling with the Aristotelian teaching the Roman law distinction between *ius naturale* and *ius gentium* according to which natural right deals only with things common to all animals (like procreation and the raising of offspring) whereas the *ius gentium* is particularly human. The Roman law distinction might seem to reflect early conventionalist teaching (cf. Democritus fr. 278). Thomas' reconciliation apparently paved the way for the conception of "the state of nature" as a status antedating human society. (Cf. Suarez, *loc. cit.* II 8 sect. 9.)

The Thomistic natural law teaching, which is the classic form of the natural law teaching, was already contested in the Middle Ages on various grounds. According to Duns Scotus, only the commandment to love God or rather the prohibition against hating God belongs to natural law in the strictest sense. According to Marsilius of Padua, natural right as Aristotle meant it is that part of positive right which is recognized and observed everywhere (divine worship, honoring of parents, raising of offspring, etc.); it can only metaphorically be called natural right; the dictates of right reason regarding the things to be done (*i.e.* natural law in the Thomistic sense) on the other hand are not as such universally valid because they are not universally known and observed.

Natural law acquired its greatest visible power in modern times: in both the American and the French revolutions, solemn state papers appealed to natural law. The change in effectiveness was connected with a substantive change; modern natural law differs essentially from pre-modern natural law. Pre-modern natural law continued to be powerful but it was adapted more or less incisively to modern natural law. The most striking characteristics of modern natural law are these: 1) Natural law is treated independently, *i.e.* no longer in the context of theology or of positive law; special chairs for natural law were established in some protestant countries; treatises on natural law took on the form of codes of natural law; the independent treatment of natural law was made possible by the belief that natural law can be treated "geometrically," *i.e.* that the conclusions possess the same certainty as the principles. 2) Natural law became more and more natural public law; Hobbes' doctrine of sovereignty, Locke's doctrine "no taxation without representation," or Rousseau's doctrine of the general will are not simply political but legal doctrines; they belong to natural public law;

they do not declare what the best political order is which by its nature is not realizable except under very favorable conditions, but they state the conditions of legitimacy which obtain regardless of place and time. 3) Natural law by itself is supposed to be at home in the state of nature *i.e.* a state antedating civil society. 4) In the modern development, "natural law" is as it were replaced by "the rights of man," or in other words the emphasis shifts from man's duties to his rights. 5) Whereas pre-modern natural law was on the whole "conservative," modern natural law is essentially "revolutionary." The radical difference between modern and pre-modern natural law appears most clearly if one studies the still-remembered great modern natural law teachers rather than the university professors who as a rule rest satisfied with compromises.

The principles informing modern natural law were established by two thinkers who were not themselves natural law teachers, Machiavelli and Descartes. According to Machiavelli, the traditional political doctrines take their bearings by how men should live and thus they culminate in the description of imaginary commonwealths ("utopias"), which is useless for practice; one ought to start from how men do live. Descartes begins his revolution with the universal doubt which leads to the discovery of the Ego and its "ideas" as the absolute basis of knowledge and to a mathematical-mechanical account of the universe as of a mere object of man's knowledge and exploitation.

Modern natural law as originated by Hobbes did not start as traditional natural law did from the hierarchic order of man's natural ends but from the lowest of those ends (self-preservation) which could be thought to be more effective than the higher ends: a civil society ultimately based on nothing but the right of self-preservation would not be utopian. Man is still asserted to be the rational animal but his natural sociality is denied; man is not by nature ordered toward society but he orders himself toward it prompted by mere calculation. This view in itself is very old but now it is animated by the concern for a natural-right basis of civil society. The desire for self-preservation has the character of a passion rather than of a natural inclination; the fact that it is the most powerful passion makes it the sufficient basis of all rights and duties. Natural law which dictates men's duties is derivative from the natural right of self-preservation; the right is absolute while all duties are conditional. Men being equal regarding the desire for self-preservation as well as regarding the power of killing others, all men are by nature equal; there is no natural heirarchy of men, so much so that the sovereign to whom all must submit for the sake of peace and ultimately of the self-preservation of each is understood as a "person," as the "person," *i.e.* as the representative or agent, of each; the primacy of the individual—of any individual—and his natural right remains intact (cf. *Leviathan* ch. 21).—The doctrine of Locke may be described as the peak of modern natural law. At first glance it appears to be a compromise between the traditional and the Hobbean doctrines. Agreeing with Hobbes, Locke denies that the natural law is imprinted in the minds of men, that it can be known from the consent of mankind and that it can be known from men's natural inclination. His deduction of natural law is generally admitted to be confusing, not to say confused, which does not prove however that Locke himself was confused. It seems to be safest to understand his doctrine as a profound modification of the Hobbean doctrine. Certain it is that, differing from Hobbes, he sees the crucially important consequence of the natural right of self-preservation in the natural right of property, *i.e.* of acquiring property, a natural right which within civil society becomes the natural right of unlimited acquisition. Property is rightfully acquired primarily only by labor; in civil society however labor ceases to be the title to property while remaining the source of all value. Locke's natural law doctrine is the original form of capitalist theory.—Rousseau too starts from the Hobbean premise. Hobbes asserted that the natural right to judge of the means of self-preservation is the necessary consequence of the right of self-preservation itself, and belongs, as does the fundamental right, equally to all men, wise or foolish. But Rousseau, differing from Hobbes, demands that the natural right to judge of the means of self-preservation be preserved within civil society as an institution agreeing with natural right: every one subject to the laws must have a say in the making of the laws by being a member of the sovereign, *i.e.* of the legislative assembly. The corrective to folly was to be found above all in the character of the laws as general both in origin and in content: all subject to the laws determine what all must or may not do. The justice or rationality of the laws is, by that generality, guaranteed in the only way compatible with the freedom and equality of all. In the society established in accordance with natural right there is no longer a need or a possibility of appealing from positive law to natural right although or because the members or rulers of that society are not supposed to be just men. Rousseau further differed from Hobbes by realizing that if man is by nature asocial, he is by nature arational; questioning the traditional view that man is the rational animal, he found the peculiarity of man in his perfectibility or, more generally stated, his malleability. This led to the conclusions that the human race is what we wish to make it and that human nature cannot supply us with guidance as to how man and human society ought to be.—Not Rousseau but Kant drew the decisive conclusion from Rousseau's epoch-making innovations: the Ought cannot be derived from the Is, from human nature; the moral law is not a natural law or derivative from a natural law; the criterion of the moral law is its form alone, the form of rationality, *i.e.* of universality; just as according to Rousseau the particular will becomes the unblameable positive law by being generalized, according to Kant the maxims of action prove to be moral if they pass the test of being universalized, *i.e.* of being possible principles of universal legislation.—At about the same time that Kant, sympathizing with the French Revolution, radicalized the most radical form of modern natural right and thus transformed natural right and natural law into a law and a right which is rational but no longer natural, Burke, opposing the French Revolution and its theoretical basis, which is a certain version of modern natural right, returned to pre-modern natural law. In doing so, he made thematic the conservatism which was implicit to some extent in pre-modern natural law. Therewith he profoundly modified the pre-modern teaching and prepared decisively the transition from the natural "rights of man" to the prescriptive "rights of Englishmen," from natural law to "the historical school."

Bibliography

1) Carlyle, R. W., and Carlyle, A. J., *A History of Medieval Political Theory in the West* (Edinburgh and London 1903–36: 6 vols.).

2) Gierke, O. von, *Political Theories of the Middle Ages* (Cambridge 1900) tr. by F. Maitland.

3) Gierke, O. von, *Natural Law and the Theory of Society, 1500 to 1800* (Cambridge 1934) tr. by E. Barker.

4) Gierke, O. von, *The Development of Political Theory* (New York 1939) tr. by B. Freyd.

5) Kelsen, Hans, "Natural Law Doctrine and Legal Positivism," in *General Theory of Law and State* (New York 1961) tr. by A. Wedberg.

6) McIlwain, C. H., *The Growth of Political Thought in the West* (New York 1932).

7) Nussbaum, A., *A Concise History of the Law of Nations* (New York 1947).

8) Rommen, H. A., *The Natural Law* (St. Louis 1947) tr. by T. Hanley.

9) Strauss, L., *Natural Right and History* (Chicago 1953).

7

Jerusalem and Athens
Some Preliminary Reflections

I. The Beginning of the Bible and Its Greek Counterparts

All the hopes that we entertain in the midst of the confusions and dangers of the present are founded positively or negatively, directly or indirectly on the experiences of the past. Of these experiences the broadest and deepest, as far as we Western men are concerned, are indicated by the names of the two cities Jerusalem and Athens. Western man became what he is and is what he is through the coming together of biblical faith and Greek thought. In order to understand ourselves and to illuminate our trackless way into the future, we must understand Jerusalem and Athens. As goes without saying, this is a task whose proper performance goes much beyond my power, to say nothing at all of the still narrower limits set to two public lectures. But we cannot define our tasks by our powers, for our powers become known to us through performing our tasks; it is better to fail nobly than to succeed basely. Besides, having been chosen to inaugurate the Frank Cohen Memorial Lectureship at the City College of the City University of New York, I must think of the whole series of lectures to be given by other men—let us hope by better and greater men—in the coming years or decades.

The objects to which we refer by speaking of Jerusalem and Athens, are today understood by the science devoted to such objects as cultures; "culture" is meant to be a scientific concept. According to this concept there is an indefinitely large number of cultures: n cultures. The scientist who studies them beholds them as objects; as scientist he stands outside of all of them; he has no preference for any of them; in his eyes all of them are of equal rank; he is not only impartial but objective; he is anxious not to distort

Reprinted from *The City College Papers*, no. 6 (The City College of New York, 1967).

any of them; in speaking about them he avoids any "culture-bound" concepts, i.e., concepts bound to any particular culture or kind of culture. In many cases the objects studied by the scientist of culture do or did not know that they are or were cultures. This causes no difficulty for him: electrons also do not know that they are electrons; even dogs do not know that they are dogs. By the mere fact that he speaks of his objects as cultures, the scientific student takes it from granted that he understands the people whom he studies better than they understood or understand themselves.

This whole approach has been questioned for some time but this questioning does not seem to have had any effect on the scientists. The man who started the questioning was Nietzsche. We have said that according to the prevailing view there were or are n cultures. Let us say there were or are 1,001 cultures, thus reminding ourselves of the Arabian Nights, the 1,001 Nights; the account of the cultures, if it is well done will be a series of exciting stories, perhaps of tragedies. Accordingly Nietzsche speaks of our subject in a speech of his Zarathustra that is entitled "Of 1,000 Goals and One." The Hebrews and the Greeks appear in this speech as two among a number of nations, not superior to the two others that are mentioned or to the 996 that are not mentioned. The peculiarity of the Greeks is the full dedication of the individual to the contest for excellence, distinction, supremacy. The peculiarity of the Hebrews is the utmost honoring of father and mother. (Up to this day the Jews read on their highest holiday the section of the Torah that deals with the first presupposition of honoring father and mother: the unqualified prohibition against incest between children and parents.) Nietzsche has a deeper reverence than any other beholder for the sacred tables of the Hebrews as well as of the other nations in question. Yet since he is only a beholder of these tables, since what one table commends or commands is incompatible with what the others command, he is not subject to the commandments of any. This is true also and especially of the tables, or "values" of modern Western culture. But according to him, all scientific concepts, and hence in particular the concept of culture, are culture-bound; the concept of culture is an outgrowth of 19th century Western culture; its application to "cultures" of other ages and climates is an act stemming from the spiritual imperialism of that particular culture. There is then a glaring contradiction between the claimed objectivity of the science of cultures and the radical subjectivity of that science. Differently stated, one cannot behold, i.e., truly understand, any culture unless one is firmly rooted in one's own culture or unless one belongs in one's capacity as a beholder to some culture. But if the universality of the beholding of all cultures is to be preserved, the culture to which the beholder of all cultures belongs, must be the universal culture, the culture of mankind, the world culture; the universality of beholding presupposes, if only by anticipating it, the universal culture which is no longer one culture among many. The variety of cultures that have hitherto emerged contradicts the oneness of truth. Truth is not a woman so that each man can have his own truth as he can have his own wife. Nietzsche sought therefore for a culture that would no longer be particular and hence in the last analysis arbitrary. The single goal of mankind is conceived by him as in a sense super-human: he speaks of the super-man of the future. The super-man is meant to unite in himself Jerusalem and Athens on the highest level.

However much the science of all cultures may protest its innocence of all preferences or evaluations it fosters a specific moral posture. Since it requires openness to all cultures, it fosters universal tolerance and the exhilaration deriving from the beholding of diversity; it necessarily affects all cultures that it can still affect by contributing to their transformation in one and the same direction; it willy-nilly brings about a shift of emphasis from the particular to the universal: by asserting, if only implicitly, the rightness of pluralism, it asserts that pluralism is *the* right way; it asserts the monism of universal tolerance and respect for diversity; for by virtue of being an -ism, pluralism is a monism.

One remains somewhat closer to the science of culture as commonly practiced if one limits oneself to saying that every attempt to understand the phenomena in question remains dependent on a conceptual framework that is alien to most of these phenomena and therefore necessarily distorts them. "Objectivity" can be expected only if one attempts to understand the various cultures or peoples exactly as they understand or understood themselves. Men of ages and climates other than our own did not understand themselves in terms of cultures because they were not concerned with culture in the present-day meaning of the term. What we now call culture is the accidental result of concerns that were not concerns with culture but with other things and above all with the Truth.

Yet our intention to speak of Jerusalem and Athens seems to compel us to go beyond the self-understanding of either. Or is there a notion, a word that points to the highest that the Bible on the one hand and the greatest works of the Greeks claim to convey? There is such a word: wisdom. Not only the Greek philosophers but the Greek poets as well were considered to be wise men, and the Torah is said in the Torah to be "your wisdom in the eyes of the nations." We must then try to understand the difference between biblical wisdom and Greek wisdom. We see at once that each of the two claims to be the true wisdom, thus denying to the other its claim to be wisdom in the strict and highest sense. According to the Bible, the beginning of wisdom is fear of the Lord; according to the Greek philosophers, the beginning of wisdom is wonder. We are thus compelled from the very beginning to make a choice, to take a stand. Where then do we stand? We are confronted with the incompatible claims of Jerusalem and Athens to our allegiance. We are open to both and willing to listen to each. We ourselves are not wise but we wish to become wise. We are seekers for wisdom, "philo-sophoi." By saying that we wish to hear first and then to act to decide, we have already decided in favor of Athens against Jerusalem.

This seems to be necessary for all of us who cannot be orthodox and therefore must accept the principle of the historical-critical study of the Bible. The Bible was traditionally understood as the true and authentic account of the deeds of God and men from the beginning till the restoration after the Babylonian exile. The deeds of God include His legislation as well as His inspirations of the prophets, and the deeds of men include their praises of God and their prayers to Him as well as their God-inspired admonitions. Biblical criticism starts from the observation that the biblical account is in important respects not authentic but derivative or consists not of "histories" but of "memories of ancient histories," to borrow a Machiavellian expression.[1] Biblical criticism reached its first climax in Spinoza's *Theological-Political Treatise*, which is frankly anti-theological; Spinoza read the Bible as he read the Talmud and the Koran. The result of his criticism can be summarized as follows: the Bible consists to a considerable extent of self-contradictory assertions, of remnants of ancient prejudices or superstitions, and of the outpourings of an uncontrolled imagination; in addition it is poorly compiled and poorly preserved. He arrived at this result by presupposing the impossibility of miracles. The considerable differences between 19th and 20th century biblical criticism and that of Spinoza can be traced to their difference in regard to the evaluation of imagination: whereas for Spinoza imagination is simply sub-rational, it was assigned a much higher rank in later times; it was understood as the vehicle of religious or spiritual experience, which necessarily expresses itself in symbols and the like. The historical-critical study of the Bible is the attempt to understand the various layers of the Bible as they were understood by their immediate addressees, i.e., the contemporaries of the authors of the various layers. The Bible speaks of many things that for the biblical authors themselves belong to the remote past; it suffices to mention the creation of the world. But there is undoubtedly much of history in the Bible, i.e., accounts of events written by contemporaries or near-contemporaries. One is thus led to say that the Bible contains both "myth" and "history." Yet this distinction is alien to the Bible; it is a special form of the distinction between *mythos* and *logos*; *mythos* and *historie* are of Greek origin. From the point of view of the Bible the "myths" are as true as the "histories": what Israel "in fact" did or suffered cannot be understood exept in the light of the "facts" of Creation and Election. What is now called "historical" is those deeds and speeches that are equally accessible to the believer and to the unbeliever. But from the point of view of the Bible the unbeliever is the fool who has said in his

1. *Discorsi* I 16.

heart "there is no God"; the Bible narrates everything as it is credible to the wise in the biblical sense of wisdom. Let us never forget that there is no biblical word for doubt. The biblical signs and wonders convince men who have little faith or who believe in other gods; they are not addressed to "the fools who say in their hearts 'there is no God.'"[2]

It is true that we cannot ascribe to the Bible the theological concept of miracles, for that concept presupposes that of nature and the concept of nature is foreign to the Bible. One is tempted to ascribe to the Bible what one may call the poetic concept of miracles as illustrated by Psalm 114: "When Israel went out of Egypt, the house of Jacob from a people of a strange tongue, Judah became his sanctuary and Israel his dominion. The sea saw and it fled; the Jordan turned back. The mountains skipped like rams, the hills like lambs. What ails thee, sea, that thou fleest, thou Jordan that thou turnst back? Ye mountains that ye skip like rams, ye hills like lambs? From the presence of the Lord tremble thou earth, from the presence of the God of Jacob who turns the rock into a pond of water, the flint into a fountain of waters." The presence of God or His call elicits a conduct of His creatures that differs strikingly from their ordinary conduct; it enlivens the lifeless; it makes fluid the fixed. It is not easy to say whether the author of the psalm did not mean his utterance to be simply or literally true. It is easy to say that the concept of poetry—as distinguished from that of song—is foreign to the Bible. It is perhaps more simple to say that owing to the victory of science over natural theology the impossibility of miracles can no longer be said to be simply true but has degenerated to the status of an indemonstrable hypothesis. One may trace to the hypothetical character of this fundamental premise the hypothetical character of many, not to say all, results of biblical criticism. Certain it is that biblical criticism in all its forms makes use of terms having no biblical equivalents and is to this extent unhistorical.

How then must we proceed? We shall not take issue with the findings and even the premises of biblical criticism. Let us grant that the Bible and in particular the Torah consists to a considerable extent of "memories of ancient histories," even of memories of memories; but memories of memories are not necessarily distorting or pale reflections of the original; they may be re-collections of re-collections, deepenings through meditation of the primary experiences. We shall therefore take the latest and uppermost layer as seriously as the earlier ones. We shall start from the uppermost layer— from what is first for us, even though it may not be the first simply. We shall start, that is, where both the traditional and the historical study of the Bible necessarily start. In thus proceeding we avoid the compulsion to make an advance decision in favor of Athens against Jerusalem. For the Bible does

---

2. Bacon, *Essays*, "Of Atheism."

not require us to believe in the miraculous character of events that the Bible does not present as miraculous. God's speaking to men may be described as miraculous, but the Bible does not claim that the putting together of those speeches was done miraculously. We begin at the beginning, at the beginning of the beginning. The beginning of the beginning happens to deal with *the* beginning: the creation of heaven and earth. The Bible begins reasonably.

"In the beginning God created heaven and earth." Who says this? We are not told; hence we do not know. Does it make no difference who says it? This would be a philosopher's reason; is it also the biblical reason? We are not told; hence we do not know. We have no right to assume that God said it, for the Bible introduces God's sayings by expressions like "God said." We shall then assume that the words were spoken by a nameless man. Yet no man can have been an eye-witness of God's creating heaven and earth;[3] the only eye-witness was God. Since "there did not arise in Israel a prophet like Moses whom the Lord saw face to face," it is understandable that tradition ascribed to Moses the sentence quoted and its whole sequel. But what is understandable or plausible is not as such certain. The narrator does not claim to have heard the account from God; perhaps he heard it from some man or men; perhaps he retells a tale. The Bible continues: "And the earth was unformed and void. . . ." It is not clear whether the earth thus described was created by God or antedated His creation. But it is quite clear that while speaking about how the earth looked at first, the Bible is silent about how heaven looked at first. The earth, i.e., that which is not heaven, seems to be more important than heaven. This impression is confirmed by the sequel.

God created everything in six days. On the first day He created light; on the second, heaven; on the third, the earth, the seas and vegetation; on the fourth, sun, moon and the stars; on the fifth, the water animals and the birds; and on the sixth, the land animals and man. The most striking difficulties are these: light and hence days (and nights) are presented as preceding the sun, and vegetation is presented as preceding the sun. The first difficulty is disposed of by the observation that creation-days are not sun-days. One must add however at once that there is a connection between the two kinds of days, for there is a connection, a correspondence between light and sun. The account of creation manifestly consists of two parts, the first part dealing with the first three creation-days and the second part dealing with the last three. The first part begins with the creation of light and the second with the creation of the heavenly light-givers. Correspondingly the first part ends with the creation of vegetation and the second with the creation of man. All creatures dealt with in the first part lack local motion; all creatures

---

3. Job 38:4.

dealt with in the second part possess local motion.[4] Vegetation precedes the sun because vegetation lacks local motion and the sun possesses it. Vegetation belongs to the earth;[5] it is rooted in the earth; it is the fixed covering of the fixed earth. Vegetation was brought forth by the earth at God's command; the Bible does not speak of God's "making" vegetation; but as regards the living beings in question, God commanded the earth to bring them forth and yet God "made" them. Vegetation was created at the end of the first half of the creation-days; at the end of the last half the living beings that spend their whole lives on the firm earth were created. The living beings—beings that possess life in addition to local motion—were created on the fifth and sixth days, on the days following the day on which the heavenly light-givers were created. The Bible presents the creatures in an ascending order. Heaven is lower than earth. The heavenly light-givers lack life; they are lower than the lowliest living beast; they serve the living creatures, which are to be found only beneath heaven; they have been created in order to rule over day and night: they have not been made in order to rule over the earth, let alone over man. The most striking characteristic of the biblical account of creation is its demoting or degrading of heaven and the heavenly lights. Sun, moon and stars precede the living things because they are lifeless: they are not gods. What the heavenly lights lose, man gains; man is the peak of creation. The creatures of the first three days cannot change their places; the heavenly bodies change their places but not their courses; the living beings change their courses but not their "ways"; men alone can change their "ways." Man is the only being created in God's image. Only in the case of man's creation does the biblical account of creation reportedly speak of God's "creating" him; in the case of the creation of heaven and the heavenly bodies that account speaks of God's "making" them. Only in the case of man's creation does the Bible intimate that there is a multiplicity in God: "Let us make man in our image, after our likeness. . . . So God created man in his image, in the image of God he created him; male and female he created them." Bisexuality is not a preserve of man; but only man's bisexuality could give rise to the view that there are gods and goddesses: there is no biblical word for "goddess." Hence creation is not begetting. The biblical account of creation teaches silently what the Bible teaches elsewhere explicitly but not therefore more emphatically: there is only one God, the God whose name is written as the Tetragrammaton, the living God Who lives from ever to ever, Who alone has created heaven and earth and all their hosts; He has not created any gods and hence there are no gods beside Him. The many gods whom men worship are either nothings

---

4. Cf. U. Cassuto, *A Commentary on the Book of Genesis*, Part I, Jerusalem 1961, p. 42.
5. Cf. the characterization of the plants as engeia ("in or of the earth") in Plato's *Republic* 491 d 1. Cf. Empedocles A 70.

that owe such being as they possess to man's making them, or if they are something (like sun, moon and stars), they surely are not gods.[6]. All non-polemical references to "other gods" occurring in the Bible are fossils whose preservation indeed poses a question but only a rather unimportant one. Not only did the biblical God not create any gods; on the basis of the biblical account of creation one could doubt whether He created any beings one would be compelled to call "mythical": heaven and earth and all their hosts are always accessible to man as man. One would have to start from this fact in order to understand why the Bible contains so many sections that, on the basis of the distinction between mythical (or legendary) and historical, would have to be described as historical.

According to the Bible, creation was completed by the creation of man; creation culminated in the creation of man. Only after the creation of man did God "see all that he had made, and behold, it was very good." What then is the origin of the evil or the bad? The biblical answer seems to be that since everything of divine origin is good, evil is of human origin. Yet if God's creation as a whole is very good, it does not follow that all its parts are good or that creation as a whole contains no evil whatever: God did not find all parts of His creation to be good. Perhaps creation as a whole cannot be "very good" if it does not contain some evils. There cannot be light if there is not darkness, and the darkness is as much created as is light: God creates evil as well as He makes peace.[7] However this may be, the evils whose origin the Bible lays bare after it has spoken of creation, are a particular kind of evils: the evils that beset man. Those evils are not due to creation or implicit in it, as the Bible shows by setting forth man's original condition. In order to set forth that condition, the Bible must retell man's creation by making man's creation as much as possible the sole theme. This second account answers the question, not of how heaven and earth and all their hosts have come into being but of how human life as we know it—beset with evils with which it was not beset originally—has come into being. This second account may only supplement the first account but it may also correct it and thus contradict it. After all, the Bible never teaches that one can speak about creation without contradicting oneself. In post-biblical parlance, the mysteries of the Torah (*sithre torah*) are the contradictions of the Torah; the mysteries of God are the contradictions regarding God.

The first account of creation ended with man; the second account begins with man. According to the first account God created man and only man in His image; according to the second account, God formed man from the dust of the earth and He blew into his nostrils the breath of life; the second account makes clear that man consists of two profoundly different ingre-

6. Cf. the distinction between the two kinds of "other gods" in Deut. 4: 15–19, between the idols on the one hand and sun, moon and stars on the other.
7. Isaiah 45:7.

dients, a high one and a low one. According to the first account it would seem that man and woman were created simultaneously; according to the second account man was created first. The life of man as we know it, the life of most men, is that of tillers of the soil; their life is needy and harsh; they need rain which is not always forthcoming when they need it and they must work hard. If human life had been needy and harsh from the very beginning, man would have been compelled or at least irresistibly tempted to be harsh, uncharitable, unjust; he would not have been fully responsible for his lack of charity or justice. But man is to be fully responsible. Hence the harshness of human life must be due to man's fault. His original condition must have been one of ease: he was not in need of rain nor of hard work; he was put by God into a well-watered garden that was rich in trees good for food. While man was created for a life of ease, he was not created for a life of luxury: there was no gold or precious stones in the garden of Eden.[8] Man was created for a simple life. Accordingly, God permitted him to eat of every tree[9] of the garden except of the tree of knowledge of good and evil (bad), "for in the day that you eat of it, you shall surely die." Man was not denied knowledge; without knowledge he could not have known the tree of knowledge nor the woman nor the brutes; nor could he have understood the prohibition. Man was denied knowledge of good and evil, i.e., the knowledge sufficient for guiding himself, his life. While not being a child he was to live in child-like simplicity and obedience to God. We are free to surmise that there is a connection between the demotion of heaven in the first account and the prohibition against eating of the tree of knowledge in the second. While man was forbidden to eat of the tree of knowledge, he was not forbidden to eat of the tree of life.

Man, lacking knowledge of good and evil, was content with his condition and in particular with his loneliness. But God, possessing knowledge of good and evil, found that "it is not good for man to be alone, so I will make him a helper as his counterpart." So God formed the brutes and brought them to man, but they proved not to be the desired helpers. Thereupon God formed the woman out of a rib of the man. The man welcomed her as bone of his bones and flesh of his flesh but, lacking knowledge of good and evil, he did not call her good. The narrator adds that "therefore [namely because the woman is bone of man's bone and flesh of his flesh] a man leaves his father and his mother, and cleaves to his wife, and they become one flesh." Both were naked but, lacking knowledge of good and evil, they were not ashamed.

Thus the stage was set for the fall of our first parents. The first move came from the serpent, the most cunning of all the beasts of the field; it seduced the woman into disobedience and then the woman seduced the man. The

8. Cassuto, *loc. cit.*, pp. 77–79.
9. One does not have to stoop in order to pluck the fruits of trees.

seduction moves from the lowest to the highest. The Bible does not tell what induced the serpent to seduce the woman into disobeying the divine prohibition against eating of the tree of knowledge of good and evil. It is reasonable to assume that the serpent acted as it did because it was cunning, i.e., possessed a low kind of wisdom, a congenital malice; everything that God has created would not be very good if it did not include something congenitally bent on mischief. The serpent begins its seduction by suggesting that God might have forbidden man and woman to eat of any tree in the garden, i.e., that God's prohibition might be malicious or impossible to comply with. The woman corrects the serpent and in so doing makes the prohibition more stringent than it was: "we may eat of the fruit of the other trees of the garden; it is only about the tree in the middle of the garden that God said: you shall not eat of it or touch it, lest you die." God did not forbid the man to touch the fruit of the tree of knowledge of good and evil. Besides, the woman does not explicitly speak of the tree of knowledge; she may have had in mind the tree of life. Moreover, God had said to the man: "thou mayest eat. . . thou wilt die"; the woman claims that God had spoken to both her and the man. She surely knew the divine prohibition only through human tradition. The serpent assures her that they will not die, "for God knows that when you eat of it, your eyes will be opened and you will be like God, knowing good and evil." The serpent tacitly questions God's veracity. At the same time it glosses over the fact that eating of the tree involves disobedience to God. In this it is followed by the woman. According to the serpent's assertion, knowledge of good and evil makes man immune to death, but we cannot know whether the serpent believes this. But could immunity to death be a great good for beings that did not know good and evil, to men who were like children? But the woman, having forgotten the divine prohibition, having therefore in a manner tasted of the tree of knowledge, is no longer wholly unaware of good and evil: she "saw that the tree was good for eating and a delight to the eyes and that the tree was to be desired to make one wise"; therefore she took of its fruit and ate. She thus made the fall of the man almost inevitable, for he was cleaving to her: she gave some of the fruit of the tree to the man, and he ate. The man drifts into disobedience by following the woman. After they had eaten of the tree, their eyes were opened and they knew that they were naked, and they sewed fig leaves together and made themselves aprons: through the fall they became ashamed of their nakedness; eating of the tree of knowledge of good and evil made them realize that nakedness is evil (bad).

The Bible says nothing to the effect that our first parents fell because they were prompted by the desire to be like God; they did not rebel high-handedly against God; they rather forgot to obey God; they drifted into disobedience. Nevertheless God punished them severely. He also punished the serpent. But the punishment did not do away with the fact that, as God

Himself said, as a consequence of his disobedience "man has become like one of us, knowing good and evil." As a consequence there was now the danger that man might eat of the tree of life and live forever. Therefore God expelled him from the garden and made it impossible for him to return to it. One may wonder why man, while he was still in the garden of Eden, had not eaten of the tree of life of which he had not been forbidden to eat. Perhaps he did not think of it because, lacking knowledge of good and evil, he did not fear to die and, besides, the divine prohibition drew his attention away from the tree of life to the tree of knowledge.

The Bible intends to teach that man was meant to live in simplicity, without knowledge of good and evil. But the narrator seems to be aware of the fact that a being that can be forbidden to strive for knowledge of good and evil, i.e., that can understand to some degree that knowledge of good and evil is evil for it, necessarily possesses such knowledge. Human suffering from evil presupposes human knowledge of good and evil and *vice versa*. Man wishes to live without evil. The Bible tells us that he was given the opportunity to live without evil and that he cannot blame God for the evils from which he suffers. By giving man that opportunity God convinces him that his deepest wish cannot be fulfilled. The story of the fall is the first part of the story of God's education of man. This story partakes of the unfathomable character of God.

Man has to live with knowledge of good and evil and with the sufferings inflicted on him because of that knowledge or its acquisition. Human goodness or badness presupposes that knowledge and its concomitants. The Bible gives us the first inkling of human goodness and badness in the story of the first brothers. The oldest brother, Cain, was a tiller of the soil; the youngest brother, Abel, a keeper of sheep. God preferred the offering of the keeper of sheep who brought the choicest of the firstlings of his flock, to that of the tiller of the soil. This preference has more than one reason, but one reason seems to be that the pastoral life is closer to original simplicity than the life of the tillers of the soil. Cain was vexed and despite his having been warned by God against sinning in general, killed his brother. After a futile attempt to deny his guilt—an attempt that increased his guilt ("Am I my brother's keeper?")—he was cursed by God as the serpent and the soil had been after the Fall, in contradistinction to Adam and Eve who were not cursed; he was punished by God, but not with death: anyone slaying Cain would be punished much more severely than Cain himself. The relatively mild punishment of Cain cannot be explained by the fact that murder had not been expressly forbidden, for Cain possessed some knowledge of good and evil, and he knew that Abel was his brother, even assuming that he did not know that man was created in the image of God. It is better to explain Cain's punishment by assuming that punishments were milder in the beginning than later on. Cain—like his fellow fratricide Romulus—founded a city, and some of his descendants were the ancestors of men practicing various arts: the city and the arts, so alien to man's original simplicity, owe their origin to Cain and his race rather than to Seth, the substitute for Abel, and his race. It goes without saying that this is not the last word of the Bible on the city and the arts but it is its first word, just as the prohibition against eating of the tree of knowledge is, as one may say, its first word simply and the revelation of the Torah, i.e., the highest kind of knowledge of good and evil that is vouchsafed to men, is its last word. One is also tempted to think of the difference between the first word of the first book of Samuel on human kingship and its last word. The account of the race of Cain culminates in the song of Lamech who boasted to his wives of his slaying of men, of his being superior to God as an avenger. The (antediluvian) race of Seth cannot boast of a single inventor; its only distinguished members were Enoch who walked with God and Noah who was a righteous man and walked with God: civilization and piety are two very different things.

By the time of Noah the wickedness of man had become so great that God repented of His creation of man and all other earthly creatures, Noah alone excepted; so He brought on the Flood. Generally speaking, prior to the Flood man's life-span was much longer than after it. Man's antediluvian longevity was a relic of his original condition. Man originally lived in the garden of Eden where he could have eaten of the tree of life and thus have become immortal. The longevity of antediluvian man reflects this lost chance. To this extent the transition from antediluvian to postdiluvian man is a decline. This impression is confirmed by the fact that before the Flood rather than after it the sons of God consorted with the daughters of man and thus generated the mighty men of old, the men of renown. On the other hand, the fall of our first parents made possible or necessary in due time God's revelation of his Torah, and this was decisively prepared, as we shall see, by the Flood. In this respect the transition from antediluvian to post-diluvian mankind is a progress. The ambiguity regarding the Fall—the fact that it was a sin and hence evitable and that it was inevitable—is reflected in the ambiguity regarding the status of antediluvian mankind.

The link between antediluvian mankind and the revelation of the Torah is supplied by the first Covenant between God and men, the Covenant following the Flood. The Flood was the proper punishment for the extreme and well-nigh universal wickedness of antediluvian men. Prior to the Flood mankind lived, so to speak, without restraint, without law. While our first parents were still in the garden of Eden, they were not forbidden anything except to eat of the tree of knowledge. The vegetarianism of antediluvian men was not due to an explicit prohibition (cf. 1:29); their abstention from meat belongs together with their abstention from wine (cf. 9:20); both were relics of man's original simplicity. After the expulsion from the garden of Eden, God did not punish men, apart from the relatively mild punishment which He inflicted on Cain. Nor did He establish human judges. God as it were experimented, for the instruction of mankind, with mankind living in freedom from law. This experiment just as the experiment with men remaining like innocent children, ended in failure. Fallen or awake man needs restraint, must live under law. But this law must not be simply imposed. It must form part of a Covenant in which God and man are equally, though not equal, partners. Such a partnership was established only after the Flood; it did not exist in antediluvian times either before or after the Fall. The inequality regarding the Covenant is shown especially by the fact that God's undertaking never again to destroy almost all life on earth as long as the earth lasts is not conditioned on all men or almost all men obeying the laws promulgated by God after the Flood: God's promise is made despite, or because of, His knowing that the devisings of man's heart are evil from his youth. Noah is the ancestor of all later men just as Adam was; the purgation of the earth through the Flood is to some extent a restoration of mankind to its original state; it is a kind of second creation. Within the limits indicated, the condition of postdiluvian men is superior to that of antediluvian men. One point requires special emphasis: in the legislation following the Flood, murder is expressly forbidden and made punishable with death on the ground that man was created in the image of God (9:6). The first Covenant brought an increase in hope and at the same time an increase in punishment. Man's rule over the beasts, ordained or established from the beginning, was only after the Flood to be accompanied by the beasts' fear and dread of man (cf. 9:2 with 1:26-30 and 2:15).

The Covenant following the Flood prepares the Covenant with Abraham. The Bible singles out three events that took place between the Covenant after the Flood and God's calling Abraham: Noah's curse of Canaan, a son of Ham; the excellence of Nimrod, a grandson of Ham; and men's attempt to prevent their being scattered over the earth through building a city and a tower with its top in the heavens. Canaan whose land came to be the promised land, was cursed because of Ham's seeing the nakedness of his father Noah, because of Ham's transgressing a most sacred, if unpromulgated, law; the curse of Canaan was accompanied by the blessing of Shem and Japheth who turned their eyes away from the nakedness of their father; here we have the first and the most fundamental division of mankind, at any rate of postdiluvian mankind, the division into a cursed and a blessed part. Nimrod was the first to be a mighty man on earth—a mighty hunter before the Lord; his kingdom included Babel; big kingdoms are attempts to overcome by force the division of mankind; conquest and hunting are akin to one another. The city that men built in order to remain together and thus to make a name for themselves was Babel; God scattered them by confounding their speech, by bringing about the division of mankind into groups speaking different languages, groups that cannot understand one another: into nations, i.e., groups united not only by descent but by language as well. The division of mankind into nations may be described as a milder alternative to the Flood.

The three events that took place between God's Covenant with mankind after the Flood and His calling Abraham point to God's way of dealing with men knowing good and evil and devising evil from their youth; well-nigh universal wickedness will no longer be punished with well-nigh universal destruction; well-nigh universal wickedness will be prevented by the division of mankind into nations in the sense indicated; mankind will be divided, not into the cursed and the blessed (the curses and blessings were Noah's, not God's), but into a chosen nation and the nations that are not chosen. The emergence of nations made it possible that Noah's Ark floating alone on the waters covering the whole earth be replaced by a whole, numerous nation living in the midst of the nations covering the whole earth. The election of the holy nation begins with the election of Abraham. Noah was distinguished from his contemporaries by his righteousness; Abraham separates himself from his contemporaries and in particular from his country and kindred at God's command—a command accompanied by God's promise to make him a great nation. The Bible does not say that this primary election of Abraham was preceded by Abraham's righteousness. However this may be, Abraham shows his righteousness by at once obeying God's command, by trusting in God's promise the fulfillment of which he could not possibly live to see, given the short life-spans of postdiluvian men: only after Abraham's offspring will have become a great nation, will the land of Canaan be given to them forever. The fulfillment of the promise required that Abraham not remain childless, and he was already quite old. Accordingly, God promised him that he would have issue. It was Abraham's trust in God's promise that, above everything else, made him righteous in the eyes of the Lord. It was God's intention that His promise be fulfilled through the offspring of Abraham and his wife Sarah. But this promise seemed to be laughable to Abraham, to say nothing of Sarah: Abraham was 100 years old and Sarah 90. Yet nothing is too wondrous for the Lord. The laughable announcement became a joyous announcement. The joyous announcement was followed immediately by God's announcement to Abraham of His concern with the wickedness of the people of Sodom and Gomorra. God did not yet know whether those people were as wicked as they were said to be. But they might be; they might deserve total destruction as much as the generation of the Flood. Noah had accepted the destruction of his generation without any questioning. Abraham, however, who had a deeper trust in God, in God's righteousness, and a deeper awareness of his being only dust and ashes than Noah, presumed in fear and trembling to appeal to God's righteousness lest He, the judge of the whole earth, destroy the righteous along with the wicked. In response to Abraham's insistent pleading, God as it were promised to Abraham that He would not destroy Sodom if ten righteous men were found in the city: He would save the city for the sake of the ten righteous men within it. Abraham acted as the mortal partner in God's righteousness; he acted as if he had some share in the responsibility for God's acting righteously. No wonder that God's Covenant with Abraham was incomparably more incisive than His Covenant immediately following the Flood.

Abraham's trust in God thus appears to be the trust that God in His righteousness will not do anything incompatible with His righteousness and that while or because nothing is too wondrous for the Lord, there are firm boundaries set to Him by His righteousness, by Him. This awareness is deepened and therewith modified by the last and severest test of Abraham's trust: God's command to him to sacrifice Isaac, his only son from Sarah. Before speaking of Isaac's conception and birth, the Bible speaks of the attempt made by Abimelech, the king of Gerar, to lie with Sarah; given Sarah's old age Abimelech's action might have forestalled the last opportunity that Sarah bear a child to Abraham; therefore God intervened to prevent Abimelech from approaching Sarah. A similar danger had threatened Sarah many years earlier at the hands of the Pharaoh; at that time she was very beautiful. At the time of the Abimelech incident she was apparently no longer very beautiful, but despite her being almost 90 years old she must have been still quite attractive;[10] this could seem to detract from the wonder of Isaac's birth. On the other hand, God's special intervention against Abimelech enhances that wonder. Abraham's supreme test presupposes the wondrous character of Isaac's birth: the very son who was to be the sole link between Abraham and the chosen people and who was born against all reasonable expectations, was to be sacrificed by his father. This command contradicted, not only the divine promise, but also the divine prohibition against the shedding of innocent blood. Yet Abraham did not argue with God as he had done in the case of Sodom's destruction. In the case of Sodom, Abraham was not confronted with a divine command to do something and in particular not with a command to surrender to God, to render to God, what was dearest to him: Abraham did not argue with God for the preservation of Isaac because he loved God, and not himself or his most cherished hope, with all his heart, with all his soul and with all his might. The same concern with God's righteousness that had induced him to plead with God for the preservation of Sodom if ten just men should be found in that city, induced him not to plead for the preservation of Isaac, for God rightfully demands that He alone be loved unqualifiedly: God does not command that we love His chosen people with all our heart, with all our soul and with all our might. The fact that the command to sacrifice Isaac contradicted the prohibition against the shedding of innocent blood, must be

10. The Bible records an apparently similar incident involving Abimelech and Rebekah (26:6–11). That incident took place after the birth of Jacob; this alone would explain why there was no divine intervention in this case.

understood in the light of the difference between human justice and divine justice: God alone is unqualifiedly, if unfathomably, just. God promised to Abraham that He would spare Sodom if ten righteous men should be found in it, and Abraham was satisfied with this promise; He did not promise that He would spare it if nine righteous men were found in it; would those nine be destroyed together with the wicked? And even if all Sodomites were wicked and hence justly destroyed, did their infants who were destroyed with them deserve their destruction? The apparent contradiction between the command to sacrifice Isaac and the divine promise to the descendants of Isaac is disposed of by the consideration that nothing is too wondrous for the Lord. Abraham's supreme trust in God, his simple, single-minded, child-like faith was rewarded, although or because it presupposed his entire unconcern with any reward, for Abraham was willing to forgo, to destroy, to kill the only reward with which he was concerned; God prevented the sacrifice of Isaac. Abraham's intended action needed a reward although he was not concerned with a reward because his intended action cannot be said to have been intrinsically rewarding. The preservation of Isaac is as wondrous as his birth. These two wonders illustrate more clearly than anything else the origin of the holy nation.

The God Who created heaven and earth, Who is the only God, Whose only image is man, Who forbade man to eat of the tree of knowledge of good and evil, Who made a Covenant with mankind after the Flood and thereafter a Covenant with Abraham which became His Covenant with Abraham, Isaac and Jacob—what kind of God is He? Or, to speak more reverently and more adequately, what is His name? This question was addressed to God Himself by Moses when he was sent by Him to the sons of Israel. God replied: "Ehyeh-Asher-Ehyeh." This is mostly translated: "I am That (Who) I am." One has called that reply "the metaphysics of Exodus" in order to indicate its fundamental character. It is indeed the fundamental biblical statement about the biblical God, but we hesitate to call it metaphysical, since the notion of *physis* is alien to the Bible. I believe that we ought to render this statement by "I shall be What I shall be," thus preserving the connection between God's name and the fact that He makes covenants with men, i.e., that He reveals himself to men above all by His commandments and by His promises and His fulfillment of the promises. "I shall be What I shall be" is as it were explained in the verse (Exod. 33:19), "I shall be gracious to whom I shall be gracious and I shall show mercy to whom I shall show mercy." God's actions cannot be predicted, unless He Himself predicted them, i.e., promised them. But as is shown precisely by the account of Abraham's binding of Isaac, the way in which He fulfills His promises cannot be known in advance. The biblical God is a mysterious God: He comes in a thick cloud (Exod. 19:9); He cannot be seen; His presence can be sensed but not always and everywhere; what is known of Him is only what He chose to communicate by His word through His chosen servants. The

rest of the chosen people knows His word—apart from the Ten Commandments (Deut. 4:12 and 5:4–5)—only mediately and does not wish to know it
immediately (Exod. 20:19 and 21, 24: 1–2, Deut. 18:15–18, Amos 3:7). For
almost all purposes the word of God as revealed to His prophets and
especially to Moses became *the* source of knowledge of good and evil, the
true tree of knowledge which is at the same time the tree of life.

This much about the beginning of the Bible and what it entails. Let us now
cast a glance at some Greek counterparts to the beginning of the Bible and in
the first place at Hesiod's *Theogony* as well as the remains of Parmenides'
and Empedocles' works. They all are the works of known authors. This does
not mean that they are, or present themselves as, merely human. Hesiod
sings what the Muses, the daughters of Zeus who is the father of gods and
men, taught him or commanded him to sing. One could say that the Muses
vouch for the truth of Hesiod's song, were it not for the fact that they
sometimes say lies resembling what is true. Parmenides transmits the
teachings of a goddess, and so does Empedocles. Yet these men composed
their books; their songs or speeches are books. The Bible on the other hand
is not a book. The utmost one could say is that it is a collection of books. But
are all parts of that collection books? Is in particular the Torah a book? Is it
not rather the work of an unknown compiler or of unknown compilers who
wove together writings and oral traditions of unknown origin? Is this not the
reason why the Bible can contain fossils that are at variance even with its
fundamental teaching regarding God? The author of a book in the strict
sense excludes everything that is not necessary, that does not fulfill a
function necessary for the purpose that his book is meant to fulfill. The
compilers of the Bible as a whole and of the Torah in particular seem to have
followed an entirely different rule. Confronted with a variety of pre-existing
holy speeches, which as such had to be treated with the utmost respect, they
excluded only what could not by any stretch of the imagination be rendered
compatible with the fundamental and authoritative teaching; their very
piety, aroused and fostered by the pre-existing holy speeches, led them to
make such changes in those holy speeches as they did make. Their work may
then abound in contradictions and repetitions that no one ever intended as
such, whereas in a book in the strict sense there is nothing that is not
intended by the author. Yet by excluding what could not by any stretch of
the imagination be rendered compatible with the fundamental and authoritative teaching, they prepared the traditional way of reading the Bible, i.e.,
the reading of the Bible as if it were a book in the strict sense. The tendency
to read the Bible and in particular the Torah as a book in the strict sense was
infinitely strengthened by the belief that it is the only holy writing or the holy
writing par excellence.

Hesiod's *Theogony* sings of the generation or begetting of the gods; the
gods were not "made" by anybody. So far from being created by a god, earth
and heaven are the ancestors of the immortal gods. More precisely, accord-

ing to Hesiod everything that is has come to be. First there arose Chaos,
Gaia (Earth) and Eros. Gaia gave birth first to Ouranos (Heaven) and then,
mating with Ouranos, she brought forth Kronos and his brothers and sisters.
Ouranos hated his children and did not wish them to come to light. At the
wish and advice of Gaia, Kronos deprived his father of his generative power
and thus unintentionally brought about the emergence of Aphrodite; Kronos became the king of the gods. Kronos' evil deed was avenged by his son
Zeus whom he had generated by mating with Rheia and whom he had
planned to destroy; Zeus dethroned his father and thus became the king of
the gods, the father of gods and men, the mightiest of all the gods. Given his
ancestors it is not surprising that while being the father of men and belonging
to the gods who are the givers of good things, he is far from being kind to
men. Mating with Mnemosyne, the daughter of Gaia and Ouranos, Zeus
generated the nine Muses. The Muses give sweet and gentle eloquence and
understanding to the kings whom they wish to honor. Through the Muses
there are singers on earth, just as through Zeus there are kings. While
kingship and song may go together, there is a profound difference between
the two—a difference that, guided by Hesiod, one may compare to that
between the hawk and the nightingale. Surely Metis (Wisdom), while being
Zeus's first spouse and having become inseparable from him, is not identical
with him; the relation of Zeus and Metis may remind one of the relation of
God and Wisdom in the Bible.[11] Hesiod speaks of the creation or making of
men not in the *Theogony* but in his *Works and Days*, i.e., in the context of
his teaching regarding how man should live, regarding man's right life,
which includes the teaching regarding the right seasons (the "days"): the
question of the right life does not arise regarding the gods. The right life for
man is the just life, the life devoted to working, expecially to tilling the soil.
Work thus understood is a blessing ordained by Zeus who blesses the just
and crushes the proud: often even a whole city is destroyed for the deeds of a
single bad man. Yet Zeus takes cognizance of men's justice and injustice
only if he so wills. (35–36, 225–85) Accordingly, work appears to be not a
blessing but a curse: men must work because the gods keep hidden from
them the means of life and they do this in order to punish them for Prometheus' theft, inspired by philanthropy, of fire. But was not Prometheus'
action itself prompted by the fact that men were not properly provided for
by the gods and in particular by Zeus? Be this as it may, Zeus did not deprive
men of the fire that Prometheus had stolen for them; he punished them by
sending Pandora to them with her box that was filled with countless evils
such as hard toils. (42, 105) The evils with which human life is beset, cannot
be traced to human sin. Hesiod conveys the same message by his story of the
five races of men which came into being successively. The first race, the

11. *Theogony* 53–97 and 886–900; cf. Proverbs 8.

golden race, was made by the gods while Kronos was still ruling in heaven; these men lived without toil and grief; they had all good things in abundance because the earth by itself gave them abundant fruit. Yet the men made by father Zeus lack this bliss; Hesiod does not make clear whether this is due to Zeus's ill-will or to his lack of power; he gives us no reason to think that it is due to man's sin. He creates the impression that human life became ever more miserable as one race of men succeeds the other: there is no divine promise, supported by the fulfillment of earlier divine promises, that permits one to trust and to hope.

The most striking difference between the poet Hesiod and the philosophers Parmenides and Empedocles is that according to the philosophers not everything has come into being: that which truly is, has not come into being and does not perish. This does not necessarily mean that what is always is a god or gods. For if Empedocles, e.g., calls one of the eternal four elements Zeus, this Zeus has hardly anything in common with what Hesiod, or the people generally, understood by Zeus. At any rate according to both philosophers the gods as ordinarily understood have come into being, just as heaven and earth, and therefore will perish again.

At the time when the opposition between Jerusalem and Athens reached the level of what one may call its classical struggle, in the twelfth and thirteenth centuries, philosophy was represented by Aristotle. The Aristotelian god like the biblical God is a thinking being, but in opposition to the biblical God he is only a thinking being, pure thought: pure thought that thinks itself and only itself. Only by thinking himself and nothing but himself does he rule the world. He surely does not rule by giving orders and laws. Hence he is not a creator-god: the world is as eternal as god. Man is not his image: man is much lower in rank than other parts of the world. For Aristotle it is almost a blasphemy to ascribe justice to his god; he is above justice as well as injustice.[12]

It has often been said that the philosopher who comes closest to the Bible is Plato. This was said not the least during the classical struggle between Jerusalem and Athens in the Middle Ages. Both Platonic philosophy and biblical piety are animated by the concern with purity and purification: the "pure reason" in Plato's sense is closer to the Bible than the "pure reason" in Kant's sense or for that matter in Anaxagoras' and Aristotle's sense. Plato teaches, just as the Bible, that heaven and earth were created or made by an invisible God whom he calls the Father, who is always, who is good and hence whose creation is good. The coming-into-being and the preservation of the world that he has created depends on the will of its maker. What Plato himself calls the theology consists of two teachings: 1) God is good and

12. *Metaphysics* 1072 b 14–30, 1074 b 15–1075 a 11; *De Anima* 429 a 19–20; *Eth. Nic.* 1141 a 33–b 2, 1178 b 1–12; *Eth. Eud.* 1249 a 14–15.

hence is no way the cause of evil; 2) God is simple and hence unchangeable. On the divine concern with men's justice and injustice, the Platonic teaching is in fundamental agreement with the biblical teaching; it even culminates in a statement that agrees almost literally with biblical statements.[13] Yet the differences between the Platonic and the biblical teaching are no less striking than the agreements. The Platonic teaching on creation does not claim to be more than a likely tale. The Platonic God is a creator also of gods, of visible living beings, i.e., of the stars; the created gods rather than the creator God create the mortal living beings and in particular man; heaven is a blessed god. The Platonic God does not create the world by his word; he creates it after having looked to the eternal ideas which therefore are higher than he. In accordance with this, Plato's explicit theology is presented within the context of the first discussion of education in the *Republic*, within the context of what one may call the discussion of elementary education; in the second and final discussion of education—the discussion of the education of the philosophers—theology is replaced by the doctrine of ideas. As for the thematic discussion of providence in the *Laws*, it may suffice here to say that it occurs within the context of the discussion of penal law.

In his likely tale of how God created the visible whole, Plato makes a distinction between two kinds of gods, the visible cosmic gods and the traditional gods—between the gods who revolve manifestly, i.e., who manifest themselves regularly, and the gods who manifest themselves so far as they will. The least one would have to say is that according to Plato the cosmic gods are of much higher rank than the traditional gods, the Greek gods. Inasmuch as the cosmic gods are accessible to man as man—to his observations and calculations—, whereas the Greek gods are accessible only to the Greeks through Greek traditions, one may ascribe in comic exaggeration the worship of the cosmic gods to the barbarians. This ascription is made in an altogether noncomic manner and intent in the Bible: Israel is forbidden to worship the sun and the moon and the stars which the Lord has allotted to the other peoples everywhere under heaven.[14] This implies that the other peoples', the barbarians', worship of the cosmic gods is not due to a natural or rational cause, to the fact that those gods are accessible to man as man but to an act of God's will. It goes without saying that according to the Bible the God Who manifests Himself as far as He wills, Who is not universally worshipped as such, is the only true god. The Platonic statement taken in conjunction with the biblical statement brings out the fundamental opposition of Athens at its peak to Jerusalem: the opposition of the God or gods of the philosophers to the God of Abraham, Isaac and Jacob, the opposition of Reason and Revelation.

13. Cf. *Laws* 905 a 4–b 2 with Amos 9:1–3 and Psalm 139:7–10.
14. *Timaeus* 40 d 6–41 a 5; Aristophanes, *Peace* 404–13; Deut. 4:19.

II. On Socrates and the Prophets

Fifty years ago, in the middle of World War I, Hermann Cohen, the greatest representative of German Jewry and spokesman for it, the most powerful figure among the German professors of philosophy of his time, stated his view on Jerusalem and Athens in a lecture entitled "The social ideal in Plato and the prophets."[15] He repeated that lecture shortly before his death. We may then regard it as stating his final view on Jerusalem and Athens and therewith on *the* truth. For, as Cohen says right at the beginning, "Plato and the prophets are the two most important sources of modern culture." Being concerned with "the social ideal," he does not say a single word on Christianity in the whole lecture. Crudely but not misleadingly one may restate Cohen's view as follows. *The* truth is the synthesis of the teaching of Plato and that of the prophets. What we owe to Plato is the insight that the truth is in the first place the truth of science but that science must be supplemented, overarched by the idea of the good which to Cohen means, not God, but rational, scientific ethics. The ethical truth must not only be compatible with the scientific truth; the ethical truth even needs the scientific truth. The prophets are very much concerned with knowledge: with the knowledge of God, but this knowledge as the prophets understood it, has no connection whatever with scientific knowledge; it is knowledge only in a metaphorical sense. It is perhaps with a view to this fact that Cohen speaks once of the divine Plato but never of the divine prophets. Why then can he not leave matters at Platonic philosophy? What is the fundamental defect of Platonic philosophy that is remedied by the prophets and only by the prophets? According to Plato, the cessation of evils requires the rule of the philosophers, of the men who possess the highest kind of human knowledge, i.e., of science in the broadest sense of the term. But this kind of knowledge, as to some extent all scientific knowledge, is according to Plato the preserve of a small minority: of the men who possess certain gifts that most men lack—of the few men who possess a certain nature. Plato presupposes that there is an unchangeable human nature. As a consequence, he presupposes that there is such a fundamental structure of the good human society as is unchangeable. This leads him to assert or to assume that there will be wars as long as there will be human beings, that there ought to be a class of warriors and that that class ought to be higher in rank and honor than the class of producers and exchangers. These defects are remedied by the prophets precisely because they lack the idea of science and hence the idea of nature, and hence they can believe that men's conduct toward one another can undergo a change much more radical than any change ever dreamt of by Plato.

15. *Hermann Cohens Jüdische Schriften,* Berlin 1924, I, 306–330; cf. the editor's note, on p. 341.

Cohen has brought out very well the antagonism between Plato and the prophets. Nevertheless we cannot leave matters at his view of that antagonism. Cohen's thought belongs to the world preceding World War I. Accordingly he had a greater faith in the power of modern Western culture to mold the fate of mankind than seems to be warranted now. The worst things that he experienced were the Dreyfus scandal and the pogroms instigated by Czarist Russia: he did not experience Communist Russia and Hitler Germany. More disillusioned regarding modern culture than Cohen was, we wonder whether the two ingredients of modern culture, of the modern synthesis, are not more solid than that synthesis. Catastrophes and horrors of a magnitude hitherto unknown, which we have seen and through which we have lived, were better provided for, or made intelligible, by both Plato and the prophets than by the modern belief in progress. Since we are less certain than Cohen was that the modern synthesis is superior to its premodern ingredients, and since the two ingredients are in fundamental opposition to each other, we are ultimately confronted by a problem rather than by a solution.

More particularly, Cohen understood Plato in the light of the opposition between Plato and Aristotle—an opposition that he understood in the light of the opposition between Kant and Hegel. We, however, are more impressed than Cohen was by the kinship between Plato and Aristotle on the one hand and the kinship between Kant and Hegel on the other. In other words, the quarrel between the ancients and the moderns seems to us to be more fundamental than either the quarrel between Plato and Aristotle or that between Kant and Hegel.

We prefer to speak of Socrates and the prophets rather than of Plato and the prophets, for the following reasons. We are no longer as sure as Cohen was that we can draw a clear line between Socrates and Plato. There is traditional support for drawing such a clear line, above all in Aristotle; but Aristotle's statements on this kind of subject no longer possess for us the authority that they formerly possessed, and this is due partly to Cohen himself. The clear distinction between Socrates and Plato is based, not only on tradition, but on the results of modern historical criticism; yet these results are in the decisive respect hypothetical. The decisive fact for us is that Plato as it were points away from himself to Socrates. If we wish to understand Plato, we must take him seriously; we must take seriously in particular his deference to Socrates. Plato points not only to Socrates' speeches but to his whole life, to his fate as well. Hence Plato's life and fate do not have the symbolic character of Socrates' life and fate. Socrates, as presented by Plato, had a mission; Plato did not claim to have a mission. It is in the first place this fact—the fact that Socrates had a mission—that induces us to consider, not Plato and the prophets, but Socrates and the prophets.

I cannot speak in my own words of the mission of the prophets. Surely here and now I cannot do more than remind you of three prophetic utterances of singular force and grandeur. Isaiah 6: "In the year that King Uzziah died I saw also the Lord sitting upon a throne, high and lifted up, and his train filled the temple. Above it stood the seraphim: each one had six wings; with twain he covered his face, and with twain he covered his feet, and with twain he did fly. And one cried unto another, and said, Holy, holy, holy is the Lord of hosts: the whole world is full of his glory. And the posts of the door moved at the voice of him that cried, and the house was filled with smoke. Then I said, Woe is me! for I am undone; because I am a man of unclean lips, and I dwell in the midst of a people of unclean lips: for mine eyes have seen the King, the Lord of hosts. Then flew one of the seraphim unto me, having a live coal in his hand, which he had taken with the tongs from off the altar: And he laid it upon my mouth, and said, Lo, this hath touched thy lips; and thine iniquity is taken away, and thy sin purged. Also I heard the voice of the Lord, saying, Whom shall I send, and who will go for us? Then said I, Here am I; send me." Isaiah, it seems, volunteered for his mission. Could he not have remained silent? Could he refuse to volunteer? When the word of the Lord came unto Jonah, "Arise, go to Nineveh, that great city, and cry against it; for their wickedness is come up before me," "Jonah rose up to flee unto Tarshish from the presence of the Lord"; Jonah ran away from his mission; but God did not allow him to run away; He compelled him to fulfill it. Of this compulsion we hear in different ways from Amos and Jeremiah. Amos 3:7–8: "Surely the Lord God will do nothing but he revealeth his secret unto his servants the prophets. The lion hath roared, who will not fear? the Lord God hath spoken; who will not prophesy?" The prophets overpowered by the majesty of the Lord, by His wrath and His mercy, bring the message of His wrath and His mercy. Jeremiah 1:4–10: "Then the word of the Lord came unto me, saying, Before I formed thee in the belly I knew thee and before thou camest out of the womb I sanctified thee, and I ordained thee a prophet unto the nations. Then said I, Ah, Lord God! behold, I cannot speak; for I am a child. But the Lord said unto me, Say not, I am a child; for thou shalt go to all that I shall send thee, and whatsoever I command thee thou shalt speak. Be not afraid of their faces; for I am with thee to deliver thee, saith the Lord. Then the Lord put forth his hand, and touched my mouth. And the Lord said unto me, Behold, I have put my words in thy mouth. See, I have this day set thee over the nations and over the kingdoms, to root out, and to pull down, and to destroy, and to throw down, to build, and to plant."

The claim to have been sent by God was raised also by men who were not truly prophets but prophets of falsehood, false prophets. Many or most hearers were therefore uncertain as to which kinds of claimants to prophecy were to be trusted or believed. According to the Bible, the false prophets simply lied in saying that they were sent by God: "they speak a vision of their own heart, and not out of the mouth of the Lord. They say. . . the Lord hath said, Ye shall have peace." (Jer. 23:16–17) The false prophets tell the people what the people like to hear; hence they are much more popular than the true prophets. The false prophets are "prophets of the deceit of their own heart" (ibid. 26); they tell the people what they themselves imagined (consciously or unconsciously) because they wished it or their hearers wished it. But: "Is not my word like as a fire? saith the Lord, and like a hammer that breaketh the rock in pieces?" (ibid. 29) Or, as Jeremiah put it when opposing the false prophet Hananiah: "The prophets that have been before me and before thee of old prophesied both against many countries, and against great kingdoms, of war, and of evil, and of pestilence." (28.8) This does not mean that a prophet is true only if he is a prophet of doom; the true prophets are also prophets of ultimate salvation. We understand the difference between the true and the false prophets if we listen to and meditate on these words of Jeremiah: "Thus saith the Lord; Cursed is the man, that trusteth in man, and makes flesh his arm, and whose heart departeth from the Lord. . . . Blessed is the man that trusteth in the Lord, and whose hope the Lord is." The false prophets trust in flesh, even if that flesh is the temple in Jerusalem, the promised land, nay, the chosen people itself, nay, God's promise to the chosen people if that promise is taken to be an unconditional promise and not as a part of a Covenant. The true prophets, regardless of whether they predict doom or salvation, predict the unexpected, the humanly unforeseeable—what would not occur to men, left to themselves, to fear or to hope. The true prophets speak and act by the spirit and in the spirit of *Ehyeh-asher-ehyeh*. For the false prophets on the other hand there cannot be the wholly unexpected, whether bad or good.

Of Socrates' mission we know only through Plato's *Apology of Socrates*, which presents itself as the speech delivered by Socrates when he defended himself against the charge that he did not believe in the existence of the gods worshipped by the city of Athens and that he corrupted the young. In that speech he denies possessing any more than human wisdom. This denial was understood by Yehudah Ha-levi among others as follows: "Socrates said to the people: 'I do not deny your divine wisdom, but I say that I do not understand it; I am wise only in human wisdom.' "[16] While this interpretation points in the right direction, it goes somewhat too far. At least Socrates refers, immediately after having denied possessing any more than human wisdom, to the speech that originated his mission, and of this speech he says that it is not his but he seems to ascribe to it divine origin. He does trace what he says to a speaker who is worthy of credence to the Athenians. But it is

16. *Cuzari* IV 13 and V 14. Cf. Strauss, *Persecution and the Art of Writing*, 105–106.

probable that he means by that speaker his companion Chairephon who is worthy of credence to the Athenians, more worthy of credence to the Athenians than Socrates, because he was attached to the democratic re-gime. This Chairephon, having once come to Delphi, asked Apollo's oracle whether there was anyone wiser than Socrates. The Pythia replied that no one was wiser. This reply originated Socrates' mission. We see at once that Socrates' mission originated in human initiative, in the initiative of one of Socrates' companions. Socrates takes it for granted that the reply given by the Pythia was given by the god Apollo himself. Yet this does not induce him to take it for granted that the god's reply is true. He does take it for granted that it is not meet for the god to lie. Yet this does not make the god's reply convincing to him. In fact he tries to refute that reply by discovering men who are wiser than he. Engaging in this quest he finds out that the god said the truth: Socrates is wiser than other men because he knows that he knows nothing, i.e., nothing about the most important things, whereas the others believe that they know the truth about the most important things. Thus his attempt to refute the oracle turns into a vindication of the oracle. Without intending it, he comes to the assistance of the god; he serves the god; he obeys the god's command. Although no god had ever spoken to him, he is satisfied that the god had commanded him to examine himself and the others, i.e., to philosophize, or to exhort everyone he meets to the practice of virtue: he has been given by the god to the city of Athens as a gadfly.

While Socrates does not claim to have heard the speech of a god, he claims that a voice—something divine and demonic—occurs to him from time to time, his daimonion. This daimonion, however, has no connection with Socrates' mission, for it never urges him forward but only keeps him back. While the Delphic oracle urged him forward toward philosophizing, toward examining his fellow men, and thus made him generally hated and thus brought him into mortal danger, his daimonion kept him back from political activity and thus saved him from mortal danger.

The fact that both Socrates and the prophets have a divine mission means or at any rate implies that both Socrates and the prophets are concerned with justice or righteousness, with the perfectly just society which as such would be free from all evils. To this extent Socrates' figuring out of the best social order and the prophets' vision of the Messianic age are in agreement. Yet whereas the prophets predict the coming of the Messianic age, Socrates merely holds that the perfect society is possible: whether it will ever be actual, depends on an unlikely, although not impossible, coincidence, the coincidence of philosophy and political power. For, according to Socrates, the coming-into-being of the best political order is not due to divine inter-vention; human nature will remain as it always has been; the decisive difference between the best political order and all other societies is that in the former the philosophers will be kings or that the natural potentiality of the philosophers will reach its utmost perfection. In the most perfect social order as Socrates sees it, knowledge of the most important things will remain, as it always was, the preserve of the philosophers, i.e., of a very small part of the population. According to the prophets however, in the Messianic age "the earth shall be full of knowledge of the Lord, as the waters cover the earth" (Isaiah 11:9), and this will be brought about by God Himself. As a consequence, the Messianic age will be the age of universal peace: all nations shall come to the mountain of the Lord, to the house of the God of Jacob, "and they shall beat their swords into plowshares, and their spears into pruning hooks: nation shall not lift up sword against nation, neither shall they learn war any more." (Isaiah 2:2–4) The best regime, however, as Socrates envisages it, will animate a single city which as a matter of course will become embroiled in wars with other cities. The cessation of evils that Socrates expects from the establishment of the best regime will not include the cessation of war.

The perfectly just man, the man who is as just as is humanly possible, is according to Socrates the philosopher and according to the prophets the faithful servant of the Lord. The philosopher is the man who dedicates his life to the quest for knowledge of the good, of the idea of the good; what we would call moral virtue is only the condition or by-product of that quest. According to the prophets, however, there is no need for the quest for knowledge of the good: God "hath shewed thee, o man, what is good; and what doth the Lord require of thee, but to do justly, and to love mercy, and to walk humbly with thy God." (Micah 6:8) In accordance with this the prophets as a rule address the people and sometimes even all the peoples, whereas Socrates as a rule addresses only one man. In the language of Socrates the prophets are orators while Socrates engages in conversations with one man, which means he is addressing questions to him.

There is one striking example of a prophet talking in private to a single man, in a way addressing a question to him. 2 Sam. 12:1–7: "And the Lord sent Nathan unto David. And he came unto him, and said unto him, There were two men in one city; the one rich, and the other poor. The rich man had exceeding many flocks and herds: But the poor man had nothing, save one little ewe lamb, which he had brought and nourished up: and it grew up together with him, and with his children; it did eat of his own meat, and drank of his own cup, and lay in his bosom, and was unto him as a daughter. And there came a traveller unto the rich man and he spared to take of his own flock and of his own herd, to dress for the wayfaring man that was come unto him; but took the poor man's lamb, and dressed it for the man that was come unto him. And David's anger was greatly kindled against the man; and he said to Nathan, As the Lord liveth, the man that hath done this thing shall surely die; And he shall restore the lamb fourfold, because he did this thing, and because he had no pity. And Nathan said to David, Thou art the man."

The nearest parallel to this event that occurs in the Socratic writings is Socrates' reproof of his former companion, the tyrant Critias. "When the thirty were putting to death many citizens and by no means the worst ones, and were encouraging many in crime, Socrates said *somewhere*, that it seemed strange that a herdsman who lets his cattle decrease and go to the bad should not admit that he is a poor cowherd; but stranger still that a statesman when he causes the citizens to decrease and go to the bad, should feel no shame nor think himself a poor statesman. This remark was *reported* to Critias. . . ." (Xenophon, *Memorabilia* I 2.32–33.)

8

Note on the Plan of Nietzsche's
Beyond Good and Evil

Beyond Good and Evil always seemed to me to be the most beautiful of
Nietzsche's books. This impression could be thought to be contradicted by
his judgement, for he was inclined to believe that his *Zarathustra* is the most
profound book that exists in German as well as the most perfect in regard to
language. But "most beautiful" is not the same as "most profound" and
even as "most perfect in regard to language." To illustrate this partly by an
example which is perhaps not too far-fetched, there seems to be general
agreement to the effect that Plato's *Republic*, his *Phaedrus* and his *Banquet*
are his most beautiful writings without their being necessarily his most
profound writings. Yet Plato makes no distinction among his writings in
regard to profundity or beauty or perfection in regard to language; he is not
concerned with Plato—with his "ipsissimosity"—and hence with Plato's
writings, but points away from himself whereas Nietzsche points most
emphatically to himself, to "Mr. Nietzsche." Now Nietzsche "personally"
preferred, not *Beyond Good and Evil* but his *Dawn of Morning* and his *Gay
Science* to all his other books precisely because these two books are his
"most personal" books (letter to Karl Knortz of June 21, 1888). As the very
term "personal," ultimately derivative from the Greek word for "face,"
indicates, being "personal" has nothing to do with being "profound" or with
being "perfect in regard to language."

What is dimly perceived and inadequately expressed through our judgement on *Beyond Good and Evil*, is stated clearly by Nietzsche in his account
of that book which he has given in *Ecce Homo*: *Beyond Good and Evil* is the
very opposite of the "inspired" and "dithyrambic" *Zarathustra* in as much as

Reprinted from *Interpretation: A Journal of Political Philosophy* 3, nos. 2 and 3 (1973).

Zarathustra is most far-sighted, whereas in *Beyond Good and Evil* the eye is compelled to grasp clearly the nearest, the timely (the present), the around-us. This change of concern required in every respect, "above all also in the form," the same arbitrary turning away from the instincts out of which a Zarathustra had become possible: the graceful subtlety as regards form, as regards intention, as regards the art of silence are in the foreground in *Beyond Good and Evil* which amounts to saying that these qualities are not in the foreground in the *Zarathustra*, to say nothing of Nietzsche's other books.

In other words, in *Beyond Good and Evil*, in the only book published by Nietzsche, in the contemporary preface to which he presents himself as the antagonist of Plato, he "platonizes" as regards the "form" more than anywhere else.

According to the preface to *Beyond Good and Evil* Plato's fundamental error was his invention of the pure mind and of the good in itself. From this premise one can easily be led to Diotima's conclusion that no human being is wise, but only the god is; human beings can only strive for wisdom or philosophize; gods do not philosophize (*Banquet* 203e–204a). In the penultimate aphorism of *Beyond Good and Evil* in which Nietzsche deline-ates "the genius of the heart"—a super-Socrates who is in fact the god Dionysos—Nietzsche divulges after the proper preparation the novelty, suspect perhaps especially among philosophers, that gods too philosophize. Yet Diotima is not Socrates nor Plato, and Plato could well have thought that gods philosophize (cf. *Sophist* 216b5–6, *Theaetetus* 151d 1–2). And when in the ultimate aphorism of *Beyond Good and Evil* Nietzsche under-lines the fundamental difference between "written and painted thoughts" and thoughts in their original form, we cannot help being reminded of what Plato says or intimates regarding the "weakness of the *logos*" and regarding the unsayable and a fortiori unwritable character of the truth (*Ep.* VII 341c–d, 342e–343a): the purity of the mind as Plato conceives of it, does not necessarily establish the strength of the *logos*.

Beyond Good and Evil has the subtitle "Prelude to a philosophy of the future." The book is meant to prepare, not indeed the philosophy of the future, the true philosophy, but a new kind of philosophy by liberating the mind from "the prejudice of the philosophers," i.e. of the philosophers of the past (and the present). At the same time or by this very fact the book is meant to be a specimen of the philosophy of the future. The first chapter ("Of the prejudices of the philosophers") is followed by a chapter entitled "The free mind." The free minds in Nietzsche's sense are free from the prejudice of the philosophy of the past but they are not yet philosophers of the future; they are the heralds and precursors of the philosophy of the future (aph. 44). It is hard to say how the distinction between the free minds and the philosophers of the future is to be understood: are the free minds by any chance freer than the philosophers of the future? do they possess an openness which is possible only during the transitional period between the philosophy of the past and the philosophy of the future? Be this as it may, philosophy is surely the primary theme of *Beyond Good and Evil*, the obvious theme of the first two chapters.

The book consists of nine chapters. The third chapter is devoted to religion. The heading of the fourth chapter ("Sayings and Interludes") does not indicate a subject matter; that chapter is distinguished from all other chapters by the fact that it consists exclusively of short aphorisms. The last five chapters are devoted to morals and politics. The book as a whole consists then of two main parts which are separated from one another by about 123 "Sayings and Interludes"; the first of the two parts is devoted chiefly to philosophy and religion and the second chiefly to morals and politics. Philosophy and religion, it seems, belong together—belong more closely together than philosophy and the city. (Cf. Hegel's distinction between the absolute and the objective mind.) The fundamental alternative is that of the rule of philosophy over religion or the rule of religion over philosophy; it is not, as it was for Plato or Aristotle, that of the philosophic and the political life; for Nietzsche, as distinguished from the classics, politics belongs from the outset to a lower plane than either philosophy or religion. In the preface he intimates that his precursor par excellence is not a statesman nor even a philosopher but the *homo religiosus* Pascal (cf. aph. 45).

Nietzsche says very little about religion in the first two chapters. One could say that he speaks there on religion only in a single aphorism which happens to be the shortest (37). That aphorism is a kind of corollary to the immediately preceding one in which he sets forth in the most straightforward and unambiguous manner that is compatible with his intention, the particular character of his fundamental proposition according to which life is will to power or seen from within the world is will to power and nothing else. The will to power takes the place which the *eros*—the striving for "the good in itself"—occupies in Plato's thought. But the *eros* is not "the pure mind" (*der reine Geist*). Whatever may be the relation between the *eros* and the pure mind according to Plato, in Nietzsche's thought the will to power takes the place of both *eros* and the pure mind. Accordingly philosophizing becomes a mode or modification of the will to power: it is the most spiritual (*der geistigste*) will to power; it consists in prescribing to nature what or how it ought to be (aph. 9); it is not love of the true that is independent of will or decision. Whereas according to Plato the pure mind grasps the truth, according to Nietzsche the impure mind, or a certain kind of impure mind, is the sole source of truth. Nietzsche begins therefore *Beyond Good and Evil* with the questioning of love of truth and of truth. If we may make a somewhat free use of an expression occurring in Nietzsche's *Second Medita-*

tion Out of Season, the truth is not attractive, lovable, life-giving, but deadly, as is shown by the true doctrines of the sovereignty of Becoming, of the fluidity of all concepts, types and species, and of the lack of any cardinal difference between man and beast *(Werke*, ed Schlechta, I 272); it is shown most simply by the true doctrine that God is dead. The world in itself, the "thing-in-itself," "nature" (aph. 9) is wholly chaotic and meaningless. Hence all meaning, all order originates in man, in man's creative acts, in his will to power. Nietzsche's statements or suggestions are deliberately enigmatic (aph. 40). By suggesting or saying that the truth is deadly, he does his best to break the power of the deadly truth; he suggests that the most important, the most comprehensive truth—the truth regarding all truths—is life-giving. In other words, by suggesting that the truth is human creation, he suggests that this truth at any rate is not a human creation. One is tempted to say that Nietzsche's pure mind grasps the fact that the impure mind creates perishable truths. Resisting that temptation we state Nietzsche's suggestion following him in this manner: the philosophers tried to get hold of the "text" as distinguished from "interpretations"; they tried to "discover" and not to "invent." What Nietzsche claims to have realized is that the text in its pure, unfalsified form is inaccessible (like the Kantian Thing-in-itself); everything thought by anyone—philosopher or man of the people—is in the last analysis interpretation. But for this very reason the text, the world in itself, the true world cannot be of any concern to us; the world of any concern to us is necessarily a fiction, for it is necessarily anthropocentric; man is necessarily in a manner the measure of all things (aph. 3 end, 12 end, 17, 22, 24, 34, 38; cf. Plato, *Laws* 716c 4–6). As is indicated sufficiently by the title of the book, the authropocentrism for which Nietzsche opts is transmoral (cf. aph. 34 and 35 with 32). At first glance there does not seem to be a connection between the grave aphorism 34 and the lighthearted aphorism 35 and this seems to agree with the general impression according to which a book of aphorisms does not have or need not have a lucid and necessary order or may consist of disconnected pieces. The connection between aphorism 34 and 35 is a particularly striking example of the lucid, if somewhat hidden, order governing the sequence of the aphorisms: the desultory character of Nietzsche's argument is more pretended than real. If the aforesaid is correct, the doctrine of the will to power cannot claim to reveal what is, the fact, the most fundamental fact but is "only" one interpretation, presumably the best interpretation, among many. Nietzsche regards this apparent objection as a confirmation of his proposition (aph. 22 end).

We can now turn to the two aphorisms in *Beyond Good and Evil* I–II that can be said to be devoted to religion (36–37). Aphorism 36 presents the reasoning in support of the doctrine of the will to power. Nietzsche had spoken of the will to power before, but only in the way of bald assertion, not to say dogmatically. Now he sets forth with what is at the same time the most intransigent intellectual probity and the most bewitching playfulness his reasons, i.e. the problematic, tentative, tempting, hypothetical character of his proposition. It could seem that he does not know more of the will to power as the fundamental reality than what he says here. Almost immediately before, in the central aphorism of the second chapter (34), he had drawn our attention to the fundamental distinction between the world which is of any concern to us and the world in itself, or between the world of appearance or fiction (the interpretations) and the true world (the text). What he seems to aim at is the abolition of that fundamental distinction the world as will to power is both the world of any concern to us and the world in itself. Precisely if all views of the world are interpretations, i.e. acts of the will to power, the doctrine of the will to power is at the same time an interpretation and the most fundamental fact, for, in contradistinction to all other interpretations, it is the necessary and sufficient condition of the possibility of any "categories."

After having tempted some of his readers (cf. aph. 30) with the doctrine of the will to power Nietzsche makes them raise the question as to whether that doctrine does not assert, to speak popularly, that God is refuted but the devil is not. He replies "On the contrary! On the contary, my friends! And, to the devil, what forces you to speak popularly?" The doctrine of the will to power—the whole doctrine of *Beyond Good and Evil*—is in a manner a vindication of God. (Cf. aph. 150 and 295, as well as *Genealogy of Morals*, Preface Nr. 7.)—

The third chapter is entitled "Das religiöse Wesen"; it is not entitled "Das Wesen der Religion," one of the reasons for this being that the essence of religion, that which is common to all religions, is not or should not be of any concern to us. The chapter considers religion with a view to the human soul and its boundaries, to the whole history of the soul hitherto and its yet inexhausted possibilities: Nietzsche does not deal with unknown possibilities, although or because he deals with religion hitherto and the religion of the future. Aphorisms 46–52 are devoted to religion hitherto and 53–57 to the religion of the future. The rest of the chapter (aph. 58–62) transmits Nietzsche's appraisal of religion as a whole. In the section on religion hitherto he speaks first of Christianity (46–48), then of the Greeks (49), then again of Christianity (50–51) and finally of the Old Testament (52). "The religiosity of the old Greeks" and above all certain parts of "the Jewish 'Old Testament' " supply him with the standards by which he judges of Christianity; nowhere in the chapter does he speak of Christianity with the respect, the admiration, the veneration with which he speaks of the two pre-Christian phenomena. The aphorisms on the Old Greeks and on the Old Testament are obviously meant to interrupt the aphorisms devoted to Christianity; the two interrupting aphorisms are put at some distance from one another in order to imitate the distance or rather opposition between what one may call Athens and Jerusalem. The aphorism on the Old Testament is immediately preceded by an aphorism devoted to the saint: there are no saints, no holy men in the Old Testament; the peculiarity of Old Testament theology in contradistinction especially to Greek theology is the conception, the creation of the holy God (cf. *Dawn of Morning* aph. 68). For Nietzsche "the great style" of (certain parts of) the Old Testament shows forth the greatness, not of God, but of what man once was: the holy God no less than the holy man are creatures of the human will to power.

Nietzsche's vindication of God is then atheistic, at least for the time being: the aphorism following that on the Old Testament begins with the question 'Why atheism today?' There was a time when theism was possible or necessary. But in the meantime "God died" (*Thus Spoke Zarathustra*, Zarathustra's Prologue Nr. 3). This does not merely mean that men have ceased to believe in God, for men's unbelief does not destroy God's life or being. It does mean, however, that even while God lived he never was what the believers in him thought him to be, namely, deathless. Theism as it understood itself was therefore always wrong. Yet for a time it was true, i.e. powerful, life-giving. In speaking of how or why it lost its power, Nietzsche speaks here less of the reasons that swayed him than of the reasons advanced by some of his contemporaries, presumably his most competent contemporaries. Not a few of his better readers will justifiably think that those reasons verge on the frivolous. In particular it is not quite clear whether those reasons are directed against natural (rational) or revealed theology. Nevertheless the most powerful anti-theistic argument which Nietzsche sketches is directed against the possibility of a clear and unambiguous revelation, i.e. of God's "speaking" to man (cf. *Dawn of Morning* aph. 91 and 95). Despite the decay of European theism Nietzsche has the impression that the religious instinct—"religiosity" as distinguished from "religion"—is growing powerfully at present or that atheism is only a transitional phase. Could atheism belong to the free mind as Nietzsche conceives of it while a certain kind of non-atheism belongs to the philosopher of the future who will again worship the god Dionysos or will again be, as an Epicurean might say, a *dionysoko-lax* (cf. aph. 7)? This ambiguity is essential to Nietzsche's thought; without it his doctrine would lose its character of an experiment or a temptation.

Nietzsche provisionally illustrates his suggestion of an atheistic or, if you wish, non-theistic religiosity by the alleged fact that the whole modern philosophy was anti-Christian but not anti-religious—that it could seem to point to something reminding of the Vedanta philosophy. But he does not anticipate, he surely does not wish, that the religion of the future will be something like the Vedanta philosophy. He anticipates a more Western, a sterner, more terrible and more invigorating possibility: the sacrificing from cruelty, i.e. from the will to power turning against itself, of God which prepares the worshipping of the stone, stupidity, heaviness (gravity), fate, the Nothing. He anticipates in other words that the better among the contemporary atheists will come to know what they are doing—"the stone" may remind us of Anaxagoras' debunking of the sun—, that they will come to realize that there is something infinitely more terrible, depressing and degrading in the offing than the *foeda religio* or *l'infâme:* the possibility, nay, the fact that human life is utterly meaningless and lacking support, that it lasts only for a minute which is preceded and followed by an infinite time during which the human race was not and will not be. (Cf. the beginning of "On truth and lie in an extra-moral sense.") These religious atheists, this new breed of atheists cannot be deceptively and deceivingly appeased as people like Engels by the prospect of a most glorious future, of the realm of freedom, which will indeed be terminated by the annihilation of the human race and therewith of all meaning but which will last for a very long time—for a millennium or more—, for fortunately we find ourselves still on "the ascending branch of human history" (F. Engels, *Ludwig Feuerbach und der Ausgang der deutschen klassischen Philosophie*): the realm of freedom, destined to perish, necessarily contains within itself the seeds of its annihilation and will therefore, while it lasts, abound in "contradictions" as much as any earlier age.

Nietzsche does not mean to sacrifice God for the sake of the Nothing, for while recognizing the deadly truth that God died he aims at transforming it into a life-inspiring one or rather to discover in the depth of the deadly truth its opposite. Sacrificing God for the sake of the Nothing would be an extreme form of world-denial or of pessimism. But Nietzsche, prompted by "some enigmatic desire," has tried for a long time to penetrate pessimism to its depth and in particular to free it from the delusion of morality which in a way contradicts its world-denying tendency. He thus has grasped a more world-denying way of thinking than that of any previous pessimist. Yet a man who has taken this road has perhaps without intending to do this opened his eyes to the opposite ideal—to the ideal belonging to the religion of the future. It goes without saying that what in some other men was "perhaps" the case was a fact in Nietzsche's thought and life. The adoration of the Nothing proves to be the indispensable transition from every kind of world-denial to the most unbounded Yes: the eternal Yes-saying to everything that was and is. By saying Yes to everything that was and is Nietzsche may seem to reveal himself as radically antirevolutionary or conservative beyond the wildest wishes of all other conservatives, who all say No to some of the things that were or are. Remembering Nietzsche's strictures against "ideals" and "idealists" we are reminded of Goethe's words to Eckermann (November 24, 1824) according to which "everything idea-like(*jedes Ide-elle*) is serviceable for revolutionary purposes." Be this as it may, "And this," Nietzsche concludes his suggestion regarding eternal repetition of what was and is, "would not be *circulus vitiosus deus?*" As this concluding ambiguous question again shows, his atheism is not unambiguous, for he had doubts whether there can be a world, any world whose center is not God (aph. 150). The conclusion of the present aphorism reminds us, through its form, of the theological aphorism occurring in the first two chapters (37) where Nietzsche brings out the fact that in a manner the doctrine of the will to power is a vindication of God, if a decidedly non-theistic vindication of God.

But now we are confronted with the fact that the vindication of God is only the inversion of the sacrificing of God to stupidity, to the Nothing, or at any rate presupposes that sacrificing. What is it that suddenly, if after a long preparation, divinizes the Nothing? Is it the willing of eternity which gives to the world, or restores to it, its worth which the world-denying ways of thinking had denied it? Is it the willing of eternity that makes atheism religious? Is beloved eternity divine merely because it is beloved? If we were to say that it must be in itself lovable, in order to deserve to be loved, would we not become guilty of a relapse into Platonism, into the teaching of "the good in itself"? But can we avoid such a relapse altogether? For the eternal to which Nietzsche says Yes, is not the stone, the stupidity, the Nothing which even if eternal or sempiternal cannot arouse an enthusiastic, life-inspiring Yes. The transformation of the world-denying way of thinking into the opposite ideal is connected with the realization or divination that the stone, the stupidity or the Nothing to which God is being sacrificed, is in its "intelligible character" the will to power (cf. aph. 36).

There is an important ingredient, not to say the nerve, of Nietzsche's "theology" of which I have not spoken and shall not speak since I have no access to it. It has been worthily treated by Karl Reinhardt in his essay "Nietzsche's Klage der Ariadne" (*Vermächtnis der Antike*, Göttingen 1960, 310–333; see also a remark of Reinhardt at the end of his eulogy of Walter F. Otto, *ib.* 379).—

It is possible but not likely that the "Sayings and Interludes" of which the fourth chapter consists, possesses no order, that there is no rhyme or reason to their selection and sequence. I must leave matters at a few observations which are perhaps helpful to some of us.

The opening aphorism draws our attention to the paramountcy of being-oneself, of being for oneself, of "preserving" oneself (cf. aph. 41). Accordingly knowledge cannot be, or cannot be good, for its own sake; it is justifiable only as self-knowledge: being oneself means being honest with oneself, going the way to one's own ideal. This seems to have atheistic implications. There occur in the chapter nine references to God; only one of them points to Nietzsche's own theology (150). There occurs only a single reference to nature (126). Instead we are confronted by nine aphorisms devoted to woman and man. Surely the knower whom Nietzsche has in mind has not, like Kant, the starred heaven above himself. As a consequence he has a high morality, a morality beyond good and evil and in particular beyond puritanism and asceticism. Precisely because he is concerned with the freedom of his mind, he must imprison his heart (87, 107). Freedom of one's mind is not possible without a dash of stupidity (9). Self-knowledge is not only very difficult but impossible to achieve; man could not live with perfect self-knowledge (80–81, 231, 249).—

The fifth chapter—the central chapter—is the only one whose heading ("Toward the natural history of morality") refers to nature. Could nature be the theme of this chapter or even of the whole second part of the book?

Nature—to say nothing of "naturalists," "physics" and "physiology"— had been mentioned more than once in the first four chapters. Let us cast a glance at the most important or striking of those mentions. In discussing and rejecting the Stoic imperative "to live according to nature" Nietzsche makes a distinction between nature and life (9; cf. 49), just as on another occasion he makes a distinction between nature and "us" (human beings) (22). The opposite of life is death which is or may be no less natural than life. The opposite of the natural is the unnatural: the artificial, the domesticated, the misbegotten (62), the anti-natural (21, 51, 55); i.e., the unnatural may very well be alive.

In the introductory aphorism (186) Nietzsche speaks of the desideratum of a natural history of morality in a manner which reminds us of what he had said in the introductory aphorism of the chapter on religion (45). But in the earlier case he led us to suspect that the true science of religion, i.e. the empirical psychology of religion, is for all practical purposes impossible, for the psychologist would have to be familiar with the religious experience of the most profound *homines religiosi* and at the same time to be able to look down, from above, on these experiences. Yet when stating the case for an empirical study, a description, of the various moralities Nietzsche states at the same time the case against the possibility of a philosophic ethics, a science of morals which teaches the only true morality. It would seem that he makes higher demands on the student of religion than on the student of morality. This is perhaps the reason why he did not entitle the third chapter "The natural history of religion": Hume had written an essay entitled "The Natural History of Religion."

The philosophers' science of morals claimed to have discovered the foundation of morals either in nature or in reason. Apart from all other defects of that pretended science it rests on the gratuitous assumption that morality must or can be natural (according to nature) or rational. Yet every morality is based on some tryanny against nature as well as against reason. Nietzsche directs his criticism especially against the anarchists who oppose every subjection to arbitrary laws: everything of value, every freedom arises from a compulsion of long duration that was exerted by arbitrary, unreasonable laws; it was that compulsion that has educated the mind to freedom. Over against the ruinous permissiveness of anarchism Nietzsche asserts that precisely long lasting obedience to unnatural and unreasonable *nomoi* is "the moral imperative of nature." *Physis* calls for *nomoi* while preserving the distinction, nay, opposition of *physis* and *nomos*. Throughout this aphorism (188) Nietzsche speaks of nature only in quotation marks except in one case, in the final mention of nature; nature, and not only nature as the anarchists understand it, has become a problem for Nietzsche and yet he cannot do without nature.

As for rationalist morality, it consists primarily in the identification of the good with the useful and pleasant and hence in the calculation of consequences; it is utilitarian. Its classic is the plebian Socrates. How the patrician Plato—"the most beautiful growth of antiquity" (Preface), whose strength and power was the greatest which hitherto a philosopher had at his disposal—could take over the Socratic teaching is a riddle; the Platonic Socrates is a monstrosity. Nietzsche intends then to overcome Plato not only by substituting his truth for Plato's but also by surpassing him in strength or power. Among other things "Plato is boring" (*Twilight of the Gods*, 'What I owe to the Ancients' nr. 2), while Nietzsche surely is never boring. Both Socrates and Plato are guided by, or follow, not only reason but instinct as well; the instinct is more fundamental than reason. By explicitly taking the side of instinct against reason Nietzsche tacitly agrees with Rousseau (cf. *Natural Right and History* 262 n.). Instinct is, to say the least, akin to nature— to that which one may expel with a hayfork but will nevertheless always come back (cf. aph. 264; cf. the italicized heading of aph. 83, the first of the four italicized headings in chapter four). We are entitled to surmise that the fundamental instinct is the will to power and not, say, the urge toward self-preservation (cf. aph. 13). What we ventured to call Nietzsche's religiosity, is also an instinct (aph. 53): "The religious, that is to say god-forming instinct" (*Will to Power* nr. 1038). As a consequence of the irrationality of the moral judgement, of the decisive presence of the irrational in the moral judgement, there cannot be any universally valid moral rules: different moralities fit, belong to, different types of human beings.

When Nietzsche speaks again of nature, supplying the term again with quotation marks (aph. 197), he demands that one cease to regard as morbid (as defectively natural) the predatory beings which are dangerous, intemperate, passionate, "tropical": it was precisely the defective nature of almost all moralists—not reason and not nature simply—, namely, their timidity which induced them to conceive of the dangerous brutes and men as morbid. These moralists did not originate the morality stemming from timidity; that morality is the morality of the human herd, i.e. of the large majority of men. The utmost one could say is that the moral philosophers (and theologians) tried to protect the individual against the dangers with which he is threatened, not by other men, but by his own passions.

Nietzsche speaks of the herd-instinct of obedience which is now almost universally innate and transmitted by inheritance. It goes without saying that originally, in pre-historic times, that instinct was acquired (cf. *Genealogy of Morals* II). While it was very powerful throughout history, it has become simply predominant in contemporary Europe where it destroys at least the good conscience of those who command and are independent and where it successfully claims to be the only true morality. More precisely, in its earlier, healthy form it implied already that the sole standard of goodness is utility for the herd, i.e. for the common good; independence, superiority, inequality were esteemed to the extent to which they were thought to be subservient to the common good and indispensable for it, and not for their own sake. The common good was understood as the good of a particular society or tribe; it demanded therefore hostility to the tribe's external and internal enemies and in particular to the criminals. When the herd morality draws its ultimate consequences as it does in contemporary Europe, it takes the side of the very criminals and becomes afraid of inflicting punishment; it is satisfied with making the criminals harmless; by abolishing the only remaining ground of fear, the morality of timidity would reach its completion and thus make itself superfluous (cf. aph. 73). Timidity and the abolition of fear are justified by the identification of goodness with indiscriminate compassion.

Prior to the victory of the democratic movement to which, as Nietzsche understands it, also the anarchists and socialists belong, moralities other and higher than the herd morality were at least known. He mentions with high praise Napoleon and, above all, Alcibiades and Caesar. He could not have shown his freedom from the herd morality more tellingly than by mentioning in one breath Caesar and Alcibiades. Caesar could be said to have performed a great, historic function for Rome and to have dedicated himself to that function—to have been, as it were, a functionary of Roman history, but for Alcibiades Athens was no more than the pedestal, exchangeable if need be with Sparta or Persia, for his own glory or greatness. Nietzsche opposes men of such a nature to men of the opposite nature (aph. 199–200). In the rest of the chapter he speaks no longer of nature. Instead he expresses the view that man must be counted literally among the brutes (aph. 202). He appeals from the victorious herd morality of contemporary Europe to the superior morality of leaders (*Führer*). The leaders who can counteract the degradation of man which has led to the autonomy of the herd, can however not be merely men born to rule like Napoleon, Alcibiades and Caesar. They must be philosophers, new philosophers, a new kind of philosophers and commanders, the philosophers of the future. Mere Caesars, however great, will not suffice, for the new philosophers must teach man the future of man as his will, as dependent on a human will in order to put an end to the gruesome rule of nonsense and chance which was hitherto regarded as "history": the true history—as distinguished from the mere pre-history, to use a Marxian distinction—requires the subjugation of chance, of nature

(*Genealogy* II. n. 2) by men of the highest spirituality, of the greatest reason. The subjugation of nature depends then decisively on men who possess a certain nature. Philosophy, we have heard, is the most spiritual will to power (aph. 9): the philosophers of the future must possess that will to a degree which was not even dreamed of by the philosophy of the past; they must possess that will in its absolute form. The new philosophers are or act, we are tempted to say, to the highest degree according to nature. They are or act also to the highest degree according to reason, for they put an end to the rule of unreason, and the high—the high independent spirituality, the will to stand alone, the great reason (aph. 201)—is evidently preferable to the low. The turn from the autonomy of the herd to the rule of the philosophers of the future is akin to the transformation of the worshipping of the nothing into the unbounded Yes to everything that was and is; that transformation would then also be evidently reasonable.

But what becomes then of the irrationality of the moral judgement, i.e. of every moral judgement (aph. 191)? Or does it cease to be rational merely because one must be strong, healthy and well-born in order to agree to it or even to understand it? Yet can one say that Nietzsche's praise of cruelty, as distinguished from Plato's praise of gentleness, is rational? Or is that praise of cruelty only the indispensable and therefore reasonable corrective to the irrational glorification of compassion (cf. *Genealogy*, preface, nr. 5 end)? Furthermore, is not Nietzsche's critique of Plato and of Socrates a grave exaggeration, not to say a caricature? It suffices to remember the difference between the *Protagoras* and the *Gorgias* in order to see that Socrates was not a utilitarian in Nietzsche's sense (cf. aph. 190). As Nietzsche says in the same chapter (202), Socrates did not think that he knew what good and evil is. In other words, "virtue is knowledge" is a riddle rather than a solution. Socrates' enigmatic saying is based on awareness of the fact that sometimes "a scientific head is placed on the body of an ape, a subtle exceptional understanding on a vulgar soul" (aph. 26); it implies awareness of the complexity of the relation between *Wissen* and *Gewissen*, to use a favorite distinction of Nietzsche which in this form is indeed alien to Socrates. To considerations such as these one is compelled to retort that for Nietzsche there cannot be a natural or rational morality because he denies that there is a nature of man: the denial of any cardinal difference between man and brute is a truth, if a deadly truth; hence there cannot be natural ends of man as man: all values are human creations.

While Nietzsche's turn from the autonomous herd to the new philosophers is in perfect agreement with his doctrine of the will to power, it seems to be irreconcilable with his doctrine of eternal return: how indeed can the demand for something absolutely new, this intransigent farewell to the whole past, to all "history" be reconciled with the unbounded Yes to everything that was and is? Toward the end of the present chapter Nietzsche gives a hint regarding the connection between the demand for wholly new philosophers and eternal return; the philosophers of the future, he says, must be able to endure the weight of the responsibility for the future of man. He had originally published his suggestion regarding eternal return under the heading "*Das grösste Schwergewicht*" (*Gay Science* aph. 341).

From the desideration of the new philosophers Nietzsche is naturally led to passing judgement on the contemporary philosophers, a sorry lot, who are not philosophers in a serious and proper sense but professors of philosophy, philosophic laborers or, as they came to call themselves after Nietzsche's death, men who "do philosophy." They are in the best case, i.e. only in rare cases, scholars or scientists, i.e. competent and honest specialists who of right ought to be subservient to philosophy or handmaidens to philosophy. The chapter devoted to this kind of man is entitled "*Wir Gelehrten*"; it is the only one in whose title the first person of the personal pronoun is used: Nietzsche wishes to emphasize the fact that apart from being a precursor of the philosophers of the future, he belongs to the scholars and not, for instance, to the poets or the *homines religiosi*. The emancipation of the scholars or scientists from philosophy is according to him only a part of the democratic movement, i.e. of the emancipation of the low from subordination to the high. The things which we have observed in the 20th century regarding the sciences of man confirm Nietzsche's diagnosis.

The plebeian character of the contemporary scholar or scientist is due to the fact that he has no reverence for himself and this in its turn is due to his lack of self, to his self-forgetting, the necessary consequence or cause of his objectivity; hence he is no longer "nature" or "natural"; he can only be "genuine" or "authentic." Originally, one can say with some exaggeration, the natural and the genuine were the same (cf. Plato, *Laws* 642c 8–d 1, 777d 5–6; Rousseau, *Du Contrat Social* I. 9 end and II. 7, third paragraph); Nietzsche prepares decisively the replacement of the natural by the authentic. That he does this and why he does this will perhaps become clear from the following consideration. He is concerned more immediately with the classical scholars and historians than with the natural scientists (cf. aph. 209). Historical study had come to be closer to philosophy and therefore also a greater danger to it than natural science. This in turn was a consequence of what one may call the historicization of philosophy, the alleged realization that truth is a function of time (historical epoch) or that every philosophy belongs to a definite time and place (country). History takes the place of nature as a consequence of the fact that the natural—e.g. the natural gifts which enable a man to become a philosopher—is no longer understood as given but as the acquisition of former generations (aph. 213; cf. *Dawn of Morning* aph. 540). Historicism is the child of the peculiarly modern tendency to understand everything in terms of its genesis, of its human production: nature furnishes only the almost worthless materials as in themselves (Locke, *Two Treatises of Government* II sect. 43).

The philosopher, as distinguished from the scholar or scientist, is the complementary man in whom not only man but the rest of existence is justified (cf. aph. 207); he is the peak which does not permit and still less demand to be overcome. This characterization applies, however, strictly speaking only to the philosophers of the future compared with whom men of the rank of Kant and Hegel are only philosophic laborers, for the philosopher in the precise sense creates values. Nietzsche raises the question whether there ever were such philosophers (aph. 211 end). He seems to have answered that question in the affirmative by what he had said near the beginning of the sixth chapter on Heraclitus, Plato and Empedocles. Or does it remain true that we must overcome also the Greeks (*The Gay Science* aph. 125, 340)? The philosopher as philosopher belongs to the future and was therefore at all times in contradiction to his Today; the philosophers were always the bad conscience of their time. They belonged then to their time, not indeed, as Hegel thought, by being the sons of their times (*Vorlesungen über die Geschichte der Philosophie, Einleitung*, ed. Hoffmeister, 149) but by being their step-sons (*Schopenhauer als Erzieher* nr. 3). As belonging to their time and their place or country if only as their step-sons, the precursors of the philosophers of the future are concerned not only with the excellence of man in general but with the preservation of Europe which is threatened by Russia and which therefore must become a united Europe (aph. 208): the philosophers of the future must become the invisible spiritual rulers of a united Europe without ever becoming its servants.

In the seventh chapter Nietzsche turns to "our virtues." Yet the "we" whose virtues he discusses there, are not "we scholars" but "we Europeans of the time after tomorrow, we firstlings of the 20th century" (aph. 214), "we free minds" (aph. 227), i.e. the precursors of the philosophers of the future. The discussion of the virtues and vices of the scholars must be supplemented by a discussion of the virtues and vices of free minds. The virtues of the free minds had been discussed in the second chapter but their vices which are inseparable from their virtues, must also be laid bare. "Our" morality is characterized by a fundamental ambiguity; it is inspired by Christianity and by anti-Christianity. One can say that "our" morality constitutes a progress beyond the morality of the preceding generations but this change is no ground for pride; such pride would be incompatible with "our" increased delicacy in moral matters. Nietzsche is willing to grant that a high spirituality (intellectuality) is the ultimate product of moral qualities, that it is the synthesis of all those states which one ascribes to men who are "only moral," that it consists in the spiritualization of justice and of that kind of severity which knows that it is commissioned to maintain in the world the order of rank, even among the things and not only among men. Being the complementary man in whom the rest of existence is justified (aph. 207), standing on the summit, nay, being the summit, the philosopher has a cosmic responsibility. But "our virtues" are not the virtues of the philosopher of the future. The concession which Nietzsche makes to the men who are "only moral" does not prevent him from treating both the reigning moral teachings (altruism, the identification of goodness with compassion, utilitarianism) as well as their critique by moralists as trivial, not to say with contempt; the superior morality which flows from that critique or which is its presupposition does not belong to "our virtues." The reigning moralities are unaware of the problematic character of morality as such and this is due to their insufficient awareness of the variety of moralities (cf. aph. 186), to these moralists' lack of historical sense. The historical sense is "our" virtue, even "our great virtue." It is a novel phenomenon, not older than the 19th century. It is an ambiguous phenomenon. Its root is a lack of self-sufficiency of plebian Europe, or it expresses the self-criticism of modernity, its longing fo something different, for something past or alien. As a consequence, "measure is foreign to us; we are titillated by the infinite and unmeasured"; hence we are half-barbarians. It would seem that this defect, the reverse side of our great virtue, points to a way of thinking and living that transcends historicism, to a peak higher than all earlier peaks. The discussion of the historical sense (aph. 223–24) is surrounded by a discussion of compassion (aph. 222 and 225): the historical sense mediates in a manner between the plebian morality which boasts of its compassion with those who have been neglected by nature (aph. 219) and which is bent on the abolition of all suffering, and the opposite morality which goes together with awareness of the great things man owes to suffering (aph. 225). The next aphorism (226) is the only one in the chapter with an italicized heading ("We immoralists"): we immoralists are "men of duty"; "our" immoralism is our virtue. "Our virtue which alone is left to us" is probity, intellectual probity; it is, one may say, the positive or reverse side of our immoralism. Probity includes and completes "our great virtue of the historical sense." Yet probity is an end rather than a beginning; it points to the past rather than to the future; it is not the virtue characteristic of the philosophers of the future; it must be supported, modified, fortified by "our most delicate, most disguised, most spiritual will to power" which is directed toward the future. Surely our probity must not be permitted to become the ground or object of our pride, for this would lead us back to moralism (and to theism).

For a better understanding of "our virtue" it is helpful to contrast it with the most powerful antagonist, the morality preached up by the English utilitarians which accepts indeed egoism as the basis of morality but contends that egoism rightly understood leads to the espousal of the general welfare. That utilitarianism is disgusting, boring and naive. While it recognizes the fundamental character of egoism, it does not realize the fact that egoism is will to power and hence includes cruelty which, as cruelty directed toward oneself, is effective in intellectual probity, in "the intellectual conscience."

To recognize the crucial importance of cruelty is indispensable if "the terrible basic text *homo natura*," "that eternal basic text" is again to be seen, if man is to be "re-translated into nature." That re-translation is altogether a task for the future: "there never was yet a natural humanity" (*Will to Power* nr. 120). Man must be "made natural" (*vernatürlicht*) together "with the pure, newly found, newly redeemed nature" (*The Gay Science* aph. 109). For a man is the not yet fixed, not yet established beast (aph. 62): man becomes natural by acquiring his final, fixed character. For the nature of a being is its end, its completed state, its peak (Aristotle, *Politics* 1252b 32–34). "I too speak of 'return to nature,' although it is properly not a going back but an ascent—up into the high, free, even terrible nature and naturalness . . ." (*Twilight of the Idols*, 'Skirmishes of an untimely man' nr. 48). Man reaches his peak through and in the philosopher of the future as the truly complementary man in whom not only man but the rest of existence is justified (aph. 207). He is the first man who consciously creates values on the basis of the understanding of the will to power as the fundamental phenomenon. His action constitutes the highest form of the most spiritual will to power and therewith the highest form of the will to power. By this action he puts an end to the rule of non-sense and chance (aph. 203). As the act of the highest form of man's will to power the *Vernatürlichung* of man is at the same time the peak of the anthropomorphization of the non-human (cf. *Will to Power* nr. 614), for the most spiritual will to power consists in prescribing to nature what or how it ought to be (aph. 9). It is in this way that Nietzsche abolishes the difference between the world of appearance or fiction (the interpretations) and the true world (the text). (Cf. Marx 'Nationalökonomie und Philosophie', *Die Frühschriften*, ed. Landshut, pp. 235, 237, 273.)

It is however the history of man hitherto, i.e. the rule of non-sense and chance, which is the necessary condition for the subjugation of non-sense and chance. That is to say, the *Vernatürlichung* of man presupposes and brings to its conclusion the whole historical process—a completion which is by no means necessary but requires a new, free creative act. Still, in this way history can be said to be integrated into nature. Be this as it may, man cannot say Yes to the philosophers of the future without saying Yes to the past. Yet there is a great difference between this Yes and the unbounded Yes to everything that was and is, i.e. the affirmation of eternal return.

Instead of explaining why it is necessary to affirm the eternal return, Nietzsche indicates that the highest achievement, as all earlier high achievements, is in the last analysis not the work of reason but of nature; in the last analysis all thought depends on something unteachable "deep down," on a fundamental stupidity; the nature of the individual, the individual nature, not evident and universally valid insights, it seems, is the ground of all worthwhile understanding or knowledge (aph. 231; cf. aph. 8). There is an order of rank of the natures; at the summit of the hierarchy is the complementary man. His supremacy is shown by the fact that he solves the highest, the most difficult problem. As we have observed, for Nietzsche nature has become a problem and yet he cannot do without nature. Nature, we may say, has become a problem owing to the fact that man is conquering nature and there are no assignable limits to that conquest. As a consequence, people have come to think of abolishing suffering and inequality. Yet suffering and inequality are the prerequisites of human greatness (aph. 239 and 257). Hitherto suffering and inequality have been taken for granted, as "given," as imposed on man. Henceforth, they must be willed. That is to say, the gruesome rule of non-sense and chance, nature, the fact that almost all men are fragments, cripples and gruesome accidents, the whole present and past is itself a fragment, a riddle, a gruesome accident unless it is willed as a bridge to the future (cf. *Zarathustra*, 'Of Redemption'). While paving the way for the complementary man, one must at the same time say unbounded Yes to the fragments and cripples. Nature, the eternity of nature, owes its being to a postulation, to an act of the will to power on the part of the highest nature.

At the end of the seventh chapter Nietzsche discusses "woman and man" (cf. aph. 237). The apparently clumsy transition to that subject—a transition in which he questions the truth of what he is about to say by claiming that it expresses merely his "fundamental stupidity deep down"—is not merely a flattery, a gesture of courtesy to the friends of woman's emancipation. It indicates that he is about to continue the theme of nature, i.e. the natural hierarchy, in full awareness of the problem of nature.

The philosophers of the future may belong to a united Europe but Europe is still *l'Europe des nations et des patries*. Germany more than any other part of non-Russian Europe has more of a prospect of a future than, say, France or England (aph. 240, 251, 255; cf. Heine ed. Elster IV 510). One could find that Nietzsche stresses in his chapter on peoples and fatherlands more the defects of contemporary Germany than her virtues: it is not so difficult to free one's heart from a victorious fatherland as from a beaten one (aph. 41). The target of his critique here is not German philosophy but German music, i.e. Richard Wagner. More precisely, European nobility reveals itself as the work and invention of France, whereas European commonness, the plebianism of the modern ideas, is the work and invention of England (aph. 253).

Nietzsche thus prepares the last chapter which he entitled *"Was ist vornehm?"* "Vornehm" differs from "noble" because it is inseparable from extraction, origin, birth (*Dawn of Morning*, aph. 199; Goethe *Wilhelm Meister's Lehrjahre* [*Sämtliche Werke*, Tempel-Klassiker, II 87–88] and *Dichtung und Wahrheit*, Vol. 2, *ed. cit.* 44–45). Being the last chapter of a prelude to a philosophy of the future, it shows the (a) philosophy of the future as reflected in the medium of conduct, of life; thus reflected the philosophy of the future reveals itself as the philosophy of the future. The virtues of the philosopher of the future differ from the Platonic virtues: Nietzsche replaces temperance and justice by compassion and solitude (aph. 284). This is one illustration among many of what he means by characterizing nature by its "Vornehmheit" (aph. 188). Die vornehme Natur ersetzt die göttliche Natur.

9

Notes on Maimonides'
Book of Knowledge

If it is true that the *Guide of the Perplexed* is not a philosophic book but a Jewish book, it surely is not a Jewish book in the same manner in which the *Mishneh Torah* is a Jewish book. Maimonides has made clear the difference between these two kinds of Jewish books by saying that the *Guide* is devoted to the science of the Law in the true sense: the *Mishneh Torah* as well as the *Commentary on the Mishna* belong to the science of the Law in the ordinary sense, i.e., the *fiqh* or *talmud*. The most obvious difference between these two kinds of Jewish books corresponds to the most obvious difference between the two kinds of science of the Law: the foundations of the Law are treated in the *Mishneh Torah* with much greater brevity than in the *Guide*, although they are alluded to in the former work in a manner that approaches clear exposition. Consequently, in the *Guide* Maimonides discusses as fully as possible the fundamental question at issue between the adherents of the Law and the philosophers—the question whether the world is eternal or has a beginning in time—whereas in his *fiqh* books he establishes the existence of God on the basis of the view, which he rejects in the *Guide*, that the world is eternal.[1] This would seem to mean that in an important respect Maimonides' *fiqh* books are more "philosophic" than the *Guide*.

Within the *Mishneh Torah* philosophy seems to be most powerfully present in the First Book, the Book of Knowledge. That Book is the only one in which the term indicating the theme is supplied with the article. More precisely, it is the only Book of the *Mishneh Torah* in which the noun

Reprinted from *Studies in Mysticism and Religion Presented to Gershom G. Scholem* (Jerusalem: Magnes Press, Hebrew University, 1967).

1. *Guide of the Perplexed* I, Introduction (6a Munk) and 71 (97a).

indicating the theme is supplied with the article both in the Introduction to the whole work and in the heading of the Book. For in the case of the Book of Sacrifices the noun indicating the theme is supplied with the article in the heading of the Book but not in the Introduction.[2] On the basis of the *Guide* this seeming irregularity could easily be understood as a hint: the Book of Knowledge deals first and above all with the foundations of the Torah; the first intention of the whole Torah is the elimination of idolatry, or the foundation of our Torah as a whole and the pivot around which it turns consists in the elimination of the opinions that support idolatry, and the primary instrument for uprooting idolatry is the Mosaic legislation regarding sacrifices.[3] On the basis of the *Mishneh Torah* alone that hint could hardly be said to approach clear exposition.

Maimonides could easily have given to the First Book of the *Mishneh Torah* the title *Sefer Madda'*. In the 70th chapter of the *Guide* he refers to what he had said on the equivocity of "soul" and "spirit" at the end of the *Sefer Madda'*. One could think for a moment that he thus refers to *Teshubah* VIII, 3; but apart from the fact that that passage could not properly be called the end of the Book of Knowledge, Maimonides does not speak there of "spirit" nor of the difficulties attending the meaning of the term "soul." He refers in *Guide* I, 70 to *Yesodē Ha-Torah* IV, 8. By this reference he suggests that there is a difference between the *Sefer Ha-Madda'* and the *Sefer Madda'*, the latter consisting only of the *Yesodē Ha-Torah* I–IV. By this hint he underlines the obvious and radical difference between those four chapters and the rest of the Book of Knowledge, to say nothing of the 13 other books of the *Mishneh Torah*. One may say that those four chapters are the Book of Knowledge *par excellence*, for they are devoted to the Account of the Chariot and the Account of the Beginning, which are identical, according to the *Guide*, with the divine science and the natural science respectively.[4]

The four chapters indicated, and only these four chapters, are devoted to the Account of the Chariot and the Account of the Beginning. These two Accounts and especially the first are a great thing, whereas the halakhic discussions are a small thing (*Yesodē Ha-Torah* IV, 13). Yet the Halakhah proper is not the only subject excluded from the two Accounts. Also excluded from the Account of the Chariot and the Account of the Beginning are the following subjects taken up in the Book of Knowledge after *Yesodē Ha-Torah* IV: the names of God (VI, 2), prophecy (VII–X), the unchangeable and absolute character of the Torah of Moses (IX,1), ethics (*De'ot*), man's free will (*Teshubah* V), particular providence (*ibid.*, IX, 1–8), the life to come (*ibid.*, VIII), and the Messianic age (*ibid.* IX, 9–10).

2. Cf., besides, *Mishneh Torah*, Bk. I, ed. M. Hyamson, 28a22 with 19a3.
3. *Guide* III, 29 and 32; cf. *M.T.* 18a3–4, and *'Abodah Zarah* II, 4.
4. *Guide* I, Introduction (3b).

In the *Mishneh Torah* the Account of the Chariot precedes the Account of the Beginning. This order is in accordance with the order of rank of the two Accounts, but it is not in accord with the fact that the Account of the Beginning (natural science) supplies the premises from which the Account of the Chariot (divine science) starts.[5] What then is the foundation of the Account of the Chariot in the *Mishneh Torah*? We note a kindred difficulty. According to Maimonides the Account of the Chariot is the doctrine of God and the angels while the Account of the Beginning is the doctrine of the creatures lower than the angels. Hence his distinction between the two Accounts blurs the fundamental difference between the Creator and the creatures. He overcomes the second difficulty to some extent by his division of the five commandments that he explains in the first four chapters; he devotes the first chapter (the chapter devoted to the doctrine of God) to the explanation of the first three commandments, and the three following chapters (the chapters devoted to the doctrine of the creatures) to the explanation of the two remaining commandments. This implies that the foundation of the doctrine of God is supplied in the Book of Knowledge, not by natural science, but by the most fundamental commandments. For instance, the first commandment—the commandment to acknowledge the existence of God—takes the place of the proof of His existence.

This must be taken with a grain of salt. Maimonides opens the body of the Book of Knowledge with the assertion that knowledge of the existence of God is the foundation of the foundations and the pillar of the sciences: he does not call it the pillar, or a pillar, of the Law, while he calls the knowledge of God's inspiring human beings with prophecy a pillar of the Law (*Yesodē Ha-Torah* VII, beginning). Accordingly he hints at the demonstration of the existence of God that starts from the sempiternal, never-beginning and never-ending, revolution of the sphere; he also refers a few times to what is "impossible." (Cf. also *Yesodē Ha-Torah* I,11, beginning.) Furthermore, according to Maimonides, knowledge of the existence of God is commanded by the words "I am the Lord, thy God"; this commandment is immediately followed by the commandment that forbids thinking or imagining that "there is another God besides this one." It is not as clear as it might be whether the words that follow immediately—namely, "this is the great root on which everything depends"—refer to both commandments or only to the prohibition (cf. *'Abodah Zarah* II, 4), nor whether the first commandment obliges us to recognize the absolute uniqueness and incomparability of God rather than His existence. At any rate, the first chapter of the *Mishneh Torah*, the theological chapter *par excellence* of the *Mishneh Torah*, sets forth that God exists, is one, and is incorporeal. God's incorporeality is not presented as the subject of a commandment; that God is incorporeal is inferred partly from His being one and partly from Biblical passages.[6]

5. *Guide* I, Introduction (5a) and 71 (98a).
6. Cf. *Guide* III, 28, beginning.

In the first chapter Maimonides had avoided the term "to create" (*bara'*) and derivatives from it. He begins to use that term when he comes to speak of the creatures. The treatment of the creatures as creatures (*Yesodē Ha-Torah* II–IV) serves the purpose of explaining the commandments to love God and to fear Him. The doctrine of the creatures is emphatically Maimonides' own,[7] at least to the extent that it does not go back to Jewish sources. Knowledge of the creatures is the way toward love of God and fear of Him because that knowledge makes us realize God's wisdom; it is not said to be required for knowing God's existence or His unity and incorporeality. Maimonides enumerates the three classes of creatures (the earthly beings, the heavenly bodies, and the angels) initially in the ascending order (*Yesodē Ha-Torah* II, 3) while he discusses them in the descending order. This change makes no difference at least in so far as in both cases the heavenly bodies occupy the central place. In his discussion of the heavenly bodies he does not speak of "creating," nor does he quote the Bible; he refers, however, to the Sages of Greece (III, 6). It is not surprising that he speaks of God's knowledge and in particular of His omniscience, not in the theological chapter proper, but when speaking of the creatures, for the problem concerns precisely His knowledge of the creatures. His knowledge of all His creatures is implied in His self-knowledge (II, 9-10). Accordingly, the angels knew God much less adequately than He knows Himself, and the heavenly bodies are aware of God still less adequately than are the angels; but as they are aware of God, so are they aware of themselves and of the angels (II, 8; III, 10). Maimonides is here silent on whether the angels and the heavenly bodies know the beings inferior to them. This is not contradicted by the fact that the angels of the lowest degree "speak with the prophets and appear to them in prophetic vision," for Maimonides speaks here "according to the language of human beings"; it suffices to say that in fact there is only one angel of the lowest degree (cf. II, 7 with IV, 6).

The Account of the Beginning is more accessible to men in general than the Account of the Chariot. The most accessible part of the Account of the Beginning is the one dealing with the sublunar creatures.[8] When discussing the characteristics of the four elements, Maimonides speaks first of the "way" of each element, then of its "custom," and only after this preparation, of its "nature" (IV, 2). He thus lets us see that "nature"—a notion pointing back to the Sages of Greece—cannot be used in the context without some preparation.[9] Maimonides calls air "spirit"; this enables him to throw light on the relation between spirit and water as stated in Gen. 1:2 and on the relation between spirit and dust as stated in Eccles. 12: 7.[10]

---

7. Cf. the "I" in *Yesodē Ha-Torah* II, 2.
8. *Yesodē Ha-Torah* IV, 11; III, end; cf. *Guide* II, 24 (54a) and III, 23 (50b).
9. Cf. Strauss, *Natural Right and History* (Chicago 1953), pp. 81–83.
10. *Yesodē Ha-Torah* IV, 2 and 9; cf. the mention of *awir* in III, 3 (*M.T.* 37a9); cf. *Guide* I, 40 and II, 30 (68a).

Knowledge of the creatures leads to love of God and to fear of Him because it leads to knowledge of His infinite wisdom and therewith to thirst and longing for knowledge of the Great Name. Yet when man considers His marvelous and great creatures themselves, he recoils and becomes afraid and realizes his littleness and lowliness and the poverty of his knowledge compared with that of God. Although knowledge of the creatures is to lead to both love and fear of God, Maimonides introduces his account of the angels as the way to love of God (II, 2). At the end of his account of the creatures other than the angels, i.e., of the bodily beings, he says that through knowledge of all creatures, man's love of God is increased; and by comparing himself with any of the great and holy bodies (i.e., the heavenly bodies) and still more with any of the pure immaterial forms (i.e., the angels) man comes into a state of fear and realizes his utter lowliness (IV,12). This seems to imply that love of God, as distinguished from fear of Him, does not altogether depend on knowledge of the creatures. This agrees with the well-known teaching of the *Guide*[11] only in so far as both teachings ascribe a higher rank to the love of God than to the fear of Him.

The highest theme of the first four chapters is God and His attributes. From God's attributes one is easily led to His names,[12] which are in a sense the theme of the next two chapters, i.e., of the central chapters of the *Yesodē Ha-Torah*. Maimonides' treatment of the names or rather of the name of God serves the purpose of explaining the three commandments to sanctify His name, not to profane it, and not to destroy things bearing His name. The opening of these two chapters makes it clear that these three commandments, in contradistinction to the study of the Accounts of the Chariot and of the Beginning (II, 12; IV, 11), are obligatory on every Jew. The discussion of the commandments regarding the sanctification and the profanation of the Name includes the discussion of the question of which prohibitions may not be transgressed under any circumstances or are in the strictest sense universally valid;[13] the strictest of those prohibitions are those against idolatry, unchastity (incest), and murder. In the seventh chapter Maimonides returns to "the foundations" by taking up the subject of prophecy to which he devotes the last four chapters of the *Yesodē Ha-Torah*. While prophecy belongs to "the foundations of the Law," it does not belong, as is indicated by the place where it is discussed, to the Accounts of the Chariot and of the Beginning. Maimonides did speak of prophecy when treating the Account of the Chariot, but only in order to reject such views of God and the angels as are based on ignorance of the character of prophetic utterances. The sole positive commandment regarding prophecy opens Maimonides' enumera-

---

11. III, 52. Cf. III, 27–28 and 51 (125a). Cf. above all the explanation of the commandments to love God and to fear Him in the *Sefer Ha-Misvot*.
12. Cf. *Guide* I, 61 ff. with I, 50–60.
13. Cf. *Melakhim* X, 2.

tion of the positive commandments regulating man's conduct toward man, as distinguished from his conduct toward God; it is there immediately followed by the commandment to appoint a king.[14] One is tempted to say that prophecy is a subject, not of theoretical, but of practical wisdom. As for the sole negative commandment regarding prophecy—the prohibition against excessive testing of claimants to prophecy—it is identical with the prohibition against testing or trying God.[15]

The plan of the *Mishneh Torah* and all of its parts must be presumed to be as rational as possible. This does not mean that that plan is always evident. That this is the case would seem to be shown sufficiently by the mere fact that Maimonides could divide all the commandments into fourteen classes in so different ways in the *Mishneh Torah* and in the *Guide* (III, 35). The plan of the first chapter devoted to prophecy (VII) is very lucid. Maimonides states first that if a man fulfills all requirements for becoming a prophet, the Holy Spirit immediately rests on him (1). As we learn from the *Guide* (II, 32), this is the view of the philosophers; it differs from the view of the Torah, according to which God may miraculously withhold prophecy from a man who is perfectly fit for becoming a prophet. Maimonides next states the characteristics of all prophets (2–4); he speaks here emphatically of "all" prophets. He then qualifies his first statement: if a man is properly prepared for prophecy, he will not necessarily become a prophet (5). While in the first statement he had stated, or almost stated, the philosophic view, he states in the repetition the view of the Torah. In the first statement he has spoken of "the Holy Spirit," which he had used synonymously with "the spirit,"[16] whereas in the repetition he speaks of the *Shekhinah*. One may compare this change with the avoidance of "creation" in chapter I and its use in the sequel. To begin with philosophy (although not *eo nomine*) and to turn almost at once to the Torah may be said to be the law governing the *Mishneh Torah* as a whole. He then qualifies his second statement: everything said about the nature, or rather the way, of prophecy is true of all prophets with the exception of Moses. Both second or qualifying statements have the same character: both introduce, or make explicit, the miraculous or supernatural. Moses' knowledge is more radically supernatural than that of the other prophets since it is angelic rather than human (6). Finally, Maimonides makes clear that signs and wonders are necessary but not sufficient for accrediting a prophet; the signs and wonders, together with the claimant's possession of wisdom and holiness, do not make certain that he is a prophet although they establish a binding legal presumption in his favor. In accordance with this Maimonides speaks rather frequently of "believing," i.e. of believing in a prophet, when discussing prophecy, while he had not spoken

14. Nos. 172–173.
15. Negative commandment No. 64.
16. Cf. his use or interpretation of Gen. 1:2 in IV, 2.

at all of "believing" when discussing the Accounts of the Chariot and of the Beginning.[17] The difficulty caused by the difference between binding legal presumption and indubitable truth is solved in the next chapter in which Maimonides shows—on the basis of the premise established in chapter VII that the prophecy of Moses is absolutely superior to that of the other prophets—that Israel believed in Moses because they were eye- and ear-witnesses of the Sinaitic revelation.[18] The authority of the other prophets is therefore derivative from the authority of the Torah.

As is sufficiently indicated by the title *Hilkhot Yesodē Ha-Torah*, the *Mishneh Torah* stands or falls by the distinction between what is a foundation or a root and what is not. Yet the fact that all commandments of the Torah are equally of divine origin and meant to be valid for ever and ever, deprives that distinction of much of its importance.[19] Therefore one ought not to expect that the fundamental distinction made by Maimonides should be entirely lucid. The foundations of the Torah in the strict sense consist of (1) what one must know regarding God, His attributes, and His names, and (2) what one must know or believe regarding the"absoluteness"of the Torah of Moses. We have seen that already the first part of these foundations consists of heterogeneous ingredients. The first four chapters of the *Yesodē Ha-Torah* (and perhaps most obviously the paragraph devoted to the bodily creatures), in contradistinction to the last six chapters, introduce philosophy into the Holy of Holies by as it were rediscovering it there. Since philosophy requires the greatest possible awareness of what one is doing, Maimonides cannot effect that fundamental change without being aware that it is a fundamental change, i.e. without a conscious, although not necessarily explicit, criticism of the way in which the Torah was commonly understood. The two parts of the *Yesodē Ha-Torah* are linked to each other by the fact that the God whose knowledge is commanded is "this God," the God of Israel.[20] Accordingly, the first section of the *Mishneh Torah* teaches that only "this God" is to be acknowledged, loved, and feared and that only His Torah is true.

On the basis of what Maimonides says in the *Guide* (III, 38) on the *De'ot*, one is inclined to suggest that with an obvious qualification the *De'ot* are devoted to man's fundamental duties toward his fellows, just as the *Yesodē Ha-Torah* are devoted to man's fundamental duties toward God. In fact all commandments discussed in the *Yesodē Ha-Torah* explicitly speak of God; yet the same seems to be true of the first two of the eleven commandments discussed in the *De'ot*. However, the second of these commandments ("to Him shalt thou cleave")[21] means according to the interpretation which

17. Cf. Albo, *Roots* I, 14 (128, 4–5 Husik).
18. Cf. the thorough discussion of this subject in Albo's *Roots* I.
19. Cf. Abravanel, *Rosh Amanah*, chs. 23–24; cf. Albo, *Roots* I, 2, end.
20. *M.T.* 34b5 and 15.
21. Deut. 10:20; the passage is not quoted in the *Guide*.

Maimonides follows, "to those who know Him (i.e., the Sages and their disciples) shalt thou cleave" (VI, 2). Accordingly one must wonder whether the first of the two commandments in question (the commandment to assimilate oneself to His ways or to walk in His ways) has an immediate theological reference. To walk in God's ways means to be gracious, merciful, just, mighty, powerful, and so on (I, 6). In order to understand the meaning of the *De'ot*, one must understand the plan of this section. The first three chapters are devoted to the explanation of the commandment to walk in the ways of God, whereas the last two chapters (VI–VII) are devoted to the explanation of the ten other commandments whose explanation Maimonides assigned to the *De'ot*. The central chapter is an appendix to the first three; it is medical rather than halakhic. The fifth chapter is another appendix to the first three, but its purport is not obvious. To understand its purport, one must first consider the chief point made in the first three chapters.

Maimonides makes there a distinction between two kinds of human goodness, which he calls wisdom and piety. Wisdom comprises all character traits that are the mean between the corresponding two faulty extremes. Piety, on the other hand, consists in deviating somewhat from the middle toward one or the other extreme, for instance in being not merely humble but very humble. One may say that what Maimonides calls wisdom is moral virtue in Aristotle's sense and that by juxtaposing wisdom and piety he in fact juxtaposes philosophic morality and the morality of the Torah. Accordingly the tension between philosophy and the Torah would here become thematic to a higher degree than in *Yesodē Ha-Torah*.[22] The tension proves on closer inspection to be a contradiction. Just as in *Yesodē Ha-Torah* VII he said in effect, first, that all prophets prophesy by means of the imagination, and then that the prophet Moses did not prophesy by means of the imagination; he says now, first, that in the case of all character traits the middle way is the right way, and then that in the case of some character traits the pious man deviates from the middle way toward one or the other extreme. More precisely, according to Maimonides the right way, the way in which we are commanded to walk, is in every case the middle way that is the way of the Lord (*De'ot* I, 3–5, 7; II, 2, 7); yet in the case of anger and pride, man is forbidden to walk in the middle way (II, 3). One obviously does not solve this difficulty by saying that Maimonides explicitly identifies the ways of the Lord only with wisdom as distinguished from piety; this act of Maimonides could be compared with his leaning toward the doctrine of the eternity of the world in *Yesodē Ha-Torah* I. The difficulty is solved somehow in the fifth chapter of the *De'ot*. That chapter is apparently devoted to "actions" of the wise man as distinguished from his character traits (and his wisdom). But the "actions" of which he speaks here cannot be dealt with separately from

22. Consider the relative frequency of "nature" in *De'ot* I, 2–3.

character traits.[23] In fact the fifth chapter differs from the chapters preceding it in that Maimonides therein moves from the theme of the wise man in the strict or narrow sense as defined above to the "disciple of the wise," i.e., the Jewish sage who is both wise and pious or in some respects wise and in others pious (cf. especially V, 5 and 9). The transition is illustrated by Maimonides' interpreting the commandment to love one's neighbor as meaning that everyone is obliged to love every Jew (VI, 3–5, 8; VII, 1, 8), as well as by his here qualifying the duty to be truthful by the requirements of peace (V, 7; cf. II, 10); furthermore, he limits, with a view to the practice of all prophets in Israel, the prohibition against publicly humiliating a Jew by the duty to proclaim his sins toward God, as distinguished from his sins toward other men (VI, 8–9). His hesitation to identify unqualifiedly the right way with the middle way may be explained by an ambiguity occurring in his source (*Pirqē Abot* V, 13–14). There it is said that he who says "what is mine is thine and what is thine is thine" is pious, but that he who says "what is mine is mine and what is thine is thine" possesses the middle character or, according to some, the character of Sodom.

The *Talmud Torah* reasonably follows immediately on the *De'ot* and thus forms the center of the Book of Knowledge. If God's demands on man—on his conduct both towards God and towards his fellow men—are delivered in the most perfect manner in the Torah and only in the Torah, knowledge of the Torah, study of the Torah is the first of all duties; for even the Accounts of the Chariot and of the Beginning form part of the study of the Torah (I, 11–12). The central section makes clear that the extreme humility demanded by the Torah does not preclude the sage's concern with being honored and enjoying other privileges, for that concern only reflects his concern with the Torah being honoured (V, 1; VI, 11–12).

The commandments explained in the *'Abodah Zarah* are mostly the immediate specifications of the first and most fundamental prohibition, namely the prohibition against thinking that there is any other god but the Lord. Accordingly, 49 of the 51 commandments discussed there are prohibitions; even the two commandments that are positive in form are in fact also negative. In order to see why the laws regarding forbidden worship form part of the Book of Knowledge, we start from the most obvious peculiarity of this section. That peculiarity is that the section is opened by an introductory chapter preceding the explanation of any of the 51 commandments in question. That chapter sets forth the relation in time of forbidden worship to the true or right worship. True worship preceded forbidden worship. This, we may say, follows necessarily from man's having been created by God in His image. Man originally knew that all beings other than God are God's creatures. This knowledge was gradually lost, with the result that the great

23. Cf. *De'ot* VI, 5 and *Sanhedrin* XVIII, 1 with *De'ot* I, 7.

majority of men became worshippers of idols while the wise men among them knew no other god but the stars and the spheres; the truth was preserved only by solitary individuals like Noah. The truth was recovered by the efforts of Abraham, who realized that the sphere cannot possibly move itself and that its mover is the creator of the whole, the only God. He fought the worship of idols as well as of the heavenly bodies by deed and by speech, his speech consisting of demonstrations. He was therefore persecuted, but saved by a miracle. This miracle is all the more remarkable since it is the only divine intervention in Abraham's recovery and propagation of the truth that is mentioned by Maimonides here. At any rate, forbidden worship—the worship of any creatures (II, 1)—is based on the most fundamental error, a demonstrably wrong view, *the* alternative to "the foundation of the foundations and the pillar of the sciences."[24] It is for this reason that forbidden worship is a proper theme of the Book of Knowledge.

It could seem that the teaching of *'Abodah Zarah* I is at variance with the teaching of the *Guide*, according to which the creation of the world is not demonstrable and the prohibition against idolatry is not accessible to reason or the intellect.[25] This would cause no difficulty since the purposes of the *Guide* and the *Mishneh Torah* differ so greatly. The case would be different if this particular difference between the two works flatly contradicted what Maimonides says in the *Guide* about the most important substantive difference between them.[26] Nor are we perplexed by his stressing the defects of the minds of most men and the ensuing necessity of establishing certainty and unanimity by means of revelation even regarding the existence of God, for what is true of most minds is not true of all (*'Abodah Zarah* II, 3). A difficulty is caused by what he says toward the end of this section (XI, 16), at the end of his discussion of the prohibitions against divination, astrology, the use of charms, and similar things: everyone who "believes" in such things and thinks that they are true and words of wisdom but to be foregone only because they are forbidden by the Torah, is a fool. One wonders whether this statement is meant to apply retroactively to idolatry proper or whether Maimonides is here suggesting a distinction between idolatry and what we would call superstition.

The last section of the Book of Knowledge is devoted to the explanation of a single commandment—the commandment that the sinner repent his sins before the Lord and make confession—as well as of the roots, or dogmas, that are "connected with [that commandment] for its sake." The dogmas in question do not belong, then, to the Accounts of the Chariot and of the Beginning. Their rationale is solely that without their acceptance repentance would be impossible; they are purely practical, i.e., they are

24. *Yesodē Ha-Torah*, beginning and *'Abodah Zarah* II, 4.
25. II, 33 (75a).
26. Cf. the beginning of this article.

more practical than the dogmas concerning prophecy and the Torah of Moses, for revelation also discloses theoretical truths; or, to use a distinction made by Maimonides in the *Guide* (III, 28), they are opinions that ought to be believed not so much on account of themselves as because they are necessary for the improvement of human living together. Besides, the heading of the last section of the Book of Knowledge implies that none of the 613 commandments of the Torah explicitly commands acceptance of the opinions in question.

The question arises, why are dogmas of this kind connected with repentance and required for the sake of repentance, as distinguished from other commanded actions, such as prayer; and which are the dogmas in question? Maimonides' codification of the particulars of the law on repentance prepares the answers to these questions. The distinction between perfect repentance and repentance as such seems to be of decisive importance. Perfect repentance requires that the sinner not again commit the repented sin although the relevant circumstances have not changed or although he is exposed to the same temptation to which he earlier succumbed: an old man cannot perfectly repent the sins he committed in his youth by virtue of his youth. From this it follows that there cannot be any perfect repentance on one's deathbed. Hence if there were not repentance pure and simple, men could not repent many of their sins. Yet they are commanded to repent all their sins. Hence repentance pure and simple requires only that man deplore his sins, confess them with his lips before the Lord, and resolve in his heart not to commit them again. Even if a man has perfectly repented a given sin, he is not for this reason free from sin, for he will commit other sins. Repentance pure and simple, as distinguished from perfect repentance, is sufficient for his sins being forgiven him (II, 1–3; cf. III, 1). Forgiveness of sins is needed because sinfulness, i.e. preponderance of one's sins over his meritorious deeds, is literally deadly, and only God knows the true weight of the various kinds of sins and meritorious deeds (III, 2). When Maimonides mentions in this context (III, 4) the fact that the sounding of the Shofar on Rosh ha-shanah is a decision of Scripture, i.e., not explicable, he gives us a hint to the effect that the commandment to repent has a reason accessible to man; that reason is the one that has just been restated. Repentance is then not possible if there is not particular providence, which in turn requires that God be omniscient. Furthermore, the crucial importance of deathbed repentance is connected with the prospect of the life to come. Accordingly Maimonides enumerates in the immediate sequel (III, 6 ff.) the kinds of men who do not have a share in the world to come; among those kinds we find him who says that the Creator does not know what men do and those who deny the resurrection of the dead and the coming of the Redeemer.

Maimonides does not explicitly introduce these three dogmas in the *Teshubah* as dogmas or roots. He speaks in the *Teshubah* of roots in the sense of dogmas only in chapters V–VI, i.e., in the central chapters of that section. "The great root" without which repentance is impossible, is man's freedom. Man is free in the sense that it depends entirely on him whether he will choose the good or the bad; it is in every man's power to be as just as Moses or as wicked as Jeroboam, to be wise or to be foolish. No other being in the world possesses this privelege. One must go beyond what Maimonides says and say that no other being possesses that privelege: God cannot be unjust or unwise. Man would not be truly free to choose good and evil, truth or error, if he did not by his own power know good or evil or truth and error. Neither God nor anyone else nor anything[27] compels man to act well or badly or draws him to either justice and wisdom or injustice and folly. Maimonides thus implicitly denies what he had asserted in the *De'ot* (I, 2) that different human beings have from their birth, by nature, inclinations to different vices; in fact, he now refrains from speaking of "nature" (*teba'*) altogether. Since the difficulty is not disposed of by silence, he replaces the statement "freedom is given to everyman" by the statement "the freedom of everyman is given to him."[28]

Man's freedom is a pillar of the whole Torah: he could not reasonably be told "do this" or "do not do that" if he were not able to do in each case the opposite of what he is told. In particular, if he lacked freedom he could not reasonably be punished for his transgressions or rewarded for his obedience. Man can avoid the punishment he deserves by repenting his evil deeds; because man is free to do evil, he is also free to repent his evil deeds. Man's freedom extends even to his knowledge or science and to his emotions. Man's freedom seems to be incompatible with God's omniscience, with His knowledge of all future things. The solution of this difficulty requires profound thought—thought that is not at the disposal of all men—and "many great roots" depend on that solution. The solution is supplied by the insight that God's knowledge differs radically from human knowledge, so much so, that God's knowledge is as unfathomable to man as His essence. But while we cannot know how God knows all creatures and their actions, we know without any doubt that man is free. This knowledge derives not merely from the acceptance of the Law but from clear demonstrations taken from the words of wisdom, i.e. from science. There remains another difficulty to the solution of which Maimonides devotes the whole sixth chapter. This difficulty is caused by many scriptural passages that seem to contradict the dogma of human freedom; in those passages God seems to be said to decree men's doing evil or good. To solve this difficulty, Maimonides explains in his own name "a great root." The explanation starts from the fact that every

27. *M.T.* 87a18.
28. Cf. *Teshubah* V, beginning with VII, beginning. The latter formulation may be the correct reading also of V, beginning; cf. Hyamson's edition and Albo, *Roots* I, 3 (59, 17–18). Cf. Pines' Introduction to his English translation of the *Guide* (Chicago 1963), p. xcv, n. 63.

unrepented sin of an individual or community requires a fitting punishment—God alone knowing which punishment is fit—in this life or in the life to come or in both lives. If the individual or the community has committed a great sin or many sins, justice requires that the sinner not escape punishment through his repentance and hence that repentance, i.e. the freedom to return from his wickedness, be withheld from him. This is what is meant by God's hardening the heart of Pharaoh and similar expressions.

Maimonides concludes the thematic discussion of repentance in the seventh chapter, in which he speaks more emphatically than before of the exalted rank of repentance: the rank of those who repent is higher than that of those who never sin; Israel will not be redeemed except through repentance; repentance brings man near to the Presence. Particularly remarkable is the suddenness with which a man through his repentance is transformed from an enemy of God into a friend of God. Those who repent have the characteristics of the pious as distinguished from the wise.

The next two chapters deal with the world to come and the Messianic age; the connection of these two themes with repentance has become clear from the thematic discussion of repentance. The life to come is the highest reward for the fulfillment of the commandments and the acquisition of wisdom. Yet, as Maimonides points out in the last chapter, as long as we fulfil the commandments of the Torah and concern ourselves with the wisdom of the Torah in order to receive any reward, we do not yet serve God properly, for we serve Him only from fear, not from love. But one can love God only to the extent to which one knows Him. Therefore one must dedicate oneself to the study of the sciences and insights that enable him to know God to the extent to which this is possible for man, "as we have made clear in the *Yesodē Ha-Torah*." With these words the Book of Knowledge ends. The reference to the *Sefer Madda'* makes it unnecessary for Maimonides to state explicitly what the required sciences or insights are.

10

Note on Maimonides' *Letter on Astrology*

The addressees of this Letter had asked Maimonides for his view about astrology. After having praised their question, he says that if they had known his *Mishneh Torah*, they would have known his opinion on the subject. He uses the first person plural when speaking of himself as the author of the *Mishneh Torah*, while when speaking of his opinion or of his *Guide* he uses the first person singular. He begins by speaking of the sources of knowledge: knowledge stems from reason (*deah*), sense, and tradition from the prophets and the just. He tacitly excludes the *endoxa* either because they deal chiefly with what one ought to do or forbear, as distinguished from what one ought to believe or not, or because they can be understood to be parts of the traditional lore. Sense occupies the central place, and among the senses the sense of touch. Maimonides exhorts his addressees to a critical posture toward anything they might be inclined to believe and especially toward opinions supported by many old books. This is not to deny the immense usefulness of the astrological literature or, since astrology is the root of idolatry, of the idolatrous literature: by studying the whole available idolatrous literature Maimonides has succeeded in explaining all commandments which otherwise seemed inexplicable and thus in explaining all commandments (see the *Guide*, III, 26 [end], and III, 49 [end]).

In Maimonides' view astrology is not a science at all but sheer nonsense; none of the wise men of the nations who are truly wise has ever written an astrological book; those books go back to the Chasdeans, Chaldeans, Canaanites and Egyptians to whose religion astrology belonged. Maimonides is silent here, as distinguished from the *Guide* (III, 37 [beginning]) on the Sabeans. But the wise men of Greece, the philosophers, held up to ridicule those four nations and refuted their tenets thoroughly. The wise men of Persia and even of India also realized the absurdity of astrology. Maimonides mentions here altogether seven nations. The reminder of the seven nations whose destruction is commanded in the Bible may not be accidental: all those nations were idolators, regardless whether their wise men were astrologers or not; this fact, I believe, was for Maimonides of greater importance than is commonly thought; the relation of astrology and idolatry is more complex than appears from the few words devoted to it in the *Letter on Astrology*. The true science of the stars is astronomy whose scope is set forth by Maimonides at considerable length.

Maimonides nexts puts the whole question on the broadest basis by speaking of the relation of the philosophers and the *Torah*. The great philosophers agree that the world has a governor, namely, the mover of the sphere. Most of them say that the world is eternal while some of them say that only its matter is eternal and others say what the prophets said that God as the only uncreated being created all creatures out of nothing. Maimonides refers to his "great compilation in Arabic" (i.e. the *Guide*) in which he had refuted the alleged proofs of the philosophers against creation and in particular creation out of nothing. By speaking of philosophers who teach creation out of nothing Maimonides reduces the difference, as stated in the *Guide*, between philosophy and the *Torah*. As appears from the context, his purpose in doing this is to present as it were a unitary front of philosophy and the *Torah* against astrology. For, as he goes on, all three groups of thinkers agree that this nether world is governed by God by means of the sphere and the stars. "Just as we say that God performs signs and miracles through the angels, so these philosophers say that all the things are always done by the nature of the world by means of the sphere and the stars, and they say that the sphere and the stars are animate and intelligent." Maimonides claims to have proved (in the *Guide*) that there is no disagreement whatever between the Sages of Israel and the philosophers regarding the general government of the world.

All the greater is the disagreement between all philosophers and the *Torah* regarding particular providence. According to the philosophers what happens to individual human beings or individual societies is altogether a matter of chance and has no cause in the stars. As against this the true religion, the religion of Moses, believes that what happens to human individuals happens to them in accordance with justice. Whereas according to the *Guide* the dividing line between the *Torah* and philosophy is their teaching regarding the eternity or non-eternity of the world or at least of matter, according to the *Letter on Astrology*, they are divided by what they teach regarding providence: even the philosophers, who teach creation out of nothing, deny particular providence. The *Torah* and all philosophers also agree as to men's actions not being subject to compulsion. Yet from this fact

Maimonides draws the conclusion that what happens to human beings is not what happens to the beasts, as the philosophers have said.

Just as there are three opinions regarding the world as a whole, there are three opinions regarding the fate of men: the opinion of the philosophers that it is a matter of mere chance, the opinion of the astrologers that it is fully determined by the stars, and the opinion of the *Torah*. The opinion of the philosophers is to be rejected on account of the acceptance of the *Torah*. There is no visible connection between the two tripartitions.

In the *Guide* Maimonides had considerably mitigated the opposition between philosophy and Judaism in regard to particular providence especially by his interpretation of the Book of Job. One may find a trace of this intention in a rather casual remark that he makes in the *Letter on Astrology* long before he comes to speak on particular providence. We lost our kingdom since our fathers sinned by turning to astrology, i.e. to idolatry, and neglected the art of war and conquest. This would seem to be an illustration of the view according to which the philosophers trace events to their proximate, not to their remote, cause. The remark referred to is at the same time a beautiful commentary on the grand conclusion of the *Mishneh Torah*: the restoration of Jewish freedom in the Messianic age is not to be understood as a miracle.

11

Note on Maimonides'
Treatise on the Art of Logic

Maimonides' *Treatise on the Art of Logic* is not a Jewish book. He wrote it in his capacity as a student of logic at the request of a master of the legal (religious) sciences, of a man of high education in the Arabic tongue who wished to have explained to him as briefly as possible the meaning of the terms frequently occurring in the art of logic. One ought therefore not to expect that Maimonides' *Logic* is an ordinary scholastic compendium, original or unoriginal. It is natural in the circumstances that he should introduce in the first chapter the terms which "we" (i.e. we logicians) use, as equivalents of the terms used by "the Arabic grammarians." In chapter 3, he mentions not only the possible, the impossible and the necessary but also the obligatory, the base and noble and the like among the modes of the proposition: is this due to an adaptation to a way of thinking to be expected from a master of the legal sciences? When he takes up in the next chapter the necessary, the possible and the impossible, he makes clear that the truly possible can only be said with a view to the future (e.g., it is truly possible that a newborn normal child will write); as soon as the truly possible is actualized, it resembles the necessary. One of the examples used in this connection deals with Abū Ishāq the Sabean. This example is not strange if one considers that the *Logic* is not a Jewish book and that Sabeanism is an alternative to Judaism. (An author, Ishāq the Sabean, is mentioned in the *Guide*, III 29.) In chapter 7, he refers without discussing them to "the legal syllogisms." He discusses there, when treating "analogical syllogism" and "inductive syllogism," syllogisms proving that heaven is created; the syllogisms in question are based on a disregard of the difference between natural and artificial things.

In chapter 8 however we learn that it is the art of rhetoric as distinguished from the art of demonstration that uses analogical syllogisms. In chapter 9 it is made clear that the philosophers—here mentioned for the first time—admit God to be only the remote cause in particular also of what befalls human beings and seek in each case for a proximate cause. In the center of chapter 10 we read that "body simply" comprises everything or is the highest genus of beings: the Sabeans knew no gods but the stars. We are reminded at the end of the chapter that the *Logic* is written for beginners. In chapter 11 Maimonides quotes the saying of a philosopher according to which "everyone who does not distinguish between the potential and the actual, the essential and the accidental, the conventional things and the natural things, and the universal and the particular, is unable to discourse."

Toward the end of chapter 11 and in chapter 13, Maimonides begins to refer again to the Arabic grammarian. In chapter 14, the concluding chapter, he speaks above all of the division of the sciences and at greatest length of political science. According to him, political science consists of four parts: self-government of the individual, government of the household, government of the city, government of the great nation or of the nations. The silence on government of a nation remains strange; perhaps Maimonides wished to exclude the government of a small nation. The expression "the great nation or the nations," as distinguished from "the great nation or all nations," may indicate that there cannot be a great nation comprising all nations. This "Averroist" view is best known to us from Marsilius of Padua's *Defensor Pacis* (I 17.10).

12

Niccolo Machiavelli

Men often speak of virtue without using the word but saying instead "the quality of life" or "the great society" or "ethical" or even "square." But do we know what virtue is? Socrates arrived at the conclusion that it is the greatest good for a human being to make speeches every day about virtue— apparently without ever finding a completely satisfactory definition of it. However, if we seek the most elaborate and least ambiguous answer to this truly vital question, we shall turn to Aristotle's *Ethics*. There we read among other things that there is a virtue of the first order called magnanimity—the habit of claiming high honors for oneself with the understanding that one is worthy of them. We also read there that sense of shame is not a virtue: sense of shame is becoming for the young who, due to their immaturity, cannot help making mistakes, but not for mature and well-bred men who simply always do the right and proper thing. Wonderful as all this is —we have received a very different message from a very different quarter. When the prophet Isaiah received his vocation, he was overpowered by the sense of his unworthiness: "I am a man of unclean lips amidst a people of unclean lips." This amounts to an implicit condemnation of magnanimity and an implicit vindication of the sense of shame. The reason is given in the context: "holy, holy, holy is the lord of hosts." There is no holy god for Aristotle and the Greeks generally. Who is right, the Greeks or the Jews? Athens or Jerusalem? And how to proceed in order to find out who is right? Must we not admit that human wisdom is unable to settle this question and that every answer is based on an act of faith? But does this not constitute the complete

Reprinted from *History of Political Philosophy*, edited by Leo Strauss and Joseph Cropsey, 2d ed. (Chicago: Rand McNally, 1972; University of Chicago Press edition, 1981). ©1963, 1972 by Joseph Cropsey and Miriam Strauss.

and final defeat of Athens? For a philosophy based on faith is no longer philosophy. Perhaps it was this unresolved conflict which has prevented Western thought from ever coming to rest. Perhaps it is this conflict which is at the bottom of a kind of thought which is philosophic indeed but no longer Greek: modern philosophy. It is in trying to understand modern philosophy that we come across Machiavelli.

Machiavelli is the only political thinker whose name has come into common use for designating a kind of politics, which exists and will continue to exist independently of his influence, a politics guided exclusively by considerations of expediency, which uses all means, fair or foul, iron or poison, for achieving its ends—its end being the aggrandizement of one's country or fatherland—but also using the fatherland in the service of the self-aggrandizement of the politician or statesman or one's party. But if this phenomenon is as old as political society itself, why is it called after Machiavelli who thought or wrote only a short while ago, about 500 years ago? Machiavelli was the first publicly to defend it in books with his name on the title pages. Machiavelli made it publicly defensible. This means that his achievement, detestable or admirable, cannot be understood in terms of politics itself, or of the history of politics—say, in terms of the Italian Renaissance—but only in terms of political thought, of political philosophy, of the history of political philosophy.

Machiavelli appears to have broken with all preceding political philosophers. There is weighty evidence in support of this view. Yet his largest political work ostensibly seeks to bring about the rebirth of the ancient Roman Republic; far from being a radical innovator, Machiavelli is a restorer of something old and forgotten.

To find our bearings let us first cast a glance at two post-Machiavellian thinkers, Hobbes and Spinoza. Hobbes regarded his political philosophy as wholly new. More than that, he denied that there existed prior to his work any political philosophy or political science worthy of the name. He regarded himself as the founder of the true political philosophy, as the true founder of political philosophy. He knew of course that a political doctrine claiming to be true had existed since Socrates. But this doctrine was, according to Hobbes, a dream rather than science. He considered Socrates and his successors to be anarchists in that they permitted an appeal from the law of the land, the positive law, to a higher law, the natural law; they thus fostered a disorder utterly incompatible with civil society. According to Hobbes, on the other hand, the higher law, the natural law, commands so to speak one and only one thing: unqualified obedience to the sovereign power. It would not be difficult to show that this line of reasoning is contradicted by Hobbes' own teaching; at any rate it does not go to the roots of the matter. Hobbes' serious objection to all earlier political philosophy comes out most clearly in this statement: "They that have written of justice

and policy in general, do all invade each other and themselves, with contradiction. To reduce this doctrine to the rules and infallibility of reason, there
is no way but first to put such principles down for a foundation, as passion
not mistrusting may not seek to displace; and afterwards to build thereon the
truth of cases in the law of nature (which hitherto had been built in the air)
by degrees, till the whole be inexpugnable." The rationality of the political
teaching consists in its being acceptable to passion, in its being agreeable to
passion. The passion that must be the basis of the rational political teaching
is fear of violent death. At first glance there seems to be an alternative to it,
the passion of generosity, that is, "a glory, or pride in appearing not to need
to break (one's word)"—but this "is a generosity too rarely found to be
presumed on, especially in the pursuers of wealth, command or sensual
pleasure; which are the greatest part of mankind." Hobbes attempts to build
on the most common ground, on a ground that is admittedly low but has the
advantage of being solid, whereas the traditional teaching was built on air.
On this new basis, accordingly, the status of morality must be lowered;
morality is nothing but fear-inspired peaceableness. The moral law or the
natural law is understood as derivative from the right of nature, the right of
self-preservation; the fundamental moral fact is a right, not a duty. This new
spirit became the spirit of the modern era, including our own age. That spirit
was preserved despite the important modifications that Hobbes' doctrine
underwent at the hands of his great successors. Locke enlarged self-
preservation to comfortable self-preservation and thus laid the theoretical
foundation for the acquisitive society. Against the traditional view, according to which a just society is a society in which just men rule, Kant asserted:
"Hard as it may sound, the problem of establishing the state [the just social
order] is soluble even for a nation of devils, provided they have sense," that
is, provided they are shrewd calculators. We discern this thought within the
teachings of Marx, for the proletarians from whom he expects so much are
surely not angels. Now although the revolution effected by Hobbes was
decisively prepared by Machiavelli, Hobbes does not refer to Machiavelli.
This fact requires further examination.

Hobbes is in a way a teacher of Spinoza. Nevertheless Spinoza opens his
Political Treatise with an attack on *the* philosophers. The philosophers, he
says, treat the passions as vices. By ridiculing or deploring the passions, they
praise and evince their belief in a nonexistent human nature; they conceive
of men not as they are but as they would wish them to be. Hence their
political teaching is wholly useless. Quite different is the case of the *politici*.
They have learned from experience that there will be vices as long as there
are human beings. Hence their political teaching is very valuable, and
Spinoza is building his teaching on theirs. The greatest of these *politici* is the
most penetrating Florentine, Machiavelli. It is Machiavelli's more subdued
attack on traditional political philosophy that Spinoza takes over bodily and

translates into the less reserved language of Hobbes. As for the sentence, "There will be vices as long as there will be human beings," Spinoza has tacitly borrowed it from Tacitus; in Spinoza's mouth it amounts to an unqualified rejection of the belief in a Messianic age; the coming of the Messianic age would require divine intervention or a miracle, but according to Spinoza miracles are impossible.

Spinoza's introduction to his *Political Treatise* is obviously modeled on the 15th chapter of Machiavelli's *Prince*. There Machiavelli says:

> Since I know that many have written (on how princes should rule), I fear that by writing about it I will be held to be presumptuous by departing, especially in discussing such a subject, from the others. But since it is my intention to write something useful for him who understands, it has seemed to me to be more appropriate to go straight to the effective truth of the matter rather than to the imagination thereof. For many have imagined republics and principalities that have never been seen nor are known truly to exist. There is so great a distance between how one lives and how one ought to live that he who rejects what people do in favor of what one ought to do, brings about his ruin rather than his preservation; for a man who wishes to do in every matter what is good, will be ruined among so many who are not good. Hence it is necessary for a prince who wishes to maintain himself, to learn to be able not to be good, or use goodness and abstain from using it according to the commands of circumstances.

One arrives at imagined kingdoms or republics if one takes one's bearings by how man ought to live, by virtue. The classical philosophers did just that. They thus arrived at the best regimes of the *Republic* and the *Politics*. But when speaking of imagined kingdoms, Machiavelli thinks not only of the philosophers; he also thinks of the kingdom of God which from his point of view is a conceit of visionaries for, as his pupil Spinoza said, justice rules only where just men rule. But to stay with the philosophers, they regarded the actualization of the best regime as possible, but extremely improbable. According to Plato its actualization literally depends on a coincidence, a most unlikely coincidence, the coincidence of philosophy and political power. The actualization of the best regime depends on chance, on *Fortuna*, that is, on something which is essentially beyond human control. According to Machiavelli, however, *Fortuna* is a woman who as such must be hit and beaten to be kept under; *Fortuna* can be vanquished by the right kind of man. There is a connection between this posture toward *Fortuna* and the orientation by how many do live: by lowering the standards of political excellence one guarantees the actualization of the only kind of political order that in principle is possible. In post-Machiavellian parlance: the ideal of the right kind necessarily becomes actual; the ideal and the actual necessarily converge. This way of thinking has had an amazing success; if someone maintains today that there is no guarantee for the actualization of the ideal, he must fear to be called a cynic.

Machiavelli is not concerned with how men do live merely in order to describe it; his intention is rather, on the basis of knowledge of how men do live, to teach princes how they ought to rule and even how they ought to live. Accordingly he rewrites, as it were, Aristotle's *Ethics*. To some extent he admits that the traditional teaching is true: men are obliged to live virtuously in the Aristotelian sense. But he denies that living virtuously is living happily or leads to happiness. "If liberality is used in the manner in which you are obliged to use it, it hurts you; for if you use it virtuously and as one ought to use it," the prince will ruin himself and will be compelled to rule his subjects oppressively in order to get the necessary money. Miserliness, the opposite of liberality, is "one of the vices that enable a prince to rule." A prince ought to be liberal, however, with the property of others, for this increases his reputation. Similar considerations apply to compassion and its opposite, cruelty. This leads Machiavelli to the question of whether it is better for a prince to be loved rather than to be feared or vice versa. It is difficult to be both loved and feared. Since one must therefore choose, one ought to choose being feared rather than being loved, for whether one is loved depends on others, while being feared depends on oneself. But one must avoid becoming hated; the prince will avoid becoming hated if he abstains from the property and the women of his subjects—especially from their property, which men so love that they resent less the murder of their father than the loss of their patrimony. In war the reputation for cruelty does not do any harm. The greatest example is Hannibal who was always implicitly obeyed by his soldiers and never had to contend with mutinies either after victories or after defeats. "This could not arise from anything but his inhuman cruelty which, together with his innumerable virtues, made him always venerable and terrible in the eyes of his soldiers, and without which cruelty his other virtues would not have sufficed. Not very considerately do the writers on the one hand admire his action and on the other condemn the main cause of the same." We note that inhuman cruelty is one of Hannibal's virtues. Another example of cruelty "well used" is supplied by Cesare Borgia's pacification of the Romagna. In order to pacify that country, he put at its head Ramirro d'Orco, "a man of cruelty and dispatch," and gave him the fullest power. Ramirro succeeded in no time, acquiring the greatest reputation. But then Cesare thought that such an excessive power was no longer necessary and might make him hated; he knew that the rigorous measures taken by Ramirro had caused some hatred. Cesare wished therefore to show that if any cruelty had been committed, it was not his doing but arose from the harsh nature of his subordinate. Therefore he had him put one morning in two pieces on the Piazza of the chief town, with a piece of wood and a bloody knife at his side. The ferocity of this sight induced in the populace a state of satisfaction and stupor.

Machiavelli's new "ought" demands then the judicious and vigorous use of both virtue and vice according to the requirements of the circumstances. The judicious alternation of virtue and vice is virtue (*virtù*) in his meaning of the word. He amuses himself and, I believe, some of his readers by using the word "virtue" in both the traditional sense and his sense. Occasionally he makes a distinction between *virtù* and *bontà*. That distinction was in a way prepared by Cicero who says that men are called "good" on account of their modesty, temperance, and above all, justice and keeping of faith, as distinguished from courage and wisdom. The Ciceronian distinction within the virtues in its turn reminds us of Plato's *Republic* in which temperance and justice are presented as virtues required of all, whereas courage and wisdom are required only of some. Machiavelli's distinction between goodness and other virtues tends to become an opposition between goodness and virtue: while virtue is required of rulers and soldiers, goodness is required, or characteristic, of the populace engaged in peaceful occupations; goodness comes to mean something like fear-bred obedience to the government, or even vileness.

In quite a few passages of the *Prince*, Machiavelli speaks of morality in the way in which decent men have spoken of it at all times. He resolves the contradiction in the 19th chapter, in which he discusses the Roman emperors who came after the philosopher-emperor Marcus Aurelius up to Maximinus. The high point is his discussion of the emperor Severus. Severus belonged to those emperors who were most cruel and rapacious. Yet in him was so great virtue that he could always reign with felicity, for he knew well how to use the person of the fox and the lion—which natures a prince must imitate. A new prince in a new principality cannot imitate the actions of the good emperor Marcus Aurelius, nor is it necessary for him to follow those of Severus; but he ought to take from Severus those portions that are necessary for founding his state and from Marcus those that are appropriate and glorious for preserving a state already firmly established. The chief theme of the *Prince* is the wholly new prince in a wholly new state, that is, the founder. And the model for the founder as founder is the extremely clever criminal Severus. This means that justice is precisely not, as Augustine had said, the *fundamentum regnorum*; the foundation of justice is injustice; the foundation of morality is immorality; the foundation of legitimacy is illegitimacy or revolution; the foundation of freedom is tyranny. At the beginning there is Terror, not Harmony, or Love—but there is of course a great difference between Terror for its own sake, for the sake of its perpetuation, and Terror that limits itself to laying the foundation for the degree of humanity and freedom that is compatible with the human condition. But this distinction is at best hinted at in the *Prince*.

The comforting message of the *Prince* is given in the last chapter, which is an exhortation addressed to one Italian prince, Lorenzo de'Medici, to take Italy and to liberate her from the barbarians, that is, the French, the

Spaniards, and the Germans. Machiavelli tells Lorenzo that the liberation of
Italy is not very difficult. One of the reasons he gives is that "extraordinary
events without example that have been induced by God, are seen: the sea
has divided itself, the cloud has led you on your way, the stone has poured
out water, manna has rained." The events without example do have an
example: the miracles following Israel's liberation from Egyptian bondage.
What Machiavelli seems to suggest is that Italy is the promised land for
Lorenzo. But there is one difficulty: Moses, who led Israel out of the house
of bondage towards the promised land, did not reach that land; he died at its
borders. Machiavelli thus darkly prophesied that Lorenzo would not liberate Italy, one reason being that he lacked the extraordinary *virtú* needed for
bringing that great work to its consummation. But there is more to the
extraordinary events without example of which nothing is known other than
what Machiavelli asserts about them. All these extraordinary events occurred before the revelation on Sinai. What Machiavelli prophesies is, then,
that a new revelation, a revelation of a new Decalogue is imminent. The
bringer of that revelation is of course not that mediocrity Lorenzo, but a new
Moses. That new Moses is Machiavelli himself, and the new Decalogue is
the wholly new teaching on the wholly new prince in a wholly new state. It is
true that Moses was an armed prophet and that Machiavelli belongs to the
unarmed ones who necessarily come to ruin. In order to find the solution of
this difficulty one must turn to the other great work of Machiavelli, the
Discourses on the First Ten Books of Livy.

Yet if one turns from the *Prince* to the *Discourses* in order to find the
solution to the difficulties not solved in the *Prince*, one goes from the frying
pan into the fire. For the *Discourses* is much more difficult to understand
than the *Prince*. It is impossible to show this without at first inducing in the
reader a certain bewilderment; but such bewilderment is the beginning of
understanding.

Let us begin at the very beginning, the Epistles Dedicatory. The *Prince* is
dedicated to Machiavelli's master, Lorenzo de'Medici. Machiavelli who
presents himself as a man of the lowest condition, as living in a low place is so
overwhelmed by his master's grandeur that he regards the *Prince*, although
it is his most cherished possession, as unworthy of the presence of Lorenzo.
He recommends his work by the observation that it is a small volume which
the addressee can understand in the shortest time, although it embodies
everything that the author has come to know and understand in very many
years and under great perils. The *Discourses* is dedicated to two young
friends of Machiavelli who have compelled him to write that book. At the
same time the book is a token of Machiavelli's gratitude for the benefits he
has received from his two friends. He had dedicated the *Prince* to his master
in the hope that he would receive favors from him. And he does not know
whether Lorenzo will pay any attention to the *Prince*—whether he would

not be more pleased with receiving a horse of exceptional beauty. In accordance with all this he disparages in the Epistle Dedicatory to the *Discourses* the custom that he had complied with in the Epistle Dedicatory to the *Prince*—the custom of dedicating one's works to princes: the *Discourses* is dedicated not to princes but to men who deserve to be princes. Whether Lorenzo deserves to be a prince remains a question.

These differences between the two books can be illustrated by the fact that in the *Prince* Machiavelli avoids certain terms that he uses in the *Discourses*. The *Prince* fails to mention the conscience, the common good, tyrants (that is, the distinction between kings and tyrants), and heaven; also in the *Prince* "we" never means "we Christians." One might mention here that Machiavelli refers in neither work to the distinction between this world and the next, or between this life and the next; nor does he mention in either work the devil or hell; above all, he never mentions in either work the soul.

Now let us come to the text of the *Discourses*. What is the *Discourses* about? What kind of book is it? There is no such difficulty regarding the *Prince*. The *Prince* is a mirror of princes, and mirrors of princes were a traditional genre. In accordance with this, all chapter headings of the *Prince* are in Latin. This is not to deny but rather to underline the fact that the *Prince* transmits a revolutionary teaching in a traditional guise. But this traditional guise is missing in the *Discourses*. None of its chapter headings is in Latin although the work deals with an ancient and traditional subject: with ancient Rome. Furthermore, the *Prince* is tolerably easy to understand because it has a tolerably clear plan. The plan of the *Discourses*, however, is extremely obscure, so much so that one is tempted to wonder whether it has any plan. In addition, the *Discourses* presents itself as devoted to the first ten books of Livy. Livy's first ten books lead from the beginnings of Rome to the time immediately preceding the first Punic war, that is, up to the peak of the uncorrupted Roman Republic, and prior to Roman conquests outside of the Italian mainland. But Machiavelli deals in the *Discourses* to some extent with the whole of Roman history as covered by Livy's work: Livy's work consists of 142 books and the *Discourses* consists of 142 chapters. Livy's work leads up to the time of the emperor Augustus, that is, the beginnings of Christianity. At any rate, the *Discourses*, more than four times as extensive as the *Prince*, seems to be much more comprehensive than the *Prince*. Machiavelli explicitly excludes only one subject from treatment in the *Discourses*: "How dangerous it is to make oneself the head of a new thing that concerns many, and how difficult it is to handle it and to consummate it and after its consummation to maintain it would be too long and exalted a matter to discuss; I shall reserve it therefore for a more appropriate place." Yet it is precisely this long and exalted matter that Machiavelli explicitly discusses in the *Prince*: "One must consider that nothing is more difficult to handle, nor more doubtful of success, nor more dangerous to manage than to make oneself the head of the introduction of new orders." It is true that Machiavelli does not speak here of "maintaining." Such maintaining, as we learn from the *Discourses*, is best done by the people, while the introduction of new modes and orders is best done by princes. From this one may draw the conclusion that the characteristic subject of the *Discourses*, as distinguished from the *Prince*, is the people—a conclusion by no means absurd but quite insufficient for one's even beginning to understand the work.

The character of the *Discourses* may be further illustrated with two examples of another kind of difficulty. In II 13, Machiavelli asserts and in a manner proves that one rises from a low or abject position to an exalted one through fraud rather than through force. This is what the Roman Republic did in its beginnings. Before speaking of the Roman Republic, however, Machiavelli speaks of four princes who rose from a low or abject position to a high one. He speaks most extensively of Cyrus, the founder of the Persian empire. The example of Cyrus is the central one. Cyrus rose to power by deceiving the king of Media, his uncle. But if he was, to begin with, the nephew of the king of Media, how can he be said to have risen from a low or abject position? To drive home his point, Machiavelli mentions next Giovan Galeazzo who through fraud took away the state and the power from Bernabò, his uncle. Galeazzo too was then to begin with the nephew of a ruling prince and cannot be said to have risen from a low or abject position. What, then, does Machiavelli indicate by speaking in such a riddling way? III 48: when one sees an enemy commit a great mistake, one must believe that there is fraud beneath; this is said in the heading of the chapter; in the text Machiavelli goes further and says "there will always be fraud beneath it." Yet immediately afterward, in the central example, Machiavelli shows that the Romans once committed a great mistake through demoralization, that is, not fraudulently.

How is one to deal with the difficulties that confront us in the *Discourses*? Let us return to the title: Discourses on the First Ten Books of Livy. The title is not literally correct but it is safe to say that the work consists primarily of Discourses on the First Ten Books of Livy. We have noted furthermore that the *Discourses* lacks a clear plan: perhaps the plan will become visible if we take seriously the fact that the work is devoted to Livy; perhaps Machiavelli follows Livy by following the Livian order. Again this is not simply true, but it is true if it is intelligently understood: Machiavelli's use and nonuse of Livy is the key to the understanding of the work. There are various ways in which Machiavelli uses Livy: sometimes he makes tacit use of a Livian story, sometimes he refers to "this text," sometimes he mentions Livy by name, sometimes he quotes him (in Latin) not mentioning or mentioning his name. Machiavelli's use of and nonuse of Livy may be illustrated by the facts that he does not quote Livy in the first ten chapters, that he quotes him in the following five chapters and again fails to quote him in the following 24 chapters. Understanding the reasons behind these facts is the key to the understanding of the *Discourses*.

I cannot treat this matter conclusively within the space at my disposal, but will deal with it through a selection of the following five chapters or quasi-chapters: I proem, II proem, II 1, I 26 and II 5.

In the proem to I, Machiavelli lets us know that he has discovered new modes and orders, that he has taken a road that was never trodden by anyone before. He compares his achievement to the discovery of unknown waters and lands: he presents himself as the Columbus of the moral-political world. What prompted him was the natural desire that he always had, to do those things that in his opinion bring about the common benefit of each. Therefore he bravely faces the dangers that he knows lie in wait for him. What are these dangers? In the case of the discovery of unknown seas and lands, the danger consists in seeking them; once you have found the unknown lands and have returned home, you are safe. In the case of the discovery of new modes and orders, however, the danger consists in finding them, that is, in making them publicly known. For, as we have heard from Machiavelli, it is dangerous to make oneself the head of something new which affects many.

To our great surprise, Machiavelli identifies immediately afterwards the new modes and orders with those of antiquity: his discovery is only a rediscovery. He refers to the contemporary concern with fragments of ancient statues, which are held in high honor and used as models by contemporary sculptors. It is all the more surprising that no one thinks of imitating the most virtuous actions of ancient kingdoms and republics, with the deplorable result that no trace of ancient virtue remains. The present-day lawyers learn their craft from the ancient lawyers. The present-day physicians base their judgements on the experience of the ancient physicians. It is therefore all the more surprising that in political and military matters the present-day princes and republics do not have recourse to the examples of the ancients. This results not so much from the weakness into which the present-day religion has led the world or from the evil that ambitious leisure has done to many Christian countries and cities, as from insufficient understanding of the histories and especially that of Livy. As a consequence, Machiavelli's contemporaries believe that the imitation of the ancients is not only difficult but impossible. Yet this is plainly absurd: the natural order, including the nature of man, is the same as in antiquity.

We understand now why the discovery of new modes and orders, which is only the rediscovery of the ancient modes and orders, is dangerous. That rediscovery which leads up to the demands that the virtue of the ancients be imitated by present-day men, runs counter to the present-day religion: it is that religion which teaches that the imitation of ancient virtue is impossible, that it is morally impossible, for the virtues of the pagans are only resplendent vices. What Machiavelli will have to achieve in the *Discourses* is not merely the presentation, but the re-habilitation, of ancient virtue against the Christian critique. This does not dispose of the difficulty that the discovery of new modes and orders is only the re-discovery of the ancient modes and orders.

This much, however, is clear. Machiavelli cannot take for granted the superiority of the ancients; he must establish it. Therefore he must first find a ground common to the admirers and the detractors of antiquity. That common ground is the veneration of the ancient, be it biblical or pagan. He starts from the tacit premise that the good is the old and hence that the best is the oldest. He is thus led first to ancient Egypt, which flourished in the most ancient antiquity. But this does not help very much because too little is known of ancient Egypt. Machiavelli settles, therefore, for that oldest which is sufficiently known and at the same time his own: ancient Rome. Yet ancient Rome is not evidently admirable in every important respect. A strong case can be made, and had been made, for the superiority of Sparta to Rome. Machiavelli must therefore establish the authority of ancient Rome. The general manner in which he does this reminds one of the manner in which theologians formerly established the authority of the Bible against unbelievers. But ancient Rome is not a book like the Bible. Yet by establishing the authority of ancient Rome, Machiavelli establishes the authority of its chief historian, of Livy, and therewith of the book. Livy's history is Machiavelli's Bible. From this it follows that Machiavelli cannot begin to use Livy before he has established the authority of Rome.

He begins to quote Livy in the section on the Roman religion (I 11–15). In the preceeding chapter he had contrasted Caesar as the founder of a tyranny with Romulus as the founder of a free city. The glory of Caesar is due to the writers who celebrated him because their judgement was corrupted by his extraordinary success, the foundation of the rule of the emperors; the emperors did not permit writers to speak freely of Caesar. Yet the free writers knew how to circumvent that restriction: they blamed Catalina, Caesar's luckless prefiguration, and they celebrated Brutus, Caesar's enemy. But not all emperors were bad. The times of the emperors from Nerva to Marcus Aurelius were the golden times when everyone could hold and defend any opinion he pleased: golden are the times when thought and expression of thought are not restricted by authority. Those remarks form in effect the introduction to Machiavelli's treatment of the Roman religion. He there treats the pagan religion as at least equal as religion to the biblical religion. The principle of all religion is authority, that is, precisely that which Machiavelli had questioned immediately before. But for the ruling class of ancient Rome, religion was not an authority; they used religion for their political purposes, and they did this in the most admirable manner. The praise of the religion of ancient Rome implies, and more than implies a critique of the religion of modern Rome. Machiavelli praises the religion of ancient Rome for the same reason for which the free writers who were subject to the authority of the Caesars praised Brutus: he could not openly blame the authority of Christianity to which he was subject. Hence if Livy's history is Machiavelli's Bible, it is his anti-Bible.

After he has established the authority of ancient Rome and shown its superiority to the moderns by many examples, he begins to intimate the defects from which it suffered. Only from this point on is Livy, as distinguished from Rome—that is, a book—his sole authority. Yet shortly before the end of Book One, he openly questions the opinion of all writers, including Livy, on a matter of the greatest importance. He thus leads us step by step to the realization of why the old modes and orders which he has rediscovered, are new: 1) The modes and orders of ancient Rome were established under the pressure of circumstances, by trial and error, without a coherent plan, without understanding of their reasons; Machiavelli supplies the reasons and is therefore able to correct some of the old modes and orders. 2) The spirit that animated the old modes and orders was veneration for tradition, for authority, the spirit of piety, while Machiavelli is animated by an altogether different spirit. The progress of the argument in Book One is indicated most clearly. While Book One begins with the highest praise of the most ancient antiquity, it ends with the expression "very young": many Romans celebrated their triumphs *giovanissimi*.

We are thus prepared for understanding the proem of Book Two. There Machiavelli openly questions the prejudice in favor of the ancient times: "men praise always the ancient times and accuse the present, but not always with reason." In truth the world has always been the same; the quantity of good and evil is always the same. What changes is the different countries and nations, which have times of virtue and times of degeneracy. In antiquity virtue resided at first in Assyria and finally in Rome. After the destruction of the Roman Empire virtue revived only in some parts of it, especially in Turkey. So that someone born in our time in Greece who has not become a Turk reasonably blames the present and praises antiquity. Accordingly, Machiavelli is perfectly justified in praising the times of the ancient Romans and blaming his own time: no trace of ancient virtue is left in Rome and in Italy. Therefore he exhorts the young to imitate the ancient Romans whenever fortune gives them the opportunity to do so, that is, to do what he was prevented from doing by the malignity of the times and of fortune.

The message of the proem to Book Two could seem to be rather meager, at least as compared with that of the proem to Book One. This is due to the fact that the proem to Book One is the introduction to the whole work, while the proem to Book Two is the introduction only to Book Two and more particularly to the early chapters of Book Two. There Machiavelli first takes issue with an opinion of Plutarch, whom he calls a weighty author—he never applies this epithet to Livy—an opinion also shared by Livy and even by the Roman people themselves: the opinion that the Romans acquired their empire through fortune rather than through virtue. Prior to the Roman conquest, the whole of Europe was inhabited by three peoples who defended their freedom obstinately and who governed themselves freely, that is, as republics. Hence Rome needed excessive virtue to conquer them. How then does it come about that in those ancient times those peoples were greater lovers of freedom than they are today? According to Machiavelli, this is ultimately due to the difference between the ancient religion and our religion. Our religion has placed the highest good in humility, abjectness, and the disparagement of the human things, whereas the ancient religion has placed the highest good in greatness of mind, strength of the body, and in all other things apt to make men most strong. But the disarmament of the world and of heaven itself is ultimately due to the destruction of the Roman Empire, of all republican life. Apart from her excessive virtue, the second reason for Rome's greatness was her liberal admission of foreigners to citizenship. But such a policy exposes a state to great dangers, as the Athenians and especially the Spartans knew who feared that the admixture of new inhabitants would corrupt the ancient customs. Owing to the Roman policy, many men who never knew republican life and did not care for it, that is, many orientals, became Roman citizens. The Roman conquest of the East thus completed what her conquest of the West had begun. And thus it came about that the Roman Republic was, on the one hand, the direct opposite of the Christian republic, and, on the other hand, the cause of the Christian republic and even the model for it.

Book Three has no proem but its first chapter performs the function of a proem. By this slight irregularity Machiavelli underlines the fact that the number of chapters of the *Discourses* equals the number of books of Livy's history, and Livy's history, as we noted before, extends from the origin of Rome until the time of the emergence of Christianity. The heading of the first chapter of Book Three reads as follows: "If one wishes that a sect or a republic live long, one must bring it back frequently to its beginning." While the heading speaks only of sects and republics, the chapter itself deals with republics, sects, and kingdoms; sects, that is, religions, occupy the center. All things of the world have a limit to their course—a limit set by heaven. But they reach that limit only if they are kept in order, and this means if they are frequently brought back to their beginnings; for in their beginnings they must have had some goodness, otherwise they would not have gained their first reputation and increase. Machiavelli proves his thesis first regarding republics, by the example of Rome's regaining new life and new virtue after her defeat by the Gauls: Rome then resumed the observance of religion and justice, that is, of the old orders, especially those of religion, through the neglect of which she had suffered disaster. The recovery of ancient virtue consists of the reimposition of the terror and fear that had made men good at the beginning. Machiavelli thus explains what his concern with the recovery of ancient modes and orders means fundamentally: men were good at the beginning not because of innocence but because they were gripped by terror and fear—by the initial and radical terror and fear; at the beginning there is not Love but Terror; Machiavelli's wholly new teaching is based on this alleged insight (which anticipates Hobbes' doctrine of the state of nature). Machiavelli turns then to the discussion of sects; he illustrates his thesis by the example of "our religion": "If our religion had not been brought back to its beginning or principle by St. Francis and St. Dominic, it would have become completely extinguished, for by poverty and the example of Christ they brought that religion back into the minds of men where it was already extinguished; and these new orders were so potent that they are the reason why the immorality of the prelates and of the heads of the religion do not ruin our religion; for the Franciscans and the Dominicans live still in poverty and have so great credit with the peoples through confession and preachings that they convince the peoples that it is evil to speak evil of evil and that it is good to live in obedience to the prelates, and if the prelates sin, to leave them for punishment to God. Thus the prelates do the worst they can, for they do not fear the punishment that they do not see and in which they do not believe. That innovation therefore has maintained, and maintains, that religion." Here the return to the beginning was achieved by the introduction of new orders. Machiavelli doubtless says this here because he did not think that the Franciscan and Dominican reforms amounted to a simple restoration of primitive Christianity, for those reforms left intact the Christian hierarchy. But the introduction of new orders is necessary also in republics, as Machiavelli emphasizes in the concluding chapter of the *Discourses*: the restoration of the ancient modes and orders is in all cases, including that of Machiavelli himself, the introduction of new modes and orders. Nevertheless there is a great difference between the Franciscan and Dominican renovation and republican renovations: republican renovations subject the whole republic, including the leading man, to the initial terror and fear precisely because they resist evil—because they punish evil visibly and hence credibly. The Christian command or counsel not to resist evil is based on the premise that the beginning or principle is love. That command or counsel can only lead to the utmost disorder or else to evasion. The premise, however, turns into its extreme opposite.

We have seen that the number of chapters of the *Discourses* is meaningful and has been deliberately chosen. We may thus be induced to wonder whether the number of chapters of the *Prince* is not also meaningful. The *Prince* consists of 26 chapters. Twenty-six is the numerical value of the letters of the sacred name of God in Hebrew, of the Tetragrammaton. But did Machiavelli know of this? I do not know. Twenty-six equals 2 times 13.

Thirteen is now and for quite some time has been considered an unlucky number, but in former times it was also and even primarily considered a lucky number. So "twice 13" might mean both good luck and bad luck, and hence altogether: luck, *fortuna*. A case can be made for the view that Machiavelli's theology can be expressed by the formula *Deus sive fortuna* (as distinguished from Spinoza's *Deus sive natura*)—that is, that God is fortuna as supposed to be subject to human influence (imprecation). But to establish this would require an argument "too long and too exalted" for the present occasion. Let us therefore see whether we cannot get some help from looking at the 26th chapter of the *Discourses*. The heading of the chapter reads as follows: "A new prince, in a city or country taken by him, must make everything new." The subject of the chapter is then the new prince in a new state, that is, the most exalted subject of the *Prince*. At the end of the preceding chapter Machiavelli had said: he who wishes to establish an absolute power, which the writers call tyranny, must renew everything. The subject of our chapter is then tyranny, but the term "tyranny" never occurs in that chapter: "tyranny" is avoided in the 26th chapter of the *Discourses* just as it is avoided in the *Prince*, which consists of 26 chapters. The lesson of the chapter itself is this: a new prince who wishes to establish absolute power in his state must make everything new; he must establish new magistracies, with new names, new authorities and new men; he must make the rich poor and the poor rich, as David did when he became king: *qui esurientes implevit bonis, et divites dimisit inanes.* In sum, he must not leave anything in his country untouched, and there must not be any rank or wealth that its possessors do not recognize as owing to the prince. The modes that he must use are most cruel and inimical, not only to every Christian life, but even to every humane one; so that everyone must prefer to live as a private man rather than as a king with so great a ruin of human beings." The Latin quotation that occurs in this chapter is translated in the Revised Version as follows: "He hath filled the hungry with good things; and the rich he hath sent empty away." The quotation forms part of the Magnificat, the Virgin Mary's prayer of thanks after she had heard from the angel Gabriel that she would bring forth a son to be called Jesus; he that "hath filled the hungry with good things, and sent the rich empty away" is none other than God himself. In the context of this chapter this means that god is a tyrant, and that king David who made the rich poor and the poor rich, was a Godly king, a king who walked in the ways of the Lord because he proceeded in the tyrannical way. We must note that this is the sole New Testament quotation occurring in the *Discourses* or in the *Prince*. And that sole New Testament quotation is used for expressing a most horrible blasphemy. Someone might say in defense of Machiavelli that the blasphemy is not expressly uttered but only implied. But this defense, far from helping Machiavelli, makes his case worse, and for this reason: When a man openly utters or vomits a blasphemy, all good men shudder and turn away from him, or punish him according to his deserts; the sin is entirely his. But a concealed blasphemy is so insidious, not only because it protects the blasphemer against punishment by due process of law, but above all because it practically compels the hearer or reader to think the blasphemy by himself and thus to become an accomplice of the blasphemer. Machiavelli thus establishes a kind of intimacy with his readers par excellence, whom he calls "the young," by inducing them to think forbidden or criminal thoughts. Such an intimacy seems also to be established by every prosecutor or judge who, in order to convict the criminal, must think criminal thoughts, but that intimacy is abhorred by the criminal. Machiavelli, however, intends it and desires it. This is an important part of his education of the young or, to use the time-honored expression, of his corruption of the young.

If space permitted it, we might profitably consider the other chapters of the *Discourses* whose numbers are multiples of 13. I shall consider only one of them: Book Two, chapter 5. The heading of this chapter runs as follows: "That the change of sects and languages together with floods and plagues destroys the memory of things." Machiavelli begins this chapter by taking issue with certain philosophers by stating an objection to their contention. The philosophers in question say that the world is eternal. Machiavelli "believes" that one could reply to them as follows: if the world were as old as they contend, it would be reasonable that there would be memory of more than 5,000 years (that is, the memory we have thanks to the Bible). Machiavelli opposes Aristotle in the name of the Bible. But he continues: one could make that rejoinder if one did not see that the memories of times are destroyed by various causes, partly originated in human beings, partly originated in heaven. Machiavelli refuted then an alleged refutation of Aristotle, of the best-known anti-biblical argument of the Aristotelians. He continues as follows: the causes originating in human beings are the changes of sects and of language. For when a new sect, that is, a new religion arises, its first concern is, in order to acquire reputation, to extinguish the old religion; and when those who establish the orders of the new sects are of a different language, they destroy the old sect easily. One realizes this by considering the procedure used by the Christian sect against the gentile sect; the former has ruined all orders, all ceremonies of the latter, and destroyed every memory of that ancient theology. It is true that it has not succeeded in completely destroying the knowledge of the things done by the excellent men among the gentiles and this was due to the fact that it preserved the Latin language, which the Christians were forced to use in writing their new law. For had they been able to write that law in a new language, there would be no record whatever of the things of the past. One has only to read of the proceedings of St. Gregory and the other heads of the Christian religion in order to see with how great an obstinacy they persecuted all ancient memories by burning the works of the poets and of the historians, by ruining the images and spoiling every other sign of antiquity; if they had joined to that persecution a new language, everything would have been forgotten in the shortest time. Through these extraordinary overstatements Machiavelli sketches the background of his own work, in particular of his recovery of his cherished Livy, the largest part of whose history has been lost owing to "the malignity of the times" (I 2). Furthermore, he here silently contrasts the conduct of the Christians with that of the Muslims whose new law was written in a new language. The difference between the Christians and the Muslims is not that the Christians had a greater respect for pagan antiquity than the Muslims, but that the Christians did not conquer the Western Roman empire as the Muslims conquered the Eastern, and were therefore forced to adopt the Latin language and therefore to some extent to preserve the literature of pagan Rome, and thereby preserve their mortal enemy. Shortly thereafter Machiavelli says that these sects change two or three times in 5,000 or 6,000 years. He thus determines the life span of Christianity; the maximum would be 3,000 years, the minimum 1,666 years. This means that Christianity might come to an end about 150 years after the *Discourses* were written. Machiavelli was not the first to engage in speculations of this kind (cf. Gemistos Plethon who was much more sanguine or apprehensive than Machiavelli).

The most important point, however, that Machiavelli makes through this statement is that all religions, including Christianity, are of human, not heavenly origin. The changes of heavenly origin that destroy the memory of things are plagues, hunger, and floods: the heavenly is the natural; the supra-natural is human.

The substance of what Machiavelli says or suggests regarding religion is not original. As is indicated by his use of the term "sect" for religion, he goes in the ways of Averroism, that is, of those medieval Aristotelians who as philosophers refused to make any concessions to revealed religion. While the substance of Machiavelli's religious teaching is not original, his manner of setting it forth is very ingenious. He recognizes in fact no theology but civil theology, theology serving the state and to be used or not used by the state as circumstances suggest. He indicates that religions can be dispensed with if there is a strong and able monarch. This implies indeed that religion is indispensable in republics.

The moral-political teaching of the *Discourses* is fundamentally the same as that of the *Prince* but with one important difference: the *Discourses* state powerfully the case for republics while also instructing potential tyrants in how to destroy republican life. Yet there can hardly be any doubt that Machiavelli preferred republics to monarchies, tyrannical or nontyrannical. He loathed oppression which is not in the service of the well-being of the people and hence of effective government, especially of impartial and unsqueamish punitive justice. He was a generous man, while knowing very well that what passes for generosity in political life is most of the time nothing but shrewd calculation, which as such deserves to be commended. In the *Discourses* he has expressed his preference most clearly by his praise of M. Furius Camillus. Camillus had been highly praised by Livy as the second Romulus, the second founder of Rome, a most conscientious practitioner of religious observances; he even speaks of him as the greatest of all *imperatores* but he probably means by this the greatest of all commanders up to Camillus' time. Machiavelli, however, calls Camillus "the most prudent of all Roman captains"; he praises him for both his "goodness" and his "virtue," his humanity and integrity, as good and wise—in a word, as a most excellent man. He has in mind particularly his equanimity, the fact that he had the same state of mind in good and in evil fortune, when he saved Rome from the Gauls and thus earned immortal glory and when he was condemned to exile. Machiavelli traces Camillus' superiority to the whims of fortune to his superior knowledge of the world. In spite of his extraordinary merits Camillus was condemned to exile. Why he was so condemned, Machiavelli discusses in a special chapter (III 23). On the basis of Livy he enumerates three reasons. But, if I am not mistaken, Livy never mentions these three reasons together as causes of Camillus' exile. In fact Machiavelli follows here not Livy but Plutarch. But he makes this characteristic change: he assigns the central place to the fact that in his triumph Camillus had his triumphal chariot drawn by four white horses; therefore the people said that through pride he had wished to equal the sun-god or, as Plutarch has it, Jupiter (Livy says: Jupiter et sol). I believe that this rather shocking act of *superbia* was in Machiavelli's eyes a sign of Camillus' magnanimity.

Camillus' very pride shows, as Machiavelli surely knew, that there is a greatness beyond Camillus' greatness. After all, Camillus was not a founder or discoverer of new modes and orders. To state this somewhat differently, Camillus was a Roman of the highest dignity and, as Machiavelli has shown most obviously by his comedy *La Mandragola*, human life requires also levity. He there praises Magnifico Lorenzo de'Medici for having combined gravity and levity in a quasi-impossible combination—a combination that Machiavelli regarded as commendable because in changing from gravity to levity or vice versa, one imitates nature, which is changeable.

One cannot help wondering how one ought to judge reasonably of Machiavelli's teaching as a whole. The simplest way to answer this question would seem to be the following. The writer to whom Machiavelli refers and deferred most frequently, with the obvious exception of Livy, is Xenophon. But he refers to only two of Xenophon's writings: *The Education of Cyrus* and the *Hiero;* he takes no notice of Xenophon's Socratic writings, that is, of the other pole of Xenophon's moral universe: Socrates. Half of Xenophon, in Xenophon's view the better half, is suppressed by Machiavelli. One can safely say that there is no moral or political phenomenon that Machiavelli knew or for whose discovery he is famous that was not perfectly known to Xenophon, to say nothing of Plato or Aristotle. It is true that in Machiavelli everything appears in a new light, but this is due, not to an enlargement of the horizon, but to a narrowing of it. Many modern discoveries regarding man have this character.

Machiavelli has often been compared with the Sophists. Machiavelli says nothing of the Sophists or of the men commonly known as Sophists. Yet he says something on this subject, if indirectly, in his *Life of Castruccio Castracani,* a very charming little work, containing an idealized description of a fourteenth century condottiere or tyrant. At the end of that work he records a number of witty sayings said or listened to by Castruccio. Almost all those sayings have been borrowed by Machiavelli from Diogenes Laertius' *Lives of the Famous Philosophers.* Machiavelli changes the sayings in some cases in order to make them suitable to Castruccio. In Diogenes, an ancient philosopher is recorded as having said that he would wish to die like Socrates; Machiavelli makes this Castruccio's saying, yet he would wish to die like Caesar. Most of the sayings recorded in the *Castruccio* stem from Aristippus and Diogenes the Cynic. The references to Aristippus and Diogenes—men not classified as Sophists—could profitably guide us if we are interested in the question of what scholars call Machiavelli's "sources."

Toward the end of the *Nicomachean Ethics* Aristotle speaks of what one may call the political philosophy of the Sophists. His chief point is that the Sophists identified or almost identified politics with rhetoric. In other words, the Sophists believed or tended to believe in the omnipotence of speech. Machiavelli surely cannot be accused of that error. Xenophon speaks of his friend Proxenos, who commanded a contingent in Cyrus's expedition against the king of Persia and who was a pupil of the most famous rhetorician, Gorgias. Xenophon says that Proxenos was an honest man and capable to command gentlemen but could not fill his soldiers with fear of him; he was unable to punish those who were not gentlemen or even to rebuke them. But Xenophon, who was a pupil of Socrates, proved to be a most successful commander precisely because he could manage both gentlemen and nongentlemen. Xenophon, the pupil of Socrates, was under no delusion about the sternness and harshness of politics, about that ingredient of politics which transcends speech. In this important respect Machiavelli and Socrates make a common front against the Sophists.

13

Review of
C. B. Macpherson
The Political Theory of Possessive Individualism
Hobbes to Locke

This serious and lucidly written book starts from the contemporary crisis in political theory which is diagnosed by the author as a crisis of the theory of liberal democracy. That crisis cannot in his view be overcome by a return to the classic theorists of liberal democracy and in particular to the seventeenth century founders of liberal democracy, because even in its original form liberalism suffered from a fundamental defect. From the beginning it fostered "possessive individualism," *i.e.* "bourgeois" individualism; its basic assumptions were "that man is free and human by virtue of his sole proprietorship of his own person, and that human society is essentially a series of market relations." Macpherson's standard of judgment is "the idea of freedom as a concomitant of social living in an unacquisitive society"—in a kind of society which, to say the least, transcends the boundaries of any "single national state." His book reads as if it were meant to show (or rather to contribute toward showing) the rationality of his ideal by laying bare the logical failures of the early theorists of possessive individualism and by tracing those failures to the contradictions of bourgeois society itself. The thinkers whom he discusses are Hobbes, the Levellers, Harrington, and Locke.

Macpherson's freedom from common prejudices is shown by the fact that he does not hesitate to begin his critical analysis of liberal theory with Hobbes. As a matter of fact, according to him "the assumptions which comprise possessive individualism . . . are clearest and fullest in Hobbes." The question which confronts the student of Hobbes at the very beginning is

Macpherson's book was published by the Oxford University Press in 1962. Strauss's review appeared in the *Southwestern Social Science Quarterly* 45, no. 1 (1964), and is reprinted by permission of the University of Texas Press.

whether his political theory necessarily presupposes, and necessarily follows from, his teaching regarding "the physiological nature of man" or his "materialism." Macpherson's answer can be summarized as follows: Hobbes' view of human nature or his "physiological postulates" supply only the major premise of his fundamental syllogism; the minor premise is supplied by "a certain model of society," *i.e.* the possessive market society. If Hobbesian men are indeed nothing but "self-moving and self-directing appetitive machines," one does not see why they should be by nature in a state of war of everybody against everybody. Yet according to Hobbes, man is distinguished from the brutes by the faculty of considering phenomena as causes of possible effects, and therefore by awareness of potentiality and power. Macpherson does not even attempt to show that the natural antagonism of all men does not follow from the peculiarity of man thus understood. Hence he fails to show that it is necessary to have recourse to a certain notion of society in order to understand Hobbes' way from man's nature to the state of nature. This is not to contradict Macpherson's assertion that Hobbes' doctrine of human nature is generally speaking favorable to the possessive market society. The reason for this, however, is not that the English society of his time had "become essentially a possessive market society" or because he thought that that kind of society is "here to stay" but that he held that kind of society to be most conducive to human well-being. Nor is Hobbes' view of men's natural competitiveness a reflex of the emerging market society; Hobbes found or would have found clear signs of that competitiveness not only in the market but in the courts of kings, in the most backward villages, among scholars, in convents, in drawing rooms, and in slave pens, in modern as well as in ancient times.

Hobbes claims to have been the first to discover the nature of human society. According to Macpherson, he has discovered only the nature of the possessive market society, and this was a great achievement indeed. Macpherson supports his assertion by the following reasoning among others. Given the urgency of knowledge of the nature of society (and, we may add, the simplicity of Hobbes' basic argument), Hobbes fails to explain why his discovery was not made much earlier, not to say in the most ancient antiquity (*cf. De Cive,* Preface, near the beginning). Hobbes explains the lateness of his discovery sufficiently by his suggestions regarding the primacy of the influence of the fear of powers invisible and regarding the basic error of ancient philosophy, anti-materialistic and materialistic (the notion of *beatitudo*). This is to say nothing of the fact that, according to Macpherson himself, Hobbes' "deriving right and obligation from fact" was "a leap in political theory as radical as Galileo's formulation of the laws of uniform motion was in natural science, and not unrelated to it." In this connection it should be mentioned that Macpherson's defense of Hobbes' derivation of right and obligation from fact against the strictures of present-day logicians belongs to the most valuable parts of his book.

The shortness of space at my disposal prevents me from speaking, however briefly, of Macpherson's analyses of the thought of the Levellers, Harrington, and Locke. His procedure is in all three cases fundamentally the same: he traces the self-contradiction of the thinkers in question to the self-contradiction of capitalist society itself. His observations deserve in all cases careful consideration. Yet one is left wondering whether they do not derive such evidence as they possess from the acceptance of his standard of judgment: if the rational society is not the universal socialist society, "the political theory of possessive individualism" must be examined in the light of a different ideal.

14

Review of
J. L. Talmon
The Nature of Jewish History—
Its Universal Significance

This is an earnest statement by a man who is both a Jew and a historian rather than a Jewish historian. According to him, the historian who studies the fate of the Jewish people cannot and need not go back behind the fact that the Jewish people was constituted by its belief in its being the chosen people; this belief made possible and in effect caused its exiles and its precarious existence throughout the ages up to the present day; for the establishment of the state of Israel has not removed "the problematic ambiguity attached to Jewish existence everywhere and at all times" (p. 9 n.). Both economic and "psychological" accounts are radically inadequate. Nor, on the other hand, is the historian as historian compelled or able to accept the theological understanding of "election." The author lays bare the parochialism informing the common notion according to which the belief in election stems from ethnic pride. The idea of "the chosen people" as of a "holy nation" or "a people of priests" expresses "what Matthew Arnold called the Jewish passion for right acting as distinct from the Greek passion for right seeing and thinking" (p. 18). It is therefore one of the two basic elements of Western civilization. It is at the root of "the fundamentally and peculiarly Western relationship between Church and State" which prevented the emergence in the West of "Oriental despotism" (p. 19). It is to be hoped that the author will develop this theme further by showing more precisely than he has hitherto done why "the passion for right acting," as distinguished from "the passion for right seeing and thinking," requires primarily a peculiar nation as its bearer.

Talmon's book was published in London by the Hillel Foundation in 1957. Strauss's review appeared in the *Journal of Modern History* 29, no. 3 (1957). ©1957 by the University of Chicago.

15

Introductory Essay for
Hermann Cohen
*Religion of Reason out of the
Sources of Judaism*

I doubt whether I am the best mediator between Hermann Cohen (1842-1918) and the present-day American reader. I grew up in an environment in which Cohen was the center of attraction for philosophically minded Jews who were devoted to Judaism; he was the master whom they revered. But it is more than forty years since I last studied or even read the *Religion of Reason*, and within the last twenty years I have only from time to time read or looked into some of his other writings. I write this Introduction at the request of the publisher and of the translator. I can do no more than to give an account of the thoughts that occurred to me at a renewed reading of *Religion of Reason*. Perhaps they will be helpful to some readers.

Present-day readers can hardly avoid feeling that *Religion of Reason out of the Sources of Judaism* (first published in German in 1919) is a philosophic book and at the same time a Jewish book. It is philosophic since it is devoted to the religion of reason, and it is Jewish since it elucidates, nay, articulates that religion out of the sources of Judaism. This impression, while correct, is not as clear as it appears at first sight.

The Jewish religion might be understood as revealed religion. In that case the philosopher would accept revelation as it was accepted by Jews throughout the ages in an uninterrupted tradition and would bow to it; he would explicate it by the means of philosophy and especially defend it against its deniers or doubters, philosophic and nonphilosophic. But this pursuit would not be philosophic since it rests on an assumption that the philosopher as philosopher cannot make or on an act of which the philosopher as philosopher is not capable. Cohen excludes this manner of understanding the

Reprinted from the English translation of Hermann Cohen, *Religion of Reason out of the Source of Judaism* (New York: Frederick Ungar, 1972).

233

relation between philosophy and Judaism by speaking of the religion of reason. "Revelation is [God's] creation of reason." Revelation is not "an historical act." For Cohen there are no revealed truths or revealed laws in the precise or traditional sense of the terms.

Let Judaism then be the religion of reason. Yet this can hardly mean that Judaism and the religion of reason are identical. Is the religion of reason found also, hence accidentally, in Judaism? Or is it the core of Judaism and only of Judaism? Cohen rejects both extremes. In particular he refuses to claim that Judaism is "the absolute religion." (This is not to deny that Cohen sometimes calls Judaism, and only Judaism, "the pure monotheism.") His solution of the difficulty is indicated by the word "source." Judaism is the source, the fountainhead of the religion of reason. The Jews "created the religion of reason." Judaism has taught mankind the religion of reason. The other religions either are altogether inadequate or they are derivative from Judaism. It is true that Judaism was not always in every respect the religion of reason. It needed the aid of Platonic and above all of Kantian philosophy to free itself completely from mythical and other irrelevancies. But this aid merely enabled Judaism to actualize fully what it meant to be from the beginning and what it fundamentally was at all times.

When one says that Cohen's *Religion of Reason* is a philosophic book, one is likely to assume that the religion of reason belongs to philosophy, that it is perhaps the most exalted part of philosophy. Yet Cohen makes a distinction between philosophy as philosophy, i.e., as scientific philosophy, and religion, and accordingly says that "Judaism has no share in philosophy" or that "Israel has no creative share in science." Nevertheless, there is according to him a kind of philosophic speculation whose matrix is religion and especially Judaism. This does not, however, do away with the fact that Cohen's *Religion of Reason* forms no part of his *System of Philosophy (System der Philosophie)*.

The relation between religion and philosophy, between the *Religion of Reason* and the *System of Philosophy*, is complicated by the fact that the central part of the *System*, the *Ethics of the Pure Will (Ethik des reinen Willens*, first published in 1904), contains, and in a way culminates in, doctrines that at first glance seem to belong to the religion of reason: the doctrines of the unique God and the messianic future. Cohen has made these doctrines integral parts of his *Ethics*; he has transplanted them out of the sources of Judaism into his *Ethics*. He solves this difficulty by distinguishing between the God of ethics and the God peculiar to religion. Yet since it is reason that shows why and how ethics must be transcended by religion, religion "enters into the system of philosophy." Accordingly, the *Religion of Reason* would have to be understood as the crowning part of Cohen's *System of Philosophy*.

However, the last part of the title ("out of the Sources of Judaism") suggests that the *Religion of Reason* transcends the boundaries of the *System of Philosophy*, or of any system of philosophy. It suffices, perhaps, to compare the full title of Cohen's work with that of Kant's *Religion within the Limits of Mere Reason.*

The obscurity that remains is ultimately due to the fact that while Cohen had a rare devotion to Judaism, he was hardly less devoted to what he understood by culture (science and secular scholarship, autonomous morality leading to socialist and democratic politics, and art); hence his insistence in particular on the "methodic distinction between ethics and religion." That distinction implies that while religion cannot be reduced to ethics, it remains dependent on "the method of ethics." Man's moral autonomy must not in any way be called in question. Cohen's goal was the same as that of the other Western spokesmen for Judaism who came after Mendelssohn: to establish a harmony between Judaism and culture, between *Torah* and *derekh eretz*. But Cohen pursued this goal with unrivaled speculative power and intransigence.

Cohen's *Ethics* and, in fact, his whole *System of Philosophy* precedes his *Religion of Reason* "methodically." Furthermore, he is compelled now and then, especially in Chapters X and XI, to take issue with the Protestant, especially German, biblical criticism of his time and with the philosophy of history on which it is based. Finally, the order of the argument within the chapters does not always have the lucidity of which it is susceptible. These facts are likely to cause considerable difficulties to the reader of the *Religion of Reason*. They can be overcome by repeated readings. In the following remarks I could not help reproducing or imitating difficulties that Cohen has left unresolved.

The *Religion of Reason* presupposes, fundamentally, the *System of Philosophy*, but it does not force the Jewish data into that system as into a Procrustean bed. Cohen follows the intrinsic articulation of that Judaism which was authoritative for him as a liberal Jew who abhorred mysticism. He interprets Jewish thought by "idealizing" or "spiritualizing" it, i.e., by thinking it through and by understanding it in the light of its highest possibilities. In so doing he claims not merely to follow the only sound rule of interpreting any worthwhile text but to continue the process that had been going on in Judaism starting with the Bible itself.

Cohen follows the intrinsic articulation of the Bible by devoting the first chapter to the uniqueness of God. For the account of creation with which the Bible opens presupposes that one knows somehow what is meant by God. The decisive elucidation of what the Bible understands by God is given in the words that "the Eternal is one" and that His name is "I am": He is the one, the only one who or what is; compared to Him, nothing else is. "There is not only no other God but altogether no being except this unique being." Nature, the world, man included, is nothing. Only God's uniqueness thus strictly understood can justify the demand that man should love God with his whole heart, with his whole soul, and with his whole might.

It would not have been in accordance with the Bible or with Cohen's *System of Philosophy* if he had opened his work with a demonstration of the existence of God. God's uniqueness excludes His having existence, existence being essentially related to sense perception. According to Cohen, the idea of God, God as an idea and not a person, is required in the first place in order to establish the indispensable harmony between nature and morality: the ethically required eternity of ethical progress, the ethically required prospect of an infinite future of ethical progress is not possible without the future eternity of the human race and therefore of nature as a whole; God "secures the ideal." It is incorrect but not altogether misleading to say that, according to Cohen, God is postulated by ethical reason.

The uniqueness of God demands or implies the rejection of the worship of "other gods." Cohen is himself animated by the prophets' "holy zeal against the false gods" when he says in his own name that "the service of other gods or of idols must be altogether exterminated." That holy zeal must overcome all hesitations stemming from the charm exerted by Greek plastics and even from compassion for the worshippers of false gods. At this point more than at any other Cohen reveals how radically he had come to question "culture" as he and his contemporaries understood it. The worship of the other gods is, according to him, necessarily worship of images. In agreement with the Decalogue, but not with Deuteronomy 4:15–19, he denies that there can be worship of sun, moon, and stars as such.

It follows furthermore from God's uniqueness that all things or beings other than God (except human artifacts) are His work. They do not come into being out of God, through emanation, for this would mean that Becoming is part of the true Being, whereas there is only and indeed "an immanent relation" of Being, the unique Being, to Becoming, of God to the world; Becoming is implied in the concept of God, in the definition of God as the unique being. It is in this way that Cohen is able to speak of creation. Creation is "the logical consequence" of the uniqueness of the divine being, nay, it is simply identical with it. Creation is therefore necessary. Cohen does not speak of creation as a free act. Nor is creation according to him a single act in or before time. Creation is continuous creation, continuous renewal. The sources of Judaism that Cohen uses for elucidating creation are almost all post-biblical. He derives his main support from Maimonides. Maimonides' doctrine of creation as set forth in the *Guide of the Perplexed* is, however, not easily recognizable in Cohen's interpretation.

Creation is above all the creation of man. But whereas creation as such is the immanent relation of God as the unique Being to Becoming, and

Becoming is coeval with God, surely man, the human race, is not coeval with God. Cohen begins to treat the creation of man in the chapter on revelation. In revelation, he says, God enters into relation with man; he had not said that in creation God enters into relation with the world. Revelation is the continuation of creation since man as the rational and the moral being comes into being, i.e., is constituted, by revelation. Revelation is as little miraculous as creation. That is to say, it is not a unique event or a number of unique events in the remote past. Cohen follows closely the first and classic document of this idealization, Moses' extensive speech in Deuteronomy in which revelation is presented as not in heaven or, as Cohen almost contends, stemming from heaven but as originating in the heart and reason of man, which are indeed God-given. "Man" here means the children of Israel. Hence, while revelation is not a unique event, it is primarily addressed to a unique people. Monotheism is to have its foundation in a national consciousness, or, more precisely, monotheism is to be the foundation of the consciousness of a nation: Israel, and Israel alone, came into being by virtue of dedication to the only God. Monotheism is not to have its foundation in the consciousness of select individuals. The outstanding individuals, in the first place Moses himself, are only the instruments of the spiritual liberation of the nation, representatives of the Jewish people, teachers of Israel, but by no means mediators between God and Israel.

Cohen had no doubt that in teaching the identity of Reason and Revelation he was in full agreement with "all," or "almost all," Jewish philosophers of the Middle Ages. He mentions in this respect with high praise, apart from Maimonides himself, Ibn Daud, who had assigned a very low status to "the prescriptions of obedience" as distinguished from "the rational principles" and had inferred from the weakness of their rank the weakness of their causes. Cohen abstracts from the fact that Ibn Daud says also—and this he says at the very end of his *Emunah Ramah*—that "the prescriptions of obedience" are superior to the rational ones since they call for absolute obedience and submission to the divine will or for faith. The perfect emblem of "the prescriptions of obedience" is God's command to Abraham that he sacrifice his only child Isaac—a command that flagrantly contradicted His previous promise and therefore transcended reason. One need not be concerned here with whether and how Ibn Daud resolved the contradiction between the thought of which Cohen approves and the thought that Cohen dismisses, but one cannot help being impressed by his attempt to find the highest or deepest ground of "the prescriptions of obedience" in Abraham's willingness to sacrifice Isaac. The religion of reason leaves no place for absolute obedience or for what traditional Judaism considered the core of faith. The reader will have no difficulty in grasping the connection between the disappearance of obedience proper and the idealization or spiritualization of creation and revelation.

Owing to its peculiar function, which was to articulate the meaning of revelation especially from Moses' speech in Deuteronomy, the chapter on revelation had left obscure the relation of revelation and hence of God to man as distinguished from Israel. This relation becomes the theme in the next chapter. Cohen takes his bearings by the second account of the creation of man (Genesis 2), which he regards as freer from myth than the first (Genesis 1). The tree of knowledge indicates that it is knowledge that distinguishes man from all other creatures and that it is knowledge, especially the knowledge of good and evil, that characterizes his relation to God. That relation is correlation. Although God is not thinkable except as creator of the world and the world is not thinkable except as God's creature, the relation of God and the world is not yet correlation. God's relation to the world points to, or is absorbed by, His relation to man. In Cohen's deliberately exaggerated expression, God's being becomes actual in and through His correlation with man. "God is conditioned by the correlation with man. And man is conditioned by the correlation with God." God cannot be thought properly as being beyond His relation to man, and it is equally necessary to understand man, the creature constituted by reason or spirit, as essentially related to the unique God Who is spirit. Reason is the link between God and man. Reason is common to God and man. But it would contradict reason if man were only the passive partner in his correlation with God. Correlation means therefore also and especially that God and man are equally, if in different ways, active toward one another. (The reader must keep in mind the question of whether Cohen has always done justice to divine activity in the correlation.) Since these insights concern man as such, the "original universalism of the spirit in Israel" leads to the final universalism of the spirit in all men without any difference of rank whatever.

The full meaning of the correlation between God and man begins to come to sight only when human action is taken into consideration. Human action must be understood in the light of divine action and vice versa. The divine attributes of action (Exodus 34:6–7), as Cohen, following Maimonides, calls them and which he reduces to love and justice, are not meant to reveal the essence of God; yet they are adequate as the norm and model for man's actions. Love and justice together are holiness. "You shall be holy, for I, the Lord your God, am holy." (Leviticus 19:2). Here the correlation is appropriately expressed, "and with the correlation mythology and polytheism cease. Holiness becomes morality." For with the progress of biblical thought Might recedes into the background and Holiness comes to the fore. As the quoted verse from Leviticus makes clear, holiness is for man a task, a never-ending, infinite task or an ideal, while it characterizes God's being; it is the ground of God's being, of His uniqueness. But God is only in regard to man: God is the Holy One for the sake of the holiness of man, which consists in man's sanctifying himself. Accordingly, the holy spirit is the spirit of man as well as of God, as Cohen tries to show by interpreting Psalm 51, "the classical passage" on the holy spirit, or rather on the spirit of holiness. To understand the holy spirit in isolation, as a person of its own, is tantamount to destroying the correlation: the holy spirit is the correlation between God and man. The competence of the holy spirit is limited to human morality— "the holy spirit is the human spirit"—but human morality is the only morality and therefore includes God's morality: there is no other standard of goodness and justice for God than for man. Cohen's notion of holiness does not seem to have much in common with "the so-called Holiness code" (Leviticus 17ff.), but—and this is of no mean significance—according to him morality, human, rational morality demands the unqualified abstention from incest.

Human action is, to begin with, action directed toward other men whom we know or believe to know from experience. The others, the men who live at our side, become inevitably those against whom we live; they are therefore not yet our fellowmen. Our fellowmen we do not know through experience pure and simple but only by virtue of the command that we love them. Only on the basis of this intrahuman correlation can the correlation of God and man become actual: in man's behavior toward men, not in his behavior toward God, the distinction between good and evil arises. It is in the light of "the social love" of our fellowmen that we must understand the love that proceeds from God and the love that is directed toward him. Cohen discusses the intrahuman relation first on the political and legal level. He takes his bearings by the talmudic concept of the sons of Noah and the seven commandments given to them. The sons of Noah do not have to adhere to the religion of Israel, i.e., they do not have to acknowledge the only God although they are forbidden to blaspheme and to worship other gods; they are not believers and yet they may be citizens of the Jewish state. In this way Judaism laid the foundation for freedom of conscience and for toleration. Cohen does not claim to have proved that Judaism has laid the foundation for the freedom of conscience of all Jews.

Cohen then goes on to discuss "the discovery of man as the fellowman" on the plane of "the social question" or, as he also says, of "the economic problem," i.e., of "the social distinction of the poor and the rich." For the prophets and the psalms it is poverty and not death and pain that constitutes the great suffering of man or the true enigma of human life. Our compassion for the poor, our love of the poor makes us understand or divine that God loves the poor and therefore in particular Israel (cf. Isaiah 41:14 and Amos 7:5), but Israel is only the symbol of mankind. God's love of the poor animates the whole social legislation of the Bible and above all the institution of the Sabbath, which prescribes rest also and in particular for servants and maids. Poverty becomes the prime object of compassion, of the affect that is a factor, nay, the factor of the moral law. In his *Ethics* Cohen had characterized the affect in general as a motor of the moral law. In his *Religion of Reason* he goes much beyond this by almost identifying the affect that fulfills that function with compassion. Here more than in the preceding chapters Cohen's heart speaks, and the fear that the Jewish heritage might be eroded vanishes. In his *Ethics* he had denied that love is the affective basis of virtue as such, and he replaced compassion by the virtue of humanity to which he devoted the last and crowning chapter. But the last and crowning chapter of the *Religion of Reason* is devoted to peace in the full Jewish meaning of *shalom*. This does not mean that he abandons the teaching of his *Ethics*; he keeps it intact as the ethical teaching; he merely supplements it by the religious teaching; but in so doing he profoundly transforms it. Humanity is among other things the virtue of art; peace is the virtue of eternity. The chapter on peace, and hence the *Religion of Reason*, concludes with an articulation of the Jewish posture toward death and the grave.

The chapter entitled "The Problem of Religious Love" is the only chapter that carries "problem" in its heading. One cannot say that this is intentional: Cohen does not write like Maimonides. But intentional or not, it is surely remarkable. Cohen speaks of the problem of religious love because he finds that religious love is taken too much for granted. Particularly striking is what he says about man's love of God. The love of God is love of an idea. To the objection that one cannot love an idea but only a person Cohen replies that "one can love only ideas; even in sensual love one loves only the idealized person." Pure love is directed only toward models of action, and no human being can be such a model in the precise sense. Pure love is love of the moral ideal. It is longing, not for union with God, but for nearness to God, that is to say, for never-ceasing, infinite sanctification of man: God alone is holy.

"The discovery of man as the fellowman," while articulated out of the sources of Judaism, belongs in itself, as one can say with some exaggeration, to the competence of ethics; the discovery of "the individual as the I" surely goes beyond that competence and is peculiar to religion. The discovery of man as the fellowman was achieved by "the social prophets"; the discovery of the individual as the I was the great progress due to Ezekiel, who seems to be unduly concerned with sacrifices and the temple and therefore to be regressive. It could seem that the discovery of the fellowman, the Thou, implies the discovery of the individual as the I. According to Cohen this is not the case, if one understands "individual"in the strict sense, "the absolute individual," "the isolated individual," whose concern transcends state and society—which are ultimately "only dark blind masses"—and therefore transcends ethics. The correlation between God and man is above all the correlation between God and the individual; the absolute individual, "the seeing individual," is man standing before God.

Regardless of whether one accepts Cohen's religion of reason, one must ponder carefully his confrontation of the seeing individual with the dark blind masses of state and society. Only in the I can the individual be discovered; only on the basis of this discovery can the fellowman be seen as an individual and thus truly become a fellowman. The reason is this: I have no right to set myself up as a moral judge of other human beings, be they poor or rich; even the judge who condemns the criminal is not meant to pass a moral judgment. But I must pass moral judgment on myself. The individual is discovered by his realization that he is morally guilty and by what that realization leads to. He cannot acquit himself, and yet he needs liberation from his feeling of guilt, i.e., purification from his guilt, his sin. Only God can liberate the individual from his sin and thus transform the individual into an I. The I liberated from sin, the redeemed I, the I redeemed before God, the I reconciled with God is the ultimate goal toward which man must strive.

For the reconciliation with God can only be the consummation of the reconciliation of man with himself. This reconciliation consists in man's "repentance," in his return from his evil ways or, more tellingly, in his making himself a new heart and a new spirit. The first step in this return is man's confession of his sin, his self-punishment, in and before the stateless congregation, i.e., together with all other members of the congregation as his fellow sinners. The return is the return to God Who alone redeems from sin. This redemptive aspect of God is what is meant by His goodness or grace as distinguished from His holiness. "It is the essence of God to forgive man's sin . . . for His essence consists in His correlation with man." When Cohen speaks, deeply moved, of God's help in reconciling man to Him, he is never oblivious of man's autonomy, which is indeed inseparable from his finiteness or frailty; he is not even oblivious of it when he interprets the verses in the prophets and the psalms in which God is compared to the shepherd and men or the souls to His lambs. But it should be noted that in speaking of God's goodness Cohen calls His good action "person-like."

Cohen confirms and deepens his doctrine of reconciliation in his discussion of the Day of Atonement, which in German is called the Day of Reconciliation, and of its primacy over all other festivals in the Jewish year. In this context he makes clear how he understands the relation of sin and punishment: the punishment is the suffering that is inseparable from human life and that leads to man's redemption provided he recognizes it as divine dispensation, as necessary for the development of his self.

The justification of suffering, and hence in particular of Israel's suffering, and not the prospect of the messianic age as the ideal goal of political and social progress, leads Cohen in his *Religion of Reason* to the discussion of "the idea of the Messiah and mankind." According to him, the idea of mankind, of all men without distinctions like those between Greeks and barbarians or between the wise and the vulgar, has at least its historical origin in religion, in monotheism; the unique God is the God of all men, of all nations. "For the Greek, man was only the Greek," despite the fact that the Stoa at any rate was "cosmopolitan," for the Stoa thought only of the individuals, not of the nations. The universalism of the prophets, which comprehends in one thought and hope all nations, is "a thought of the boldest and world-political courage"; the prophets thus became "the originators of the concept of world history," nay, of "the concept of history as the being of the future," for they placed the ideal, which is opposed to all present and past reality, not beyond time but in the future. Mankind as one, because unified in its highest aspiration, never was or is, but will be; its development never comes to an end; that development is progress. By turning toward the future the prophets completed the break with myth that had been achieved by monotheism, the message of the unique God as the God of morality. Israel, the eternal people, is the symbol of mankind. Israel had to survive the destruction of the Jewish state; it has to survive for all times because it is the creator of the Bible, and creation is in this case, too, a never-ending renewal. The Jewish state as one state among many would not point as unmistakably to the unity of mankind as the one stateless people dedicated uniquely to the service of the unique God, the Lord of the whole earth.

This is the meaning of Israel's election: to be an eternal witness to pure monotheism, to be *the* martyr, to be the suffering servant of the Lord. The misery of Jewish history is grounded in messianism, which demands humble submission to suffering and hence the rejection of the state as the protector against suffering. Israel has the vocation not only to preserve the true worship of God but also to propagate it among the nations: through its suffering Israel acquires the right to convert them; the freely accepted suffering makes manifest the historic worthiness of the sufferer. For the prophets and by the prophets Israel became the rest or remainder of Israel, the ideal Israel, the Israel of the future, that is to say, the future of mankind. The patriotism of the prophets is at bottom nothing but universalism.

In this spirit Cohen discusses the messianic passages in the prophetic books. In his idealizing interpretation there is no place for the hope that Israel will return to its own country, to say nothing of the restoration of the temple. He justifies this interpretation in particular by the fact that Jeremiah foretold the return from captivity of Israel's bad neighbors who had also been deported, but this does not do away with the fact that he brought the same good message to Israel. Nor does Ezekiel's prophecy that after Israel's "merely political restoration" it will extirpate the abominations, do away with the fact that he prophesied also and in the first place Israel's "merely political restoration." It is perhaps more important to note that according to Cohen's interpretation of Isaiah 9:6–7 the day of the Lord can no longer seriously be thought to be imminent, for the new time is meant to be a new eternity: could not eternity, even a new eternity, be imminent? Cohen himself admits that the prophets did not explicitly place the end of the days in a wholly remote future; he traces that fact to the preponderance of their concern with a political future of their own nation and of mankind. He, however, regards as the essence of messianism the "supra-sensuousness"— the eternal futurity—of the earthly future of mankind within its natural development, which is a progressive movement.

The concern with the earthly and natural (nonmiraculous) future seems to be weakened by the beliefs in the immortality of the soul and in the resurrection of the body. These beliefs are unacceptable to Cohen in their traditional, "dogmatic" form. He is therefore compelled to examine the sources of Judaism on these subjects and to idealize what they say as much as possible. Belief in the survival of the souls is in an early stage connected with the worship of ancestors. In this stage the grave is of utmost importance, as it still is in the biblical stories of Abraham and Joseph. Dying is understood in the Bible as going to one's fathers: the individual soul goes or enters into the soul of the people, and the people does not die. Immortality means, therefore, the historical survival of the fathers, i.e., of the individual in the historical continuity of his people. Cohen uses this apparently redundant expression in order to exclude any thought of the survival of the souls in the literal sense. On the basis of messianism, immortality comes to mean the survival of the soul in the historical process of the human race. Even more than immortality can the "image" of resurrection convey the thought of the eternal sequence of generations of men in the historical unity of the peoples in general, and of the messianic people in particular. This does not mean that the individual is only a link in a chain, for through the discovery of the individual in the light of holiness, i.e., morality, resurrection takes on the purely moral meaning of rebirth, of self-renewal; the link gives life to the chain of the generations.

It is characteristic of monotheism, as distinguished from myth, that it seeks a meaning of death only for the sake of the morally concerned individual. Accordingly, Koheleth says that when man dies the soul returns to God Who has given it—and not to the nether world of myth. Only in this way can one reconcile death with the infinite task of morality or self-purification. This infinite endeavor must be understood in the spirit of messianism: the other life is the historical future, the future in the unending history of the human race. Under "Persian influence" the beliefs in immortality and resurrection combined, became active in the Jewish mind, and were identified with the belief in the messianic age throughout rabbinical antiquity; hence the historical character of the messianic future became endangered: the messianic future, which is to come by virtue of man's actions, was in danger of being understood as the shadowy kingdom of heaven in the Beyond for whose coming one can only wait and pray. This danger was averted in Judaism, however, because of the persistent awareness of the difference between the messianic age, on the one hand, and immortality and resurrection, on the other; that awareness was most clearly expressed by Maimonides in his *Code*.

Cohen especially loathed the notion of hell; concern with eternal punishment, as more obviously the concern with reward, stems from man's natural eudemonism and is therefore incompatible with ethics proper. It is true that justice, and hence also punitive justice, is thought to be an attribute of God; but, as Cohen says, tacitly but all the more remarkably deviating from Maimonides (*Guide of the Perplexed* I 54), His justice, as distinguished from His love, cannot be the model of human action; His punitive justice remains entirely His mystery and cannot be the concern of morally concerned men. For an understanding of this assertion one must consider that, according to Cohen, Maimonides asserts for the messianic time "in precise clarity the principle of socialism"; he probably means by this the disappearance of all obstacles to the knowledge of God. He is, of course, silent about the "Laws concerning Kings and Their Wars" with which Maimonides so impressively concludes his *Code*. It is therefore all the more praiseworthy that Cohen accepts the notion, so deeply rooted in Jewish piety, of "the merit of the fathers": "the patriarchs alone have every merit that their descendants can acquire." Here enthusiasm for the future gives way to gratitude for the past; it would be better to say that enthusiasm for the future reveals its being rooted in a past to which veneration and gratitude are due. These apparently contradictory tendencies are reconciled by an idealizing interpretation or by the fact that the religion of reason is the religion of reason out of the sources of Judaism. Under no circumstances must the merit of the fathers be permitted to cast the slightest doubt or veil on the autonomy of the individual.

The most obvious difficulty to which Judaism is exposed in modern times is caused by its being Law, an all-comprehensive, sacred law. Cohen was assisted in overcoming these difficulties by his failure to take into consideration the extreme questioning of law as such as it was known to him from Plato's *Statesman*. He has the courage to say that Revelation and Law are identical. According to him, the Law is either the moral law or is meant to contribute to man's moral education. More precisely, all particular commandments concern means; their suitability is therefore subject to examination. In the last analysis the Law is symbol. The only danger entailed in the universal supremacy of the Law, the subservience of everything a man does to the ideal of holiness, is that it leaves no room for man's theoretical and esthetic interests, for "culture" in one sense of the term; but these interests lack the firm center that only the unique God of Jewish monotheism can supply. Besides, this danger can be reduced, and partly has been reduced, by correctives that do not render questionable the Law as a whole.

Cohen admits that, indirectly through Moses Mendelssohn and directly through the Reform movement through which the Jews gained access to the culture of the nations in whose midst they live, the power of the Law has been weakened, but he insists that it has not been destroyed. The survival of Judaism still calls for a certain self-isolation of the Jews within the world of culture and therefore for the Law, however much its scope and its details may have to be modified; it calls for such an isolation "as long as the Jewish religion stands in opposition to other forms of monotheism" or the other forms of monotheism stand in opposition to the Jewish religion, in other words, as long as the messianic age has not yet come.

Yet isolation is not the sole purpose of the Law; its main purpose is the idealization or sanctification of the whole of human life through the living correlation with God. In the chapter on the Law, Cohen engages in a critique of Zionism about which it is not necessary to say anything since it is easily intelligible to every reader. As the reader can hardly fail to notice, in the same context Cohen seems almost to face the possibility actualized not long after his death by national socialism. But his "optimism" was too strong.

The soul and inwardness of the Law is prayer. Prayer gives life to all actions prescribed by the Law, so much so that one may doubt whether prayer is commanded in any of the 613 particular commandments of which the Law is traditionally held to consist. Prayer is the language of the correlation of man with God. As such it must be a dialogue while being a monologue. It is this because it expresses man's love of God as an actual experience of the soul, for the soul is given by God and hence is not exclusively the human soul; therefore it can speak to God and with God. Love of God is the highest form of human love; it is longing for God, for nearness to Him. This must not make one forget that man's longing for God is longing for his redemption, for his moral salvation—a longing that originates in anguish. But man is not merely his soul; all human cares and sorrows become legitimate themes of prayer. Above all, the dangers to intellectual probity are impenetrable for man; if all other purposes of prayer could be questioned, its necessity for veracity, for purity of the soul cannot: God alone can create in man a pure heart. Cohen speaks with emphasis of the danger to veracity that comes from one's fear of being despised by flesh and blood for confessing and professing the religious truth. The Jewish notion of prayer is characterized by the fact that the synagogue is not called a house of prayer but a house of learning or study, for that house is built not for the individual who prays in solitude but for the congregation that lives in anticipation of the messianic kingdom of God; for its coming "in your lives and in your days and in the life of the whole house of Israel" Jews pray in the Kaddish. Yet the congregation cannot be preserved without the Law and therefore without the study of the Law.

The headings of the last five chapters are the only ones that are identical or almost identical with chapter headings in the *Ethics*. The chapter entitled "The Virtues" takes the place of the chapters of the *Ethics* that are entitled

"The Concept of Virtue," "Truthfulness," and "Modesty." The reason for this change is the following. In the *Ethics* Cohen had said that, according to the prophets, God is truth, and they meant by this that "the true God is the ground of morality." But he had continued: "But this is the difference, this is the gulf between religion and ethics, that in ethics no extraneous foundation can be laid; even God must not be for ethics the methodic ground of moral knowledge." Accordingly, in the *Religion of Reason* the true God becomes the ground of morality or more specifically of the virtues; the discussion of the virtues in general and of truth and truthfulness in particular cannot even externally be separated from one another. This is not to deny that even in the *Religion of Reason*, while insisting that "religion must be truth," he still says: "what would truth be without scientific knowledge as its foundation?" It is possible, though, that he means here by "scientific knowledge" rational knowledge and in particular ethical knowledge. Since God is the truth, He cannot in any way be or become a symbol. Truthfulness or intellectual probity animates Judaism in general and Jewish medieval philosophy, which always recognized the authority of reason, in particular. But truthfulness requires knowledge, and our knowledge is imperfect. Therefore truthfulness must be accompanied by modesty, which is the virtue of skepticism. In his *Religion of Reason* Cohen makes no distinction between modesty and humility except to say that he who is humble before God is modest toward men. In his *Ethics* he had said that modesty keeps unimpaired the feeling of one's own worth whereas humility makes the assumption of one's own worthlessness.

In the chapter on fidelity in the *Ethics* Cohen had said that religion must transform itself or be transformed into ethics: religion is a state of nature while the state of maturity is ethics. The transformation must be prepared by the idealization of religion. But this presupposes in the first place fidelity to religion, fidelity to one's religion. In the same chapter he comes to speak of the apparent conflict between fidelity to one's "lost nationality" and fidelity to the state: did he have in mind the Jews in particular? He speaks of gratitude only to the state. In the much shorter chapter on fidelity in the *Religion of Reason* he speaks much more fully of the connection between fidelity and gratitude; he quotes there "If I forget thee, let my right hand forget me." A peculiarly Jewish act of fidelity is the study of the Torah. "Fidelity in the study of the Torah did not permit that the noble character of the folk soul perish amidst the oppression of millennia." He does not speak of the moral obligation not to desert one's people especially when they are in need—and when are Jews not in need?—because for him this went without saying. Almost his whole work, his whole life bears testimony to this fidelity and his gratitude to the Jewish heritage—a fidelity limited only by his intellectual probity, by a virtue that he traced to that very heritage.

Cohen was a faithful warner and comforter to many Jews. At the very least he showed them most effectively how Jews can live with dignity as Jews in a non-Jewish, even hostile, world while participating in that world. In showing this he assumed indeed that the state is liberal or moving toward liberalism. Yet what he said about Jewish martyrdom provided, without his being aware of it, for the experience that the Jews subject to Hitler were soon to undergo. He did not provide what no human being could have provided, a way of dealing with a situation like that of the Jews in Soviet Russia, who are killed spiritually by being cut off from the sources of Judaism. It is a blessing for us that Hermann Cohen lived and wrote.

Leo Strauss
1899–1973
A Bibliography

Asterisked entries are reprinted in the present volume.

1921

Das Erkenntnisproblem in der philosophischen Lehre Fr. H. Jacobis. Unpublished dissertation, University of Hamburg. Pp. 1–71. Printed abstract.

1923

"Antwort auf das 'Prinzipielle Wort' der Frankfurter." *Juedische Rundschau* (Berlin) 28(9):45.
"Anmerkung zur Diskussion über 'Zionismus und Antisemitismus.' " *Juedische Rundschau* (Berlin) 28(83/84):501.
"Das Heilige." *Der Jude* (Berlin) 7:240–42.
"Der Zionismus bei Nordau." *Der Jude* (Berlin) 7(10/11):657–60. See 1980.

1924

"Paul de Lagarde." *Der Jude* (Berlin) 8(1): 8–15.
"Soziologische Geschichtsschreibung?" Review of S. M. Dubnow, *Die neueste Geschichte des jüdischen Volkes.* III Band. *Der Jude* (Berlin) 8(3):190–92.
"Cohens Analyse der Bibel-Wissenschaft Spinozas." *Der Jude* (Berlin) 8(5/6):295–314.
Review of A. Levkowitz, *Religiöse Denker der Gegenwart. Vom Wandel der modernen Lebensanschauung. Der Jude* (Berlin) 8(7):432.
"Zur Auseinandersetzung mit der europäischen Wissenschaft" *Der Jude* (Berlin) 8(10):613–17.

1925

"Biblische Geschichte und Wissenschaft." *Juedische Runschau* (Berlin) 30(88):744–45.

1926

"Zur Bibelwissenschaft Spinozas und seiner Vorläufer." *Korrespondenzblatt* (des Vereins zur Gründung und Erhaltung einer Akademie für die Wissenschaft des Judentums) 7:1–22. Reprinted in Kurt Wilhelm, ed., *Wissenschaft des Judentums im deutschen Sprachbereich. Ein Querschnitt.* Tübingen: J. C. B. Mohr. 1967. 1:115–37.

1930

Die Religionskritik Spinozas als Grundlage seiner Bibelwissenschaft: Untersuchungen zu Spinozas Theologisch-politischem Traktat. Berlin: Akademie-Verlag.

1931

Moses Mendelssohn Gesammelte Schriften: Jubiläumsausgabe. Coeditor. Vol. 2. Introductions
   to "Pope ein Metaphysiker!" "Sendschreiben an den Herrn Magister Lessing in Leipzig,"
   "Kommentar zu den 'Termini der Logik' des Mose ben Maimon," and "Abhandlung über
   die Evidenz." Berlin: Akademie-Verlag.
Review of Julius Ebbinghaus, *Über die Fortschritte der Metaphysik. Deutsche Literaturzeitung,*
   no. 52 (December 27), cols. 2451–53.

1932

Moses Mendelssohn Gesammelte Schriften: Jubiläumsausgabe. Coeditor. Vol. 3, pt. 1. Intro-
   ductions to "Phädon," "Abhandlung von der Unkörperlichkeit der menschlichen Seele,"
   "Über einen schriftlichen Aufsatz des Herrn de Luc," and "Die Seele." Berlin: Akademie-
   Verlag.
"Anmerkungen zu Carl Schmitt, *Der Begriff des Politischen." Archiv für Sozialwissenschaft
   und Sozialpolitik* 67, no. 6 (August-September):732–49. See 1976.
"Das Testament Spinozas." *Bayerische Israelitische Gemeindezeitung* (Munich) 8, no. 21
   (November 1):322–26.

1933

"Quelques remarques sur la science politique de Hobbes." *Recherches Philosophiques* 2:
   609–22.

1934

"Maimunis Lehre von der Prophetie und ihre Quellen." *Le Monde Oriental* (Uppsala) 28:99–
   139. Reprinted in *Philosophie und Gesetz,* 1935.

1935

Philosophie und Gesetz: Beiträge zum Verständnis Maimunis und seiner Vorläufer. Berlin:
   Schocken. See final entry.

1936

"Quelques remarques sur la science politique de Maïmonide et de Farabi." *Revue des Etudes
   Juives* 100:1–37.
"Eine vermisste Schrift Farabis." *Monatsschrift für Geschichte und Wissenschaft des Judentums*
   80:96–106.
The Political Philosophy of Hobbes: Its Basis and Its Genesis. Translated from the German
   manuscript by Elsa M. Sinclair. Foreword by Ernest Barker. Oxford: Clarendon Press.
   Reissued with a new preface, 1952. Chicago: University of Chicago Press.

1937

"Der Ort der Vorsehungslehre nach der Ansicht Maimunis." *Monatsschrift für Geschichte und
   Wissenschaft des Judentums* 81:93–105.
"On Abravanel's Philosophical Tendency and Political Teaching." In *Isaac Abravanel,* edited
   by J. B. Trend and H. Loewe, 93–129. Cambridge: Cambridge University Press.

1939

Review of Moses Hyamson's edition of Maimonides, *The Mishneh Torah*, book 1. *Review of Religion* 3, no. 4 (May): 448–56.

"The Spirit of Sparta or the Taste of Xenophon." *Social Research* 6, no. 4 (November): 502–36.

1941

Review of James T. Shotwell, *The History of History*. *Social Research* 8, no. 1 (February): 126–27.

Review of R. H. S. Crossman, *Plato Today*. *Social Research* 8, no. 2 (May): 250–51. Reprinted in *What is Political Philosophy?* 1959.

Review of C. E. Vaughan, *Studies in the History of Political Philosophy*. *Social Research* 8, no. 3 (September): 390–93. Reprinted in *What is Political Philosophy?* 1959.

Review of Karl Löwith, *Von Hegel bis Nietzsche*. *Social Research* 8, no. 4 (November): 512–15. Reprinted in *What Is Political Philosophy?* 1959.

"Persecution and the Art of Writing." *Social Research* 8, no. 4 (November): 488–504. Reprinted in *Persecution and the Art of Writing*, 1952.

"The Literary Character of *The Guide for the Perplexed*." In *Essays on Maimonides*, edited by S. W. Baron, 37–91. New York: Columbia University Press. Reprinted in *Persecution and the Art of Writing*, 1952.

1942

Review of C. H. McIlwain, *Constitutionalism, Ancient and Modern*. *Social Research* 9, no. 1 (February): 149–51. Reprinted in *What Is Political Philosophy?* 1959.

Review of E. E. Powell, *Spinoza and Religion*. *Social Research* 9, no. 4 (November): 558–60. Reprinted in *What Is Political Philosophy?* 1959.

1943

Review of S. B. Chrimes' edition of Sir John Fortescue, *De Laudibus Legum Angliae*. *Columbia Law Review* 43, no. 6 (September): 958–60. Reprinted in *What Is Political Philosophy?* 1959.

Review of John Dewey, *German Philosophy and Politics*, revised edition. *Social Research* 10, no. 4 (November): 505–7. Reprinted in *What is Political Philosophy?* 1959.

"The Law of Reason in the *Kuzari*." *Proceedings of the American Academy for Jewish Research* 13:47–96. Reprinted in *Persecution and the Art of Writing,* 1952.

1945

"Farabi's *Plato*." In *Louis Ginzberg Jubilee Volume,* 357–93. New York: American Academy for Jewish Research. Reprinted in abridged and modified form as the Introduction to *Persecution and the Art of Writing*, 1952.

"On Classical Political Philosophy." *Social Research* 12, no. 1 (February): 98–117. Reprinted in *What Is Political Philosophy?* 1959.

1946

Review of John O. Riedl's edition of Giles of Rome, *Errores Philosophorum*. *Church History* 15, no. 1 (March): 62–63.

Review of Leonardo Olschki, *Machiavelli the Scientist*. *Social Research* 13, no. 1 (March): 121–24. Reprinted in *What Is Political Philosophy?* 1959.

Review of Heinrich A. Rommen, *The State in Catholic Thought: A Treatise in Political Philosophy*. *Social Research* 13, no. 2 (June): 250–52. Reprinted in *What is Political Philosophy?* 1959.

Review of Anton C. Pegis' edition of *Basic Writings of Saint Thomas Aquinas*. *Social Research* 13, no. 2 (June): 260–62. Reprinted in *What Is Political Philosophy?* 1959.

"On a New Interpretation of Plato's Political Philosophy." *Social Research* 13, no. 3 (September): 326–67. (A review article on John Wild, *Plato's Theory of Man*.)

Review of Zera S. Fink, *The Classical Republicans: An Essay on the Recovery of a Pattern of Thought in Seventeenth Century England*. *Social Research* 13, no. 3 (September) 393–95. Reprinted in *What is Political Philosophy?* 1959.

Hebrew translation of "Political Philosophy and History." *Eyoon. Hebrew Journal of Philosophy* (Tel Aviv) 1, nos. 2–3 (November): 129–46. (See 1949.)

1947

Review of Ernst Cassirer, *The Myth of the State*. *Social Research* 14, no. 1(March):125–28. Reprinted in *What Is Political Philosophy?* 1959.

Review of Alfred Verdross-Rossberg, *Grundlinien der antiken Rechtsund Staats-philosophie*. *Social Research* 14, no. 1 (March): 128–32. Reprinted in *What Is Political Philosophy?* 1959.

"On the Intention of Rousseau." *Social Research* 14, no. 4 (December): 455–87. (A review article on George R. Havens' edition of Jean-Jacques Rousseau, *Discours sur les sciences et les arts*.)

1948

"How to Study Spinoza's *Theologico-Political Treatise*." *Proceedings of the American Academy for Jewish Research* 17:69–131. Reprinted in *Persecution and the Art of Writing*, 1952.

On Tyranny: An Interpretation of Xenophon's Hiero. Foreword by Alvin Johnson, "On Xenophon and Dr. Strauss." New York: Political Science Classics. Reprint. Glencoe, Ill.: Free Press, 1950.

1949

"Political Philosophy and History." *Journal of the History of Ideas* 10, no. 1 (January): 30–50. Reprinted in *What Is Political Philosophy?* 1959.

1950

Review of J. W. Gough, *John Locke's Political Philosophy*. *American Political Science Review* 44, no. 3 (September): 767–70. Reprinted in *What Is Political Philosophy?* 1959.

"On the Spirit of Hobbes' Political Philosophy." *Revue Internationale de Philosophie* 4, no. 14 (October): 405–31. Reprinted in *Natural Right and History*, 1953.

"Natural Right and the Historical Approach." *Review of Politics* 12, no. 4 (October): 422–42. Reprinted in *Natural Right and History*, 1953.

1951

"The Social Science of Max Weber." *Measure* 2, no. 2 (Spring): 204–30. Reprinted in *Natural Right and History*, 1953.

Review of David Grene, *Man in His Pride: A Study in the Political Philosophy of Thucydides and Plato*. *Social Research* 18, no. 3 (September): 394–97. Reprinted in *What Is Political Philosophy?* 1959.

Hebrew translation with English summary of "On Husik's Work in Medieval Jewish Philosophy." *Iyyun. Hebrew Philosophical Quarterly* (Jerusalem): 215–23, 259–60. (See 1952.)

1952

"The Origin of the Idea of Natural Right." *Social Research* 19, no. 1 (March): 23–60. Reprinted in *Natural Right and History*, 1953.

I. Husik's Philosophical Essays: Ancient, Medieval and Modern. Coeditor. Introduction, "On Husik's Work in Medieval Jewish Philosophy." Oxford: Basil Blackwell.

"On Collingwood's Philosophy of History." *Review of Metaphysics* 5, no. 4 (June): 559–86. (A review article on R. G. Collingwood, *The Idea of History*.)

Persecution and the Art of Writing. Glencoe, Ill.: Free Press. (A collection of five previously published essays.)

Review of Yves R. Simon, *Philosophy of Democratic Government*. *New Scholasticism* 26, no. 3 (July): 379–83. Reprinted in *What Is Political Philosophy?* 1959.

"On Locke's Doctrine of Natural Right." *Philosophical Review* 61, no. 4 (October): 475–502. Reprinted in *Natural Right and History*, 1953.

The Political Philosophy of Hobbes, with a new Preface. Chicago: University of Chicago Press.

1953

"Walker's Machiavelli." *Review of Metaphysics* 6, no. 3 (March): 437–46. (Review of L. J. Walker, S.J.,'s edition of *Discourses of Niccolò Machiavelli*.)

Natural Right and History. Chicago: University of Chicago Press. (The Walgreen lectures, delivered at the University of Chicago in October, 1949, parts of which were previously published.)

"Maimonides' Statement on Political Science." *Proceedings of the American Academy for Jewish Research* 22:115–30. Reprinted in *What Is Political Philosophy?* 1959.

1954

Droit naturel et histoire (French translation of *Natural Right and History*). Paris: Librairie Plon.

De la tyrannie (French translation of *On Tyranny*, with "Restatement on Xenophon's *Hiero*"; additional material by Alexandre Kojève). Paris: Librairie Gallimard. "Restatement" reprinted in *What Is Political Philosophy?* 1959.

Hebrew translation with English summary of "The Mutual Influence of Theology and Philosophy." *Iyyun. Hebrew Philosophical Quarterly* (Jerusalem) 5, no. 1 (January): 110–26. Originally the third (last) lecture in a series, "Progress or Return," 19 November 1952, at the B'nai B'rith Hillel Foundation, University of Chicago. See 1979.

"Les fondements de la philosophie politique de Hobbes" (French translation of "On the Basis of Hobbes' Political Philosophy"). *Critique* (Paris) 10, no. 83 (April): 338–62. English original printed in *What Is Political Philosophy?* 1959.

"On a Forgotten Kind of Writing." *Chicago Review* 8, no. 1 (Winter-Spring): 64–75. Reprinted in *What Is Political Philosophy?* 1959.

1955

Hebrew translation with English summary of "What Is Political Philosophy?" *Iyyun. Hebrew Philosophical Quarterly* (Jerusalem) 6, no. 2 (April). (Revised version of the Judah L.

Magnes lectures, Hebrew University, Jerusalem, 1954–55.) English original printed in *What Is Political Philosophy?* 1959.

1956

"Che cosa è la filosofia politica?" (Italian translation of "What Is Political Philosophy?"). *Il Politico* (Milan), 21(2):359–73.
"Kurt Riezler, 1882–1955." *Social Research* 23, no. 1 (Spring): 3–34. Reprinted in *What Is Political Philosophy?* 1959.
"Social Science and Humanism." In *The State of the Social Sciences,* edited by Leonard D. White, 415–25. Chicago: University of Chicago Press.
Hebrew translation with English summary of "Social Science and Humanism." *Iyyun. Hebrew Philosophical Quarterly* (Jerusalem) 7, no. 2 (April): 65–73.

1957

Diritto naturale e storia (Italian translation of *Natural Right and History*). Venice: Neri Pozza.
Part of "What Is Political Philosophy?" *Journal of Politics* 19, no. 3 (August): 343–68.
"How Farabi Read Plato's *Laws.*" In *Mélanges Louis Massignon,* vol. 3: 319–44. Damascus: Institut Français de Damas. Reprinted in *What Is Political Philosophy?* 1959.
"Machiavelli's Intention: *The Prince.*" *American Political Science Review* 51, no. 1 (March): 13–40. Reprinted in *Thoughts on Machiavelli,* 1958.
*Review of J. L. Talmon, *The Nature of Jewish History—Its Universal Significance. Journal of Modern History* 29, no. 3 (September): 306.

1958

"Locke's Doctrine of Natural Law." *American Political Science Review* 52, no. 2 (June): 490–501. (A critical note on W. von Leyden's edition of Locke, *Essays on the Law of Nature.*) Reprinted in *What Is Political Philosophy?* 1959.
Thoughts on Machiavelli. Glencoe, Ill.: Free Press.

1959

"The Liberalism of Classical Political Philosophy." *Review of Metaphysics* 12, no. 3 (March): 390–439. Review article on E. A. Havelock, *The Liberal Temper in Greek Politics.* Reprinted in *Liberalism Ancient and Modern,* 1968.
What is Political Philosophy? Glencoe, Ill.: Free Press.
"What Is Liberal Education?" Commencement address at University College, University of Chicago, 6 June. Chicago: University of Chicago. Reprinted in *Education for Public Responsibility,* edited by C. Scott Fletcher, 43–51. New York: Norton, 1961. Also in *Liberalism Ancient and Modern,* 3–8, 1968.

1961

Comment on W. S. Hudson, "The Weber Thesis Re-examined." *Church History* 30, no. 1 (March): 100–102.
" 'Relativism.' " In *Relativism and the Study of Man,* edited by Helmut Schoeck and J. W. Wiggins, 135–57. Princeton: Van Nostrand.

1962

"Liberal Education and Responsibility." In *Education: The Challenge Ahead*, edited by C. Scott Fletcher, 49–70. New York: Norton. Reprinted in *Liberalism Ancient and Modern*, 9–25, 1968.

"An Epilogue." In *Essays on the Scientific Study of Politics*, edited by Herbert J. Storing, 307–27. New York: Holt, Rinehart and Winston. Reprinted in *Liberalism Ancient and Modern*, 1968.

"Zu Mendelssohns 'Sache Gottes oder die gerettete Vorsehung.' " In *Einsichten: Gerhard Krüger zum 60. Geburtstag,* 361–75. Frankfurt am Main: Vittorio Klostermann.

1963

"Replies to Schaar and Wolin" (no. 2). *American Political Science Review* 57, no. 1(March):152–55.

History of Political Philosophy. Coeditor. Introduction, "Plato," and "Marsilius of Padua." Chicago: Rand McNally. "Marsilius of Padua" reprinted in *Liberalism Ancient and Modern*, 1968.

On Tyranny. Revised and enlarged, including Alexandre Kojève, "Tyranny and Wisdom." New York: Free Press of Glencoe.

"How To Begin To Study *The Guide of the Perplexed*." In *Maimonides' Guide of the Perplexed*, translated by Shlomo Pines, xi–lvi. Chicago: University of Chicago. Reprinted in *Liberalism Ancient and Modern*, 1968.

" 'Perspectives on the Good Society,' a Report on a Jewish-Protestant Colloquium Sponsored by the Divinity School of the University of Chicago and The Anti-Defamation League of B'nai B'rith." *Criterion* 2, no. 3 (Summer): 1–8. Reprinted in *Liberalism Ancient and Modern,* 1968.

1964

The City and Man. Chicago: Rand McNally. (Enlarged version of the Page-Barbour lectures given at the University of Virginia, 1962.)

"The Crisis of Our Time" and "The Crisis of Political Philosophy." In *The Predicament of Modern Politics*, edited by Harold J. Spaeth, 41–54, 91–103. Detroit: University of Detroit Press.

*Review of C. B. Macpherson, *The Political Theory of Possessive Individualism*. Southwestern Social Science Quarterly* 45, no. 1 (June): 69-70.

Meditacion sobre Maquiavelo (Spanish translation of *Thoughts on Machiavelli*). Madrid: Instituto de Estudios Politicos.

1965

Spinoza's Critique of Religion. New York: Schocken Books. Translated from *Die Religionskritik Spinozas*, 1938; extensive new English preface reprinted in *Liberalism Ancient and Modern*, 1968.

Hobbes politische Wissenschaft. Neuwied am Rhein and Berlin: Hermann Luchterhand Verlag. (The German original of *The Political Philosophy of Hobbes*, 1936, with a new preface.)

"On the Plan of the *Guide of the Perplexed*." In *Harry Austryn Wolfson Jubilee Volume*, 775–91. Jerusalem: American Academy for Jewish Research.

1966

Socrates and Aristophanes. New York: Basic Books.

1967

*"Jerusalem and Athens. Some Preliminary Reflections." (The Frank Cohen Public Lecture in Judaic Affairs.) The City College Papers, no. 6. New York: The Library, The City College, The City University of New York.

"Jerusalem and Athens. Some Introductory Reflections." *Commentary* 43:45–57. (Abridged from the Frank Cohen lecture cited above.)

La tirannide. Saggio sul "Gerone" di Senofonte (Italian translation of *On Tyranny*). Milan: Giuffrè Editore.

"John Locke as 'Authoritarian.' " *Intercollegiate Review* 4, no. 1 (November–December): 46–48. (Review of Philip Abrams, ed. and trans., *John Locke: Two Tracts on Government.*)

"Liberal Education and Mass Democracy." In *Higher Education and Modern Democracy*, edited by Robert A. Goldwin, 73–96. Chicago: Rand McNally. (A composite of "What Is Liberal Education?" and "Liberal Education and Responsibility.")

"A Note on Lucretius." In *Natur und Geschichte: Karl Löwith zum 70. Geburtstag*, 322–32. Stuttgart: W. Kohlhammer Verlag.

*"Notes on Maimonides' Book of Knowledge." In *Studies in Mysticism and Religion Presented to Gershom G. Scholem*, 269–83. Jerusalem: Magnes Press, Hebrew University.

1968

*"Natural Law." *International Encyclopedia of the Social Sciences.*

"Greek Historians." *Review of Metaphysics* 21, no. 4 (June): 656–66. (A critical study of W. P. Henry, *Greek Historical Writing: A Historiographical Essay Based on Xenophon's "Hellenica."*)

Liberalism Ancient and Modern. New York: Basic Books. (Includes "On the *Minos*," not published elsewhere, and "Notes on Lucretius," of which only the first section was published previously as "A Note on Lucretius"; see 1967.)

1969

Prawo naturalne w świetla historii (Polish translation of *Natural Right and History*). Warsaw: Pax.

Hebrew translation with English summary of "Philosophy as Rigorous Science and Political Philosophy." *Iyyun. Hebrew Philosophical Quarterly* (Jerusalem) 20, nos. 1–4 (January–October): 14–22, 315–14 (*sic*). (Shlomo Pines Sixtieth Anniversary Volume.) (See 1971.)

1970

Xenophon's Socratic Discourse: An Interpretation of the "Oeconomicus." Ithaca: Cornell University Press.

"Machiavelli and Classical Literature." *Review of National Literatures* 1, no. 1 (Spring): 7–25.

¿Que es filosofia politica? (Spanish translation of *What Is Political Philosophy?*). Madrid: Ediciones Guadarrama.

*"On the *Euthydemus*." *Interpretation* 1, no. 1 (Summer): 1–20.

"A Giving of Accounts" with Jacob Klein. *The College* (Annapolis and Santa Fe) 22, no. 1 (April): 1–5.

1971

*"Philosophy as Rigorous Science and Political Philosophy." *Interpretation* 2, no. 1 (Summer): 1–9. (See 1969).

Prirodno pravo i istorija (Croatian translation of *Natural Right and History*). Translated by Milica Lučič. Sarajevo: Veselin Masleša, Biblioteka Logos.

1972

Xenophon's Socrates. Ithaca: Cornell University Press.

*"Machiavelli." In *History of Political Philosophy*, 2d ed., edited by Leo Strauss and Joseph Cropsey. Chicago: Rand McNally.

*"Introductory Essay." In Hermann Cohen, *Religion of Reason Out of the Sources of Judaism*, xxiii–xxxviii. New York: Frederick Ungar.

1973

*"Note on the Plan of Nietzsche's *Beyond Good and Evil*." *Interpretation* 3, nos. 2–3 (Winter): 97–113.

1974

*"Preliminary Observations on the Gods in Thucydides' Work." *Interpretation* 4, no. 1 (Winter): 1–16.

Moses Mendelssohn Gesammelte Schriften: Jubiläumsausgabe. Editor. Vol. 3, pt. 2. Introductions to "Sache Gottes oder die gerettete Vorsehung" (see 1962), "Morgenstunden," and "An die Freunde Lessings." Stuttgart–Bad Cannstatt: Friedrich Frommann Verlag (Gunther Holzboog).

1975

The Argument and the Action of Plato's Laws. Chicago: University of Chicago Press.

"The Three Waves of Modernity." In *Political Philosophy: Six Essays by Leo Strauss*, edited by Hilail Gildin, 81–98. Indianapolis and New York: Bobbs Merrill/Pegasus.

*"Xenophon's *Anabasis*." *Interpretation* 4 no. 3 (Spring): 117–47.

1976

"Comments on Carl Schmitt's *Der Begriff des Politischen*" (translation of "Anmerkungen zu Carl Schmitt, *Der Begriff des Politischen*"). In *The Concept of the Political by Carl Schmitt*, edited and translated by George Schwab. New Brunswick, N.J.: Rutgers University Press. (See 1932.)

*"On Plato's *Apology of Socrates* and *Crito*." In *Essays in Honor of Jacob Klein*. Annapolis: St. John's College.

1978

"Correspondence with Hans-Georg Gadamer Concerning *Wahrheit und Methode*." In *The Independent Journal of Philosophy / Unabhängige Zeitschrift für Philosophie* 2:5–12. Vienna.

"Letter to Helmut Kuhn." In *The Independent Journal of Philosophy / Unabhängige Zeitschrift für Philosophie* 2: 23–26. Vienna.
"On a Forgotten Kind of Writing." In *The Independent Journal of Philosophy / Unabhängige Zeitschrift für Philosophie* 2: 27–31. Vienna. Reprinted from *Chicago Review*, 1954.

1979

"The Mutual Influence of Theology and Philosophy." In *The Independent Journal of Philosophy / Unabhängige Zeitschrift für Philosophie* 3:111–18. Vienna.
"La persécution et l'art d'écrire" and "Un art d'écrire oublié" (French translations of "Persecution and the Art of Writing" and "On a Forgotten Kind of Writing"). In *Poétique: Revue de Théorie et d'Analyse Littéraires* (April) 229–53.

1980

O tiraniji (Serbo-Croatian translation of *On Tyranny*, including A. Kojève, "Tyranny and Wisdom" translated as "Tiranija i mudrost"). Zagreb: Grafički zavod Hrvatske.
"Zionism in Max Nordau" (translation of "Zionismus bei Max Nordau"). In *The Jew: Essays from Martin Buber's Journal, "Der Jude," 1916–1928*, edited by Arthur A. Cohen, and translated by Joachim Neugroschel. University, Alabama: University of Alabama Press. (See 1923.)

1981

"On the Interpretation of *Genesis*" with French translation. In *L'Homme: Revue française d'anthropologie* (Paris) 21, no. 1:5–36.
"Progress or Return? The Contemporary Crisis in Western Civilization." In *Modern Judaism* 1:17–45. (Two lectures delivered at the B'nai B'rith Hillel Foundation, the University of Chicago, November 5 and 12, 1952.)
Die Religionskritik Spinozas als Grundlage seiner Bibelwissenschaft, with an introduction to the reprinted edition by Norbert Altwicker. Hildesheim: Georg Olms Verlag.

1982

"Théologie et philosophie: leur influence réciproque" (French translation of "The Mutual Influence of Theology and Philosophy"). In *Le temps de la réflexion*, vol. 2. Paris: Gallimard.
Pensées sur Machiavel, with an introduction by M.-P. Edmond (French translation of *Thoughts on Machiavelli*). Translated by Michel-Pierre Edmond and Thomas Stern. Paris: Payot.

1983

"Correspondence Concerning Modernity" Exchange of letters with Karl Löwith beginning October 1, 1946. In *Independent Journal of Philosophy/Revue Indépendante de Philosophie* 4:105–19. Paris.

Forthcoming

Philosophy and Law. Philadelphia: The Jewish Publication Society of America. Translated from *Philosophie und Gesetz*, 1935.

Index of Authors